Unsustainable

Unsustainable

AMAZON, WAREHOUSING, AND
THE POLITICS OF EXPLOITATION

Juliann Emmons Allison
and Ellen Reese

UNIVERSITY OF CALIFORNIA PRESS

University of California Press
Oakland, California

© 2023 by Juliann Emmons Allison and Ellen Reese

Cataloging-in-Publication Data is on file at the Library of Congress.

ISBN 978-0-520-38837-6 (cloth)
ISBN 978-0-520-38838-3 (pbk.)
ISBN 978-0-520-38839-0 (ebook)

32 31 30 29 28 27 26 25 24 23
10 9 8 7 6 5 4 3 2 1

We dedicate this book to warehouse workers
and their communities.

Contents

List of Illustrations   ix

Acknowledgments   xi

1. Opening the Box: Amazon's Impact on Warehousing,
    Workers, and Communities   1

2. Boxing In Our Community: Amazon Expands
    Inland Southern California's Warehouse Empire   26

3. Behind the Box: Exploitative Conditions
    in Amazon's Warehouses   64

4. Boxed In: Discipline, Control, and Mechanisms
    of Exploitation in Amazon Warehouses   93

5. Moving Boxes Together: Inequalities and Social
    Relations among Warehouse Workers   115

6. Boxed and Bruised: Warehouse Workers' Injuries
    and Illnesses   147

7. Boxing Lessons: Community Resistance to Amazon
    and Warehousing in Inland Southern California   183

8. Beyond the Box: Confronting Amazon and the Politics
    of Exploitation and Inequality   222

    Methodological Appendix: Amazon Warehouse
    Worker Interviews   253
    Notes   263
    References   289
    Index   331

Illustrations

FIGURES

1.1.	People's Council Tribunal, September 7, 2021, San Bernardino, CA	2
1.2.	Cranes and containers at Long Beach Harbor	15
2.1.	Amazon air cargo FC at March Air Reserve Base, Moreno Valley, CA	42
2.2.	Amazon Prime cargo plane at March Air Reserve Base, Moreno Valley, CA	43
7.1.	Amazon FC, Bloomington, CA	193
7.2.	Semi-truck traffic at automated Amazon FC, Eastvale, CA	210
7.3.	Press conference and rally to support AB 701 (the Warehouse Quotas law), September 7, 2021, San Bernardino, CA	211
7.4.	Public march to support AB 701 (the Warehouse Quotas law), September 7, 2021, San Bernardino, CA	211
7.5.	Amazon Prime semi-truck at regional air hub at San Bernardino International Airport	213
8.1.	Amazon FC in Beaumont "area of interest," Riverside County, CA	251

MAPS

1.1.   Southern California counties   14

2.1.   Amazon FC and air cargo facilities in "Metro" Inland
       Southern California   51

TABLES

2.1.   Amazon Facilities in Inland Southern California   49

2.2.   Spatial Inequality in Southern California by Metropolitan
       Statistical Area   57

3.1.   Interviewees' Common Concerns   69

3.2.   Interviewees' Job Assessment   71

5.1.   Interviewees' Perceived Inequalities, Divisions, and Relations 119

6.1.   Interviewees' Health Concerns   151

A.1.   Interviewees' Social Characteristics   258

A.2.   Interviewees' Job Characteristics   260

Acknowledgments

First and foremost, we thank all of the Southern California warehouse workers who completed interviews or surveys about their employment and working conditions for this book, as well as labor, environmental justice, and other community activists in the region. Without their assistance and insights, this book would not have been written. In addition, we are extremely thankful for each and every one of the Sociology 197 students at UCR who helped us with research for this book. They played critical roles in translating surveys; collecting surveys or interviews from warehouse workers; transcribing interviews; and/or analyzing or coding data, sharing personal insights, and assisting with various other background research discussed in this book. We thank Fernando David Márquez Duarte and Sofia Rivas for their careful assistance with copyediting earlier drafts of this manuscript. We also want to recognize Reiley Allison, who verified Amazon facility locations and helped to create our maps. Staff, members, and other affiliates of the Black Workers Center network, Center for Community Action and Environmental Justice (CCAEJ), IE Labor Council, the International Brotherhood of Teamsters, the People's Collective for Economic Justice (PC4EJ), the San Bernardino Airport Communities (SBAC), the Sierra Club, Uni Global Union, the

Warehouse Workers Resource Center (WWRC), and Warehouse Workers United (WWU) were also very helpful in sharing important information, insights, conversations, and perspectives that helped to give birth to this book. We are also grateful for previous research advice and collaborations with affiliates of the Black Workers Center network, the WWRC, and the UCLA Labor Center.

We are extremely grateful to our editor, Naomi Schneider, and our reviewers for UC Press for their helpful feedback and suggestions on earlier drafts of this book and other book materials. We are also very grateful to many wonderful colleagues and UCR alumni over the years for research assistance, support, advice, conversations, feedback, and previous research collaborations that helped us to carry out research related to this book and helped to inspire and shape our writing. Among others, these include Arman Azedi, Jake Alimahomed-Wilson, Saman Banafti, Marissa Banuelos, Elizabeth Bingle, Rudolph Bielitz, Marissa Brookes, Edna Bonacich, Christopher Chase-Dunn, Michael Chavez, Randol Contreras, Kevin Curwin, Mirella Deniz-Zaragoza, Juan De Lara, Edwin Elias, Johnnyra Esparza, Alfonso Gonzalez Toribio, Erica Gonzalez, Catherine Gudis, Joel Herrera, Luis Higinio, Mila Huston, Francesco Massimo, Julisa McCoy, Ruth Milkman, Jessica Moronez, Hali Pinedo, Evelyn Pruneda, Karthick Ramakrishnan, Anthony Roberts, Dylan Rodriguez, Asbeidy Solano, Becca Spence Dobias, Alexander Scott, Jason Struna, Chikako Takeshita, Devra Weber, and Susan Zieger. They also include a number of other colleagues at UC Riverside, including affiliates and alumni of the Center for Social Innovation, the Center for Latino and Latin American Studies Research Center (including members of the Latino Labor Working Group), the Center for Ideas and Society (CIS), the Departments of Sociology and Gender and Sexuality Studies, the Global Studies program, the Labor Studies program, and the Environment, Sustainability, and Health Equity Initiative.

Research for this project was financially supported through various research grants from the UC Center for Collaborative Research for an Equitable California (UCCREC), UC California Studies Consortium of the UC Humanities Research Institute (UCHRI), and the UC Institute for Research on Labor and Employment. It also benefited from previous research collaborations and conversations on related topics with various staff affiliated with UCR's Center for Social Innovation (CSI) and the UCLA Labor Center.

Finally, Juliann wishes to thank her friends and family, especially Raymond, Reiley, and Olivia Allison, for their enduring patience throughout the process of envisioning and writing this book. Ellen also wishes to thank her friends and family, especially Ernest Savage, Xavier Reese-Savage, and her parents, Emmy and William Reese, for their patience, support, and additional sources of news and information as we developed and wrote this book.

1 Opening the Box

AMAZON'S IMPACT ON WAREHOUSING,
WORKERS, AND COMMUNITIES

On a hot September day in 2021, about seventy people gathered together in a public park in San Bernardino, California, for the first People's Council Tribunal on the region's warehouse industry (see figure 1.1). Signs posted around the panel of community speakers read: "Support Amazon Workers" and "End Warehouse Injuries." Three Latina women opened the event by describing the physical dangers they faced while working for low pay at Amazon warehouses. Yesenia Barrera, a former Amazon seasonal employee and organizer for the Warehouse Worker Resource Center (WWRC), described the stress that workers experience every day, forced to work at an unbearable pace to meet the company's high productivity quotas. Unable to keep up with the required work rate, she had been "fired by the algorithm." When she showed up to work the next day, her work badge no longer allowed her to enter the building. Another worker, a machine operator, testified about the difficulty she faced in using the bathroom while working at Amazon. Her machine never stopped, and she had to obtain permission from her supervisor to leave her workstation, but the supervisor wasn't always nearby. In response, she felt compelled to reduce her water intake, putting her at risk of dehydration. The third woman described how working full-time at Amazon left her physically exhausted and in pain, and injured her wrists.

Figure 1.1. People's Council Tribunal, September 7, 2021, San Bernardino, CA.
Left to right: Brenda Huerto Soto (PC4EJ and WWRC), Veronica Alvarado (WWRC),
Daisy Lopez (WWRC), and Yesenia Barrera (WWRC). Photo by Ellen Reese.

Responding to the workers' powerful testimonies, the mother of a former Amazon warehouse worker also testified, describing her daughter's
experience. After her long work shifts, which often lasted ten hours or
more, the daughter became frustrated because she was forced to push
carts that were too heavy for her. She was only given a thirty-minute training session on her first day and was frequently assigned to new positions
without adequate training, which made it difficult for her to work safely.
Robert Martinez, a United Parcel Service employee and longtime member
of the International Brotherhood of Teamsters Local 63, also responded to
the workers' testimonies. He described how he enjoyed better pay, more
employee benefits and a better health-care plan, greater workplace safety,

and other rights and protections than the workers employed by Amazon, which he attributed to being covered by a union contract.

The People's Council Tribunal, which gave public voice to growing community concerns about the impacts of Amazon and warehousing in the region, preceded a public march, rally, and press conference that called for the passage of a state bill to better protect warehouse workers' health and safety, ability to use the restroom, and other rights in the context of high work quotas. These events drew together a broad array of local activists, including representatives from unions and other labor organizations; student groups; and immigrant rights, environmental justice (EJ), faith-based, and other community organizations.[1]

Brenda Huerta Soto, from the People's Collective for Environmental Justice (PC4EJ), also spoke during the morning event. Her testimony drew attention to the environmental health issues associated with the warehousing and logistics industries in the region, which are engaged in storage, order management and fulfillment, and distribution to customers and retail stores. Calling for an end to the human and community exploitation by these industries, she described how their rapid expansion had worsened the region's very high levels of air pollution, especially in neighborhoods located close to warehouses.[2] Soto's call to action echoed concerns that have been raised by many other Inland Southern California residents over the years. The air quality in Inland Southern California communities located closest to the region's freeways and warehouse complexes has become so bad that journalists, physicians, and activists alike commonly refer to them as "diesel death zones." As one journalist described it, the air smells like "a lit cigarette dropped into a bottle of orange Fanta."[3] Inland Southern California resident Angela Balderas told that same reporter that she had sought hospital care more than five times in 2019 for chest tightness and difficulty breathing: "I feel drained, my chest feels tight, I have difficulty breathing, and everything takes more energy."[4]

These activists' claims reflect long-standing concerns that the effects of warehousing and logistics on workers and communities are unsustainable in Inland Southern California, a region that includes both Riverside and San Bernardino Counties. The increased number of unionized warehousing and logistics jobs and overwhelming presence of warehouses, distribution centers (DCs),[5] and delivery stations in the region represent multiple and overlapping threats to workers' rights, labor standards, the public's health, natural landscapes, and social and environmental justice. Demands by community, EJ, and labor activists alike have increased to include curtailing the warehouse industry's further expansion altogether in the region. The WWRC, PC4EJ, and Teamsters are part of a broader coalition of community organizations established in 2019 in opposition to the expansion of the San Bernardino International Airport to accommodate Amazon's newly developed air cargo facility. The San Bernardino Airport Communities (SBAC) and its member organizations have since organized numerous actions in support of their demands for "clean air and good jobs." For example, they have engaged in community picketing that slowed down Amazon deliveries at a major warehouse on Cyber Monday in 2019, urged local policy makers to establish a community benefits agreement for the air cargo facility and to enact a temporary moratorium on new warehouse developments, conducted a lively protest inside a warehouse developer's office, and even filed an environmental lawsuit against the construction of the air cargo facility to say "enough" to unabated warehouse development in the region.[6]

Within a year of SBAC's formation, Inland Southern California had become the national and global epicenter of the growth of Amazon's warehouse and delivery services, and the COVID-19 pandemic had arrived, forcing millions of people to stay at home as much as possible to protect their own and others' health. The popularity of Amazon's electronic shopping platform, already rising rapidly, skyrocketed. By 2022, Amazon claimed to have about 300 million customers worldwide.[7] The far-reaching impacts on workers and communities motivated labor, environmental, social justice, and community organizations, like those in San Bernardino, to organize and confront Amazon. Among many other demands, they have called upon Amazon to engage in stronger climate action; respect workers' right to organize; and implement better COVID-19 protections for workers, more than 20,000 of whom had tested positive for the disease by the end of 2021.[8]

The impacts of Amazon's rapid growth during the first two years of the COVID-19 pandemic (2020–2022) in Inland Southern California, as elsewhere in the nation and world, were highly unequal. In contrast to the millions of Americans who lost their jobs amid the worst economic crisis since the Great Depression, Amazon's founder and longtime chief executive officer (CEO), Jeff Bezos, remained among the top two richest men on earth and became even wealthier.[9] Like other "tech titans," Bezos profited enormously from the pandemic. By August 2020, Bezos's net worth had reached $202 billion—greater than McDonald's corporation, Exxon Mobil corporation, and Nike Inc. In a single day in July 2020, Bezos earned a record $13 billion. His ex-wife, Mackenzie Bezos, by then the thirteenth richest person and fourth richest woman in the world, gained $4.6 billion that same day, a consequence of her 25 percent interest in Amazon stock.[10] At the time, Amazon's stock had increased by 86 percent since the previous January, driving the corporation's value up $87 billion.[11] Bezos's wealth has enabled him to purchase a spectacular series of luxurious homes located across the United States, worth an estimated $500 million; invest in Blue Origin, his private space travel company; and even travel to the moon and back in 2021.[12] Although Bezos' fortunes later declined, he remained the second richest man on earth, with a net worth of $135.5 billion in July 2022.[13]

The enormous wealth of Bezos and Amazon's major investors contrasts sharply with the earnings of Amazon warehouse employees. Despite Amazon's relatively high entry-level wage for a warehouse associate in the United States ($15 per hour on average), the corporation's median annual salary is $32,000 for a worker employed full-time and year-round.[14] This salary is slightly more than half the median household income in the city of San Bernardino, California, in 2019 ($48,062), where Amazon's full-time salary would cover the living wage only for a single worker with no children.[15] Although Amazon was among the US companies that temporarily offered workers hazard pay, an extra $2 per hour, to compensate them for the elevated risk of contracting the virus at work, the corporation retracted this additional pay within months, despite rising COVID-19 cases, as soon as it had met its labor recruitment goals.[16]

Median annual household incomes throughout Southern California—ranging from $45,834 in San Bernardino County to $95,934 in Orange County—are less than 1 percent of Bezos' $13.4 million hourly income.[17] These disparities belie his purported loyalty to consumers, represented by an empty "customer's" chair at every Amazon meeting.[18] Not surprisingly, prevailing analyses of Amazon's growth and Bezos's business success emphasize the entrepreneur's innovative ideas and cunning and ruthlessness toward the company's competitors and workers.[19] This prior research is insightful, yet it neglects the political forces and systemic inequalities that contribute to Bezos's wealth and Amazon's status as the "most valuable" corporation in the world.[20]

In contrast to such accounts, we argue that the rise of Amazon, and of warehousing more generally, is based on the unsustainable exploitation of, or taking advantage of, workers' labor and communities' resources.[21] This exploitation generally depends upon systemic inequalities, namely neoliberal global capitalism and multiple, and often intersecting, social, spatial, and workplace inequalities. Throughout this book, we document how Amazon's rapid rise, as well as the concentrated growth of warehousing and logistics more generally in the region, has negatively affected workers, their families and communities, and the natural environment, and how workers and their communities are fighting back against these harms. We build this argument mainly through a community case study of these dynamics in Inland Southern California, but also consider similar trends underway across the United States and in other nations. Inland Southern California is home to one of the world's largest logistics clusters, or geographic concentration of logistics-related companies and activities, where Amazon has become the largest private sector employer.[22] We argue that the region therefore provides a particularly compelling example of the socioeconomic and environmental threats associated with the largely unfettered growth of warehousing, as well as the challenges and prospects for grassroots mobilization and coalition building to counteract them.

Although Amazon and Inland Southern California have distinct features, many of the trends we highlight—such as rising levels of wealth and income inequality, increased corporate welfare, e-commerce and workplace automation, the use of subcontracted and temporary labor, the exploitation and hypersurveillance of workers and communities of color, and rising levels of air pollution—are part of national and global trends found in the contemporary economy. Amazon has played a major role in actively promoting many of these trends, combining them with "one-click instant consumerism." Amazon has played such a leading and role in the United States, Europe, and other parts of the world that our era has arguably become one of "Amazon capitalism."[23] As the second US

company to employ more than a million people worldwide, and whose facilities and workforces are continuing to grow and spread, Amazon's impacts
on workers and communities have become both increasingly apparent and
controversial.[24] While many people worldwide continue to idolize Amazon
and Bezos, they have also become well-known icons of corporate greed.

This book critically examines the consequences of Amazon's dominance
of warehousing from the perspective of warehouse workers and their communities, and why and how workers and other community activists have
confronted this corporate giant. While we pay particular attention to Amazon's impacts in Inland Southern California, we do so while maintaining
an eye on similar trends in the United States and other nations. How does
the growth of Amazon and the warehouse industry and its concentration
in certain regions depend upon and help to reproduce social and regional
inequalities by constraining employment, educational, and other opportunities for local residents? How has the rise and concentration of warehousing in low-income communities of color contributed to air pollution and
related environmental and public health disparities across communities?
How do warehouse workers experience their working conditions, and how
do their work experiences vary across race, ethnicity, nativity, gender, and
age? What role has community and labor organizing played, or could it
play, in transforming Amazon and the warehousing industry? Our book
responds to these questions by combining information from ethnographic
fieldwork, in-depth interviews with Amazon warehouse workers, and other
sources.

This chapter introduces our theoretical perspective and the key con-
cepts and ideas that guide our analysis of workplace inequalities in Amazon and the warehouse industry, and why Amazon warehouses have
become so concentrated in certain regions, such as Inland Southern California, more than others. We then explain our data and methodology and
conclude with an overview of the remainder of the book.

A CRITICAL LENS ON WAREHOUSING AND LOGISTICS

Logistics originated with ancient systems designed to supply the Roman
legions. During the Middle Ages, the concept was adapted to characterize

economic supply systems that included roads, warehouses, forts and castles, and storage depots. Developments in transportation and communications to facilitate waging the world wars in the twentieth century catalyzed the creation of modern logistics, which integrate and coordinate purchasing, manufacturing, transportation, warehousing, returns, and other activities to maximize profits across the entire supply chain, including purchasing, operations, resource management, and information workflow as well as logistics.[25] These systems include multiple modes of transport—for example, ships, trains, planes, and trucks—warehousing and storage, and distribution. While early research on logistics focused on economic and technological developments and applications, more recent, critical scholarship illuminates the social and political implications of logistics growth.[26]

Our critical lens challenges conventional reductions of logistics to an apolitical understanding of cargo transport and supply chain management by illuminating the social and embodied consequences of this essentially "spatial and material practice."[27] More specifically, we draw upon two lines of critical theory and analysis—intersectionality and human geography—to explore the social and spatial injustices inherent in Inland Southern California's warehousing industry and related transportation services. Intersectionality is a concept originally developed by Black feminist scholars to account for the ways that systemic inequalities—including those based on race, ethnicity, gender, sexuality, class, and immigrant status, among others—intersect and interact to generate distinct effects on individuals and groups, as well as resistance.[28] Building on these insights, we join critical human geographers who are beginning to theorize and explore how multiple, and often intersecting, social inequalities operate in and through spaces and places to produce location-based inequalities.[29]

We further review the central ideas informing our analysis of how Amazon and warehousing in Inland Southern California impacts workers and communities. First we explain central themes associated with intersectional feminist scholarship that can help us to understand workplace inequalities in Amazon and the broader warehouse industry. Our intersectional analysis builds upon previous research that describes and explains the dependence of longshore work and supply chains, respectively, on processes of extraction based on race, gender, and sexuality to include differences in individual and social identity—for example, ethnicity, socio-

economic class, and nativity—that are particularly germane to the Inland
Southern California logistics cluster.[30] Next we explore elements of critical
geography and show how they can account for "spatial injustices" related
to the uneven spread of warehouses across neighborhoods and regions, especially their concentration in low-income communities of color, a dynamic that is especially evident in Inland Southern California.[31]

Workplace Inequalities at Amazon and throughout the Warehouse Industry

As Susila Gurusami persuasively argues, contemporary capitalism is intersectional because it "exploits race, gender, and other modes of identity
to stratify labor and reproduce forms of capital from particular bodies."[32]
In regional labor markets, workers are treated and paid unequally by their
employers and managers based on their social identities as well as their
employment contracts, occupations, industries, and job titles. This situation yields a highly patterned "hyper-exploitation" of multiply marginalized workers, such as immigrant Latinas, who tend to earn less than
men, white women, *and* native-born Latinas.[33] Inequalities in educational
attainment and work experience contribute to, but do not fully explain,
such patterns. Rather, racism, patriarchy, and other inequalities continue
to combine in complex ways to shape labor market outcomes through
various mechanisms, including unequal capitalist investments across regions and neighborhoods, employer discrimination, residential segregation, unequal access to education and training, occupational and job-level
segregation, personal networks, and wage-setting processes.[34]

Applying an intersectional feminist perspective to the case of Amazon provides clarity on the effects of racial, ethnic, and gender inequality
within the corporation. Although women and people of color have been
making slight gains at the top of Amazon in recent years, they remain
grossly underrepresented. Of the twenty-eight members of Amazon's top
executive "S-team" in 2021, only four were women (14 percent), up from
one out of eighteen in 2019 (4 percent).[35] The "S-team" is simply the very
top of Amazon's leadership structure. Men made up 77.9 percent of its senior leaders globally and 77.2 percent of senior leaders in the United States
in 2020. And among senior leaders in the United States, 70.7 percent were

white, 20 percent were Asian, 3.9 percent were Latino, 3.8 percent were
Black, 1.4 percent were multiracial, and 0.2 percent were Native American.
Amazon's managers were more diverse than its senior leaders, but most
(56.4 percent) were white, while another 19.5 percent were Asian, compared to 10.4 percent who were Black and 9.5 percent who were Latino.

At the bottom of Amazon's workforce, women made up 48.5 percent of
tier 1–3 "field and customer support" staff worldwide and 50.5 percent of
those workers in the United States in 2020. In the United States, fully 71.5
of these lower-level workers at that time were workers of color: 31.0 percent were Black, 26.4 percent were Latino, 8.7 percent were Asian, 3.7 percent were multiracial, and 1.7 percent were Native American.[36] Amazon's
most recent report to the federal Equal Employment Opportunity Commission provides a bit more detail on these lower-level workers, showing that as of 2018, workers of color made up 68 percent of "laborers and
helpers," which include but go beyond blue-collar warehouse workers. Of
these, 33 percent were Black and another 22 percent were Latino. In contrast, 71.4 percent of top executives and senior-level employees that year
were white.[37]

In Southern California, including Riverside and San Bernardino Counties as well as Los Angeles and Orange Counties, data from 2017 indicate
that about 54 percent of Amazon warehouse workers were Latino, 34 percent were white, 7 percent were Black, 4 percent were Asian American,
and 1 percent were of other races. About 84 percent of these line workers
lacked college degrees. While about 44 percent of these workers were
under the age of 30, another 44 percent were between the ages of 30 and
54, and the remaining 12 percent were age 55 or older. With respect to
gender, 59 percent were men, and 41 percent were women.[38] The proportion of women employed by Amazon appears to be growing and varies
across departments and facilities. According to some Amazon warehouse
workers in the region, women appear to make up about half or more of the
warehouse workers they observe at work.

The inequalities observed at Amazon, where workers of color are concentrated in the lowest-paid positions, can also be found in warehouses
throughout the United States. Nationally, by 2019 most blue-collar and
line warehouse workers were men, but women constituted about 28 percent of those employed in traditional warehouses and 44 percent of those

employed in the e-commerce warehouses. More than half of nonmanage-rial and nonprofessional warehouse workers were then under the age of 35. Across US regions, the specific racial composition of frontline warehouse workers varies, although workers of color are overrepresented nationally in these occupations compared to their share of the general workforce.[39] For example, Latino warehouse workers outnumber Blacks in the South-ern California and New Jersey logistics clusters, but the reverse tends to be true in the Chicago logistics cluster and less complex logistics hubs sur-rounding other midwestern and southeastern cities. Although warehouse workers nationwide are mostly native born, many are immigrants.[40]

Our book also highlights the hyper-exploitation of temporary and sea-sonal warehouse workers. Such workers are often denied the same em-ployment benefits, pay, and job security as permanent and directly hired employees. Our earlier research with Jason Struna and Joel Herrera shows that in Inland Southern California the wages and annual salaries of blue-collar warehouse workers, mostly Latino, differed and depended upon their employment status (as temporary agency or direct hires) as well as their immigrant status and gender.[41] This book revisits the role of ex-ploitative hiring practices in warehousing by examining how they operate within Amazon in particular, including the corporation's heavy reliance on seasonal employees.

Earnings in the warehouse industry tend to be low relative to other industries, and Amazon warehouse earnings are even lower than the in-dustry average.[42] Although Amazon's minimum wage is $15 per hour, the median annual salary for Amazon warehouse employees is $28,000, which is well below the average $32,000 annually for permanent, full-time warehouse workers in Inland Southern California in 2018.[43] Nationally, re-search shows that earnings in the warehouse industry, already low relative to other industries, tend to be further depressed when Amazon enters a county.[44] Research also finds that Amazon's arrival in a county tends to in-crease the level of warehouse employment by 30 percent but does not boost overall private sector employment due to job losses in other industries.[45]

Providing a comprehensive analysis of the full range of the exploitative practices used by Amazon and other logistics companies—which affects a variety of workers, including high-tech employees, lower-level managers, engineers, market analysts, clerical workers, and delivery drivers, among others—is beyond the scope of this book. This limitation also applies to analyses of Amazon's labor and environmental practices in the many cities and regions around the world where this corporation operates. Instead, this book provides a critical, in-depth examination of Amazon's exploitative practices, including its reliance on electronic surveillance of workers, where they are perhaps the most evident: among its Inland Southern California warehouse workforce.

As critics point out, the rise of warehousing and Amazon has constrained employment opportunities in Inland Southern California, where more than half of workers are employed in jobs that are neither good (providing middle-class wages) nor promising (entry level with career pathways to middle-class jobs).[46] By 2020, Amazon was employing more than 20,000 workers and about to hire another 4,900 employees, representing about one-fifth of the 102,000 warehouse and other logistics workers who were employed in the region in 2019.[47]

Our book explores how, in the context of Amazon and warehousing both in and beyond Inland Southern California, workers experience exploitative working conditions as well as employment discrimination, harassment, and other forms of intersecting social inequalities, including those based on race, gender, immigrant status, and age. In addition, we document how workers are fighting back against the inequalities and exploitation they face at Amazon in various ways. Many workers have resisted Amazon's exploitative working conditions in warehouses by simply refusing or quitting these jobs. Along with public pressure and worker protests, tight labor market conditions during the COVID-19 pandemic put pressure on Amazon and other low-wage employers to raise wages. Other forms of Amazon worker resistance have been more collective in nature, such as engaging in strikes, protests, petitions, unionization drives, and other types of workplace actions, which have helped to win various improvements in working conditions. Amazon workers have also demanded improvements in antidiscrimination and labor policies and their enforcement through policy advocacy and legal complaints. Given high worker turnover rates in Amazon warehouses, the heavy reliance on temporary and seasonal workers by Amazon and other warehouse employers, and employer retaliation against worker activists, formerly as well as currently employed warehouse workers have played critical roles in worker organizing and other forms of resistance targeting Amazon and the broader warehouse industry.[48]

Spatial Injustice and Warehouse Siting:
Amazon in Inland Southern California

Amazon, as other corporations and entire industries often do, exploits workers, natural resources, and public infrastructures of certain communities more than others. Critical, political analyses of geographic space provide a foundation for understanding such spatial inequalities.[49] Corporations, including logistics companies, frequently relocate all or part of their operations to places where land and labor are cheap. This spatialization of capitalist expansion produces international, regional, and local inequalities manifest in the exploitation of specific, identifiable people, communities, and places by others at the discretion of corporate elites often headquartered far away.[50]

Wilma Dunaway explains that "capitalists maximize profits by externalizing production costs to households and to the ecosystems that provision them."[51] Likewise, capitalism naturally externalizes the costs of distribution, or the transportation of goods from factories to warehouses and DCs, onto families and communities. Logistics involves many private, capitalist enterprises responsible for the purchasing, manufacturing, transportation, warehousing, returns, and other activities that maximize profits across the entire supply chain.[52] Yet its success depends on the capacity of these companies to exploit workers, use public infrastructure such as roads and highways, degrade natural resources, and take advantage of communities and even households. Amazon and other warehouse employers take advantage not only of the workers they directly employ, but also of the caregiving labor in households, often carried out by women of color, who feed their families, watch children during work hours, and care for sick and injured workers for little or no pay.[53]

Research finds that in the United States most of Amazon's warehouses are located in low-income neighborhoods of color.[54] Quan Yuan similarly concludes that the costs of logistics are most often born by low-income communities of color located nearby warehouses and delivery stations in Inland Southern California.[55] According to Yuan, spatial injustice is

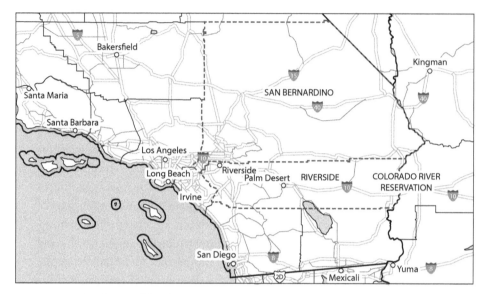

Map 1.1. Southern California counties

manifest in the disproportionate location of warehouses, fulfillment centers (FCs), and transportation operations in Inland Southern California,
which is less socioeconomically advantaged than neighboring Orange, Los
Angeles, and San Diego Counties (see map 1.1).[56] As Yuan argues, "unregulated logistics expansion" is responsible for reduced green space, greater
air pollution, and related health threats—especially asthma and other respiratory diseases—across communities differentiated by social and economic factors.[57]

Amazon dominates the Inland Southern California logistics cluster.[58]
The corporation opened more than fifty warehouses and related facilities
in the region between 2012, when Amazon's first California FC was established in San Bernardino, and the end of 2021.[59] Amazon's Inland Southern California "push" proved to be a "game changer" for warehousing,
distribution, and transportation in the region. The expansion of logistics
and warehousing in the region, underway since 1980, has both accelerated
and changed due to the growth of Amazon and other e-commerce operations and the integration of online and brick-and-mortar transactions—
that is, omni-channel fulfillment, which might pair online purchasing with

Figure 1.2. Cranes and containers at Long Beach Harbor. Photo by Parker Allison.

in-store pickup.[60] By 2015, more than 598.3 million tons of freight valued at $1.7 trillion moved from the Los Angeles and Long Beach megaports through the region's one-billion-plus square feet of warehouse and DC space annually (see figure 1.2).[61] Half of this freight was processed in Amazon FCs.[62]

Amazon's influx into Inland Southern California was not surprising given that the region had already become a "warehouse empire."[63] The region had a particular spatial geography and other features considered ideal for warehousing, distribution, and transportation companies.[64] Most significantly, the western edge of Inland Southern California, which includes Riverside and San Bernardino Counties, is conveniently located about sixty miles east of the expansive Los Angeles and Long Beach ports. Moreover, the region had long been characterized as having affordable real estate; proximity to rail freight corridors, interstate highways, and airports; a concentration of low-wage industries that put downward pressure on wages; access to a large customer market; and relatively conciliatory policy makers.[65]

The rise of Amazon and of warehousing more generally in the region was not simply an economic project of big box retailers, logistics companies, and warehouse developers, but also a political project carried out by policy makers in a region that despite recent political gains made by progressives has long been dominated by Republicans and conservative Democrats.[66] Local and county governments in the region generally welcomed and paved the way for Amazon's entrance into the region, just as they did for other warehouse developers for decades.[67] The construction of Inland Southern California's first Amazon warehouse in in 2012 followed and coincided with the loss of state funding for economic redevelopment and municipal governments' increased reliance on tax revenues, in addition to government grants, for economic growth and development. This public finance bind, in part, accounts for the collusion between politicians and business interests that has made regulatory laxity and corporate tax breaks de rigueur for Amazon and other major retailers and warehousers throughout the state.[68] Cities where Amazon FCs are located have returned as much as 80 percent of California sales tax earned to the corporation as an incentive.[69]

Politicians supported by the region's business communities have approved such incentives because they regard Amazon and other warehouse developers as key to the region's economic growth—most importantly, a source of jobs for working-class people in inland counties, where unemployment rates have historically been high relative to coastal counties and the state.[70] Political and economic leaders also anticipated increasing tax revenues, household incomes, and ancillary revenues and other improvements. According to the chief economist for the Inland Empire Economic Partnership, John Husing, Amazon's investment "'moved through inland outlets like local hair salons, restaurants, industrial supply firms, and grocery stores, generating a secondary [boon] of $2.7 billion'" by 2016.[71] Fans of the corporation similarly point to how the development of Amazon facilities stimulated improvements in street and traffic control, upgrades in landscaping, and other essential infrastructure, overlooking their costs for the region.

Such political dynamics, while particularly pronounced in Inland Southern California, are not isolated to the region, as revealed by Amazon's well-publicized bidding war among cities for the location of Amazon's second headquarters, or HQ2. In that bidding war, US cities competed over which city could provide the most generous financial incentives and subsidies to Amazon while asking very little in return, in order to attract the corporation to invest in their community. According to research on US state and local subsidy deals by Good Jobs First, Amazon, Inc. has received "about 20 economic development subsidy packages a year since 2012 for its warehouses and data centers—$3.7 billion and counting as of December 2020."[72]

Neoliberal policies, on the rise since the late 1970s, and increases in corporate political influence paved the way for these lavish corporate giveaways. Neoliberal policies tend to support business interests at the expense of workers, low-income people, and the environment. Examples of neoliberal policies include increases in business subsidies and tax breaks, reductions or eliminations of price controls, reductions in environmental regulations, rollbacks in capital and labor market regulations, and the lowering of trade barriers. Such measures encouraged corporations, including Amazon and other big box retail companies' logistic and warehouse operators, to encourage profitability through minimizing environmental protections, labor costs, and workers' rights.[73]

Amazon's exceptional growth has illuminated the unsustainability of industries, markets, and economies that generate far too high personal and social costs relative to any benefits provided to workers, communities, and the environment. The increasingly negative impacts of Amazon, and of warehousing more generally, on workers, communities, and natural environments have resulted in outrage and inspired resistance, especially in the regions where they are concentrated, including Inland Southern California.[74] According to Anthony Victoria, communications director of the Center for Community Action and Environmental Justice (CCAEJ), "The pollution outweighs the economic development."[75] Local residents also complained as the development of Amazon's sprawling FCs and other facilities brought increased traffic, damaged city streets, and replaced open spaces and desert landscapes in outer suburbs and rural areas.

We recognize these impacts of Amazon and other warehousing, transportation, and distribution enterprises on Inland Southern California, as well as the intersecting social inequalities that shape the experiences of, and inequalities among, warehouse workers in the region. Although we mainly focus on Amazon's warehouses in Inland Southern California in this book, we also reflect on the corporation's assault on other areas and the impact of contemporary logistics on human societies and natural environments more generally. Likewise, we consider the rise of community as well as labor resistance to Amazon and the warehouse and logistics industries both regionally and globally, arguing that it provides significant lessons for our future.

ETHNOGRAPHIC COMMUNITY CASE STUDY METHODOLOGY

Through this book, we seek to raise public consciousness about the social, economic, health, and environmental harms associated with the rapid rise of Amazon and the warehousing industry, and how and why workers and communities are fighting back against those harms. We do so by providing an ethnographic, in-depth community case study of warehousing, especially Amazon warehouses, in Inland Southern California, and building upon our decades-long research on this topic. We argue that Amazon's warehouses in this region provide a stark example of many of the harms associated with e-commerce logistics to workers, communities, and the natural environment, and have become a growing target of popular discontent. Our community study uses an extended, mixed-methods observational research strategy intended to generate knowledge about the lives of women and other socially, economically, and/or spatially disadvantaged groups in *specific* contexts.[76]

Our interest in warehousing, and in Amazon in particular, grows out of our experiences of living and working in Inland Southern California, where the social, economic, and environmental impacts of the southland's logistics industry are both visible and visceral. Diesel-powered semitrailers and smaller delivery trucks, increasingly emblazoned with the Amazon logo, crowd already congested freeways; the brown haze characteristic of photochemical smog due to automobile exhaust and factories conceals 10,000-foot mountains on summer days. Nearly everyone in the region at least knows someone who has worked in a warehouse or elsewhere in logistics, among the top five employing industries in the region.[77] In fact, this book's first author's father maintained and operated the cranes used for (un)loading shipping containers and designed a conveyor for unloading container cargo, and her daughter spent a summer working in an Amazon warehouse.

Our experiences and interest in understanding and resisting the practically unmitigated expansion of an industry that knowingly exploits the region's workers, communities, and environments has engendered the relationships and insights necessary to generate a compelling community case study of Amazon and warehousing in two of California's largest counties. This book is the result of more than a decade of predominantly community-based research that has included formal in-depth interviews; countless conversations with current and former Amazon warehouse workers, labor and community activists, and public officials; original surveys of warehouse workers; and analyses of scholarly and gray literature on logistics, warehousing, and Amazon, including news articles, government and proprietary data, and other observational data. Much of our research involved collaboration with labor and community activists and other scholars in the region and required our ongoing participation with community and labor organizations, including CCAEJ, PC4EJ, and the WWRC. In addition, we supervised student and worker interns who worked directly with community and labor organizations, helping them to document their concerns about the impacts of Amazon and the regional impacts of warehousing on workers, the economy, the natural environment, and other aspects of community sustainability. This book represents a critical, intersectional feminist reexamination of the results of this previous research. We highlight how intersecting social inequalities, especially those related to race, immigration status, class, and gender, bear on the specific labor, community, and environmental issues associated with Amazon's entry into the region's warehousing, distribution, and transportation operations.

Our data on warehouse workers' experiences draw heavily on eighty-two in-depth interviews with Amazon warehouse workers employed in Riverside and San Bernardino Counties. The first wave of interviews was collected between 2018 and 2019, before the COVID-19 pandemic, while the second wave of interviews was collected during this pandemic, in the fall of 2020. Recruiting workers in low-wage jobs for interviews about their views and experiences at work is often challenging because they are vulnerable to employment retaliation by current or future employers. Given this constraint, and following the methods used by other researchers studying other types of vulnerable workers in low-wage jobs, we relied upon workers' personal networks to recruit respondents.[78] Because Amazon relies so heavily on the labor of our students and their friends and families, we recruited a team of student research assistants who were trained and offered course credit to help to recruit, collect, and transcribe interviews with current and former Amazon warehouse workers. Interviews mainly focused on respondents' personal experiences as Amazon employees as well as their assessments of the job and their treatment by the corporation and coworkers. In the second wave of interviews respondents were also asked new questions regarding workplace health and safety related to the COVID-19 pandemic. The methodological appendix provides more details about our recruitment method and the interview sample, including workers' social characteristics, jobs, and employment experiences.

These interviews provide rich insights into the employment and workplace experiences of blue-collar Amazon warehouse workers in Inland Southern California, including the impact of the COVID-19 pandemic on this vulnerable population. The interview sample included twenty-three workers with only a high school or technical degree, eleven workers in their thirties and forties, ten married workers, twenty parents, fourteen immigrants, eight non-Latino white workers, six Asian workers, four Black workers, eleven mixed race workers, and a transgender worker. In addition, the sample also included nineteen part-time workers, eleven temporary agency workers, and workers employed in a variety of specific tasks and jobs.

This diversity of interview respondents notwithstanding, the typical interviewee in our sample was a single, native-born Latino worker in their early twenties with some college education, who was employed full-time and worked directly for the corporation. Slightly more women than men were interviewed. This typical worker had worked more than seven months at Amazon and had been converted from a seasonal to a permanent worker. Relying on student researchers' personal networks to recruit research participants contributed to certain biases in our interview samples. Younger, female, student, and childless workers were oversampled by our student research assistants, most of whom were women, while older, male, and nonstudent workers were underrepresented when compared to what is known about Amazon warehouse workers in Southern California.[79]

Given that these biases in our sample limit our ability to generalize about all Amazon warehouse workers, we compare our findings on Inland Southern California workers' experiences and views, expressed in their interviews, with those on Amazon warehouse workers from relevant secondary research, legal cases, and news reports. Relying on such secondary information helps us to overcome the limitations of our interview sample and also provide a broader context for our research. Despite their limits, our interviews do capture the everyday work experiences and perspectives of a subset of actual Amazon warehouse workers. Collectively, they also facilitate the development of a better understanding of how workers' experiences vary across gender, race, immigration status, sexual orientation, parental and student status, and age, as well as their employment status and jobs. Finally, the interviews reveal how workplace experiences and workers' views shifted during the COVID-19 pandemic.

Our research on efforts to organize warehouse workers in Inland Southern California is based on participant observation of the Warehouse Workers United (WWU) campaign; the WWRC; the Teamsters; and the coalition of labor, environmental, and social justice organizations that constitute the SBAC. Since the founding of the WWRC in 2011, the second author has served as a member of its board of directors. Along with other volunteer work for WWU and WWRC, the second author has participated in multiple actions, meetings, presentations, and events organized and carried out by CCEAJ, the Sierra Club, WWU, and WWRC staff between 2008 and 2020. This field research is supplemented with information from media and internet stories of activism as well as information provided to us by organizational staff; student interns; community leaders; and volunteers affiliated with WWU, WWRC, Teamsters 1932, the Sierra Club, CCAEJ, and other labor and community organizations.

BOOK OVERVIEW

Chapter 2 introduces our case study of Amazon in Inland Southern California and provides a historical and regional context for the rest of the book. We begin with a political-economic history of the region, discussing the long and racialized history of logistics in the region based on the state's colonial past and catalyzed by the arrival of the transcontinental railroad in Inland Southern California, which was essential to the region's citrus and tourism industries. Latino, Black, and Asian immigrant workers were heavily exploited in the construction of the railroad, the production of agricultural and other goods it transported, and tourist and related service industries.[80] We then discuss how and why the logistics industry grew and shifted over time as the region became a center of warehousing. Between 2012 and 2021, Amazon built nearly fifty warehousing and related facilities in Inland Southern California. Amazon and other warehousing, distribution, and transportation facilities created blue-collar jobs for many local residents, but these gains came with high costs in terms of increased traffic congestion, air pollution, loss of green space, and associated threats to public health.

The next four chapters draw upon our eighty-two in-depth interviews with Amazon warehouse workers to explore various aspects and consequences of the exploitative working conditions and workplace inequalities in Amazon's warehouses. Where relevant, we compare our regional findings with those of academic, journalistic, and legal research on Amazon warehouse workers and their concerns in the United States. In chapter 3 we examine the exploitative working conditions in Amazon's warehouse from the perspective of workers, most of whom are Latino. In contrast to Bezos's personal fortune, warehouse workers' pay was often just above minimum wage and below unionized warehouse workers' earnings. Additionally, workers hired through temporary agencies or seasonally were paid lower wages than direct hires and denied benefits. Our interviews suggest that many warehouse workers, facing limited employment options in the region for workers without college degrees, considered their Amazon job as better than their previous work experiences in terms of providing more work hours and slightly better wages and benefits. Participants nonetheless expressed many concerns about their working conditions and their low pay relative to the high cost of living.

Chapter 4 describes various mechanisms by which warehouse operators exploit blue-collar warehouse employees and how those workers experienced them. Some of these methods, such as providing workers with periodic small raises as incentives for them to work hard and stay on the job and the use of warnings, coaching, and threat of termination to discipline

OPENING THE BOX   23

workers, are fairly standard; others are more novel, such as "algocratic" forms of management that rely on electronic devices to monitor workers' productivity against computer-generated algorithms.[81] Many of our interviewees considered Amazon's productivity standards to be unreasonable and electronic surveillance under the threat of termination to be very stressful. Although many of these techniques appeared to be effective in generating hard work among Amazon warehouse workers in the short run, they contribute to high levels of worker dissatisfaction and high rates of employee turnover.

Chapter 5 examines relationships among warehouse workers and how they experience social inequality, favoritism, and harassment on the job. Here we explore workers' experiences with sexism, racism, xenophobia, heteronormativity, and ageism on the job, putting interviewees' stories into the context of legal complaints about employment discrimination and harassment filed by Amazon employees. We also examine other types of workplace constraints that shape workers' relationships, many of which were more severe during the first months of the COVID-19 pandemic. These include workplace competition, isolating work tasks, and prohibitions against workplace socializing. Along with high employee turnover and social inequalities and tensions among workers, these features of work life create serious challenges for efforts to organize Amazon warehouse workers.[82] Yet friendly relationships among coworkers were still very common, and the feelings of solidarity, trust, mutuality, and loyalty they generate provide valuable resources for worker organizing.

Chapter 6 compares Amazon warehouse workers' health and safety concerns before and during the 2020 pandemic. We find that nearly all research participants interviewed, both before and during the pandemic, were concerned about the unreasonably high standards for work pace and accuracy and the use of electronic monitoring to enforce them. Pressure to work quickly contributed to workplace stress and encouraged high rates of workplace injury, consistent with findings from research analyses of Amazon's injury records, which show its injury rates to be higher than the rates for the overall warehouse industry.[83] Noisy machinery had led to permanent hearing loss for several interviewees. Although some workers appreciated the corporation's use of material rewards and competition to motivate workers, other workers complained about workplace competition and were unimpressed by the rewards being offered. Workers also complained about extremely isolating working conditions, further exacerbated by the implementation of social distance rules during the COVID-19 pandemic and frequent rotation of workers across positions. Warehouse workers had many concerns about their potential exposure to COVID-19 and the corporation's failure to do enough to protect workers' health and safety on the job. Overall, Amazon warehouse workers discussed many ways in which their grueling and stressful working conditions took a toll on their mental and physical health. Such concerns have motivated many Amazon workers to take action through legal complaints, petitions, and protest regionally and globally.

Chapter 7 considers how community activists have responded to the threats posed to communities and workers by the expansion of Amazon and warehousing in Inland Southern California. EJ and community activists have relied on legal settlements to provide pollution mitigation for new warehouse developments in cities such as Fontana and Moreno Valley.[84] EJ activists, local residents, and their allies also successfully urged the South Coast Air Quality Management District (SCAQMD) to create new rules requiring large warehouses and other facilities that become identified as indirect sources of hazardous air pollution to adopt measures to reduce these emissions or to pay fines.[85] We also examine efforts by labor activists to organize warehouse workers and improve their working conditions through collective action, policy advocacy, and legal complaints. With assistance from the WWRC, warehouse workers won a series of favorable rulings from state regulatory agencies against various labor law violations by warehouse employers, including Amazon. Warehouse workers and their allies also engaged in workplace organizing, protests and other actions, as well as policy advocacy. By doing so, they gained political support for new state laws designed to better protect warehouse workers' rights and put pressure on warehouse employers, most recently Amazon, to improve wages and working conditions. Finally, we consider how labor, EJ, and other community organizations built alliances across movements. Responding to the various threats to workers and residents associated with the rapid rise of Amazon in a region already inundated by warehousing, they mobilized workers and residents and engaged in joint actions in support of "clean air and good jobs." Activists have not yet won their main demands for a warehouse moratorium in San Bernardino and more community and labor benefits from Amazon's new air cargo facility at the San Bernardino airport. Yet they have won local warehouse moratoria in other Inland cities, temporarily pausing further warehouse developments there, and gained support for community benefits agreements (CBAs) elsewhere in the city. Their grassroots organizing and coalition building has also helped to transform local and regional politics in ways that could pave the way for future organizing campaigns and victories for workers and communities.

Chapter 8 reflects on the meaning of Amazon's rise and the status of its ascendance in Southern California and beyond and situates popular resistance to Amazon and warehousing in the context of broader regional, national, and transnational opposition to Amazon. Recent opposition includes efforts to organize workers for better wages and working conditions in cities across the United States and in Europe; local campaigns to block the further expansion of Amazon; and national and transnational protest campaigns targeting Amazon for its environmental, business, and labor practices. At the time of this writing, there has only been one successful formal union election among Amazon warehouse workers in the United States (by the Amazon Labor Union in Staten Island, New York, which Amazon is challenging through a legal complaint). Yet as Alec MacGillis argues, the process of organizing unions among these workers has just begun; unionization efforts by steelworkers and autoworkers took decades to succeed.[86] We conclude that while confronting Amazon and the larger warehouse and logistics industry involves enormous challenges, doing so remains vital for those seeking a more just, equitable, and environmentally sustainable economy.

2 Boxing In Our Community

AMAZON EXPANDS INLAND SOUTHERN
CALIFORNIA'S WAREHOUSE EMPIRE

In March 1870, John W. North, an abolitionist who had served as surveyor-general of the Nevada Territory under President Abraham Lincoln, issued a broadside seeking investors for "A Colony for California." North envisioned a communitarian, temperance colony that would consist of "intelligent, industrious and enterprising people, so that each one's industry will help promote his neighbor's interests as well as his own."[1] Together with Dr. James P. Greves, North recruited colonists and incorporated the Southern California Colony Association in San Bernardino, which purchased 8,600 acres of the former Rancho Jurupa from the California Silk Center Association in September of the same year. At the association's first shareholder's meeting in December, colonists adopted the name "Riverside" because of their new home's proximity to the Santa Ana River. Water diverted from that river via canals would provide irrigation for the colony's citrus groves.

The Riverside colony was designed as an alternative to the "rampant exploitation of people and resources" that North, Greves, and the other social reformers had experienced in the eastern and midwestern United States. It flourished, but not without compromise. An 1895 Board of Trade publication characterized the city of Riverside at the time as "largely

composed of well-to-do horticulturalists and substantial businessmen engaged in occupations . . . connected with or dependent upon [the citrus
industry]."[2] Riverside's first orange trees were planted in 1871. A decade
later, nearly half of California's million citrus trees were grown in the city's
groves, just in time for the extension of rail freight and passenger service
to the region in 1882 (Riverside) and 1883 (San Bernardino).

The Southern Pacific Railroad and the Atchison, Topeka and Santa Fe
Railroad "carried entire trains of cars filled solely with oranges" to markets nationwide.[3] In 1895 the *Los Angeles Herald* reported that the city
of Riverside alone had produced "3,000 carloads of 300 boxes [of citrus]
each," valued at $1.5 million ($4.9 million in 2021 dollars), which contributed to its renown as the wealthiest city per capita.[4] The article failed to
recognize the hard labor performed by thousands of "economically, politically, and socially powerless" Californios, Native Californians, Mexicans,
Chinese, Japanese, Koreans, Filipinos, European "fruit tramps," and Black
farmworkers.[5] Nor did it acknowledge the increasing air pollution due to
orchard heaters and smudge pots used to heat orange groves and the exhaust from coal-fired steam engines.[6]

The class-based, racial, and ethnic tensions and environmental degradation associated with Inland Southern California's historic citrus industry are manifest as well in the region's contemporary socioeconomic
landscape. Allan Olmstead and Paul Rhode argue that the juxtaposition
of great wealth and labor exploitation inherent in the region at the turn
of the century reflects "two contrasting legends about California's agricultural history. One recognizes the state's farmers as "progressive, highly
educated, early adopters of modern technologies, and unusually well organized to use irrigation to make a 'desert' bloom . . . [the other regards
the] agricultural system as founded by landgrabbers whose descendants
continue to exploit migrant workers and abuse the Golden State's natural
environment."[7]

While nineteenth-century logistics, meaning the railroad's ascendance
over stagecoaches and mule freighters, *enabled* the citrus industry to grow,
the expansion of warehousing, distribution, and transportation services
has ingrained logistics as Inland Southern California's defining industry.[8]
The last pre–COVID 19 Inland Empire Business Activity Index reported
that "while the healthcare industry contributes the greatest number of

jobs to the region, transportation and warehousing are the most competitive local industrial sectors nationally, [and] contribute the fourth largest number of jobs, behind health care, retail, trade, and accommodation."[9] With over fifty warehouse-related facilities in Riverside and San Bernardino Counties, Amazon had become not only the region's largest private employer by 2021, but also a major contributor to the impoverishment of blue collar warehouse workers and the poor health of Inland Southern California residents impacted by the bad air quality and other health risks associated with goods movement.[10]

This chapter reviews the political-economic history of Inland Southern California, paying particular attention to the class, racial/ethnic, gender-based, and other intersecting inequalities and policies and events that combined in the region. For many years, workers and communities of color, racially diverse but increasingly Latino, have generally been exploited by mostly white men of affluence who historically gained control of the most of the productive property; invested in agriculture, railroads, manufacturing, and other low-wage industries; and dominated the region's political agenda.[11] These same workers and residents have also suffered the brunt of the external costs of warehousing and the logistics industry, including traffic congestion, noise and air pollution, water contamination, and threats to public health.

This brief history is followed by a discussion of the logistics industry's growth during the twenty-first century, emphasizing the rapid expansion of Amazon's warehouse facilities and their impacts on the environment and job quality in the region.[12] Amazon, like other warehousing, distribution, and transportation employers, created mainly blue-collar jobs for Inland Southern California residents. Latino and Black workers are disproportionately represented among warehouse workers generally, and among Amazon's frontline warehouse employees in particular.[13] Their relatively low wages and high risk of workplace injury beg the question of Amazon's successful contribution of "good" jobs to the economy. In addition, warehousing, distribution, and transportation enterprises typically increase traffic congestion and air pollution at the cost of green space. While these environmental costs are borne by the region as a whole, its poorer communities, often disproportionately Latino or Black, are most at risk of respiratory illnesses and cancer due to their proximity to logistics activities. This chapter illuminates the spatial injustice and long-term un-sustainability of Inland Southern California's logistics industry, providing a historical foundation for understanding the experiences of the region's warehouse workers and communities, including their collaboration and resistance, which are the focus of the rest of the book.

BRIEF POLITICAL AND ECONOMIC HISTORY OF INLAND SOUTHERN CALIFORNIA

Inland Southern California is an Amazon "warehouse town," character-ized by proximity to major interstate highways and railways and within a plausible commute for residents who are desperate for work.[14] The cross-country I-10 and north-south I-15 provide freight trucks with nationwide access from the Ports of Los Angeles and Long Beach through Riverside and San Bernardino Counties. Intermodal facilities for both the expansive BNSF Railway and Union Pacific Railroad located in the region service the western two-thirds of the United States to connect with eastern rail lines. The region is also home to a large working-class labor pool, more than half of which was constituted by migrant and second-generation Latinos when the first Amazon warehouse was constructed.[15]

The region's logistics industry originated with the extension of the intercontinental railroad to Riverside and San Bernardino Counties in the 1890s, which ended the region's isolation from the rest of the United States and, in combination with the widespread use of refrigerated rail cars, facilitated the growth of the citrus industry. Like the region's citrus boom, today's transportation and warehousing sector has exacerbated the region's history of socioeconomic discrimination on the basis of racial and ethnic difference, which arose along with the colonization of the coastal territory that would become California. The impact of the logistics indus-try on the region's natural environment and public health has been far more devastating than navel orange production was.

The following brief political and economic history of Inland Southern California is divided into three major periods: (1) colonial Inland South-ern California, covering the periods of Spanish and Mexican rule; (2) early California statehood, which includes the role of the gold rush in catalyzing economic growth and development; and (3) California's "Orange Empire," emphasizing the socioeconomic, racial/ethnic, and environmental threads connecting the region's citrus history to its warehousing present. Each section provides a historical snapshot of the period's major economic changes, central industries, labor configurations, and impacts on the natural environment and public health.

Colonial Inland Southern California

Prior to Spanish colonization, Native Californians living in what is now Riverside and San Bernardino Counties were intimately connected to their environments. The Luiseño, Cahuilla, Serrano, and Cupeño peoples used fire and hand tools to shape the landscape they called home so that it provided all the food, fiber, and medicine they required. They foraged for nuts, seeds, berries, roots, bulbs, and tubers rather than investing in agricultural production and hunted deer, rabbit, game birds, and fish.[16]

Beginning in 1769, Spanish colonists established four presidios, or military forts, and twenty-one missions near existing Native Californian settlements, each staffed by two Franciscan priests and a small complement of soldiers for defense. The purpose of the missions included subduing Native Californians—whom the Spanish referred to as *gente sin razon* or "uncivilized people"—and providing food and supplies for themselves and the soldiers garrisoned in the presidios. Consequently, Native Californians' lands were taken, and they were baptized and held captive in the missions, where they learned Spanish and the tenets of Catholicism and were trained in skills—such as brickmaking and construction, cattle herding, and farming and fieldwork—that would be useful in colonial society. Their successful cultivation of grains, fruits, vegetables, herbs, and nuts and production of meat (beef, pork, mutton, and goat) provided the foundation for pueblos and ranchos. Yet many Native Californians did not survive the harsh conditions of mission life, which included overcrowding, flogging, and other forms of corporal punishment; exposure to European diseases; and restrictions on their cultural practices. Historical records indicate that the population of up to 100,000 Native Californians in the coastal "mission zone" declined by as much as two-thirds between 1769 and 1834.[17]

Following Mexico's independence from Spain in 1821, Alta California colony, which included today's Nevada and Utah and parts of Arizona, New Mexico, Colorado, and Wyoming, became a Mexican province. Alta California's second provincial governor, José Maria de Echeandía, emancipated Native Californians in 1826 and proclaimed them eligible for Mexican citizenship.[18] However, many opted to remain in the missions rather than attempt survival in fractured communities and a landscape that had been transformed by irrigation systems and new transportation corridors and degraded by invasive species. Governor José Figueroa secularized and closed the missions in 1834, a process that was supposed to include distribution of mission lands and other property to the Native Californians who had resided there.[19] In fact, the lands were sold to immigrants or granted to wealthy landowners and other elite Mexican families to increase settlement of the province. The Mexican land grant system created 470 ranchos between 1822 and 1848 in Alta California, which provided a livelihood for the people who owned and worked on them.

While most rancho owners were male Californios (Spanish and Mexican settlers), sixty-six women, who were entitled to property rights under Spanish and Mexican law, and a small number of Native Californians were also granted ranchlands. For example, Mission Sobrante de San Jacinto in Riverside County was granted to María del Rosario de Aguierre; three additional Inland Southern California ranchos were patented to women who were the widows or heirs of the original grantees.[20] No Native Californians owned ranchos in Riverside or San Bernardino Counties.[21] In what would later become Inland Southern California, as was typical elsewhere in the province, Native Californians continued to provide low-cost ranch labor.

Early California Statehood

The road to California's statehood began with the Bear Flag Revolt in May 1846, a "mini war of independence" involving about thirty gun-toting white, male American settlers, who occupied Sonoma Plaza, raised a flag that depicted a bear and a lone red star, and proclaimed the independence of the Republic of California. California's nationhood ended twenty-five days later when the United States absorbed California into the union, following the navy's seizure of Monterrey in the course of its war with Mexico. Californios ceded Alta California to the United States less than a year later, and the region was formally annexed from Mexico in 1848.[22] California was never organized as a territory but rather administered by a federal military authority until its admission into the United States in 1850.

California's rapid and unorthodox entry into the United States was a consequence of governance challenges associated with the gold rush and enduring congressional and cultural conflicts over slavery. The discovery of gold flakes in the American River near Coloma, California, in 1848 was "one of the most significant events" to shape the state, and the nation during the nineteenth century.[23] The impact of the gold rush was not confined to the Sacramento Valley—miners struck gold near Barstow in San Bernardino County, for instance—but coal, iron, tin, silver, and borax were more common in Inland Southern California. Tens of thousands of prospective gold miners and other settlers poured into California from Australia, China, the Pacific Islands, and Europe as well as nearby Oregon and the United States.

This extraordinary influx of immigrants—an estimated 300,000 by the mid-1850s—generated rapid economic growth; the emergence of mining boomtowns; and unprecedented demand for railroads, banks, and other critical infrastructure that enabled California to leapfrog over territorial status and qualify for statehood by the end of 1849. California's population easily exceeded the 60,000 necessary for statehood applications, and the overcrowded, lawless mining camps and towns demanded a level of governance that exceeded the capacity of distant federal authorities. Despite the eagerness of Californians and Americans alike to establish the state, the organization of Alta California into territories, which normally preceded statehood, was a major source of contention between slave and free states. The Compromise of 1850 included the admission of the westernmost portion of Alta California as a free state (California) and the organization of the Utah and New Mexico territories, where residents would decide for themselves whether or not slavery would be permitted.[24]

Population growth due to the gold rush and associated manufacturing, construction, and service industries, in addition to increased agricultural production and cattle and sheep ranching, drastically altered California's demographics and social hierarchies. The 1852 state census recorded 260,959 inhabitants: mostly Californios (non-native *and* born in California,

Latin America, or Spain) and Anglos (Caucasians), but also 1,678 free Blacks, 31,266 domesticated Native Californians, and 45,803 "foreigners."[25]

According to that census, 10 percent of California's population was female, reflecting a doubling of the number of women and girls statewide that is generally attributed to the gold rush.[26] Miners' wives and other female family members represented some of the first women to "amble," rather than rush, to California during this period.[27] They were followed by women from nearby Southern California and Mexico as well as from throughout the United States, South America, Asia, and Europe, who arrived in and around the gold boomtowns seeking work and marriage. While most of these women were employed as domestics, schoolteachers, nurses, and entertainers, others operated boarding houses, gambling parlors, theaters, and related businesses, and some were employed in less traditional positions, including photographer, stagecoach driver, and bullfighter.[28] White women generally had greater access than women of color to higher status positions. Women, regardless of their race, ethnicity, immigration status, or social class, retained their skills and experiences when they traveled south to Los Angeles and Inland Southern California as the gold fields closed.

The 1852 census did not record citizenship. In contrast to Mexico, which had guaranteed citizenship to all *gente de razon* (or "civilized people"—i.e., Catholic, Spanish-speaking people who served the community), regardless of racial or ethnic background, the 1849 California state constitution "established hierarchies of difference that justified the categorization of members of non-white groups as non-citizen subjects."[29] Because American citizenship excluded people of African and Indigenous descent, Anglo and elite—that is, powerful, landholding—Californio delegates to the state's Constitutional Convention struggled with how to incorporate Californios, due to their European, Indigenous, and African ancestry. They finally agreed to recognize Mexicans who opted to stay in California, pursuant to the Treaty of Guadalupe Hidalgo that ended the Mexican-American War, as citizens; however, they extended suffrage only to white men who were Mexican (of Spanish/European descent) or American. The 1849 Constitution also gave the legislature authority to grant suffrage to Native Californians and their descendants. Black people in California, as elsewhere in the nation, were excluded from US citizenship.

Elite Californios arguably colluded with Anglos to secure their own standing as Americans, at the expense of other Mexican citizens and inhabitants of Alta California; however, most were ultimately unable to hold onto the land and other wealth that had determined their elevated status.[30] In violation of promises to protect full property rights to Mexicans' lands in California codified in the Treaty of Guadalupe Hidalgo, the California Land Act of 1851 required rancheros to document their claims to land via an extensive confirmation process that took an average of seventeen years to complete.[31]

Although most claims (604 of 813) were eventually confirmed, many rancheros lost their properties due to missing titles, unclear boundaries, or the return of former mission lands to the Catholic Church. Many of those who "won" their claims had to sell some of their property to cover legal costs. Others lost their land entirely due to mortgage default, bankruptcy, squatters—who could legally preempt others' claims to land by paying $1.25/acre for up to 160 acres—or as a consequence of "climactic misfortunes."[32]

Natural disasters contributed to additional shifts in land use and ownership. The 1861–62 megaflood dumped ten feet of rain and snow on California over just forty-three days. In Inland Southern California the Santa Ana River overflowed, creating an inland sea that destroyed riverside agriculture; drowned hundreds of thousands of cattle; and swept away Agua Mansa, once the largest settlement between Santa Fe and Los Angeles. This disaster was followed by the great drought of 1862–65. California received no more than four inches of rainfall annually throughout this period, resulting in the loss of as much as 70 percent of the cattle in some parts of the Southland, ending the state's "pastoral," rancho period.[33] Most rancheros subdivided their vast properties and sold the parcels to settlers.

The catastrophic loss of livestock and grazing lands due to the Great Flood of 1862, and the drought of 1863–64 that followed it, pushed California to adopt a new economy—initially farming, which was facilitated by the arrival of the transcontinental railroad. Other commercial enterprises, construction, manufacturing, transportation, and tourism would follow. Though squatters, and later homesteaders, successfully acquired relatively small plots, most of the best agricultural lands continued to be owned by the wealthiest rancheros or were purchased by rich, white Americans and religious or utopian colonists. Mormon colonists purchased Rancho San Bernardino in 1851, and North's collective purchased the former Rancho Jurupa almost twenty years later. While individual farmers and tight-knit colonies were often self-sufficient in terms of inputs, available family or community labor, and yield, larger agricultural operations required irrigation systems—especially in California's arid inland valleys—day laborers, and ready markets for their produce.

California's Orange Empire

The availability of large tracts of former ranchero lands for purchase and an expanding population of dispossessed ranchers and migrant farmworkers contributed to Riverside colonists' anticipated agricultural success. Additionally, they required: products suited to the region's Mediterranean climate, a reliable irrigation system to offset annual dry seasons, and a means of transporting their products to eastern markets. As much as 95 percent of California produce was sold in cities located along the Missouri and Ohio Rivers, the Great Lakes, and the Atlantic Ocean.[34]

Although Spanish missionaries had introduced citrus crops in the mid-1700s, it was the seedless, navel orange that put Riverside and other Inland Southern California locations on the map. Riverside colonist Eliza Tibbets is credited with planting the region's "parent" Washington orange tree in 1873.[35] The lack of water that oranges and other subtropical produce require to thrive prompted Riverside colonists to build irrigation canals, including the twenty-mile-long (Matthew) Gage Canal, constructed by the Riverside Water Company (which superseded the Southern California Colony Association) between 1874 and 1889. The San Antonio Water Company, established in 1892 by Canadian engineer and San Bernardino colonist George Chaffey, provided supplemental water to the region. In combination with regular freight rail service, water enabled the commercial success of citrus agriculture and contributed to the late nineteenth-century Southern California real estate boom. The "California Dream" of owning a home and farm out West attracted predominantly white, ethnically European migrants from across the United States to the Orange Empire, solidifying the region's shift from ranching to farming.[36] The accompanying growth of cities and other settlements throughout the region brought tourists, who tended to be white, along with the hotels, restaurants, shops, health spas, and other attractions typically staffed by Native Californians, Mexicans, and Irish immigrants.[37]

Though Riverside and San Bernardino constituted Southern California's primary agricultural areas throughout the early twentieth century, orange groves "carpeted the foothills of the San Gabriel and San Bernardino Mountains from Pasadena to Redlands."[38] Because the fruit produced in these expansive groves had to be picked by hand, the rise of the Orange Empire demanded a vast seasonal workforce that initially included Native Californians, previously conscripted into land work on Spanish missions, and Latinos, then called "Hispanics" (white landowners ordinarily did not distinguish among Mexican Americans, Californios, and migrant Mexicans). Chinese immigrants, most of whom had been lured by the promise of gold or recruited to complete construction of the transcontinental railroad between Promontory Point, Utah, and Sacramento, California, traveled south, where their horticultural knowledge and skills were widely recognized and exploited. Chinese farm and packinghouse workers comprised 80 percent of California's citrus labor force at the turn of the century. Increased participation in citrus production by Korean, Filipino, Japanese, and European immigrants and poor Americans—both Black and white—followed passage of the Chinese Exclusion Act in 1882.[39] Farmworkers were typically male, and increasingly Mexican as a consequence of the Alien Land Laws (1913 and 1920), which prohibited noncitizens from owning land, and the Mexican Revolution (1910–20), which drove a northbound immigration boom.[40]

In contrast, by the 1890s most of those who worked in packinghouses were female and white, due to anti-Asian sentiment combined with the feminization of the less strenuous, washing, sizing, grading, wrapping, and packing processes that were moved indoors from the early outdoor packing "tents."[41] This gendered agricultural labor segregation broke down during World War I, when the Women's Land Army of America's "farmerettes" worked in both the fields and packinghouses, full-time and at wages equal to men's. Yet the social hierarchy in the citrus industry continued to reflect nationality: "At the top, the growers, native-born white; at the bottom, the foreign-born migrants, or their children."[42] Resistance was limited, due in part to restrictions on worker militancy associated with California's Red Scare. Riverside packinghouse workers and orange pickers nonetheless engaged in a historic strike in 1917 organized by the Industrial Workers of the World (IWW). The strike was broken by a court injunction and strike-breakers from Redlands.

Citrus farming peaked in the mid-1940s and declined through the 1970s due to changes in the national citrus industry and regional economy, a reduced supply of farm labor, and environmental challenges. Florida was the primary beneficiary among the US citrus-producing states (Arizona and Texas, in addition to California and Florida) of the US Armed Forces' demand for a palatable source of vitamin C for troops stationed overseas during World War II. Though the Spanish introduced citrus to Florida as well as California, and both states produce many of the same orange varieties, Florida's subtropical climate yields sweeter, juicier fruit compared to the hardier, thick-skinned oranges that grow in California. Unsurprisingly, the majority of Florida's oranges are used for juicing, and the wartime demand for juice motivated that state to invest heavily in technologies for making orange juice concentrate, a product that maintained its popularity for more than thirty years.[43]

World War II contributed to the diversification and industrialization of Southern California's economy, which benefited from "massive federal defense" spending for the production of warships, planes, electronics, and communications tools as well as food, metals, oil, and other raw materials.[44] Military employment and wartime production generated more than a million jobs statewide for a racially and ethnically diverse workforce. Two of Inland Southern California's historically major employers established during the 1940s—the Kaiser Steel mill in Fontana, the largest on the West Coast, and Norton Air Force Base in San Bernardino—were the beneficiaries of this investment. As was the case during World War I, the region's women of all races and ethnicities filled workforce gaps created by men's military service.[45] Wartime job growth spurred the construction and transportation industries into high gear. Construction of housing developments, shopping centers, freeways, and strip malls spurred growth in retail, services, and transportation in Inland Southern California as it did elsewhere in the state.[46] Employment opportunities for women, especially Latina and Black women, declined significantly as servicemen returned from World War II, and women of all races and ethnicities were encouraged to take up domestic roles during the early postwar period.[47]

These broad economic changes contributed to agricultural labor shortages that made citrus production much less profitable than it had been during the preceding decades. Increasing employment opportunities in manufacturing, natural resource extraction, construction, and the military—all of which paid better than citrus farming and processing—diminished the supply of agricultural workers.[48] The internment of ancestral Japanese residents during World War II further reduced that supply. During that war and subsequently, Inland Southern California's citrus farmers became increasingly reliant on Mexican Americans and undocumented Mexican immigrants. The region's farmers also benefited through the early 1960s from the Bracero program, begun during World War II, which supported the legal migration of millions of Mexican guest workers who were paid the relatively low prevailing wages in agriculture.[49]

In addition to labor challenges, citrus farmers had to manage groves that were under threat from drought, parasitic diseases, and increasing air pollution from automobile travel and trains. Inland Southern California's air pollution is primarily a consequence of its location at the intersection of two "atmospheric sewers."[50] Prevailing westerly winds blow polluting emissions through the hills and mountains from Los Angeles and Orange Counties to settle inland, where they are trapped by the San Gabriel, San Bernardino, and San Jacinto Mountains. This baseline impact was increasingly exacerbated by polluting emissions associated directly with citrus production—smudge pots and grove heaters as well as freight rail—resulting in local smog and associated public health impacts in the region. Inland Southern California residents as well as atmospheric scientists recognized the everyday effects of smog—historically, a mix of smoke and fog or air pollution that reduces visibility. "You'd blow your nose, and it would be black," said an early California pollution control official.[51]

Studies conducted as early as 1970 suggest that exposure to air pollution may lead to a reduction in maximal attained lung function by early in adult life.[52] In 1972 the *New York Times* reported, "Smog blights everything in Riverside—work, recreation, plants, mental and physical health."[53] Such findings helped to catalyze clean air legislation both in California and nationally.[54] Over time, the costs of air pollution mitigation, in addition to increasing labor costs, relative to declining revenues from citrus and other agricultural revenues, prompted many farmers to sell their land to industrial developers, residential homebuilders, and real estate speculators, although some fruit and vegetable farming persists in the region, especially in Riverside (citrus), Temecula (grapes), Coachella (dates), and Blythe (cotton).[55]

AMAZON IN THE WAREHOUSE EMPIRE

Amazon's predominance in Inland Southern California's economy, where it became the largest private employer by mid-2021, further accelerated the rise in warehousing in the region that has been underway since the 1980s.[56] This expansion followed the global economic restructuring initiated during the 1970s, which featured the movement of manufacturing to Asia, Latin America, and other locations where production costs were lower. Innovations in logistics and retail sales resulted in geographically extensive supply chains linking foreign production to American consumption.[57] With the rise of "just in time" retail, warehousing, distribution, and transportation services replaced manufacturing as the economic basis for growth in many localities and regions, including Inland Southern California.

Los Angeles and Long Beach port authorities, freight transport companies, and professional logistics organizations recognized that Inland Southern California's "favorable regulatory climate and devalued land markets made it easier and less expensive to build large numbers of megawarehouses" than would be possible in Los Angeles.[58] Riverside and San Bernardino county supervisors and city planning commissions throughout the region, many of which were dominated by Republicans and conservative Democrats, collaborated with warehouse developers in this visioning exercise to deploy a project that bound the region's socioeconomic future to the rising flow of imported goods from the ports.[59]

The region's first storage warehouses were constructed in the early 1980s, just as thousands of workers lost their jobs when Kaiser Steel closed in 1982. Kaiser Steel, the first steel plant in the West, transformed the city of Fontana, in San Bernardino County, from an agricultural colony like Riverside and other Southland cities built on former Spanish and Mexican ranchos into to a manufacturing powerhouse during World War II.

During the decade that followed, warehouses surrounded the residential communities and shopping centers originally envisioned to support residents working for local manufacturers, like Kaiser, as well as higher-wage employers in coastal communities.

This spatial conversion of the region's economy coincided with the city's, and the region's, demographic transition from predominantly white in 1970 (82 percent for Riverside, 65 percent for San Bernardino) to approaching one-third Latino by 2010 (27 percent for Riverside, 33 percent for San Bernardino).[60] By the end of this period, Latinos—both immigrants and US citizens—became concentrated in warehouse jobs. Warehouse workers in Inland Southern California earned as much as 27 percent less than logistics workers at or near the ports, who were more highly skilled and more commonly unionized.[61] In addition to experiencing regional wage disparities, Inland Southern California's non-white communities have also been heavily impacted by the increased air pollution associated with the uptick in warehousing, a situation that continues to prevail, in part because both industrial and residential developers tend to chase the same "cheap land."[62]

Amazon opened its first California FC, a specialized warehouse that combines short-term storage, packaging, and shipping, in San Bernardino in 2012. Although the region had officially recovered from the housing crisis by then, the city's unemployment rate was 14 percent, and the city council had recently filed for bankruptcy protection. Local officials, including the city's Democratic mayor, Pat Morris, viewed Amazon's entry into the city as an important source of new jobs and economic growth.[63]

Amazon's arrival also coincided with a key moment in the region's political "blue shift" that accompanied increases in non-white voter registration. Over half of registered voters in San Bernardino registered Democrat in 2012. Although a majority of the region's increasingly racially diverse registered voters began supporting democratic presidential candidates in 2008 and continued to do so throughout the decade, Republicans and conservative Democrats won city council elections in the region and dominated the county boards of supervisors in both Riverside and San Bernardino until at least 2016.[64] By 2020, although racial gaps in voter participation persisted, they were closing, and a more demographically and politically diverse body of candidates had begun to achieve more electoral success locally, due in part to California's sharp lean toward Democrats. Even so, conservative Democrats remained politically influential in both Riverside and San Bernardino Counties, especially when compared to other parts of California. This situation provided generally favorable political conditions for Amazon and other warehouse developers, although local electoral shifts eventually provided new opportunities for activists to slow the expansion of warehousing in certain cities, as we discuss more fully in chapter 7.[65]

In the following discussion we further analyze the growth of warehousing and Amazon's move to dominate e-commerce and logistics in Inland Southern California. We begin by providing an overview of the rise of warehousing that emphasizes the spatial impacts of e-commerce on contemporary logistics. Next we discuss Amazon's expansion in the region, given this economic and spatial context. We then discuss the economic and EJ issues that have spurred community action and public resistance to warehousing and Amazon, discussed more fully in chapter 6.

The Rise of Warehousing

The end of the postwar economic boom hit Inland Southern California hard. The sun-setting of federal protections for manufacturing and investment in industrialization related to the military contributed to reduced economic growth and job creation in mining and manufacturing throughout the region. Union and other cooperative labor activity generally declined through the 1980s as the United States institutionalized its neoliberal adoption of free-market capitalism and strict limits on public investment and ownership. Until very recently, the US political economy was characterized by increased dependence on overseas manufacturing, the outsourcing of service jobs, and the realignment of military bases, processes that would continue into the twenty-first century.[66] This economic transition led to declines in higher-paying, often unionized manufacturing jobs and an increase in lower-paid and generally nonunion jobs in the service-providing and logistics industries. Specifically, the conversion to a peacetime service economy cost Inland Southern California tens of thousands of factory jobs, including 4,500 layoffs when the unionized Kaiser Steel mill closed in 1983, and 32,000 military positions associated with the closures of Norton Air Force Base and Pomona's guided missile factory and the transition of March Air Force Base into the March Air Reserve Base,

Figure 2.1. Amazon air cargo FC at March Air Reserve Base, Moreno Valley, CA. Photo by Parker Allison.

which has served as an Amazon Air gateway since 2018 (see figures 2.1 and 2.2). These losses reduced regional demand for small businesses and service providers, leading to additional job losses, including overall reductions in retail and management jobs. Public sector, health-care, construction, and trucking jobs, some of which were unionized, increased in subsequent decades. Yet many workers, including new residents moving into the region, found their employment options increasingly narrowed to lower-skilled jobs, such as those offered by big box retailers, temporary employment agencies, and warehouse employers.[67]

Job losses and falling wages, together with rising interest rates implemented to combat the "great inflation" of the 1970s, resulted in declining homeownership and overall social mobility, especially in communities of color, where incomes were lower, contributing to rising race- and ethnicity-based disparities in homeownership.[68] For example, in 1975 the median income for white families in the United States was $14,270; the comparable statistics for Black and Latino families that year were $8,780

Figure 2.2. Amazon Prime cargo plane at March Air Reserve Base, Moreno Valley, CA. Photo by Parker Allison.

and $9,550, respectively.[69] California voters responded to inflation in part by passing Proposition 13—"The People's Initiative to Limit Property Taxation"—in 1978. Prop. 13, promoted by anti-tax business groups, imposed strict limits on property taxes and capped annual increases in assessed property values.[70]

The intervention failed to improve home affordability for those living in Inland Southern California, where median family incomes remained insufficient to purchase a single-family home into the 1980s. But it did reinforce the differential costs of homeownership in Los Angeles, Orange, and San Diego Counties compared to Riverside and San Bernardino Counties.[71] In 1984 the average price for a new home in Riverside or San Bernardino was $106,000 or $89,000, respectively, compared to $165,000 for a new home in Orange County or $144,000 in Los Angeles. The region's relatively affordable housing fueled a phenomenal increase in Inland Southern California's population; nearly one billion people moved to Inland Southern California between 1970 and 1985. The region's new residents included large numbers of Black and Latino residents, contributing to a trend toward greater racial and ethnic diversity.[72] Given the lack of high-paying jobs with benefits in the region, many of these newcomers, along with other residents, commuted to and from work in Los Angeles, Orange, and San Diego Counties, contributing to freeway congestion and air pollution and motivating the development of transportation corridors that changed the landscape.

Business associations representing the Los Angeles and Long Beach ports and Inland Southern California, including the Distribution Management Association (DMA) of Southern California and Inland Empire Economic Partnership (IEEP), considered the rise of warehousing in Riverside and San Bernardino Counties to be inevitable, given the region's high demand for jobs and low property values. Scholars have been less sanguine. Juan De Lara argues that "markets are produced, not naturally occurring phenomena."[73] According to De Lara, Southern California's emergence as a "Warehouse Empire" is the result of a regional balance of political power dominated by Republicans and conservative Democrats, and business interests that maintained control in many city and county governments despite the demographic transition to majority Latino, and a concerted campaign to promote logistics and warehousing development.[74] Logistics and warehouse boosters developed and circulated policy papers, planning studies, and jointly funded intergovernmental and public-private development projects, many sponsored by the Southern California Association of Governments (SCAG). SCAG develops long-range regional transportation plans that impact the sustainability and public health of communities across six counties (Imperial, Los Angeles, Orange, Riverside, San Bernardino, and Ventura) and 191 cities.

Port expansions—such as the dredging to deepen the port and acquisition of land to accommodate container terminals—began with the development of the 1980 Port (of Los Angeles) Master Plan. This build-out was supported by the construction of the Alameda Corridor, the SCAG-sanctioned and federally funded freight rail expressway connecting the Los Angeles and Long Beach ports with transcontinental mainlines that terminate near downtown Los Angeles. Together with the growth of inexpensive offshore production and the availability of containerized shipping, these innovations in logistics enabled the volume of imports entering the Long Beach and Los Angeles ports to triple. The Port of Los Angeles alone surpassed the Port of New York and New Jersey in terms of container volume in 1990, a position it still holds, ranking just ahead of the Port of Long Beach.[75]

Port expansions, which have continued into the twenty-first century, and efficient freight rail service inland from the ports catalyzed the extension of warehousing, distribution, and transportation services into Riverside, and then San Bernardino, Counties. Industrial developers, facing opposition in Los Angeles to air pollution from diesel-fueled trucks, trains, and ships and increasing demands for fairer labor practices, looked inland, where land was "dirt cheap."[76] They invested heavily in the construction of increasingly large warehouses and DCs to accommodate the influx of goods arriving at the Los Angeles and Long Beach ports—as much as 40 percent of all imports to the United States since the mid-1990s—almost all along rail and highway transportation routes through Inland Southern California.[77] While storage warehouses had dotted the region's landscape since the 1908s, the construction of Costco's Mira Loma FC in 1997 marked the arrival of contemporary, high-tech, multifunctional DCs.[78] Warehouse construction has paused only once since that enormous facility was constructed, when the housing bubble burst in fall 2008.[79]

Warehousing, along with jobs in food, retail sales, and administrative and health-care services, contributed heavily to the phenomenal growth of employment opportunities in the region during the 1990s. By the decade's end, nonfarm employment had grown by 130,000 jobs, and the region was just beginning to experience the rise of a reverse commute—workers driving *to* Inland Southern California to work.[80] Small manufacturing operations as well as warehouses replaced dairies and farmlands along I-15, and the Ontario Mills outlet shopping center attracted more visitors than Disneyland the year it opened in 1997.[81] The abundance of low-wage work increasingly distinguished Riverside and San Bernardino Counties from the state overall, which was rapidly becoming known for its professional, scientific, and high-tech industries. This situation raised concerns about the quality of the region's jobs—especially in warehousing, distribution, and transportation.[82]

Warehouse workers grew in number in the 1990s and early 2000s. Along with long-term residents, many moved to Inland Southern California from Mexico and Central America as well as from economically depressed neighborhoods in Los Angeles and throughout the Southwest. Nicholas Allen, a prominent union organizer, characterized these workers, mostly Latino, as "vital . . . to the pumping heart of the vascular system of the world's largest retail corporations on the planet, yet their conditions are miserable and their prospects for achieving the American Dream are slim."[83] The median annual salary for logistics workers employed full-time in transportation and material-moving occupations in Riverside and San Bernardino Counties has consistently run about 85 percent of the region's overall median annual salary since the early 2000s. Compensation was much lower for part-time and temporary employees.[84]

Residential construction developers joined warehousing and other industrial developers in buying up large land parcels in Inland Southern California. By the late 1990s, expanded access to higher-risk home mortgages as well as the region's proximity to high-wage coastal cities and the persistently low land costs in the region incentivized residential development. Riverside and San Bernardino Counties became one of the nation's largest migration destinations. This generalization was especially true for lower-income Black and Latino households, which were aggressively targeted by subprime lenders.[85] Between 2000 and 2006, residential developers constructed more than 170,000 new single-family homes in Riverside County alone to meet the housing demand, fueled largely by people who sought to escape from crime, blight, and outrageous housing prices in Los Angeles and other cities further west.[86]

Due to the combined effects of logistics expansion and population growth, even Inland Southern Californians who did not work in or near warehouses or distribution facilities were ultimately impacted—by both rising traffic congestion and air pollution, especially fine particulate matter ($PM_{2.5}$) associated with the combustion of diesel fuel in semi-trucks. $PM_{2.5}$ pollution is associated with high rates of asthma and respiratory illnesses in the region and contributes to premature deaths.[87] These health risks are particularly salient for children, who inhale higher quantities of pollutants, and residents of low-income communities of color, who often experience higher than average exposure to air pollution due to living near transit corridors and industrial sites.[88] Inland Southern California residents generally suffer more from poor air quality than their coastal neighbors do. Population growth in the region coincided with a demographic transition from majority white to majority Latino, along with a rising share of residents who are Black and Asian. Thus, many of those impacted by Inland Southern California's poor air quality are Latino or Black.[89]

Boxed In by Amazon

Inland Southern California was among the regions hardest hit by the Great Recession, which cost the region more than 146,000 jobs between 2008 and 2010, and unemployment hit a record high of 14.5 percent.[90] Though it was recovering steadily by January 2012, just months before Amazon's first Inland Southern California FC opened, the unemployment rate in the region remained high at 12.5 percent. Unemployment continued to fall, to a historic low of 4.1 percent in 2018. This decline was due in part to rising employment in construction, local government, higher education, and health care, as well as light manufacturing and the high-tech industry. Still, the largest numbers of new jobs created in Riverside and San Bernardino Counties between 2011 and 2017 were in logistics and e-commerce, including the operations of multiple Amazon FCs and other distribution facilities.[91]

Similar to what occurs nationally, Amazon's FCs and related facilities in Inland Southern California are disproportionately sited in low-income communities of color along supply routes where access to air, rail, and truck freight services makes it easier than elsewhere to transport goods.[92] Despite the increasingly obvious risks to residents of these communities— increased traffic congestion, poor air quality, and health threats—regional policy makers habitually count on public support for Amazon developments, which promise jobs for the region's abundant blue-collar workforce and sales tax revenue. Declines in federal funding for urban and housing development and Prop 13 limits on property taxes compel local governments to rely on sales tax revenue.

In California, sales tax is collected by the state government and returned to the jurisdiction where the sale occurred according to the "situs rule."[93] Municipal and county decision makers lure developers and retailers, including warehousing facilities, that serve as the point of sale for online consumers, with local tax incentives, abatements, and subsidies. Sales taxes generally provide local governments in California with their fourth largest source of revenue, after charges for services, intergovernmental aid, and property taxes.[94] Yet cities where Amazon FCs are located, beginning with San Bernardino, have returned up to 80 percent of state sales tax earned to the corporation.[95] In California, roughly a tenth of the state's 7.25 percent sales tax is directed to the city or jurisdiction where a retailer operates; the remainder goes to the relevant counties and the state. Until Amazon opened its first DC in San Bernardino, sales tax generated by Amazon sales to California residents was shared among all of the state's cities; immediately afterward, it was shared between San Bernardino and Patterson, where Amazon opened its second FC. Amazon had designated these two cities as its legal "points of sale," meaning they earned 100 percent of the tax—about $8 million annually *each*—collected for Amazon sales in California. $6.4 million is a hefty price to pay for the presence of an "aggressive retailer [that grows] at the expense of existing retailers."[96]

The diversity of Amazon's facilities in Inland Southern California, summarized in table 2.1, enables the benefits of vertical integration across the corporation's various distribution operations. Amazon owns and operates increasing elements of the supply chain—from inventory management, to warehousing and distribution, to customer service—related to the corporation's fulfillment partners and customers. By the end of 2021 there were more than fifty Amazon warehousing and fulfillment facilities in the region, located primarily along major transportation corridors and near airports, as depicted in map 2.1.[97] These facilities included twenty-nine of the previously defined FCs and crossdock centers (IXDs)—the "epitome of [just in time delivery]" that minimize shipping by moving products directly from receiving to shipping docks—two storage facilities, and an Amazon Fresh/Pantry, which provides short-term storage for, and distributes, groceries and single-serving items to Amazon Prime members.[98] At that time there were also twelve facilities devoted to "last mile" delivery, including sortation centers, where orders are aggregated for delivery, and delivery stations that increasingly coordinate independent contractors to supplement delivery services provided by FedEx, United Parcel Services (UPS), and other delivery partners.[99] There were also seven air cargo service locations exclusively for Amazon.[100] Finally, Amazon operated a printing service in the region to allow users to create printing projects for their Amazon Photo collections. Amazon's proprietary "empire" of geographically distributed, functionally specialized FCs and IXDs, sortation center

Table 2.1   Amazon Facilities in Inland Southern California

Facility Code	Location	Year Opened	Type
		Warehouses (N = 32)	
ONT2	San Bernardino	2012	FC
ONT4	San Bernardino	2012	Amazon Prime Fresh/Pantry
XIX2	San Bernardino	2013	IXD
ONT8	Moreno Valley	2014	IXD
ONT6/HLA3	Moreno Valley	2014	FC
ONT9	Redlands	2014	FC
SNA4	Rialto	2015	FC
LGB5	San Bernardino	2016	FC
SNA6/SNA9	Eastvale	2016	FC
LGB4	Redlands	2017	FC
LGB8	Rialto	2017	IXD
LGB6	Riverside County	2018	FC
LGB3	Eastvale	2018	FC
XUSV	Redlands	2018	FC
LAX9	Fontana	2019	IXD
LGB7	Rialto	2019	FC
PSP1	Beaumont	2019	FC
PCA3/XIX6	Fontana	2019	IXD
SBD2	San Bernardino	2020	FC
PCA2	Perris	2020	FC
SBD3	San Bernardino	2020	IXD
LGB9	Perris	2020	FC
TEN2/XUSJ	Rialto	2020	FC
HLA9/XLX3	Perris	2020	FC
DFX4	Victorville	2021	FC
SBD1	Bloomington	2021	IXD
SLA5/SLA6	Eastvale	2021	Amazon Fresh warehouse
VUPQ	Fontana	2021	FC
IONT	Jurupa Valley	2021	DC (storage)
XUSO	Perris	2021	FC
ONT7	San Bernardino	2021	FC
KRB7	Beaumont	2021	FC

(continued)

Table 2.1   (Continued)

Facility Code	Location	Year Opened	Type
		Delivery (N = 12)	
ONT5	San Bernardino	2013	Sortation center
DLA5	Riverside	2016	Delivery station
DCA2	Eastvale	2016	Delivery station
DLA7	Chino	2017	Delivery station
HLA3	Moreno Valley	2020	Delivery station
DCX1	Riverside	2020	Delivery station
DIB6	Redlands	2021	Delivery station
DUR9	Temecula	2021	Delivery station
ONT1	Jurupa Valley	2020	Sortation center
CNO5	Chino	2020	Sortation center
DJW8	Cathedral City	2021	Delivery station
HLA4	Perris	2021	Delivery station
		Amazon Air (N = 7)	
AAONT	Ontario	2016	Amazon Air
KRB1/XIX7	San Bernardino	2016	Amazon Air
KRIV	Moreno Valley	2018	Amazon Air
KRB4	Perris	2020	Amazon Air
AASBD	San Bernardino	2021	Amazon Air
KONT	Ontario	2021	Amazon Air
KSBD	San Bernardino	2021	Amazon Air
		Printing (N = 1)	
ONT3	San Bernardino		Printing

NOTE: All locations verified by authors.

and delivery stations, and air freight facilities is designed to ensure rapid fulfillment of customer orders.

Amazon Prime members have enjoyed free, two-day delivery since 2005; free same-day delivery became available in some locations as early as 2009.[101] Fulfillment by Amazon makes this popular model available to

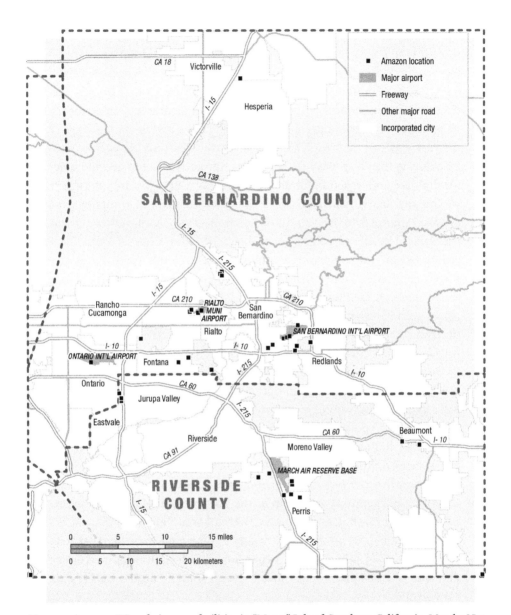

Map 2.1. Amazon FC and air cargo facilities in "Metro" Inland Southern California. Map by Nat Case, INCase LLC. *Source:* US Census TIGER data.

other companies. For a fee, Amazon stores users' products until they are sold and then takes responsibility for picking, packing, shipping, and customer service for the sale. The sheer volume of Amazon's e-commerce and complexity of omni-channel fulfillment, which covers other brands' distribution needs, require "larger footprints" and greater logistics capacity to satisfy consumers' unpredictable buying habits and demand for quick delivery and easy returns. The average "warehouse" size more than doubled during the 2007–2017 decade to 184,000 square feet to provide space for multiple and varied fulfillment activities as well as product storage.[102] In comparison, Amazon FCs and IXDs are monstrous—ranging from 600,000 square ft to over 4 million square feet (the corporation's largest warehouse) in Inland Southern California.[103] These large facilities foster economies of scale by processing more goods at lower costs due to low wages, automation, and extended hours of operation, which reduces payroll.[104] Amazon facilities operating in Inland Southern California by the end of 2021 had significantly reduced delivery times and costs throughout the state's heavily populated and predominantly suburban areas from Los Angeles to the US-Mexico border.[105]

Despite the undesirability of large-scale distribution activities in coastal counties' dense population centers, consumer demand for fast delivery and the advent of green, or at least less environmentally impactful, logistics processes has drawn some distribution and transportation services, including small delivery stations, into Los Angeles, Orange, and San Diego Counties. Regional policy makers, such as Riverside County chief executive Jay Orr, nonetheless continue to see Inland Southern California as a natural extension of the ports. Likewise, logistics boosters, including IEEP president and CEO Paul Granillo, argue that the region is unique in its proximity to twenty million consumers and capacity to accommodate planned port expansions.[106] More than 40 percent of the nation's consumer goods move through Inland Southern California annually.[107]

When the COVID-19 pandemic led to rising demand for home-delivered goods in 2020 and 2021, Amazon opened seventeen warehouses and eight delivery facilities—a third of its total operations in Inland Southern California. While this expansive fulfillment infrastructure cost billions, Amazon's profits nearly doubled in 2020 over the previous year and increased

220 percent in 2021.[108] Amazon captured forty-one cents of every dollar spent online in the United States in 2021.[109]

ENVIRONMENTAL AND ECONOMIC
IMPACTS OF AMAZON'S TAKEOVER

Amazon's dominance among Inland Southern California's e-commerce companies and logistics operations makes the corporation complicit in sustaining the spatial injustice that has long plagued the region.[110] Spatial (in)justice recognizes the social, economic, and environmental conditions that both reflect and enable the prioritization of some individual, group, and corporate demands over the needs of communities and societies.[111] Consumer demand for immediate receipt of competitively priced goods, combined with the technological innovations and infrastructure developments necessary to support global supply chains, "reconfigured" the Inland Southern California landscape to expand and politicize "intersecting spatial scales—the warehouse, the diesel-poisoned body, the foreclosed home, the racialized state."[112]

Feminist geographers underscore intersectional impacts on the embodiment of spatial inequities in individuals and by communities. Ellen Kohl argues, for example, that it can be impossible for residents of communities characterized by race, ethnicity, class, and/or gendered behaviors to "take off" the "hats" that constitute their position vis-à-vis environmental (in)justice. This insight easily extends to struggles for social justice more generally among the region's warehouse workers and the communities impacted by Amazon, which have been shaped by the embodied experience of living and working in Inland Southern California today.[113] Many warehouse workers of color, along with working-class people who sought employment in the region's first DCs, condemned early warehousing opponents, who tended to be white, middle-class homeowners who feared the impact of logistics on property values and livelihoods. For example, construction of the 1.8-million-square-foot Skechers shoe warehouse in Riverside County's Moreno Valley in 2012 pitted predominantly Latino proponents of warehouses, which promised "jobs now!," against white, anti-warehouse activists concerned that the massive facility would "encroach on their pastoral lifestyles."[114] Chapter 7 explores this phenomenon, which is often characterized pejoratively as NIMBY (Not In My Back Yard) opposition, including its Inland Southern California origins in activism by working-class white women.

In contrast, the increasingly socially and economically diverse and collaborative resistance to Amazon today reflects a shared experience of vulnerability to exploitation among members of labor, community, and environmental groups, and those who support them, that is less strictly defined by race or ethnicity, economic class, gender norms, and/or other social differences.[115] The toxic air pollution and low wages associated with warehousing, distribution, and transportation especially impact those living in the region's poorer communities of color located nearest transportation corridors. Yet the psycho-ethical, physically and emotionally unhealthy, and logistical challenges of living and working in Inland Southern California are more widespread. It is therefore not necessarily surprising that the SBAC, a multiracial and ethnic, interfaith, intergenerational, social justice, labor rights, and environmental action coalition, was established in 2019 in response to the proposed expansion of the airport to support Amazon's air freight operations; coalition members intentionally united around demands for both good jobs for local residents *and* pollution mitigation associated with the project. The remainder of this section relates the origins of resistance to Amazon to the overwhelmingly negative impacts of warehousing on many Inland Southern California communities.

Impacts on the Environment and Health Disparities

Journalist Noah Smith aptly characterizes Inland Southern California's predominant workplaces—warehouses, delivery operations, and transportation services—and communities as the Southland's "back lot."[116] In the film industry context, "back lot" refers to an area behind or adjoining a set where outdoor scenes are shot. Smith argues that Inland Southern California provides the vast logistics staging ground and distribution hub that primarily serves the more prosperous counties on its borders. Amazon's siting of fulfillment operations in Inland Southern California to serve consumers in more prosperous Southland regions, especially coastal counties, is consistent with the disproportionate siting of warehouses in socioeconomically disadvantaged communities throughout Southern California.[117] Ivette Torres and collaborators from both the PC4EJ and the University of Redlands found that warehouses in Southern California are consistently approved for construction in poor communities that are notably also heavily impacted by pollution from existing facilities and operations.[118] Both Alec MacGillis's reportage in *Fulfillment* and a recent collaboration between Consumer Reports and *The Guardian* on Amazon's expansion strategy extend this generalization to the nation.[119] That report simply states that "Amazon opens most of its warehouses in neighborhoods with a disproportionately high number of people of color," most of which also have a greater share of low-income residents than is the norm for their metro area. The report contrasts Amazon warehouse locations with its Whole Foods and other retail outlets, which tend to be placed in wealthier, whiter neighborhoods.[120] The relationship is even more evident for Amazon's corporate offices, which are located in zip codes with very low percentages of Black, Latino, and Indigenous residents, according to a report by Amazon employee activists.[121]

This spatial injustice is further evidenced by socioeconomic, demographic, and air quality data for California's southern counties. The summary provided in table 2.2 indicates that, in contrast to the coastal counties—especially Orange and San Diego Counties—Inland Southern California is younger; browner; poorer; more dependent on warehousing, distribution, and transportation services; and subject to higher levels of air pollution. The Riverside-San Bernardino-Ontario Metropolitan Statistical Area (MSA) is the only Southern California region where residents who identify as Hispanic or Latino represent the majority ethnic group. The median household income in Orange County is more than $10,000 higher than any of the comparable figures for the other Southland regions. Poverty is much higher in the Riverside-San Bernardino-Ontario and Los Angeles-Long Beach MSAs than in the other Southland regions, though young women of the majority race or ethnicity constitute the poorest demographic in every region. More than twice as many residents of the Riverside-San Bernardino-Ontario MSA are employed in warehousing and transportation services as is the case in either Orange County or the San Diego-Carlsbad MSA. Although none of the Southland regions represented in table 2.2 have attained National Ambient Air Quality Standards

(NAAQS), there are stark differences in the air pollution experiences of residents in Riverside and San Bernardino Counties versus those living in Los Angeles, Orange, or San Diego Counties.

Table 2.2 includes American Lung Association analyses for ozone, which contributes to chest pain, coughing, shortness of breath, throat irritation and long-term lung damage, and fine particulates ($PM_{2.5}$), which are associated with premature death from heart and lung disease.[122] The annual weighted average number of "high ozone" days, when ozone exceeds the "moderate" threshold of 70 parts per billion (pbb), in San Bernardino County was ten times higher than in neighboring Orange County during the period 2017–2019. The comparable figures were eight and six times higher for Riverside and Los Angeles Counties. While Los Angeles County experienced the greatest annual weighted average number "high $PM_{2.5}$" days, when $PM_{2.5}$ exceeds the 3.2-day standard, Riverside and San Bernardino Counties also experienced much higher levels of $PM_{2.5}$ than did Orange and San Diego Counties during the period 2017–2019. While such health problems cut across genders, women tend to provide the most care, both paid and unpaid, for children, the elderly, and sick relatives affected by these public health problems.[123]

Research on the relationship between warehousing, distribution, and associated transportation activities and social, environmental, and health disparities in poor communities of color supports the insights suggested by table 2.2.[124] The relationship between spatial injustice and Amazon's expansion in Inland Southern California may be an artifact of e-commerce retailers' and other warehouse-dependent enterprises' demand for the same relatively inexpensive land desired by developers of low-income housing. Quan Yuan's longitudinal analysis of warehouse sitings in Southern California suggests that "unregulated logistics expansion" contributes to environmental disparities across communities differentiated by social and economic factors.[125] The analysis suggests that siting decisions were based on the availability of affordable space with proximity to rail freight corridors, interstate highways, and airports; access to Southern California's large customer market; and the promise of a large, blue-collar labor pool.[126] Yuan also argues that affordable land independently incentivizes the construction of low-income housing near warehouse complexes, which naturally attracts low- and lower-middle-income people, often also of color.

Table 2.2 Spatial Inequality in Southern California by Metropolitan Statistical Area

	Riverside-San Bernardino-Ontario	Los Angeles-Long Beach-Anaheim	Orange County	San Diego-Carlsbad
Race/ethnicity				
Asian	7%	16%	21%	12%
Black	7%	6%	2%	5%
Latino	52%	45%	34%	34%
White	31%	29%	40%	45%
Median age	35	37	39	36
Median income	$71,000	$78,000	$96,000	$84,000
Poverty	15%	14%	11%	12%
Poorest demographic	Latinas, 25–34	Latinas, 25–34	White women, 18–24	Latinas, 25–34
Major industries (% residents)				
Education	9%	—	9%	—
Health care	13%	12%	12%	—
Management	—	—	—	11%
Manufacturing	—	10%	11%	—
Office/administration	—	—	—	9%
Retail trade	12%	10%	10%	—
Sales	—	—	—	10%
Science-technology	—	—	9%	—
Warehouse	8%	5%	3%	3%
High ozone days (2017–2019)	SB: 173 Riv: 136	107	17	37
High PM days (2017–2019)	SB: 10 Riv: 10	14	6	3

NOTE: An earlier version of this table appears in Emmons Allison (2020).

SOURCE: Data USA (2019); American Lung Association (2019).

PM = particulate matter

Social justice activists both in Inland Southern California and elsewhere in the United States agree that Amazon and other e-commerce retailers include economic analyses in their siting decisions.[127] Quinta Warren, Consumer Reports associate director for sustainability policy, argues that these enterprises nonetheless take "advantage of a national legacy of racist policies that have kept cities across the country segregated for generations, [resulting in] disproportionate health and environmental impacts to communities of color."[128] Zoning laws fail to insulate residential developments from industrial uses, including warehouses and related logistics operations, and lax—or inadequately enforced—air quality regulations and public nuisance laws. Chapter 7 explores the role this problem plays in catalyzing resistance to warehousing in Inland Southern California.

Political context also plays a role in warehouse siting decisions by shaping the interactions among logistics companies, real estate agents, and municipal and county governments.[129] Local governments develop and implement the zoning restrictions, tax and other economic incentives, and environmental regulations that encourage or discourage proposed warehouse developments; once a warehouse, DC, or logistics center gains approval and is under construction, commercial realtors mediate negotiations between the developers or owners of these facilities and prospective tenants. Amazon's interactions with municipalities and developers, in particular, capitalize on wealthy millennials' reliance on e-commerce.[130] The Riverside County Board of Supervisors, long recognized as politically conservative if not also Republican, and increasingly criticized for its failure to represent Latino residents, approved dozens of these facilities for construction in unincorporated areas.[131]

Due to larger systemic racial and class inequities, residents of the primarily low-income communities of color most directly impacted by warehouses and the fulfillment operations they support have historically participated at low levels in the policy decisions that directly impact their health and safety. Racial and ethnic gaps in political participation persist, even after accounting for educational attainment, income, homeownership, and other socioeconomic considerations. Latinos, who represent the majority of residents in Inland Southern California's poorer communities, have attended meetings related to local politics and policy less than half as often as the region's white residents have.[132] Chapter 7 documents recent actions by community organizations created specifically to resist warehouse development that challenge this generalization.

The warehouses and DCs that are essential to Amazon and other e-commerce companies are distinct from the usual "locally undesirable land uses" (LULUs) because their negative environmental and public health impacts flow primarily from their appearance and role in traffic congestion rather than from their operations. Some warehouses do store flammable, explosive, and/or and toxic goods; however, warehouses and DCs more often alter or degrade (sub)urban landscapes.[133] Warehousing, distribution, and transportation are associated with local warming, increased air pollution and related respiratory illnesses, and road damage.[134] The public health consequences associated with diesel truck traffic and congestion pose the greatest threat to Inland Southern California neighborhoods adjacent to, or along transportation corridors connecting, warehouses in the region. A recent analysis by the SCAQMD indicates that the population living within half a mile of at least one large warehouse is 62 percent Latino and 8 percent Black, compared with a population that is 45 percent Latino and 7 percent Black across Los Angeles, Orange, Riverside, and San Bernardino Counties.[135]

The air pollution—especially ozone and particulates—these Southland residents experience is high enough to warrant their designation as "diesel death zones" for the multitude of health issues residents face. According to the SCAQMD, communities located within half a mile of Southland transportation corridors are in the 64th percentile for asthma and 65th percentile for heart attacks, compared to 53rd and 57th percentile for asthma and cardiovascular disease incidence rates, respectively, for Los Angeles, Orange, Riverside, and San Bernardino Counties.[136] Regional social justice advocate Penny Newman referenced the region's notoriously high levels of deadly ozone and particulate matter to explain why "children born in San Bernardino or Riverside county will be exposed to as many carcinogens in the first 12 days of their life as most people are in 70 years."[137] These physical ailments compound the emotional and physical labor involved in caring for those who are ill, which is disproportionately born by women, either in their familial roles or as employed health-care providers.[138]

The magnitude of Amazon's fulfillment operations makes the corporation accountable for much of the increasing truck (and delivery van) traffic congestion, air pollution, and incidences of respiratory illnesses in Inland Southern California. In addition to Amazon's contribution to these impacts from fulfillment-driven transportation services, the corporation is more directly responsible for emissions and related health disparities associated with its deliveries, 45 percent of which are handled directly by Amazon.[139] Amazon's initial investment in sortation and delivery centers included dual gasoline-diesel fuel Mercedes Benz Sprinter Vans, which was criticized by more climate-forward competitors, including Walmart and UPS, and its own employees, as well as environmental activists.[140] A year later, after "thumbing its nose" at climate action, Amazon's 2019 Climate Pledge to have at least half its shipping operations carbon neutral by 2040 includes transition from Sprinter Vans to electric Rivians beginning in 2021.[141]

Amazon's pivot is consistent with the logistics industry's expectation that electrification and sustainability will be central to the future of warehousing, distribution, and transportation, in part due to recent regulatory requirements discussed further in chapter 7.[142] Yet Amazon's overall carbon footprint rose 19 percent in 2020 to 61 million metric tons, and the company's fossil fuel use increased by 69 percent while total carbon intensity decreased by 16 percent.[143] Amazon blames these increases on the unprecedented demands on e-commerce associated with the COVID-19 pandemic. The pandemic is associated with a $183 billion increase in online spending between March 2020 and February 2021. That "COVID bump" was nearly equivalent to the 2020 holiday e-commerce spending, which represented a 33 percent increase over 2019.[144]

Impacts on the Economy

Amazon's public relations staff, politicians, and other fans of the corporation argue that Amazon's impact on Inland Southern California's environment and the health of its residents, especially those who belong to the region's communities of color, is outweighed by the benefits associated with jobs.[145] The catch is that Amazon warehouse jobs do not necessarily increase overall employment growth; each Amazon FC or IXD increases warehousing jobs by 30 percent, gains that are entirely offset by job losses in other industries.[146] Moreover, the region's higher employment rate has not been accompanied by increased earnings. While the median annual salary for the logistics industry as a whole is a lower-middle-class $48,000, the average annual salary *in* Inland Southern California warehouses, including Amazon facilities, is just over $31,000.[147] The associated $15 per hour minimum wage barely qualifies as a living wage in Inland Southern

California, and then only for a single adult, a working couple, or a family of three in which two adults are employed full-time.[148]

There is little evidence to support the claim that the region's warehouse jobs represent the bottom rungs of ladders to the middle class.[149] Advancement at Amazon, in particular, requires scoring a shift that makes—traditional or onsite—higher education or additional training possible, an advantage that is attenuated by race, ethnicity, and gender.[150] As we discussed in chapter 1, most of Amazon's managerial and higher paid corporate employees in the United States are white and male, while most of its frontline warehouse workers are Black or Latino. In Inland Southern California, most warehouse workers are Latinos, and most lack college degrees. While they are mostly men, women make up a significant and growing share of these workers, who carry out backbreaking, grueling work under tight surveillance and experience high rates of workplace injury.[151]

The official narrative that warehouse work provides a path to the middle class is further imperiled by increasing reliance on automation in warehousing and fulfillment processes, especially at Amazon. The contemporary consumers' demand for smaller, individualized packages, at irregular intervals if not immediately, is expensive for e-commerce companies. Trips to the mall or supermarket have been replaced by online order fulfillment: picking, packing, and delivery, typically completed by paid, working-class people of color, whose pay must be low to ensure the system's profitability. Had it not been for automation, Amazon arguably would not have been able to afford its 2018 across-the-board minimum hourly wage increase to $15 or its COVID-19 pandemic era hazard pay (an additional $2 per hour) and other hiring incentives ($18 per hour with hiring bonuses as high as $3,000 in some locations). Amazon's increasing reliance on robots means that "fewer workers are needed to . . . ship $100 million worth of stuff."[152]

Amazon will require a number of highly skilled employees to install, service, and operate its growing robot workforce, but not enough to offset the loss of warehouse work.[153] Consequently, Amazon's futuristic "robotic" FC in Eastvale, a regionally wealthy city built on the remains of a dairy farm in Riverside County, evokes fears of another Skechers debacle. In 2010, Skechers—a California-based lifestyle and performance footwear company—closed five DCs in Ontario to open a 1.8-million-square-foot, highly-automated Skechers warehouse in Moreno Valley. The new facility was supposed to employ 1,000 people—500 new hires and up to 500 transfers. Two years later, 600 people, mostly transfers, worked at the new Skechers DC.[154] This occurrence is not unusual. According to a survey of warehouse operators by Peerless Research Group, 79 percent of warehousing and storage operations, and up to 59 percent of order fulfillment activities industry-wide, had been automated by mid-2019.[155]

Jobs lost to automation are notably *in addition to* those sacrificed to the "Amazon effect," or the disruption of retail markets caused by consumers' increasing reliance on e-commerce and retailers' scrambling to compete with Amazon's mammoth selection, fast and often free shipping, generous return policy, and subscription services.[156] In combination with other features of the retail landscape—including an oversupply of shopping outlets and changes in spending habits—the Amazon effect contributed to the "retail apocalypse," referring to the wave of brick-and-mortar store closures, especially major chains. These closures have occurred alongside retail resurgence manifest in mall retrofits, retail downsizing—such as small-format Target, Sears, and Ikea stores—and the emergence of new "consumer retention tactics," including parking lot delivery, drop-off returns, and personal shoppers to make shopping more convenient.[157] Such adaptations by retail stores also occurred in Inland Southern California, but mostly in response to retail store closures and consequent ongoing changes in consumer behavior associated with the COVID-19 pandemic. Even before these changes, the region's retail vacancy rate in 2019 was among the highest in the nation and nearly twice as high as in neighboring Orange and Los Angeles Counties.[158]

THE UPSHOT OF AMAZON'S BUILDOUT

Amazon's Inland Southern California build-out capitalizes on the region's history of racial and ethnic, class, gender-based, and other intersecting inequalities and conflicts. These socioeconomic inequalities were codified via settlers' ordinances during the period of Spanish and Mexican colonization, the federal Bracero program from the 1940s through the early 1960s, and a suite of state and local tax and other policies throughout California's history. Beginning in the 1980s, when manufacturing waned and military activity ramped down in the region, conservative and business-friendly officials embraced warehousing at the expense of spatial justice and long-term environmental and economic sustainability. The Great Recession fueled the fire for their commitment. Amazon appeared to solve one of the region's biggest problems at the time: double-digit unemployment.

Amazon did generate thousands of blue-collar jobs for Inland Southern California residents, especially Latinos; however, the relatively low wages offered and the difficult working conditions in Amazon FCs, combined with the corporation's rapid geographic expansion and absorption of desperately needed sales tax revenues, have undermined the corporation's benefits to the region. The experiences of Amazon workers and community residents heavily impacted by the corporation's warehouses and delivery facilities helped to galvanize resistance among warehouse workers and a wide range of other activists and air quality regulators, concerned about warehousing's negative socioeconomic and environmental impacts. The chapters that follow explore Amazon warehouse workers' experiences; regional efforts to organize warehouse workers; and the rise of collaborative, community-based resistance to the warehouse industry.

3 Behind the Box

EXPLOITATIVE CONDITIONS
IN AMAZON'S WAREHOUSES

Thirty-eight year-old Julio immigrated to the United States from Mexico as a child and earned a high school degree before he began working in an Inland Southern California warehouse. Julio is a devoted husband and father of two teenage daughters who said he was motivated to work at Amazon because it allowed him "to support my family, support myself, and have a roof over my head."

Despite having about sixteen years of experience in the warehouse industry before joining Amazon, Julio was initially hired at an entry level (tier 1) position helping to receive packages in inbound, because "when you get hired at Amazon, you start off from the bottom." He moved up slowly over the course of six years, to a tier 3 position, in which he worked on supply orders. Julio was employed in various other positions along the way, including assisting the manager and supervisor as a "process guide," training employees to operate forklifts, and serving as a safety committee member. He enjoyed learning new work skills, including how to use computers, send emails, and prepare spreadsheets. Like many Amazon warehouse workers, he worked full-time: four ten-hour shifts. He often worked overtime during the holiday peak season (October through December) and around Amazon's Prime Day in the summer.

Although Julio felt exhausted at the end of his shift and sometimes felt intense foot pain, he still believed that his job at Amazon was, in many respects, much better than his previous warehouse jobs. Julio explained,

> I'm extremely satisfied especially because my whole building is actually temperature controlled, say it could be like 120 degrees outside but you don't even feel it, it could be 75 inside because they have all the walls padded and they have AC, or vice versa, it could be minus 20 degrees outside and it's hot in there. . . . I've been doing this 18–20 years of warehouse work, and all the warehouses I'd worked at previously, the conditions were horrible. Sometimes you'd have to be in there, it was 100 degrees outside, and it would feel like 120 degrees inside, you know? So right here, I'm in heaven. That's one of the primary things, you know. . . . There's a bunch of water stations, they have a bunch of vending machines where you can buy yourself a snack, they have two break rooms, they have four bathrooms, one in every corner like a box.

Julio appeared to be fortunate in these respects; other workers have reported that Amazon warehouse facilities, and even different locations within facilities, varied in their quality, and workers sometimes lacked access to various amenities, including good temperature control.[1] Julio also appreciated other employment benefits that Amazon offers its permanent workers, such as forty hours of paid time off (PTO) per year, which could be used for a vacation or to cover any time an employee arrived late or missed a day of work. In addition, "You get 401k, you get the whole nine yards the first day you become permanent. . . . Health insurance, dental insurance, life insurance, they have pet insurance, 401k of course. They have a lot of stuff you can take advantage of." Even so, Julio admitted that his pay at the time, $18.75 per hour, was still too low for the high cost of living in the region, and that his family relied on insurance through his wife's job rather than his own because of the cost of Amazon's insurance plan. He described the daily financial struggles that millions of US workers experience in this way:

> It seems like everyday, on a daily basis, everything's going up: food and health insurance, and of course, the companies they need to compensate you better in order for you to make a living, you know? Because if not, sooner or later, we're just going to be working to pay our health insurance or stuff like that, you know? We're not going to have enough money to survive on our own.

Julio concluded, "I think Amazon should pay a little bit more."

Julio's conclusion does not simply express his personal desire to earn a higher wage so that he can support his family given the growing costs of living. It also reminds us that Amazon's profits, like those of other companies, depend on underpaying or exploiting its workers. Much of the mainstream press and popular writing about the rise of Amazon attributes the corporation's profitability and overall success to its founding CEO, Jeff Bezos, who is portrayed as a particularly shrewd, ruthless, and innovative businessman. While these individual personality traits may have contributed to Amazon's rise, we argue that the corporation's phenomenal growth is also structural; as in most corporations in the United States, Bezos and other Amazon leaders have taken advantage of workers in the context of enduring inequalities and lax government oversight of labor markets and workplaces.

As we argued in chapter 1, systemic social inequalities in neoliberal global capitalism, including those related to gender, race, ethnicity, immigrant status, and class, interact in multiple and complex ways to shape local and regional labor markets.[2] In the case of Amazon in Inland Southern California, most warehouse workers are workers of color, mostly Latino, who lack college degrees.[3] In contrast, those at the very top of Amazon's corporate hierarchy are mostly wealthy, well-educated, white men who do not live in the region.[4]

The sheer concentration of so many warehouses in the region and absence of other, higher-paying industries creates an informal "school to warehouse" pipeline that brings tens of thousands of young workers of color, mostly Latinos, along with their older counterparts, into blue-collar warehouse employment.[5] In addition, there are also formal career pipelines in the region that help to recruit students to warehouse employment. For example, Amazon invested $50,000 in an "Amazon logistics and business management pathways program" at Cajon High School in San Bernardino.[6] Most warehouse workers lack a college degree and other technical skills or certifications that might help them to gain employment in higher-paying jobs. There is also an absence of higher-paying jobs in the region, a situation that was particularly evident during the COVID-19 pandemic. While other businesses and workplaces shut down or reduced hours in response to the pandemic, business was booming in warehouses, especially Amazon FCs and delivery stations. Amazon built additional FCs, delivery stations, and sortation centers and engaged in a hiring spree, increasing its global workforce by 75 percent between March 2020 and September 2021.[7]

While Amazon's exploitative employment practices depend on the social and regional inequalities that shape and constrain the employment options for workers of color without college degrees in Inland Southern California, it also operates *inside* the workplace itself. As a result, Amazon warehouse workers face exploitative employment contracts that pay workers poverty-level wages and render many of them precarious through temporary or seasonal employment contracts.[8]

In this chapter, we begin to explore the working conditions in Amazon warehouses in Inland Southern California from the perspective of warehouse workers, most of whom are Latino and lack a college degree. We do so by analyzing findings from the eighty-two in-depth interviews completed between 2018 and 2020 with current and former blue-collar Amazon warehouse workers employed in the region, and by putting these interview findings into the context of relevant research and journalism on Amazon warehouse workers' views and experiences. In particular, we detail workers' low pay relative to the high cost of living, insufficient employment benefits, and inequalities in pay and benefits among both seasonal and so-called permanent employees. We find that warehouse workers often express multiple concerns about their working conditions, and most do not plan to stay in them long. Yet like Julio, many workers express satisfaction with their jobs and would recommend them to other workers because they compare favorably to previous jobs they have held in terms of pay and other benefits. Finally, we explore how workers' schedules and working conditions negatively impact their lives outside of the warehouse, including their family and school lives.

COMMON CONCERNS AMONG WORKERS

Amazon takes advantage of workers' need to make money, low minimum wages set through policy, and the limited job alternatives in regional labor markets, especially for workers without a college degree or technical training. Working conditions in Amazon warehouses are notorious for being physically grueling, so it is not surprising that many Amazon warehouse workers interviewed for this book expressed multiple concerns about their working conditions.

Table 3.1 summarizes interviewees' most common concerns. When asked if they experienced pain or fatigue at the end of their work shift, 93 percent of those interviewed for this book, both before and during the pandemic, agreed.[9] Similarly, another survey of Amazon warehouse workers employed in the region finds that 77 percent of respondents expressed concerns related to fatigue or exhaustion, while 60 percent reported aches and pain.[10] In our interview sample, most of the handful of workers reporting no pain or fatigue at the end of their shifts worked part-time. Pain and fatigue was especially intense among those employed full-time, who typically worked a ten-hour shift, four days a week, and those working overtime and on night shifts. Describing his job as a stower, Angelo said, "We had to lift a lot of heavy boxes, and stay awake until 4 am." Stowers scan and store items on shelves and in bins so that other workers, employed as pickers, can find and retrieve them to fill customers' orders. Workers employed as pickers in less-automated facilities describe walking for about sixteen miles by the end of their shifts. Other jobs, such as packing or sorting, and even picking and stowing, in facilities relying on robots to store or retrieve items, require workers to stand in place most of their shifts, which also takes a toll on the body, often in the form of foot pain and sore muscles from repeatedly bending and reaching.

As table 3.1 shows, most interviewees (nearly 66 percent) did not look forward to coming to work the next day, a finding that remained consistent throughout the COVID-19 pandemic. Many Amazon workers described their warehouse jobs as mentally draining, socially isolating, highly repetitive, and boring, while others focused more on the stress and physical pain associated with doing the job. Just over half of those interviewed, both before and during the pandemic, agreed that they had concerns with the pressure to work fast, while just under half expressed personal concerns about their ability to "make rate," or meet Amazon's high productivity standards. When directly asked, many of the workers also agreed that their jobs were stressful, dangerous, and difficult, and the percentages of respondents agreeing with these three concerns were especially high

Table 3.1 Interviewees' Common Concerns

Concern	Prepandemic Sample			Pandemic Sample			Both Samples		
	Frequency	Valid Responses	%	Frequency	Valid Responses	%	Frequency	Valid Responses	%
Pain/fatigue after shift	40	43	93.02	28	30	93.33	68	73	93.15
Not looking forward to work	28	43	65.12	20	30	66.67	48	73	65.75
Pressure to work fast	23	41	56.10	16	30	53.33	39	71	54.93
Worried about making rate	19	40	47.50	15	30	50.00	34	70	48.57
Work stress	17	43	39.53	21	31	67.74	38	74	51.35
Dangerous job	16	38	42.11	16	29	55.17	32	67	47.76
Job is difficult	13	39	33.33	17	30	56.67	30	69	43.48
Inability to use restroom	13	41	31.71	11	28	39.29	23	69	33.33
Income concern	11	39	28.21	13	31	41.94	24	70	34.29
Promotion concern	12	41	29.27	11	29	37.93	23	70	32.86

during the pandemic. As table 3.1 shows, a majority of those interviewed during the pandemic agreed with these concerns, compared to less than half before the COVID-19 pandemic. This result might reflect the additional stresses and challenges related to working during the pandemic, including added health risks and the need to follow new safety rules while still working quickly. Similarly, another survey found that 72 percent of Amazon warehouse workers and delivery drivers in the region believed it was more stressful to make rate during the pandemic than before it.[11] About one-third of interviewees agreed that they had concerns about their ability to use the restroom when needed, with their incomes, and with their opportunities to receive raises or promotions.

Despite interviewees' frequent concerns about the negative impact of the job on their mental and physical health, nearly half (49 percent) said their Amazon job was better than other low-wage jobs they had held, as shown in table 3.2. When asked about the other jobs they had held, interviewees listed a wide variety of occupations. Most commonly, they mentioned employment in food services (36 percent), retail (34 percent), warehousing (25 percent), office or administrative support occupations (13 percent), customer service (11 percent), and campus service jobs (11 percent). When directly asked, about 37 percent reported previous employment experience in the warehouse or logistics industry.[12] Although some workers had less work experience than others, many had worked in a number of low-wage jobs in the region. For example, describing his work experience prior to his Amazon job, Samuel said: "I worked at Home Depot for like four years and then, I did like temporary jobs, like at Toyota, a warehouse in Ontario. I worked at retail in Target for a couple years." As we discuss more fully in the next section, compared to other low-wage jobs in the region, Amazon's wages were often slightly better, its work schedules were more predictable, and it provided workers with more hours.

Perhaps these relative benefits of working at Amazon and the promise of obtaining bonuses for helping to recruit workers, in combination with the lack of better employment alternatives in the region, explains why most workers interviewed said that they would (at least sometimes) recommend the job to another worker, as shown in table 3.2. The table also indicates that when directly asked whether or not they were satisfied with their jobs overall, nearly half (46 percent) said, "yes," although this view

Table 3.2 Interviewees' Job Assessment

	Prepandemic Sample		Pandemic Sample		Both Samples	
	Frequency	*Percentage*	*Frequency*	*Percentage*	*Frequency*	*Percentage*
Comparison to former job						
Better	19	45.24	17	54.84	36	49.32
Worse	15	35.71	4	12.90	19	26.02
About the same	7	16.67	4	12.90	11	15.07
Don't know; better & worse	1	2.38	6	19.35	7	9.59
Total valid responses	*42*		*31*		*73*	
Do you recommend Amazon?						
Yes	14	32.56	14	45.16	28	37.84
Sometimes or it depends	16	37.21	12	38.71	28	37.84
No, never	13	30.23	5	16.13	18	24.32
Total valid responses	*43*		*31*		*74*	
Satisfied with job (overall)?						
Yes	25	56.82	10	31.25	35	46.05
Sometimes or partly	4	9.09	0	0.0	4	5.26
No	15	34.09	22	68.75	37	48.68
Total valid responses	*44*		*32*		*76*	

was more common prior to the COVID-19 pandemic than during it, when working conditions became even more stressful and isolating than usual and more current workers were interviewed. That said, most interviewees, who were disproportionately young compared to most Amazon warehouse workers in the region, regarded their Amazon job as simply a short-term way to earn money rather than as a long-term career.[13] Many interviewees had specific criticisms of their working conditions, even when they viewed the job as relatively better than other job options available to them. For example, Juan, who was previously employed in construction, explained:

> In the past, I've had a lot of bad jobs so working here [at Amazon] isn't that bad compared to other jobs I've had. Here I get more things than I would in past employments, for example, health insurance. I'm used to doing hard labor for less, so compared to my past experiences, Amazon is kind of a step up. They even give us free coffee! I feel like this is okay for right now, but I still don't agree with the way they treat their employees. . . . The way they run their warehouses can be dehumanizing!

Juan's mixed assessment was fairly common among workers in the sample. Compared to other job options available to them, many viewed Amazon's pay, hours, and benefits as relatively better, but regarded working conditions at Amazon to be worse in other ways, such as being more stressful, alienating, and physically draining.

AMAZON'S WAGES AND BENEFITS

In response to public pressure, labor market pressure, and worker organizing, Amazon has made efforts to position the corporation as a fair wage leader. In October 2018 Amazon raised its entry-level pay for warehouse workers in the United States to $15 per hour, including those employed part-time and in seasonal positions, both to alleviate political pressure and to attract applicants for the coming holiday season. At that time, the average pay for Amazon warehouse workers was about $13 nationwide, and the corporation was coming under fire by Senator Bernie Sanders and others for its low wages and employees' use of federal assistance programs. Explaining this decision to the press, Bezos said, "'We listened to our critics, thought hard about what we wanted to do, and decided we wanted to lead.'" Amazon executives also joined others calling for a higher federal minimum wage.[14] Yet even as it raised its minimum wage for warehouse workers, Amazon eliminated their stock options and incentive pay, or bonuses for high productivity, which it had previously offered to its warehouse associates.[15]

As journalist Dean Baker and others suggest, Amazon's decision to raise its entry-level wage to $15 per hour was not simply a good way to counter public criticism. It was a strategic way to attract workers in a historically tight labor market characterized by an unemployment rate of 3.7 percent at the end of 2018.[16] Amazon's warehouse workers earn even more than $15 per hour if they work the night shift and overtime or in places where the cost of living is high and workers are in high demand. They also receive small raises over time for seniority, which vary across sites and depend on workers' rank. Workers interviewed for this study reported receiving periodic raises of $0.15 or $0.25 per hour.

At the start of the COVID-19 pandemic in March 2020, Amazon offered $2 per hour "hazard pay," a temporary pay boost used to recruit workers despite the additional health risks associated with working long hours indoors and in close proximity to others. At the time, Amazon was in the midst of hiring about 100,000 new employees to meet the surging demand for home-delivered products. Workers were disappointed when the corporation reversed this hazard pay at the end of May 2020 even though reported coronavirus cases, including among Amazon workers, continued to climb.[17] By then unemployment levels and Amazon's newly recruited workforce had risen enough that additional, across-the-board pay incentives for employee recruitment were no longer needed.[18] As Olivia said, "We did get a two dollar raise when we first started, so I thought that was kind of nice. . . . It helped a little bit more with . . . my expenses and then it was suddenly just, you know, taken out." Although able to pay her bills, she lamented her "low budget." Similarly, Daniella, 46 years old and partially responsible for supporting her 22-year old daughter and 2-year old granddaughter, remarked:

> Amazon should have been paying more just because they're a really big company and we're only getting paid $15 . . . for the amount of working time we

were there . . . especially because, just 'cause Amazon makes so much money in the day, I know they can pay people more, but the only time they paid us more was during the virus for about a month only. They raised it up to $17 an hour, but then right after that month finished, we're just going back to $15. . . . Wow! Working during a pandemic and still only getting paid $15 an hour!

Daniella's remark reveals that many Amazon warehouse employees are conscious of, and are morally opposed to, the exploitative nature of the corporation.

Consistent with Daniella's assessment that Amazon could afford to pay warehouse workers more than the corporation did during the COVID-19 pandemic, research by the Brookings Institution finds that Bezos's wealth increased by $75.6 billion between March and December 2020, about forty-two times the cost of dollars that Amazon spent on hazard pay for about one million workers, which totaled $1.8 billion. Likewise, the average hourly pay increase for Amazon's frontline workers during this same period was about 99 cents, compared to an hourly wealth increase of $11.5 million for Bezos. The researchers conclude, "Amazon and Walmart could have more than quadrupled the COVID-19 compensation to frontline workers and still earned more profit than last year."[19]

Amazon raised workers' pay again, but not until the spring of 2021, when the demand for labor was rising as more businesses and workplaces reopened and Amazon was coming under heavy attack for opposing a failed unionization campaign in Bessemer, Alabama. In April 2021 it announced a series of pay raises for its employees, ranging from $0.50 per hour to $3 per hour.[20] And in May 2021 Amazon announced a new hiring spree, seeking to hire an additional 75,000 employees in warehousing and transportation. At some locations it advertised a wage of up to $17 per hour, plus a sign-on bonus of as much as $1,000.[21] By October 2021 Amazon was offering up to $18 per hour entry-level wages, depending on shifts and locations, and up to $3,000 in sign-on bonuses as it sought to recruit 150,000 employees nationwide for the upcoming holiday season.[22]

Many of the "permanent" full-time workers interviewed for this study said that the pay and employment benefits offered by Amazon, including its health and dental insurance plans and its 401K plan, are better than those offered by many other low-wage employers in the region. As noted previously, interviewees' prior work experience was most commonly in food service and retail, which are the other major sources of employment in Inland Southern California.[23] Although Indeed ranks average base salaries for food service (e.g., $17.43/hour in San Bernardino) and retail jobs (e.g., $18.93/hour in San Bernardino) in the region at about the national average, respectively, these jobs typically provide too few hours, unpredictable schedules, and no benefits.[24] Destiny, who previously worked in retail and customer service before working at Amazon and became permanently injured at her Amazon job, recalled that "the one thing I liked about Amazon was, if I needed hours, they were there." For workers such as Viviana, Amazon warehouse work also provided a welcome break from interacting with "rude customers."

In addition to their Amazon warehouse jobs, about 37 percent of interviewees had previous work experience in the warehouse or logistics industry, and at least 25 percent mentioned being employed in other types of warehouses.[25] For some of these workers, Amazon's wages and benefits package were also better than what they were offered by other warehouse employers in the region at the time. As Brianna put it, "As far as any warehouse, Amazon probably pays one of the best!" Indeed, many other nonunionized warehouse employers pay less than Amazon does, employ workers through temporary agencies, and do not provide benefits. Consequently, the region's logistics industry is generally considered exploitative. As other research finds, the concentration of transportation and warehouse jobs in the region contributes to low earnings and poverty in Inland Southern California.[26] As surveys and official statistics have also shown, low wages and precarious employment—whether through temporary agencies or seasonal contracts—are especially common among the region's blue-collar warehouse workers.[27]

Unionized warehouse workers earn more than nonunionized Amazon warehouse workers, however. For example, Joey Alvarado, a warehouse worker employed by Stater Brothers in Moreno Valley, California, reported to *Bloomberg News* in 2021 that he earned $30 per hour in Moreno Valley, California, thanks to his Teamsters Local 63 union contract. He also had a pension and a good health insurance plan for his family, one that does not require him to pay any premiums.[28] Another Teamsters 63 member whom we interviewed in 2018, Linda, similarly reported that she was earning good pay ($26 per hour) due to her seniority plus another $13 per hour during periods in which she exceeded the productivity standard. Like Joey, Linda also enjoyed the good health insurance plan her union contract provided to her and her husband, who also worked for Stater Brothers. Both her pay and the terms of this health insurance plan were far better than the employment package offered to her daughter, a warehouse worker employed by Amazon, who continued to rely on her parents' health insurance plan because she could not afford to pay the monthly premium for Amazon's health insurance plan.[29]

By 2022 other major warehouse employers in the region, even non-union ones such as Target and Walmart, were apparently offering higher wages than Amazon as they competed with one another to recruit and retain workers as labor market conditions improved in the aftermath of the pandemic.[30] Even prior to this, a few Amazon workers interviewed for this book described warehouse jobs with better pay and working conditions than at Amazon. For example, Doug, who was fired by Amazon for his inability to make rate, was later hired as a forklift operator for another company. Explaining why he preferred his current job to his Amazon job, he said: "The work that I'm doing now I feel is easier. You get paid better. . . . The company is family oriented. You get almost every major holiday off with pay and, it's just a better work environment."

Nationally, warehouse industry wages tend to fall in US counties where Amazon opens facilities, more than 6 percent in the first two years, and only reach their previous levels five years later.[31] Of course this pattern of flat or falling wages for warehouse workers varies among counties due to local conditions and unionization rates. For example, in Robbinsville, New Jersey, warehouse workers' average earnings were $24 in 2014, when Amazon opened its first FC there; nearly six years later, average warehouse wages in the township and nearby municipalities were down to $17.50 per hour, a decrease that reflects, in part, a lack of unionization among Amazon warehouse workers, even in this historically pro-union region.[32]

Most interviewees for this book were keenly aware that Amazon's pay rate was too low relative to the high cost of living in Southern California, even among those who viewed Amazon's pay and benefits as relatively better than their previous low-wage jobs. For example, Sofia explains why she would recommend the job only for younger workers fresh out of high school: "If it's just yourself, then I think it's a good job, but to support a family, I wouldn't really recommend it." Research for MIT's living wage calculator suggests that a worker like Julio, living in a household with two adults working and two dependent children, needed to earn $24.45 per hour in 2020 to cover basic living costs in San Bernardino.[33] Similar data analyses indicate that an employee needed to earn $24.79 per hour to afford the fair market rent on a two-bedroom apartment in the Riverside-San Bernardino-Ontario metropolitan area.[34] These wages are well above the $18.75 per hour that Julio, the top-earning Amazon warehouse worker in our interview sample, reported at the time of his interview. Most interviewees reported earning entry-level wages or just above them.

When asked about the most desirable job improvements many interviewees, like Julio, mentioned pay raises. According to Josh, warehouse workers' low wages are "the biggest flaw at Amazon." Even workers who were childless lamented the low wages offered by Amazon. As Hannah put it, "I think there should be more room for getting the raise, which it doesn't seem like there is." Although she lives in a small desert city, where housing costs are less expensive than at other places in the region, she still found it difficult to pay her bills. As she explained, "There's always stuff that comes up, unexpected stuff, like with my car. . . . When a big expense comes up, it's kind of hard cause I don't have savings." Hannah explained that car expenses were essential because she had to travel more than thirty miles to get to her Amazon job and had been unable to find work closer to home.

As these workers' perspectives illustrate, Amazon's low wages are particularly problematic because they make it difficult, at best, for many of their warehouse employees to live independently from their parents, let alone support a family. Research finds that about 41 percent of Amazon warehouse workers employed in Southern California were doubled up with family members or roommates, while about 21 percent lived with their parents in multigenerational households. About 33 percent lived in overcrowded housing situations, in which there was more than one person per room or more than two people per bedroom.[35] Nationwide, wages, especially among workers without a college education, have not kept up with rising housing costs, making it increasingly difficult for many working-age adults to live independently. No wonder "doubling up," a lifestyle strategy in which two or more unmarried working-age adults live together, including adult children living with their parents, has been on the rise generally across the nation. The doubling-up trend to pay housing costs has been especially pronounced in Inland Southern California; by 2016, 44 percent of adults between the ages of 23 and 65 lived in a doubled-up household in the Riverside metropolitan region, compared to 30 percent nationally.[36] Most of our interviewees lived in such households, usually with their parents. About 52 percent of the prepandemic sample and 66 percent of the pandemic sample were adults who lived with their parents.

Relative to their wages, the cost of health insurance benefits offered to warehouse workers is also expensive, especially for those who need health insurance for their children and other family members. Many workers rely on family members, such as a spouse or parent, for their own health insurance or all or part of their children's health insurance. For example, Elvia provided only vision and dental insurance for her two sons, who relied on their father for their basic medical insurance; splitting the insurance coverage in this way kept it affordable for her. Jimmy, a student worker in his thirties who was married and had a child, reported, "I had insurance through the school so I did not utilize Amazon's insurance. The school insurance covered more and the deductible was less." Other college students unable to rely on their parents' health insurance plans reported relying on their school's health insurance plan as well.

Meanwhile, some workers, especially single mothers in our interview sample, relied on Medicaid (subsidized health insurance). According to the Government Accounting Office, a total of 4,218 Amazon workers across six states (out of nine states examined) relied on the Supplemental Nutrition Assistance Program (SNAP, formerly known as food stamps) in 2020. This same report found that a total of 4,155 Amazon workers received Medicaid in five out of the six states examined.[37] Research finds that most, or 59 percent, of Amazon warehouse workers in Los Angeles, Orange, Riverside, and San Bernardino Counties have children.[38] Although Amazon offers a 401K plan, it does not offer its workers a pension plan, putting older workers at risk of poverty given that Social Security benefits among workers in low-wage jobs typically are insufficient to prevent poverty in the United States.[39]

Like other researchers examining the perspectives of contemporary workers in the United States, we found that a class critique was often

absent in many of the interviews, even when workers described their economic hardships or difficult working conditions. This finding is not too
surprising given the historical absence of a strong labor movement in US
society and the persistent cultural influence of the "American dream" ideology and myths surrounding meritocracy; those cultural ideas suggest
that one's financial success is largely the result of individuals' hard work or
talent and divert attention away from the role of systemic class, race, and
other social inequalities.[40]

Yet some workers interviewed, including some of those quoted previously, did offer very pointed critiques of their exploitative working conditions, Bezos's greed, and the race and class divisions they observed in
Amazon warehouses and the broader corporation. Two interviewees, one
of whom was Latino and the other Black, compared their Amazon warehouse jobs to slavery. For example, Daniel said: "When I would describe
my job to my friends and family, I would say that I thought slavery was
dead but this was a prime example how . . . capitalism is the new slavery
bro'. . . . That's how I would describe my job. That job is slavery." Similarly,
Destiny claimed that her Amazon warehouse job was similar to being in
a "slave factory." Amazon warehouse worker activists, including Christian
Smalls, president of Amazon Labor Union, have similarly used the metaphor of slavery to publicly criticize Amazon warehouse jobs, draw attention to the disproportionate number of Blacks employed in them, and how
they reproduce systemic race and class inequalities.[41] The use of the slave
metaphor in the United States is controversial but also a long-standing
practice, to strongly criticize, and portray as illegitimate, various harsh
conditions of state-sanctioned unfreedom, including oppressive and exploitative working conditions associated with racialized class oppression.[42]

Other warehouse workers criticized the exploitative nature of Amazon by contrasting their low wages with the incredible profits of the corporation or the wealth of its founder and longtime CEO, Bezos, whom
Forbes identified as the richest man on the planet for four years before he
was overtaken by Elon Musk in 2022.[43] When Roberto was asked what
he would do to improve Amazon for workers if he were a superhero, he
responded, "give everybody $100 raises. And that's all on Bezos' dime be-
cause he can afford it." Further elaborating on this point, he said, "Jeff
Bezos is greedy. If he'd stop being greedy, then that's basically it. He could

literally, with his pocket change, end poverty for us, probably throughout the world and still be one of the richest people ever and he just doesn't. He just gets richer, and it's annoying." Estella responded similarly to the question of what changes she would like to make at Amazon:

> I . . . would increase pay to help everyone there. No risks or consequences in paying workers more. Jeff Bezos would only have not more money but more people would be less job insecure. I remember someone having to take an Uber every day to work because her car broke down. Avoiding job insecurity would help a lot of workers.

Humberto summed up the sentiment of many interviewees when he said, "For a $1 trillion company, we aren't paid a lot."

TEMPS AND SEASONAL WORKERS

Many of Amazon's workers are precariously employed, a situation that is institutionalized, in part, through workers' employment contracts. As early as 1997 Amazon, like many other warehouse employers in the nation, relied on temporary agencies to employ workers. This arrangement was convenient for keeping labor costs low and the size of its workforce flexible to meet surging demand for "just in time" goods during major shopping seasons. In 2016 researchers estimated that, similar to the national warehouse industry generally, about 40 percent of Amazon's warehouse workforce in the United States was hired through temporary agencies, although this practice appeared to be more common in particular locations and to increase during the holidays.[44] Similarly, an analysis of surveys from 2009 to 2013 finds that in Inland Southern California, between 46 and 63 percent of blue-collar warehouse workers were temporary agency workers, or temps.[45]

Compared to warehouse workers who are directly hired, temps tend to be paid less per hour, are employed for fewer weeks per year, and are less likely to have employer-provided health insurance than workers directly hired by warehouse and logistics employers.[46] Interviewees who were initially hired as temporary agency workers for Amazon report that they earned somewhere between fifty cents and a dollar less than permanent employees for doing the same kind of work. A review of fifty job ads from across the nation in 2016 similarly found that Amazon warehouse workers employed through temporary agencies were paid between fifty cents to one dollar less per hour.[47]

Paola, who worked for nearly one year for Amazon in 2015 and 2016, provides a rich description of the inequalities and visible tensions she observed between Amazon warehouse workers who were employed by temporary agencies and those employed directly by Amazon:

> People who were hired through the company felt they had a privilege or a higher position than the workers who were coming in as temp workers; they (temp workers) were getting paid less, sent home when they made the 40 hours, and they didn't get any benefits. Whenever a temp worker had a job that no one really wanted, people would mock them and they would be told, "Ha-ha! You are only getting paid for this job $11.00!" "Damn they are only paying you that and you are not even getting benefits." I could feel that the temp workers didn't really like the people hired through the company, but they (temp workers) also didn't fight them because they knew the company workers had a privilege for being directly employed.

The inequalities between temporary agency workers and those directly hired by Amazon were more than simply differences in pay, hours, and benefits; they included a difference in status. As Alejandra observed, "The temps would always be like, talked down to. Blue badges were always like that." For Tyler, who was employed as a temp and built workstations for other workers, status differences among workers based on their employment status was reinforced through unequal access to restrooms. He observed that the "red hats, the people who were hired by the temp agency, had to go outside to use the porta-potties." Reflecting back on his Amazon work experience, Tyler concluded, "Amazon has been the worst job experience I have ever had. I'm able to make more [at my new job], work flexible hours, and use the restroom."

Amazon's reliance on temporary agencies to hire warehouse workers helped to minimize its labor costs in other ways besides simply reducing the cost of wages and benefits. It reduced the cost of recruiting and screening workers and other human resource tasks. It reduced the cost of federal unemployment benefits and time spent in unemployment appeals hearings. It also complicated efforts to unionize warehouse workers and reduced the corporation's legal liabilities for workplace accidents and other labor law violations. For example, Ronald Smith, a 57-year-old temporary Amazon employee who worked in Avenal, New Jersey, died after being dragged and crushed to death by a conveyor belt. The Occupational Safety and Health Administration (OSHA) cited four staffing agencies and the contractor who operated the facility for Amazon, but not Amazon itself, for the incident.[48]

Despite the corporate benefits of using temporary agencies, by 2017 Amazon either stopped or greatly reduced its reliance on temporary agencies to hire workers in Inland Southern California. None of the warehouse workers interviewed for this book who were employed after 2016 were hired through temporary agencies, nor did they know of any warehouse workers hired through temporary agencies in later years. It is not clear why Amazon made this shift, but it may be related to a series of legal cases and settlements against Amazon and the temporary agencies it used to hire warehouse workers. For example, one such court case alleging that Amazon and SMX had engaged in wage and hour violations by failing to pay workers for the time they spent going through security screenings before work and during lunch breaks was settled in 2015 for $3,700,000.[49] A few of the workers interviewed for this study had personally received or knew someone who had received small checks related to some of these legal settlements with SMX. Amazon now exclusively hires its own workers in California, at least, but often initially as "seasonal workers" despite the time of year. Seasonal workers can be terminated when their employment contracts expire and they are no longer needed. As Anong put it, "When you are a white badge it's tough to know if you're going to have a job tomorrow."

For Amazon workers, the division between seasonal and permanent employees is made visible through their work badges. Seasonal workers wear white badges while permanent workers wear blue badges, and workers identify their own and other workers' employment status by referring to these badge colors. Interviewees offered various accounts of how workers could become permanent workers, suggesting that the conversion process varies over time, work sites, or jobs or is not clearly communicated to workers. According to Erica, seasonal workers can become permanent within as few as thirty days if they perform well on the job and are able to meet expected work requirements, they follow corporation and workplace rules, and there is sufficient demand. This probationary period, however, was longer for some workers than for others. Some workers were frustrated when they watched coworkers transition more quickly than they did to permanent status. Additionally, some workers were hired as permanent, full-time employees immediately during the pandemic. As Camila put it, "As far I know, the last hiring group, they completely converted them from the moment they walked in." Managers' decisions about who was hired as a permanent employee thus appeared arbitrary to many workers. Workers interviewed before the pandemic, when the demand for workers was more variable, reported more examples than did those hired during the pandemic of workers being laid off at the end of their seasonal contracts. Given how challenging Amazon found it to keep up with its demand for workers during the COVID-19 pandemic, it is likely that conversions from white to blue badges depended less on work performance than on how many workers Amazon needed.[50]

IMPACTS ON FAMILY LIFE, EDUCATION, AND ASPIRATIONS

Motivations to work among our interviewees and to endure difficult and stressful working conditions and precarious employment were intimately tied to their lives outside of the workplace. They had to pay their bills, had to support their families, or needed additional income to help pay for the costs of higher education so that they could pursue better-paying jobs or future career paths. Yet the exploitative working conditions that warehouse workers experienced also took a toll on their lives outside of the warehouse. Their low wages, lack of good benefits, long and unpredictable work hours, and sheer exhaustion from doing physical labor for long hours constrained their lives outside of the warehouse. As Camila put it:

> Too many hours that we are required to work, so that can interfere a lot with your day, your personal life, like school sometimes, for example. I know a lot of workers and friends of mine who have worked at Amazon and they've had to quit because it was just too much. It was just way too much. They don't think about the workers in the sense that they do have outside lives, or that

there's just too much work, for example 12 hours for five days a week. That tires out anybody's body, any body, mentally and physically. . . . The workload or the amount of hours they still require us to work a week can be exhausting. So, five days every other week would be okay, but five days every week, your life is practically at the warehouse.

Overtime hours are more common for full-time workers, especially during peak shopping seasons. Some of these overtime hours are voluntary; workers are notified electronically of the opportunity to work more hours and can agree to work them if others do not volunteer for them first. Other overtime hours, known as "mandatory extra time," are required. Veronica, a 21-year-old Latina employed as a sorter and a problem solver, reported that she was sometimes required to work sixty hours per week and that she could not refuse the overtime. Such long work hours did not leave any time for personal activities, and her work routine became "repetitive and tiring." In the following discussion we explore more fully the challenges that Amazon warehouse employment presents, first for family life and then for college students' school life.

Family Life

Amazon often portrays itself as a "family friendly" corporation, and it does provide some good family benefits to its employees, including its warehouse associates.[51] Most notably, Amazon provides paid family leave policies that are generous relative to most major employers: up to twenty weeks of paid maternity leave and six weeks of paid paternity leave, which can be shared with partners not employed by Amazon. The corporation also provides eight weeks of reduced hours after employees return to work through its "ramp back" program.[52]

Yet other aspects of working in Amazon warehouses are not so family friendly. For example, Amazon has been charged with pregnancy discrimination by at least seven former Amazon warehouse employees. Managers refused to approve their requests for pregnancy-related accommodations, such as allowing them to spend more time in the bathroom or reducing the hours they spent on their feet, and then fired them after their pregnancy was known.[53] Pregnancy discrimination appears to be fairly common in the warehouse industry, according to other accounts by warehouse workers.[54]

Warehouse workers' long, physically draining work hours often left them with little time and energy for family life, especially on the days that they worked for ten hours or more. As Julio put it, "There's actually days when you get home and you don't wanna do nothing. . . . But how do I balance it? . . . I think about my family first." Research shows that about 59 percent of Southern California line workers in Amazon warehouses support children.[55] Working parents made up about one-third of the prepandemic interview sample and about 14 percent of the pandemic interview sample. Their stories provide a haunting look at family life among Amazon warehouse employees.

Working parents in our interview sample often felt motivated to work to support their children, but their long hours of laborious work took a toll on their parenting. For example, Adriana, a single Latina mother in her early thirties, reported that physical exhaustion and the pain in her feet from her ten-hour shifts as a full-time Amazon packer interfered with her ability to give her two children (ages 10 and 13) much time and energy on the days that she worked. She said, "It could be hard sometimes when I'm tired and I don't want to do anything. . . . I just want to go upstairs and lay down." She tried to make it up to her children during the other three days when she was off work. She has remained in the job for almost five years, seeing no other alternative: "I have bills and I have kids. So it's like I have no choice." In addition to her children, Adriana lived with her mother, her boyfriend, her sister, and her brother-in-law. Even with her family's help paying bills and providing free childcare for her children, she was unable to afford Amazon's health insurance plan for her family and relied on Medi-Cal instead.

Elvia, another single Latina mother in her thirties with two children (ages 7 and 8), who was employed during the pandemic, was able to secure a work schedule that accommodated family responsibilities. She worked about forty hours per week: eight hours per day, five days a week, including weekends. Although she wished that she could work only thirty hours per week so that she could spend more time with her children, she preferred her current work schedule over her previous full-time schedule of ten-hour work shifts for four days, which is more typical among Amazon warehouse workers. Working only eight hours per day allowed her to help her children with their homework at night. While she was at work, she relied on her mother, whom she lived with, to take care of her children. "My mom pretty much helps me with the kids with putting them in their [distance learning] classes, so she babysits throughout the day for me. I pay her for babysitting at the same time as I pay for the bills for the house and stuff of that nature." She was also grateful that Amazon allowed her to take unpaid personal time (UPT) off when her children got sick. When asked if she could afford to pay for childcare if she didn't have her mother's help, Elvia responded, "I don't think it's affordable on the Amazon salary." She went on to describe how much she paid her mother for watching her two children: "With my mom, I give her 300 a month, if that, sometimes four [hundred], just depends on how much I make that month." Her rent and other bills were also fairly low, since she lived with her parents and was one of three adult wage earners in her household. Other working parents interviewed similarly relied on other family members or friends, often women of color, to help out with childcare for no cost or below-market rates. This finding corroborates the insight of materialist feminist scholars, such as Wilma Dunaway, who argue that employers frequently rely on unpaid household labor to minimize the costs of labor.[56]

In contrast to Elvia's experience, however, other parents reported greater difficulties juggling their parental obligations with their Amazon work schedules. This was especially true for single mothers with less family help or those employed full-time, working graveyard shifts, working over-time, or with very young children. Clara, a single mother employed as a process assistant, often worked more than forty hours per week. During peak season, she worked up to seventy hours per week. She relied on her sister to watch her son while she worked. After her shift she would pick up her young son from her sister's house, often when he was already asleep. "So I would just watch him sleep. That was the only time I would get to see him." She regretted that she was not able to get him involved in sports because of her work schedule. Similarly, Vanessa, another single mother, said, " I feel as if I miss out on a lot of my son's young age."

The graveyard shift itself also took a toll on family life. Destiny, a single mother who worked the graveyard shift in San Bernardino—6:30 p.m.– 5:00 a.m., four days per week—had a care provider to watch her children at night in Riverside, where she lived (about thirty minutes away from her workplace). Getting enough sleep was a challenge for her family. As she describes, "I would pick them up around 5:30 a.m. I would sleep in the parking lot at my kids' school, have them dressed and ready to go, and I would then drop them off at school by 8 in the morning." Kelly, another mother employed on a graveyard shift, struggled to take her infant daughter to daytime medical appointments and feared something might happen to her daughter if she fell asleep while watching her. After Amazon's management denied all four of her requests for a daytime shift, she finally accepted Amazon's "Pay to Quit" offer, which compensates workers who agree to quit and never work for the corporation again.

Both current and former workers also discussed the difficulties of juggling their Amazon work schedules with their need to help take care of sick relatives. For example, Brianna, a current employee, described the strains on family life caused by working overtime during peak season:

> I have somebody right now in my house going through cancer, and I only see them on Sunday, and that is my overtime day, apparently, so I have no time to see my loved ones, no time to visit anybody because you're pretty much with Amazon. Amazon controls your life November until January because we're trying to make customer promises.

Some former workers also reported losing their jobs because they were incompatible with their family obligations, such as helping to take care of an ill family member. For example, Jesus was fired because he used up too much UPT. At the time he was facing family problems, including having to help his mother, who needed surgery. He was given no additional time off despite presenting the corporation with written doctors' notes about the situation. Similarly, Andrea, who had already realized her warehouse job was making her "unhappy," decided to quit because "my dad got sick and he needed someone to start taking him to the doctor's office and his appointments." The challenges of caring for disabled loved ones can be just as difficult for Amazon employees as caring for family members who are ill. Research indicates that about 22 percent of Amazon workers in Southern California had a family member with a disability.[57]

Education, Training, and Future Aspirations

Most interviewees had at least some college education, and many indicated during their interviews that they were enrolled in college at the time, typically at the University of California, Riverside (UCR), although some were community college students.[58] Student status was only directly queried among those interviewed during the pandemic. Among that sample, 51 percent of interviewees were enrolled students at the time of their interview in the fall of 2020. Compared to all UCR students that quarter, greater percentages of student interviewees were Latino (66.7 percent versus 38.7 percent) and Black (11.1 percent versus 3.0 percent), and smaller percentages were Asian (11.1 percent versus 30.8 percent) and white (5.6 percent versus 12.9 percent).[59] About 59 percent of these interviewees were raised in Inland Southern California, a percentage that is likely to be greater than the general UCR student population, which is drawn from across the state, and 7.5 percent of which identified as international students that quarter.[60]

While some college students, mostly those employed part-time or during the summers, described their Amazon job as compatible with their school schedules, others reported difficulty juggling college with their Amazon job. This situation was especially true among those employed full-time at night. Long work hours and the physical and mental exhaustion from work made it very difficult for many students to succeed academically.

Felipe, employed on a night shift, attended college classes during the day. This combination made it difficult for him to obtain sufficient sleep:

> [It] is dangerous, especially when you are driving home afterwards, that's dangerous. . . . We would work long hours, and it was always at the end of the day. You don't get much sleep. . . . Lots of sleep deprivation. It's very dangerous. . . . I almost hit a pole once, because I passed out. . . . Yeah, I didn't sleep. My sleep schedule would be between classes, from 11–1, and then I would go home and sleep from 2–7 or 4–7.

As Camila, another college student who worked full-time on the graveyard shift, put it, "You're tired when you wake up, you're tired when you go in, and you're obviously tired when you come out." Some students wanted to work part-time but could only find full-time jobs available at Amazon. Others who worked full-time during summer months reported that they tried unsuccessfully to secure part-time jobs at Amazon during the academic year. One student reported losing his job when managers converted his part-time position into a full-time job.

Even students who were employed part-time found it hard to combine warehouse employment with their schoolwork. Viviana, a Latina in her early twenties who was taking an extra class in order to graduate on time, while working part-time at Amazon, said:

> With taking so many classes right now, it's kind of a hard thing. . . . And it's only part time. It's five hours, but with me like in the mornings, I have to do my homework and then before I know it, I have to get myself ready for work, go to work, come in, come back . . . and I eat and then I do my homework until it's pretty late. And then I go to bed. It's just continuous and . . . for midterms when they come up, it's been kind of a lot.

Between the hours she spent on work and schoolwork, she found little time to talk with her family or do anything for enjoyment. And even though it was only part-time, her job limited her ability to study and complete all of her school assignments.

Ana, who transferred from a community college to a four-year public university, decided to quit her part-time Amazon job because the hours were incompatible with her new school schedule.

> The hours I had were midnight to 6 AM and then I was gonna start [university]. . . . I was like, "How am I gonna do that?". . . I had labs, so I was gonna be getting out at 5 and having to work at midnight. . . . That's the reason I got out. The hours they changed, so they changed from . . . like 4 to 10 AM. It still wasn't gonna work. Yeah, they work with you [to change your schedule] but at the same time, if it doesn't fit you, they honestly don't care 'cause you're such an easy replacement.

In the prepandemic interview sample, at least five student workers reported that they had to quit or were fired due to the challenges related to juggling work and school. Some quit their jobs in order to spend more time on their schoolwork and get more sleep. Others were fired from their Amazon jobs because they missed too much work due to school. Various college students, some still employed, reported that working for Amazon took a toll on their grades because it reduced their time and energy for schoolwork.

Amazon offers a tuition assistance program, which pays for part of the cost of an AA degree and certain types of technical certificate programs, but it is only available to full-time employees and not to students in four-year degree programs. Maria, who tried this tuition assistance program, found it difficult to combine full-time work with college. She reported:

> I find myself putting [my dreams] on hold. I was going to community col-
> lege and then I started working. . . . I had other responsibilities popping up
> and I'm expected to be an adult. Then it's overwhelming and you feel like
> you do not have time anymore for school. I loved school and learning but
> once I started working, it felt like I put school on a back burner.

Although some college students were able to quit their jobs in order to devote more time to their education, some workers could not afford to do that, especially if their incomes were needed for basic household expenses. They struggled to juggle school and work, or they quit school or put it on hold.

Most interviewees viewed their Amazon warehouse jobs as short-term jobs that they took in order to earn money, to help pay their bills or their school expenses, or to help their families financially. During the pandemic, Amazon warehouse jobs seemed to be the only ones readily available to workers in the region because retail shops, hotels, college campuses, and restaurants closed or reduced their work hours. Most interviewees were well aware of the limitations of Amazon jobs. For example, when asked if she would recommend her Amazon job to other workers, Esther said, "If it was someone who like really needed a job like they needed money, then definitely. I'd be like, 'Work Amazon.' But if it was someone who . . . wanted to . . . further themselves or find like a nice job, then I would not recommend it." Similarly, Erica said, "I would love to be a teacher. But Amazon is a very good job. That's a good like starting job for anyone that just needs to make money."

Like Erica, most of the young workers (under the age of 30) who were interviewed described various types of long-term career goals that were completely unrelated to their Amazon warehouse jobs, most commonly in education and social services or in business or business administration.[61] Compared to their younger counterparts, the career goals of the older workers (30 or more years of age) were fairly similar but not as diverse.[62] About twice the percentage of these older workers compared with workers under 30 did not identify a long-term career goal or dream job (16 percent versus 7 percent).[63]

Notably, only eight workers, or nearly 10 percent of the eighty-two workers interviewed, expressed any interest in a long-term career at Amazon. About three times the share of older workers than younger ones (21 percent versus 7 percent) expressed interest in a possible career at

Amazon. Paola, in her twenties, told us, "I hope that one day I can go back to Amazon and change things." In her interview she described various concerns with working conditions inside Amazon's warehouses, including the fast pace of work, the corporation's lack of regard for worker safety, and its hostility toward unions. Another worker initially wanted to become a buyer for Amazon but had doubts about this career goal after interacting with other buyers and gaining more work experience with the corporation. Other workers indicated that they sought to be long-term employees for Amazon, several of whom had already been promoted beyond tier 1 and, like Julio, had long-term experience in the warehouse industry. A few of these workers mentioned that they would pursue other jobs if they were unable to advance much at Amazon, however.

Life after Amazon varied considerably among former Amazon workers, who made up about 51 percent of the interview sample. About 40 percent were unemployed at the time of their interviews. Although the causes of their unemployment varied, many of these unemployed workers were either actively searching for work or full-time students. Several had suffered from severe workplace injuries at their Amazon jobs that had left them disabled. Employed former workers held a variety of jobs after leaving Amazon, most commonly in warehouses for another employer or on college campuses where they were enrolled as students. Three former workers found work in food services; several found retail jobs; and others became employed in a wide variety of jobs (construction worker, office worker, tow truck dispatcher, care provider, barber, mechanic, loan officer) or found jobs in social services, higher education, or customer service.

Former workers who were not pursuing their preferred careers or college degrees described various structural barriers that blocked them from doing so, including the lack of money to pay for school or invest in their own business or a lack of job opportunities in their field. Some young women mentioned the need to take time off from school or work in order to take care of their young children, while other workers described quitting school or work in order to take care of adult family members who were disabled or sick, problems that are related to the lack of publicly subsidized childcare and long-term care in the United States. During the pandemic, some young workers did not enroll in school because they did not like distance or online learning. Without additional education and training, many of these workers faced few other alternatives to warehouse employment in the region that paid as well or offered as many benefits and work hours, especially when many campuses closed and businesses shut down or downsized during the pandemic.

Even with a bachelor's degree in hand, young workers find constraints in terms of job availability, especially when faced with pandemic-related work closures. Olivia, a recent college graduate with a degree in business administration who was seeking a career in accounting, explained why she was working at Amazon in this way:

> I felt like I had things going on track. I was graduating from college. I had an internship. And then when the whole pandemic happened, my internship was . . . closed down. I really got unmotivated . . . scared to even go out of my home. . . . My mom feared for like our safety. Because of the pandemic so she told me. . . . "Please don't work right now. I want you to be safe." . . . That's what stopped me from, you know, reaching out and applying to other places. . . . Now I have just settled for Amazon, because you know I'm getting paid. I feel like it was an easy way in, you know. I got the job on [the] spot, and then now I'm just trying to find . . . that motivation to pursue my dream job.

Many months later and still in the midst of the pandemic, Olivia had begun to apply for jobs in accounting, but without success. Older workers employed by Amazon also described having to put their career plans on hold. For example, Elvia, who was in her thirties at the time of her interview and still employed by Amazon, had attended trade school for eight months to become a pharmacist but then had to put that dream on hold. She gave birth to two children and had to work to support them, and she could no longer afford trade school. Like so many other US workers, Elvia found her upward mobility blocked by the lack of affordable education and training, childcare, and good jobs with internal career ladders for workers without college or technical degrees.

Although workers' immediate need for income and the lack of good alternative employment options were the primary mechanisms that rendered Amazon warehouse workers available to be exploited, managers still had to compel workers to work hard and fast in order for them to actually be exploited. In the next chapter we explore the various techniques that Amazon managers and supervisors used to motivate, control, and discipline warehouse employees.

4 Boxed In

DISCIPLINE, CONTROL, AND MECHANISMS
OF EXPLOITATION IN AMAZON WAREHOUSES

Like many young people in Inland Southern California, Paola began working at the age of 16 for a series of low-wage employers. She worked as a cashier for a fast-food restaurant and a big box retail company, then worked for a major manufacturing company through a temporary agency. Paola began her fourth job, as an Amazon warehouse worker, after graduating from a local high school. Her motivation was simple: "I needed to make some sort of income without bothering my parents because I was heading to college." Paola's parents worked long hours for low wages. To cover household bills, they often depended on wages earned by her older sister, and Paola too, when she was employed.

Paola lived with her girlfriend's family, a household of seven that included several teenagers and five employed adults. Paola's girlfriend, who had already been working at Amazon as a warehouse worker a few months, recommended the job to her. Initially, Paola was excited about her new job:

> I was pretty naïve. I said, "Amazon pays 12 dollars," which at the time minimum wage was I believe 8 dollars. I thought "it was a really good job," and I heard a lot of people speak about how they had good work safety practices and really good benefits. So, I applied. . . . They just made themselves seem

like the best company in the logistics industry, which they were not. I remember what lured me into the company was that they said that after
working with the company for a year and you graduated with a degree they
had listed, you were guaranteed a position with the company to work in
that field. . . . I thought that I was going to graduate [with one of those
degrees].

Less than six months later, Paola was disenchanted with the job, which
she later viewed as dangerous, exhausting, depressing, stressful, and exploitative. About nine months after she was hired, Amazon fired her because she stopped showing up to work. By then, Paola was struggling to
stay off academic probation and looking for a better job, one that would
be more compatible with her school schedule. While she worked on her
schoolwork and looked for another job, her girlfriend scanned her badge
in and out for her so it appeared as if she were working, even though she
was not. At that time, she was assigned to work as a water spider, which
was less tightly monitored than other warehouse positions. Paola managed to get paid for several months when she was not actually working.
By the third month, Amazon figured out what was going on and fired her.

While working for Amazon, Paola worked as a case receiver, stower,
and water spider:

> As a case receiver my job was to stay in the assembly line. It was a long line
> where boxes were coming and we had to open each box, count each item,
> scan each item into our computer, and place all the items back into the
> boxes, and put the packages in the conveyer belt. The following job I moved
> up to was carrying boxes, so I would scan boxes and put them into their
> certain designation, so they would have carts for one area and carts for an-
> other area and I would scan each box and place them into whatever case
> they belonged to.

Her next position, as a water spider, was less surveilled than her jobs as a
case receiver and stower had been, but was still very difficult: "If I'd go to
the restroom or go get water it was an inconvenience for the team because
we were all just trying to get our boxes delivered. . . . It was not easy to go to
the restroom and drink water." Even worse, the water spider job was dangerous; it involved "pushing 10 to 12 boxes that weighed 50 to 60 pounds
and I would push them all around the warehouse. I knew that if I would've
bumped into another crate of boxes, that would be really bad."

During the peak holiday season (in November and December), Paola was required to work overtime. By the end of the fall term, she was put on academic probation. Then she realized, "There was no way I was going to complete my degree and stay working there. That was not going to happen. . . . I asked for a part-time [job], and they would not offer it." Paola's warehouse job was also taking a toll on her physical health: "I had bruises all over my legs because of the boxes I was throwing around. My mom was telling me, 'When you get older you will not be able to move, you are going to die early, because you are putting on so much work and you are young.'" Her job also caused her chronic pain in her feet, hands, and wrists and was stressful:

> Standing on your feet for 10 hours, people would tell me, "you will get over the pain after a month," but it never went away. It was just something you had to deal with. . . . Your hands and wrists start to hurt, because you scan each item individually. That pain never went away either. The mental abuse from people that were ambassadors. . . . [They] kind of run a "dictator-type" of work place. That is how I saw it. They would tell us if we were on the company's goal or if we were lacking and we had to pick up the work. A lot of them were very abusive with that power. . . . My body was definitely done. I had bruises, my legs would hurt every day, the working conditions were terrible, and the stretches didn't do anything.

During a ten-hour shift, "We would have two 15-minute breaks, which weren't really 15-minutes, because you still had to walk all the way to the front, pass security, pass to the locker room, and still try to get through everybody, so not really 15-minutes."

On top of the pain and exhaustion she experienced, Paola and her girlfriend both experienced sexual harassment and were also hassled by fellow workers for being lesbians. Her girlfriend filed a formal complaint about sexual harassment. After many months of inaction, the human resources (HR) department finally moved her girlfriend's harasser to another part of the warehouse, but she continued to be harassed during breaks until she finally quit. Discouraged by the inaction of the HR department on her girlfriend's complaint, Paola never reported her own experiences of being harassed by male workers.

As Paola became more aware of just how difficult her warehouse job was, the wages seemed more unfair. She and her fellow workers were told that at most they would only earn $14.00 per hour as a warehouse worker. Moreover, there were very limited opportunities for upward mobility within the corporation. Only a few out of hundreds of warehouse workers would ever become promoted to a higher managerial position; workers would simply be assigned to another position in the warehouse rather than be given a higher-paying job with greater responsibility. Meanwhile, "the CEO is the richest man in the world."

Paola described at length the various techniques that managers at Amazon, who she noted were mostly white, used to motivate warehouse workers, who she recalled as being mostly Black and brown, to work hard, beginning with the mandatory group meetings at the beginning of each shift known as "stand up meetings": "They (Amazon managers) would tell us the goal of the day, and the percentage of how many numbers we made. It was kind of a pep talk that was annoying. I never listened to it because it was boring and mundane." Workers would be updated about twice per day "how we were doing in our percentages." We would be told, "you are at this percentage, you are on rate, or you are not on rate." One of her friends received a "write-up" after three warnings "for not meeting the goal at the end of the day." If they obtained too many "write-ups," workers faced termination:

> There was a lot of pressure to meet rate. One day I was called on and I was told to pick up my rate, because I was in the 40's and 50's and I was getting made fun of because my rate was very low compared to everyone else. I guess making rate would be 70 percent and being on top of the goal number was at a 100 percent. The numbers [of items] were at millions. I remember a million something, because they would always play this annoying song from Lil Wayne, "a million" and get us excited to meet our goal. . . . During holiday time they really picked it up with the incentives. I believe everyday they were rallying off cards, and when we had really heavy days they [managers] would rally off a TV. Everyone would go crazy for it. . . . [W]hen the big items came, they wouldn't come as often as the regular gift cards[;] people just started working much harder and there was also a lot of work.

To motivate them to work hard during the Thanksgiving holiday, workers were offered pies. Informal competitions among workers also helped to motivate them to work extra hard:

> People would fight for the bigger boxes because these boxes had a higher number of items, and when you had higher number of items you would be able to reach the goal a lot faster. . . . The max number of items in a box was

1,000 and the least was 1. My coworkers, to make it less boring, we would try to grab the bigger boxes. At the end of the day, it would help us reach their goal. It was fun to fight over the bigger boxes with the bigger number of items, even though, that meant the most amount of work.

Despite such moments of "fun" among her coworkers, Paola found her working conditions to be generally oppressive:

> It was very depressing on those 11-hour workdays to go in when it was dark and to leave when it was already getting dark again. It was four consecutive days; a big chunk of my life was going into this depressive work place. There were no windows, only bright lights and big boxes, and everyone was in these orange vests. . . . It felt really wrong to know that there is a work place like this where people are putting so much work of their lives and getting so little back. It was like seeing an episode of the "Black Mirror." . . . Even as a recent high school graduate, it felt wrong and terrible.

After Paola was fired from her Amazon warehouse job, she experienced several "hard" months of being unemployed, which she was able to survive because she was living with her girlfriend's family. She eventually found another job as a bank teller through her girlfriend's sister and graduated from college. She felt terrible for many of the older workers who had "no other opportunity and option," except to continue to work at Amazon for their income.

As Paola's observations suggest, the financial need to work—whether to pay for basic survival needs, such as food, clothing, transportation, and shelter, or to pay for other desired items, including money for school books, car payments, discretionary spending, or a cell phone—and limited employment options, the focus of the last two chapters, are among the fundamental mechanisms that position workers to be exploited by unscrupulous employers. Once hired by Amazon, they become subject to that corporation's managerial techniques of workplace discipline and control that entice or compel them to work hard.

In Amazon's FCs, delivery stations, and warehouses, workplace discipline is maintained through both "carrots," positive incentives for working hard, and "sticks," or punishment for underperforming. Managers rely heavily on impersonal computer codes, or algorithms, and electronic surveillance and communication to monitor and discipline workers, but often combine these systems with in-person communication.[1] Before the pandemic and implementation of social distancing rules, managers would speak with workers directly at the beginning of their work shifts in group "standup meetings" in which they would discuss the goals for that day and respond to workers' questions. Workers would also do exercises and stretch together to prepare their bodies for the tough day of work ahead. Workers' productivity was often measured electronically, through hand-held scanners or other devices, enabling managers to reward and punish workers depending on their performance measures. Scholars refer to such styles of management as "algocratic," or "rule by algorithm," when they rely heavily on computer-generated mathematical programs.[2]

This chapter explores workers' experiences with, and many concerns about, discipline and control in Amazon warehouses, the daily mechanisms through which Amazon seeks to maximize its profit by maximizing labor productivity and efficiency while minimizing its labor costs, including the costs of supervising and managing large numbers of workers: thousands of workers per shift at some facilities. We first discuss workers' perspective on being electronically monitored for their productivity and "ruled by algorithm" under the threat of termination. We then discuss various other techniques and incentives that, in addition to pay raises and minor promotions, Amazon managers have used to try to motivate and discipline warehouse workers to work hard and fast, namely, workplace competition, games, and giveaways. Finally, we discuss Amazon's "Pay to Quit" program, which encourages disgruntled workers to agree to quit and never return by offering them one-time payments; this program arguably helps to cement loyalty among remaining workers.[3] Our interview findings, in the context of other research, suggest that highly similar mechanisms of labor exploitation are used across Amazon's worldwide network of warehouse facilities, which tend to result in a "high churn" model of employment that keeps workers productive in the short run but often fails to sustain long-term employment.[4]

ELECTRONIC SURVEILLANCE AND RULE BY ALGORITHM

Amazon uses algorithms and electronic devices to monitor warehouse workers' ability to keep up with productivity standards, including their ability to "make rate" and the time they spend off task. Summarizing the requirements for promotion to permanent employee, Esther said: "Do your job and make rate, also always be on time." As Erica, a sortation associate, put it, "They could write you up for like quite a few things." Elaborating on this point and explaining which seasonal (or "white badge") workers are invited to convert to permanent (or "blue badge") status and which workers are fired, she said: "So if you're just not doing your job, you just leave early. . . . If you have a certain amount of write ups, you can be fired." According to data reported by Amazon, the corporation was terminating more than 10 percent of its warehouse employees annually, solely for productivity reasons, in 2019, a statistic that suggests "thousands lose their jobs with the company annually for failing to move packages quickly enough."[5]

Working under constant surveillance with the threat of termination is stressful. As Brianna put it, "The fact that they can fire you for any little thing now gives me serious anxiety like everyday. . . . Any wrong move and you can get fired. I've seen people that have been there years like I have and they get fired for the littlest thing."

Work rates are monitored electronically, typically through scanners (which used to be fairly heavy and strapped to workers' arms but are now lighter and handheld), or computer software.[6] As Stella described: "You're being tracked on what you're doing all the time. . . . You have to scan your badge to let the system know that you are doing that job and then from that moment forward it's tracking everything you do. Down to the second." This electronic monitoring enables just a few higher-paid managers to discipline and control a large number of workers. As Angel put it, "If they didn't have the technology that they had, they wouldn't be able to learn who's doing what."

Managers often rely on lower-level supervisors, usually recruited from more experienced workers and known as "process associates" or "ambassadors," to carry out most of the personal communication with workers. As Paola reports, "The managers were the ones who would only give us the morning announcements, walk around, and scare people but they didn't really do much. The only people yelling at us, and talking to us one-on-one to tell us our rates were the ambassadors." Many warehouse workers found their relationships with managers to be very impersonal and alienating.

For example, Olivia reported, "I dislike that management is not as involved as I would like them to be. . . . You're just like a number to them."

As Camila put it, "The relationship is between you and the machine, not your manager." Similarly, other workers claimed that their managers only cared about whether or not they were meeting their "numbers" or required work and error rates. Elvia, who had worked at Amazon for seven years, did not even know who her current manager was. Several workers recalled instances in which it was difficult to actually find a manager when one was needed to resolve an issue because the buildings were so large and the managers were so few in number.

Required work rates tend to be high, requiring workers to work very quickly. The particular rates required varied across workers depending on their jobs and over time, especially with the introduction of greater automation. Stella reported that packers need to pack at least 180 items every hour, while Olivia, who worked in the receiving department, said that she was expected to scan at least 220 items per hour. Ana, who used a finger scanner, was expected to scan about 300 items per hour. Miguel reported, "In stowing, you're supposed to be at a rate of 275 cases per hour and 11 second takt time which is how fast you grab an item from the tote and to the bin on the pods." Daniel describes his experience as a picker and packer this way:

> They will show you something on the scanner and you have to go find it in that place and you had to pretty much have to run to it. . . . There was a time on the scanner so you had to get there quickly. . . . We were running around. . . . We were working ten-hour shifts. That was a picker. . . . Then for the packer . . . you would stay in one spot but the speed at which they had you pack or package the items. . . . That was more demanding even though you were standing still. The rate they wanted you to go at, I felt like it was more demanding. They wanted you to help with 130 packages per hour, so it was pretty fast. . . . You just package everything as fast as you can.

Jimmy recalled, "Everyone there is concerned with making rate. It is the only thing that mattered. . . . We had to move 4 boxes of items per minute. It doesn't sound like a lot but it is basically 4 times 60 including walking to the corresponding pallet." For some jobs, work rate standards sometimes vary by the day and season, depending on the number of customer orders or how many workers actually show up that day. As Erica, a sortation associate, describes:

> When we prepare for the same day, we put the racks out. . . . When I started working . . . people weren't really ordering much, we will start up with like 40 racks . . . but as time went on the numbers got bigger and recently . . . there were 90 racks and that like kind of extended past the conveyor belt, so we had to use a different conveyor belt but it was just like a lot of moving around and getting everything situated for that. And in the end, not all 90 drivers came through to pick up their routes so we had 60 routes leftover. . . . We had to move it to "night sort," which is like a hassle for us. . . . You can't really predict how many routes you're gonna have or how many drivers are actually going to show up.

Similarly, Erica, who worked at a delivery station, said that "especially now, since Christmas is coming up, a lot of people have been ordering a lot of stuff, so we have about 90 routes over 5,000 packages to scan through and put away." Keeping up with these work rate standards is often difficult for workers, and many find the rates expected of them to be unreasonable. As Esther put it, making rate was "stressful and tiring." Karen, a picker, said, "I was always scared every day, because I wasn't meeting rate."

Learning how to "make rate" requires a certain amount of skill and experience, which can be difficult for new workers to acquire quickly, even after their initial training, which only lasts a few days. Daniel reported,

> They would keep track of your rate per hour and you had to keep a certain rate to keep them happy. If you go under that, they would be on your ass. . . .The first day, the rate was like 120, 130 packages per hour and I was going like as fast as I possibly could, if not faster, and I was barely getting the minimum, and I was like, "Oh no!" . . . After a while, it got easier, but in the beginning, they are really on your ass.

Daniel's description points to how workplace discipline often relies on personal pressure by supervisors and managers in addition to electronic monitoring. Workers also typically rely on "learning ambassadors" or other coworkers to help them learn the tricks of the trade for "making rate" successfully in the first few weeks or months of their job or when they are reassigned to a new position.

When workers fail to "make rate" they face verbal reminders, repri-
mands, or coaching from their immediate supervisors or managers. As
Julio reported, "They [managers] rely on technology like that to fire
people, to actually talk to them, 'Hey you know your rate is slow, pick it
up.'" Another worker, Angel, described the combination of electronic and
personal communication used to discipline workers in this way:

> You'd get messages on your scanner and that's when you would have to go
> see them. Everyone would look at you like, "Damn, what did you do?!" If it
> was the main manager at the desk, you'd go there and they would tell you
> what you're doing wrong and very rarely if you're doing something right.

Various workers reported that employees' work rates were monitored
multiple times a day, as well as assessed over the course of the whole day
and week. Jacky recalled a situation in which she was ridiculed because
she had the lowest work rate on her shift. In other instances, workers were
yelled at for failing to make rate. In contrast, workers who performed
above rate and work shifts that were especially productive were verbally
praised during standup meetings. In March 2020, Amazon claimed that
it had suspended the practice of providing productivity, or rate, feedback
nationwide during the pandemic, and extended this policy indefinitely
during the pandemic, but managers did not clearly communicate this
change in policy to their employees.[7] Many interviewees who were employed during the pandemic were unaware of this change in policy.

In addition to pressuring workers to work quickly through direct verbal communication, managers also publicly post employees' work rates.
As Jorge put it, "Everybody felt pressure to be fast. . . . Before and after
breaks they would have a list of people who are doing the best. . . . At
some point you know everybody's ID card and of course, you know everybody's name so it is easy to tell like, 'This guy is doing terrible today.' So,
it [was] very public." As Ana put it: "They would like post your rate like
trying to get you guys to compete with each other to see how fast or slow
you're going."

Although workers are supposed to be warned before they are issued a
write-up for failing to "make rate," some managers skip that step, according to our interview respondents. According to Jessica, "That is unfair but
human resources didn't do anything about it." Similarly, Laura reported

that, "I don't even remember why I got my first write up. I think I didn't make rate and he was supposed to give me a warning, but instead he just wrote me up and then kinda told me, 'oh, I'm gonna take your write up off,' but it never came off."

Implementation of disciplinary procedures often appeared arbitrary to workers and to depend on managerial discretion. Jorge commented:

> I felt bad for the supervisors and managers 'cus like they were stuck in this middle place where they were working for the corporation, which only saw us as like robots, but they also had to work with us directly and they couldn't just see us as robots. So, they had to . . . work in between, saying, 'Hey work impossibly fast, but also, how are you?'

Workers reported considerable variation among managers and supervisors, however, noting that some were more lenient and personable than others.

Some of the workers interviewed were fired for too many failures to "make rate." As Doug, employed by Amazon for nine months, said, "I got terminated supposedly because my rate was too low, even though I was told by a supervisor that . . . my rate was fine." Another worker, Katie, had an anxiety attack in response to the pressure to "make rate" and was later fired because her work rate was too low. Other workers report quitting because they were on the verge of being fired for failing to make rate. According to Diana, "They expected a lot of raised numbers and for it to constantly be going up. So they would keep hiring people and they would not be able to get to those numbers." Similarly, Andrea observed, "I think they were letting go a lot of people who were actually responsible at their job. They just couldn't meet the rate." Another worker recalled that a friend was fired for performing just 1 percent below the required rate.

Workers are under pressure to not only "make rate" but to have a low rate of errors. On pressure to minimize errors, Josh notes: "The only stress is kinda when I make errors, so it can be a little high. . . . Like if you count two thousand units and you have one error you're fine compared to having counted six hundred units and one error, then it's gonna be all huge, like the ratio." Jorge observed that "they focused mostly on speed," but sometimes would ask workers to focus on "efficiency" if they had too many errors. "That was really hard 'cus now you want us to be fast and focused." Similarly, Samuel recounted, "Being a slam operator, you see everybody's mistakes and people who make rate above expectations they are getting packages kicked out. . . . They want fast pace, but they want quality which is sometimes unobtainable."

Workers are also monitored electronically in terms of their time off task (TOT). According to Fernando, "So if you got over thirty minutes per week you were given a write-up. So every time, every six minutes they start counting time against you. So if you like even use up two minutes, two minutes they count you as two minutes off task." Other research based on surveys and interviews with warehouse workers finds that TOT is usually counted after about six minutes of "idle time," although this varies somewhat across positions.[8] According to Elvia, TOT would begin to be counted if she had three minutes between scans. Workers would receive a warning for an hour of TOT and would be fired if they spent two hours off task per day. As Olivia described:

> You haven't been in your station for like ten minutes, more than ten minutes, like someone does come around your desk and see where you are, were you doing your work, or where you have been during that time that you had been missing or not working. They do go to your desk and ask you where you've been or why you have time off task.

As she describes, managers do not simply rely on electronic monitoring but combine it with in-person supervision to enforce the TOT rules.

Camilla also reported that she was once unfairly reprimanded for too much TOT due to a lack of work or completing her assigned task more quickly than expected:

> You can get written up because you're not working, but if there's no work to do, then what do you do? Or you finish your work because you're fast, so what do you do? You sit and wait for work, but that is counted as "time off task." . . . I had an instance where I stayed on my wall because I am a pretty fast packer. One of the PA's [process assistants or supervisors] comes up to me, she tells me that I have seventeen minutes of time off task. . . . If I accumulate 30 minutes, I was going to be written up. . . . [That] frustrated me because it didn't make any sense. . . . How am I supposed to work if I don't have any work and I finished all my work?

As Mia, who worked in fluid load, said: "Sometimes there isn't enough work to make rates. Sometimes . . . there are reasons for you to have TOT that is not like you're just out there wandering or doing nothing."

Mia and other workers cited various instances in which failures to meet TOT or work rates were not due to their lack of work effort, but instead involved workers being unfairly held accountable for work stoppages or mechanical failures. According to Olivia, "Sometimes our time off task is calculated and it's not our fault, like when there's a problem with the conveyors, or like a jam or something like that." Similarly, Mia explained that the scanners "glitch and caused many errors." Other workers reported frequent problems with the scanners due to depleted batteries, inconsistent internet, or bad barcodes. Others noted how equipment, such as automatic tape dispensers, sometimes malfunctioned. In such situations, workers were at the mercy of managers' or supervisors' discretion in terms of whether or not they would be excused for failing to hit their expected rates or TOT. June recalled a particular incident when she was written up for failing to meet her hourly rate due to a problem with her scanner. For weeks she tried to get this incident off her work record, but her managers dismissed her concerns. Similarly, Kelly recounted, "It was annoying because the conveyors broke down all the time and if you got a bad scanner you were still responsible to make rate."

Measures of TOT are based on very narrowly defined and highly repetitive work tasks, overlooking time spent on other types of work tasks. For example, Camila reported that time spent completing the health surveys, which were required of workers during the pandemic, could also sometimes lead workers to accumulate too much TOT. As she explained, "You go by your rate and the items you scan, and if these surveys pop up before that, it just takes longer, and it takes time that shows that you aren't working."

Under pressure to "make rate" and not spend "too much time off task," Amazon warehouse workers work quickly and have little time for breaks. Not only do these constraints contribute to their high rates of workplace injury, they also encourage many warehouse workers to pee in bottles in the aisles rather than use the restroom.[9] The practice of peeing in bottles among warehouse workers hit the news partly thanks to the undercover research of British journalist James Bloodworth, who publicized his firsthand experiences of being employed as an Amazon warehouse worker.[10] A survey of 102 Amazon warehouse workers in Britain also found that fully 74 percent of respondents agreed that they avoided the toilet while at work due to fears of missing their work rates or being fired.[11] In our own sample, about one-third of workers interviewed expressed concerns about being able to use the restroom when needed. It is unclear, however, how many workers did not have those concerns because they either peed in the aisles or reduced their consumption of water during work hours, two strategies found to be common among warehouse workers.[12]

In 2021 Amazon's public relations team angered workers when it tweeted, "You don't really believe in the peeing in bottles thing, do you?" Amazon's warehouse workers and delivery drivers alike fired back with personal stories and photographs to publicly document their use of pee bottles.[13] As Ana explained, Inland Southern California warehouse workers resorted to peeing not only in bottles but also in trashcans:

> Like once a week you'd be passing through an aisle, and I'll have to go get this pick right, and then out of nowhere a bad smell hits and there's only one thing and it's like you'd have to call someone and be like, "Yo! Someone did some shit." It's like instead of going to the bathroom they'd piss in the trash can cause they didn't want to take the time to go and waste all that time.

Describing the pressure that warehouse workers experience due to TOT monitoring, Angelo said:

> Fuck no, I would not recommend Amazon to anyone! I hated that. It was so bad because literally you'd only have such a limited amount of time to not be doing your task, so you can't really have a break. Even to use the bathroom literally it takes at *least* 5 minutes to go to the bathroom on a forklift. It was so bad they'd all be really bitchy and total power complex. . . . So, the person of the day who had the most time off task would be talked to. . . . There's been people fired for that.

As Angelo explained, some warehouses were as big as "four football fields put together," making it difficult to use the restroom quickly. Paola recalled, "There were only two restrooms in the whole building and the building was huge. . . . If you were to take too long, it would be counted against you because you were still logged in." Diana reported, "If you are in the bathroom for more than four minutes then they will be able to see that and then ask you why you were gone for so long."

Esther, who worked as a splitter sorting packages by region as they come down a conveyor belt, explained what would happen if she were to use the bathroom this way:

> It'll mess everything up like it'll mess up the whole line. I don't have the ability to leave. And if I wanted to leave, there's no one that I could tell, like there's no one next to me. . . . So usually if I like have to go to the restroom, I just wait till the packages get really slow and then I'll go really quick so that when I come back it doesn't really affect my work too much.

Felipe similarly reported, "They tell you, 'Stop going to the bathroom! What are you doing?!" Likewise, Samuel reported, "They tell you, 'They give you breaks for a reason.' . . . When you have to use the bathroom, you normally don't make rate." Yet as Camila explained, if workers actually use the restroom, or get water or snacks during their work breaks, it is difficult to rest because of the time required to walk across the massive facility to do so and then return to their workstations. For Jorge, the inability to use the bathroom while at work was "probably one of the biggest issues."

Clara, a Latina employed by Amazon for four years who was promoted to process assistant, discussed how she personally advocated for workers facing termination due to too much TOT:

> Every time we would check the times on the computer we would see that they would be off task. If you would ask them like, "Where were you?," they would be like, "In the restroom," and I would fix it, but most managers wouldn't. They would be like, "That's Time Off Task." Like I remember there was this girl that always went to the restroom, and she was a good packer, but when we had our daily meetings at the end of the day they were like, "Fire her." . . . She has a lot of TOT . . . and I would be like, "No, whoa." . . . I had to cover for certain people because I still felt like they were working hard and just go to the bathroom a lot.

Like many of the workers quoted here, Clara recalled that at the end of the day most managers insisted that the time workers spent going to the bathroom should still be counted as TOT. Facing public criticism from workers and in response to several lawsuits, Amazon eventually suspended and loosened its implementation of its productivity standards in 2020 and

2021 in order to give workers additional time to comply with pandemic-related safety standards. By then, thousands of Amazon workers had already been fired for failing to meet those standards.[14]

In addition to productivity standards, work schedules and rules about unpaid and paid time off were also strictly enforced and monitored electronically. As Daniel recalls,

> One day they sent me an email saying to go 15 minutes earlier. . . . They said it was going to go into effect tomorrow, so I misread the date. . . . I went and clocked in 15 minutes early and so I clocked out 15 minutes early as well and I ended up getting two points that day. . . . I worked exactly . . . ten hours, yet they took 2 points because I clocked in early and clocked out early.

Daniel wanted to explain the situation but was unable to do so because "it was pretty hard to get a meeting with HR." Pedro reported that he was unfairly fired as a result of a computer error related to his hours. Although the online scheduling system indicated that he had worked enough hours to earn a vacation, he was notified that this was incorrect when he returned to work. He was actually five hours below the required number of hours needed to take his vacation. He was then fired even though the mistake appeared to be due to inaccurate corporate records.

Given the volatility in consumer demands, workers are expected to "flex up" or "flex down," sometimes on short notice. Anong, a South Asian man in his midtwenties who was hired before the pandemic, describes a common dilemma that many warehouse workers faced when they arrived at work only to learn that there was not enough work to do:

> From January to April is when it is least busy and because of that there will be times when they ask people to leave, like two hours into the shift. When they ask you to leave, it's not like they have the power to force you to get out. They ask volunteers, for who wants to go home early. For my department for ship dock, since we don't have a rate, it just depends on the individual. But in other departments . . . they have a quota they have to meet. If not enough people leave then a majority of people will not be making rate . . . and will get a write up. Then they're in danger of getting fired. That's the hard part. . . . Then you're like, "Well do I lose $100 bucks tonight so I can have a job tomorrow or do I risk it and hopefully I can make it through?"

Work rate requirements thus not only help to ensure that workers are highly productive but also create incentives for workers to voluntarily leave when there is insufficient work. Other workers recounted times when they were asked toward the end of a shift to stay a few hours late in order to get a large batch of deliveries out on time. Sometimes this overtime was voluntary, but sometimes it was mandatory, and workers who refused it would lose their UPT. If workers accumulated too much UPT, they faced termination.

INCENTIVES TO WORK HARD: COMPETITION, GAMES, GIVEAWAYS, AND OTHER REWARDS

In addition to fear of the stick, workers were also motivated to work hard through competitive pressure and positive incentives. Workplace competition was reinforced through managerial praise for especially fast and efficient workers and work shifts and even by encouraging workers to compete across facilities and work shifts in terms of their productivity.

The emphasis on "making the numbers" also prompted informal competition among workers. As Daniel described,

> I worked in horrible conditions horrible jobs but I feel like Amazon was still somehow more difficult. . . . They created a hostile environment between your own friends and your own co-workers. . . . I am very competitive and having a rate system in place, really made it like, "Hey I am beating you." It was more of a toxic environment. They wanted people to compete to do better you know? I can see the psychology behind it. . . . But at least for me, it's what made it a little harder. I had harder physical jobs but they were not pushing you the way Amazon pushes you.

Similarly, a Moreno Valley man employed as a stower for Amazon, in an interview for *The Atlantic*, described how workers are forced to compete against other workers every day when they must match or exceed the standard work rate or face termination if they are unable to do so. As he put it, "'They make it like the Hunger Games. That's what they actually call it.'"[15]

Many workers learned that they could make rate more easily by "cherry picking" the boxes with more items. This bred workplace competition over such boxes, coordination among friendly coworkers, and resentment among workers excluded from other workers' help. Elizabeth reports:

I noticed that since they give you a rate, there is a lot of competition among ourselves. I noticed that since they require that rate and require us to keep working, there was always a lot of shade within the employees, especially if you don't have friends. I made friends in Amazon and when they would get a good box, they were so kind with me, and they would give me a small portion of it.

Andrea likewise described how workers who were packing the chutes would sometimes steer the boxes with more items, the "big ships," toward their friends: "I thought that was really, really unfair because you know, everybody had to make their rate.... We all have families to feed you know. We all depend on that job." She observed, "Oh my god, one day one of these girls, she almost beat me up 'cus I grabbed one of them [the 'big ships']. Yeah, people got mad. They almost fought you for it and I thought it was pretty stupid." Likewise, Elvia explained that as a stower, how many items you could stow depended not just on your ability to work quickly but also on the "people you know because they would bring you the good work, or small items versus big items where it's hard for you to make rate." Such strategies bred resentment among workers, however. For example, a picker, Jimmy, reported, "There were a couple of folks I was not very fond of because they would pick light stuff, like envelopes. They were making rate but not pulling their weight physically."

Amazon also offered its warehouse associates periodic raises tied to seniority and the promise of being promoted to more favorable tasks or from a seasonal to a permanent position. In addition, managers sometimes offered additional small incentives or giveaways. As Hannah reported: "We get the Swagbucks for doing a good job and then we can buy what we want with it." Similarly Samuel observed: "In peak season, they'll try to do little giveaways for people who are over-performing." Another worker, employed as a picker, claimed they would run competitions during "Power Hour" in which the fastest picker would receive a prize, such as a cookie, or be entered into a raffle for a gift card.[16] Supervisors would also sometimes buy workers food when work was especially heavy or during the holiday season. As Erica explained:

When there's a hard day on the next day or next week that we work, our managers bring us food like Jersey Mikes, Dominos. They've brought us

coffee. They really . . . understand the struggles that we are going through
'cause they're going through the same one, so they try to make it known that
they appreciate that we've been working.

Another incentive to work hard was built into work schedules. Although
workers complained about their ten-hour work shifts, they were motivated
to work long hours because it gave them three days off from work each
week. Extra pay for overtime also motivated workers to volunteer for it.

AMAZON'S "HIGH CHURN" EMPLOYMENT MODEL

Although interviewees suggest that Amazon is effective at motivating
warehouse employees to work hard during their shifts, it is not very good
at motivating them to stay on the job or in the corporation for very long.
Amazon's "high churn" employment model is characterized by very high
rates of employee turnover due to a combination of high numbers of
employees quitting, being fired, getting laid off, or losing employment
through serious injury. An analysis of warehouse workers' annual turnover
rates in California counties in 2017 finds that these rates were, on average,
about 100.9 percent in counties where Amazon warehouses are located,
compared to 83 percent in all warehouses and 69.8 percent in all California industries that year. Moreover, warehouse worker turnover rates were
only 38.1 percent in 2011, the year prior to Amazon's entrance in California.[17] A follow-up analysis by the *New York Times* similarly found that in
all US counties where Amazon had opened warehouse facilities, worker
turnover rates increased by 30 percent within two years compared to two
years prior to Amazon's arrival.[18] Subsequent corporate records revealed
that national turnover rates in Amazon's warehouses were even greater
than earlier estimates and rose during the pandemic, from 123 percent in
2019 to 159 percent in 2020, compared to 46 and 59 percent in 2019 and
2020 respectively for the US transportation and warehousing industries.[19]
    Researchers attribute Amazon's "extreme high churn" employment
model to a combination of factors, including the high numbers of workers
quitting (often in response to bad working conditions), the firing of workers
unable to "make rate" or otherwise failing to comply with the corporation's

demanding work standards and strict rules, heavy reliance on temporary and seasonal workers, and high rates of workplace injury (discussed more fully in chapter 5). In addition, inadequate human resources staff give workers little recourse to contest unfair firings that sometimes result from small misunderstandings or glitches in computer programs or machinery.[20] Martina, a former Amazon warehouse associate who was employed in the HR department at the time of her interview, confessed that "sometimes there's so many concerns, we can't handle all of them at once."

Amazon's "high churn" model has both costs and benefits for the corporation. On the one hand, high employee turnover, coupled with rising demand for e-commerce, keeps the demand for warehouse workers high, puts upward pressure on wages, and even creates labor supply problems.[21] On the other hand, high employee turnover benefits Amazon by replacing disgruntled and injured employees with fresh new workers; it also creates obstacles for worker organizing and unionization that reduce workers' capacity to negotiate even higher wages.

Amazon routinely lays off seasonal workers, especially those who underperform, after their seasonal contracts end. Amazon also routinely provides financial incentives, or buyouts, for warehouse workers to leave their jobs. Each year, warehouse workers are given "the offer" for a one-time payment through the corporation's Pay to Quit program, an idea that Amazon borrowed from Zappos, the online shoe and clothing company it acquired in 2009. The first year, they are offered $2,000 to quit Amazon and agree to never work for the corporation again, and the payment increases by $1,000 each year, up to a maximum payment of $5,000. Explaining the reasoning behind this program to his shareholders in 2014, Bezos explained that it was not "healthy" for workers and the corporation if workers remained at a job they did not truly want. Arguably, the program encouraged disgruntled workers to move on while fostering feelings of loyalty among those who choose to stay.[22]

Similarly, Amazon executives offer free in-house training programs and tuition reimbursements for technical or two-year degrees in high-demand fields for workers interested in pursuing careers outside of Amazon. It did so even as it chose to offer very limited opportunities for warehouse associates to move into higher-paying professional and managerial positions within the corporation. As Martina observed, Amazon tended to hire young workers "fresh out of college" as managers rather than valuing the work experience of warehouse workers without college degrees, some of whom, like herself, had years of previous experience in warehouse work and management. According to David Niekerk, the former vice president of Amazon's HR, Amazon's head of operations preferred hiring college graduates rather than hourly employees for leadership positions. Bezos viewed long-term employment among Amazon's hourly workforce as a "'march to mediocrity'" and purposely sought to avoid workplace discontent in part by offering warehouse workers incentives to leave rather than developing pathways to upward mobility within the corporation.[23]

Developing internal career ladders for warehouse workers, like unionization and other measures to improve working conditions, could entail additional short-term labor costs for the corporation, which it probably seeks to avoid, but it could help to reduce the corporation's turnover costs and labor supply problems.[24] In the meantime, workers, their families, and communities pay the price of Amazon's "high churn" employment model. High turnover rates among Amazon warehouse workers contribute to unemployment and poverty, especially in communities, like Inland Southern California, where warehouses, especially Amazon warehouses, are concentrated.[25]

In addition to quitting their jobs, Amazon warehouse workers described small acts of individual-level resistance on the job. Although Amazon monitored workers closely, some workers, and even managers, stole items, ate candy when an open bag was discovered, or momentarily escaped surveillance cameras to engage in nonwork activities. Paola's story, in which her girlfriend clocked her in and out of an Amazon warehouse so that she could get paid without actually being at work, was particularly dramatic. Other workers described smaller acts of escaping workplace monitoring to socialize. Angelo, a forklift driver, reported, "Me and my friends would always go to the top of the shelves on forklifts, up high and just have conversations." Another worker described how a group of older ladies discovered a way to leave the facility during their shifts without being noticed and return to work before their shifts were over to clock out. Although these women initially got away with this during an especially busy peak period, they eventually got caught. Some of these actions, through which workers defied workplace rules, resulted in firings, reminding workers that they faced termination for not following the rules.

In the next chapter we further explore how workers' social identities shaped their experiences on the job. While most of the Amazon workers we interviewed faced highly exploitative working conditions that took a toll on their physical and mental health, workers of color, many of whom were immigrants, women, and older workers, often faced harassment and discrimination at work, which created additional sources of stress and tension among workers. We also explore positive workplace relations among workers and the ways in which coworkers supported and befriended one another, despite a highly competitive, isolating, and impersonal workplace environment.

5 Moving Boxes Together

INEQUALITIES AND SOCIAL RELATIONS AMONG WAREHOUSE WORKERS

Alejandra is a naturalized US citizen who was born in Mexico and entered the United States when she was an infant. Her family came to the United States so that her father could find a better-paying job. In Mexico, her father struggled financially, and even when he worked two or three jobs, he could not earn enough for everyone to eat regularly. Raised in Southern California (Los Angeles and then Fontana), Alejandra graduated from high school and then attended a community college. She was nearly 24 years old at the time of her interview and just a few classes shy of earning her associate's degree. She was living with seven other family members, including her parents, her significant other, her sister's significant other, her sister's four-month-old baby, and several teenage relatives. Her family was close and often enjoyed spending time with each other and helped each other with chores and childcare.

Alejandra was a former Amazon warehouse worker who had worked in the logistics industry for about six years, including about two and half years in Amazon warehouses in San Bernardino between 2013 and 2016. She found out about the job through a good friend from high school and had been excited about the opportunity to get employment benefits. She was initially hired in an entry-level associate position. After working at several positions, including as a stower and water spider, Alejandra was promoted to learning ambassador, then process associate (PA), and was being trained as an area manager before quitting because of growing concerns about the job.

What Alejandra enjoyed the most about her job was her coworkers. As she recalled, when she first began her job, "My good friend. . . . She taught me a lot throughout the warehouse. . . . She'd guide me in everything. . . . Really never, no AM [area manager] reached out to me or an ambassador." Although some employees were not very cooperative, she had good relationships with many coworkers and enjoyed talking with them, even after being promoted to area manager in training. She earned the workers' respect by treating them with dignity, listening to their stories and concerns, being friendly to them, and helping to train them. As she put it, "I've always loved helping people, training them, teaching them new things that I know." Alejandra fondly recalled, "The people I worked with made it fun." Some of the workers even brought her gifts in appreciation for her help at work.

When Alejandra became an area manager in training, however, she did not like how managers dismissed and failed to address warehouse workers' formal complaints, injury reports, and concerns expressed in corporate surveys. Nor did she like the employment discrimination that she observed and encountered over the years. She sometimes advocated for various workers, encouraging other managers to give them more opportunities to succeed, and became frustrated when they did not. Her concerns about managers' unfair treatment of workers and fear of retaliation for speaking up about it eventually led her to quit her Amazon job.

Alejandra described various examples of employment discrimination by race and gender as well as workers' weight and physical appearance. According to Alejandra, workers "were racially profiled, by upper-higher [managers], not, like I said, not all of them, some of them." Elaborating on this point, she said:

> It also depended on the HR person. Sometimes they did have their preferences. . . . They'd ask if you were Hispanic, white, African-American, Latino, all that. And, I feel like, they'd kinda go through all that, and just have a group of Latinos, two Hispanics in the back, and like an African-American and a white, and I'd be like "ok." But, then . . . there were days that they were

all just mixed, and it was beautiful like having everybody be mixed because we can learn from them, you know?

Describing gender discrimination against women warehouse workers, mostly women of color, by trainers and supervisors in the inbound and outbound departments, Alejandra said:

> There was a lot of discrimination. They would just be sexist . . . like they said . . . "Women don't, like the girls, they won't go as fast as they can and they walk" . . . which I thought was very sexist, you know? . . . Inbound, outbound, they just wanted more men, not females because it was trailers. . . . Because the males, they have them more on the equipment . . . or doing more like heavy lifting type of things.

Alejandra told several stories about other supervisors or PAs who were biased in favor of attractive young women associates because of their physical appearance, gender, and age rather than because of their work performance. She personally experienced this kind of discrimination when she was newly hired. Her supervisor "would just stare at me. You know when someone will just stare at you and stare at you?" When this supervisor promised to get her a better job assignment ("in the mids") even though she had one of the worst scan rates, "girls started saying, 'Oh he wants to just get in your pants . . . that's how you get promotions here.'" About a week later, after she started her new job assignment, the supervisor approached her in the parking lot and asked her for a date, which she turned down. She claimed that this was not an isolated incident: "I noticed that as a PA, that's how a lot of people, a lot of females moved their way up more." Another PA she worked with, who was 27, showed favoritism toward physically attractive younger women, whom he would assign to preferred jobs in the warehouse. Another female worker complained about this unfair practice to Alejandra, "She said, 'And I don't think that's fair for us. We don't have the body, we don't show too much cleavage, or you know, our undergarments don't show when we're bending over.'" Alejandra also observed that overweight workers were overlooked for more preferred job assignments.

Alejandra never submitted any formal complaints about these incidents of employment discrimination and sexual harassment because she sought to avoid retaliation for doing so. As she explained, "I would worry a lot [about] speaking up because I felt like my job was on the line." Over time she became increasingly uncomfortable with how workers were treated unfairly but did not feel like she had the option of speaking up about it, even as an area manager in training. Such concerns eventually led to her resignation.

Alejandra's story touches upon many of the themes addressed in this chapter, which focuses on Amazon warehouse workers' social relations, including their experiences with, and observations of, workplace diversity and inequality. In Inland Southern California, more than half (54 percent) of Amazon warehouse workers are Latino, 34 percent are white, 7 percent are Black, 4 percent are Asian American, and the remaining 1 percent are other races. Although most are men, 41 percent are women. Most, about 84 percent, lack college degrees. These workers also tend to be young. About 44 percent of these workers are below the age of 30, another 44 percent are between the ages of 30 and 54, and the remaining 11 percent are 55 or older.[1] According to our interviewees, most workers appear to be below the age of 50.

We begin this chapter by examining Amazon warehouse workers' experiences and observations of workplace discrimination and inequity. Brianna summarized the feelings of many interviewees when she said, "I feel like everybody is not treated equally at that place." When directly asked, nearly 49 percent of all the current and former workers interviewed for this book perceived problems related to fairness, while nearly 41 percent reported problems related to discrimination, as shown in table 5.1. Nearly one in four (24 percent) of those asked claimed there were problems of racism and/or sexism, and 55 percent expressed concerns about workplace divisions. These findings were reasonably consistent across samples, although concerns related to fairness were more common in the prepandemic sample, perhaps due to the greater ease of communicating before the pandemic or more time on the job in that sample.[2] Workers discussed various kinds of unfairness and differential treatment of warehouse workers. In addition to racism and sexism, workers described problems related to favoritism, sexual harassment, heterosexism, transphobia, racialized xenophobia, and ageism. In the following discussion we explore their experiences with, and observations of, these social inequalities, including intersecting inequalities, such as favoritism toward younger women or prejudice against immigrants of color.

Table 5.1 Interviewees' Perceived Inequalities, Divisions, and Relations

	Prepandemic Sample			Pandemic Sample			Both Samples		
Variable	Frequency	Valid Responses	%	Frequency	Valid Responses	%	Frequency	Valid Responses	%
Concern: fairness	26	42	61.90	9	30	30.00	35	72	48.61
Concern: discrimination	16	41	39.02	12	28	42.86	28	69	40.58
Concern: racism/sexism	11	42	26.19	6	28	21.43	17	70	24.29
Workplace divisions (any)	27	44	61.36	14	31	45.16	41	75	54.67
Divisions: gender	12	45	26.67	5	28	17.86	17	73	23.29
Divisions: race	4	44	9.09	3	29	10.34	7	73	9.59
Coworker friendships	35	42	83.33	21	33	63.63	56	75	74.67
Coworker relationships									
Positive	36	44	81.82	16	28	57.14	52	72	72.22
Negative	3	44	6.82	3	28	10.71	6	72	8.33
Neutral or mixed	5	44	11.36	9	28	32.14	14	72	19.44

We then examine other types of workplace constraints on their social relations, such as workplace competition, the isolating nature of certain jobs, and rules restricting workplace socializing. These constraints make it difficult, but not impossible, for Amazon warehouse workers to challenge the norms and expected—unfair and discriminatory—behaviors common to their positions. We also discuss workers' experiences with various kinds of friendly and supportive relationships with their coworkers. Despite constraints on workplace socializing and the unequal and competitive nature of the work environment, 75 percent of warehouse workers interviewed for this study claimed they had friends at work, while 72 percent of interviewees reported that they had positive relationships with their coworkers. We conclude by recognizing the power of these relationships to establish workers' solidarity and motivation for collective action.

FAVORITISM

When asked if they had experienced or observed any unfairness at work, workers frequently complained about favoritism, or behavior by someone in a supervisory or other leadership position that favors one or more employees over others for personal reasons. Various workers reported that managers and supervisors exercised favoritism when assigning workers to different tasks and jobs. For example, Camila responded,

> I've witnessed where somebody's preferred some of us to an easier area or an area they prefer better than somebody who's better at their job. Because they favor them. . . . Those are your leads, so if they . . . don't get along with you, they can put you in positions wherever they want and there's some positions that are least liked or least desirable.

Similarly, Roberto reported that due to favoritism, "Some people get pulled to do the easier tasks more often than others . . . a less labor intensive task, so cleaning the scanners instead of walking around all day, picking up trash, for the most part, it's just less labor intensive stuff." According to Olivia: "I do notice like some of the supervisors telling one person to do, you know, a certain task and then they're even saying that like, 'you're my favorite,' like they actually do verbally say it!"

Workers also perceived favoritism in terms of promotions. For example, Juanita observed that supervisors and managers choose their favorite workers for promotions and opportunities to learn new positions and technologies, even when those workers had not been there long or proven to be good workers. She believed that she was overlooked for a promotion, which was given to another, less-experienced worker. Like Juanita, Camila observed that managers and PAs were not always the most qualified workers: "What I dislike the most is sometimes how it's run . . . and honestly who they hire as managers and PAs. . . . I know that there's people way more qualified, with more knowledge of their work." Similarly, Michelle remarked, "I wish it was easier to get a raise or a promotion that's based on what you know, not who you know."

In addition to supporting their favorites for easier job assignments and promotions, managers and supervisors might not discipline them for failing to comply with work rules or productivity standards. For example, Jose observed workers out of favor were reprimanded for not following COVID-19 safety protocols, while favored workers were not. According to Elvia, "You've had managers pick smaller items and give 'em to, you know the people that they like. Or if they see people talking, they don't say anything to them." Similarly, Julio observed, "Some people get talked to more than others. Some people will be like, 'Hey why is your rate so low?' and then some people, their rate is low but they don't actually get talked to the same ways some other people get talked to, you know what I mean?"

Many workers believed that favoritism by managers and supervisors contributed to workplace tensions and resentments among workers. Workers also described how coworkers played favorites with one another, providing additional help to those they liked. As discussed in chapter 4, workers gave their friends smaller items that were easier to carry, or boxes with more items to scan, to help them "make rate." In contrast, coworkers were rude toward workers they disliked.

SEXISM AND SEXUAL HARASSMENT

Previous research on blue-collar warehouse workers indicates they are stratified by gender.[3] For example, among blue-collar warehouse workers in Inland Southern California, women, especially Latina immigrants, are concentrated in packing and packaging occupations, while a significantly greater number of Latina immigrants are employed through temporary agencies compared to their male counterparts.[4] US temporary agencies have also steered women and men into gender-typed warehouse jobs by referring to women as "lights" and "small hands" and men as "heavies" and "big hands."[5] Surveys collected in Will County, Illinois, find that female temporary warehouse workers report being excluded from opportunities to be trained as forklift drivers and overlooked for laborer jobs, while male warehouse workers avoid packing jobs because they view them as paying too little for the work involved.[6] The gender division of labor in warehouses contributes to inequality in hourly pay; temporary warehouse and packing and packaging jobs in which women are more commonly employed tend to be associated with lower pay than male-dominated laborer and forklift driving positions.[7] Even greater pay differentials by gender are linked to men's greater concentration in managerial occupations in the warehouse industry.[8]

When asked, nearly one in four (or 23 percent) of the warehouse workers interviewed for this book agreed that there were divisions among workers based on gender (see table 5.1). According to Clara, who was employed for years at Amazon, managers were mostly men. Similarly, Josh observed, "A lot of the managers are men. . . . Lately, they started hiring more females and people of color [as managers] recently . . . but for a while, when I first started, it was like all white guys." Some workers noted exceptions to these general trends, however. For example, Erica, employed during the 2020 pandemic, said, "I see some more girls . . . as full time. Like there's a lot of shift supervisors and managers that are girls."

Although Amazon associates tend to be cross-trained and be paid the same wage rates across warehouse tasks, a gender division of labor similar to that identified by researchers among blue-collar warehouse workers in the overall industry was described in interviews collected for this book. For example Jimmy, employed in 2013, said: "I think women were asked to do the inbound and the guys got shoved to do the trucks. Women were tasked to do more of the scanning or problem control. . . . I saw more women being hired as temps." During our tour of the San Bernardino Amazon warehouse in 2019, we observed a gender division of labor in the warehouse. Most of the workers unloading trucks were men, and the only forklift driver in sight was a man. In contrast, we observed many women picking and packing.

Many interviewees described how women warehouse workers were subjected to gender-based and sexual harassment by male coworkers, supervisors, and managers. Similar to other blue-collar workplaces such as port docks, heavy machinery was associated with men and masculinity, and male coworkers commonly harassed women who used it.[9] Interviewees for this book claimed that women employed as forklift drivers or leads experienced gender harassment or felt distinct performance pressures as token women. For example, Jimmy claimed, "They trained a few women for forklift, but it is unusual to train women to do that task. Women were always being stereotyped as bad drivers or unable to perform that task." Elizabeth, another former employee, recalled:

> The forklift drivers were mainly guys. So, I did get extremely discriminated [against] because I was a female forklift driver. I would come home pissed because guys would hit on me. They would harass me and say things like, "Oh you grabbed the wrong fork, go put it back and grab the right one," like they're trying to put me in my place.

Similarly, Maria recalled, "For a female, you had to prove yourself. You had to prove yourself that you were a good worker, you could lead a department, and you weren't being a bitch, if you could lead a department and not be a little hoe. Before I came along, there were only males leading." Other workers recounted frustrations among women in terms of being overlooked for male-stereotyped warehouse positions. For example, Samantha expressed frustration about seeking but failing to become a dockworker even though she had filled out the paperwork and consulted with a manager about it.

There were, of course, exceptions to the overall gender division of labor. For example, Maria expressed appreciation for Amazon for giving her the opportunity to prove herself in a traditionally male-stereotyped job:

> I get to go home and just feel accomplished. Especially when I feel that people underestimate me based on my looks because I'm small and I'm a girl. They wouldn't expect me, in a million years, to be packing thirty-pound boxes at a fast pace for ten hours. This job has given me the opportunity to prove myself.

Estella, a woman who was assigned to work on the docks, observed, "Men would carry heavy ones for me." As these quotes reveal, even when the gender division of labor was broken, gender still shaped workplace experiences and practices in Amazon warehouses.

Interviewees also varied in their opinions in terms of whether Amazon's female workers, mostly women of color, were subject to employment fairness, discrimination, or favoritism. While such variation may reflect differences in workers' gender consciousness, it is also likely that problems of employment discrimination varied across supervisors, managers, and facilities. Anong claimed that women workers "do tend to be pushed aside." Similarly, Jorge recalled that "some of the girls were treated differently. . . . More blame would be put on them if something went wrong. . . . Like if they weren't filling their quotas."

In contrast to Jorge's account, both male and female workers reported that some supervisors treated women, especially attractive women, better than men. As Samuel put it, "Some supervisors would favor the prettier girls like you know, people that they're cool with." Similarly, Paola claimed, "It was mainly the most attractive girls were getting the easy way." Likewise, Xavier reported, "Some women moved up and were promoted faster because of favors or relationships with some of the managers." Briana similarly noted, "I know a lot of women that do things to get promoted." Another woman initially employed as a warehouse associate who later became an assistant manager agreed with these assessments.

Various workers also claimed that supervisors were more likely to select women, particularly attractive women, to become either "problem solvers" or "ambassadors." When describing supervisors' favoritism toward women, Samuel reported, "There was some favoritism with . . . supervisors picking problem solvers. At first they were generally mostly women. So there was kind of a thing [rumor] going around like, 'you only pick the pretty girls to learn how to problem solve.'" Jimmy similarly noted, "Sometimes women would be promoted faster to ambassadors but it's hard to say if that was the reason. It was kind of favoritism with a cost." As several workers noted, the problem solver and ambassador positions were coveted, as they were considered somewhat less onerous and less tightly monitored compared to other jobs, such as picking or packing, and were key positions for becoming promoted to supervisory positions.

Workers, both male and female, observed the challenges for Amazon's blue-collar female workers in terms of the male-dominated or masculine culture in warehouses. Various workers also discussed the problem of male warehouse workers sexually harassing their female colleagues. Estella recalled, "Some men made women uncomfortable and go up to you and talk to you. . . . Uncomfortable because you couldn't really move positions unless told to." Jorge reported:

> Working at a warehouse is probably like the most, the most like sexist jokes of any other place. . . . It's a macho-like environment . . . with all this heavy machinery and stuff. Like the women were kind of encouraged to be like more manly. . . . They had to like to put on this persona like you can't fuck with me.

Given the masculine work culture and hostile climate for women warehouse workers, it is probably not too surprising that during work breaks, Julio usually observed "girls hanging out with girls, guys hanging out with guys."

A number of workers recalled various instances of sexual harassment experienced by themselves or coworkers. For example, Destiny observed, "Some men, not all, were like, 'Ok since I'm working at a warehouse, I can hit up any one of these females.' And the women who work there usually wear like workout clothes. So, women were usually seen as sex objects." Samuel likewise reported, "There's a lot of . . . things that go there as far as sexual talk and you know, verbal things that happened in between employees and sometimes supervisors." Similarly, Jimmy observed, "I think there [was] generally a lot of flirting, between younger people or older men with younger women. It was sometimes consensual or non-consensual." According to Fernando,

> Within the workers and the management, there is a lot of like not overt harassment, but there's . . . a sense of like uncomfortability that is placed among the women. . . . There [was] a lot of attention toward specific women. . . . If they were like really . . . attractive . . . you see like a lot of men gathered toward them, which I think would make it very difficult for them to do their job.

Mateo similarly recalled, "Sexual harassment, unwanted sexual comments, compliments, and conversations that made you feel uncomfortable," and that contributed to workplace "drama": "There was female attraction within coworkers and then there's multiple people arguing and fighting, lots of sexual harassment that shouldn't be taking place but it does happen and people don't do anything about it." Anong likewise observed that "a lot" of women workers experienced sexual harassment.

Some workers chose not to report the sexual harassment they experienced or observed to the HR department. For example, Camilla shared, "I've personally experienced sexual harassment, where they just say inappropriate things." Camilla feared getting fired if she filed complaints about sexual harassment and employment discrimination. She continued to work at Amazon because she needed the income to support her family, including her grandmother, who was sick.

Even when workers did complain to the HR department about sexual harassment, management did not adequately address their complaints or required witnesses, which was often difficult given the isolated nature of many warehouse tasks. As one worker put it:

> Sexual harassment is not taken seriously, from my experience with my coworkers. . . . They've been to HR and HR doesn't do much about it, or from what I've been told. HR doesn't do much and tells them to switch departments if they can't work with that person. It seems like supervisors and managers tend to cater more toward what the company needs than what the employee needs. As a tier 1, it feels like you're left off on your own and there is not a lot of security there. I think it sucks that a lot of the female coworkers have to experience that. It's a really common thing. When they try to report to HR, they say they need concrete evidence, like telling us that if someone said something inappropriate, it isn't enough. You need to have witnesses, but it's hard when you do work since you're out there by yourself.

Warehouse work is often socially isolating, and interviewees recalled various instances in which workers were harassed when no one else was in sight or earshot, such as in empty bathrooms or aisles.

Josh recalled that after a worker had filed a sexual harassment complaint against a man who showed naked pictures of her to other coworkers, "the whole thing got really messy and they didn't do anything to him. He ended up switching to a different department to avoid it. . . . I understand they had nothing to prove what he did, but she obviously was feeling intimidated and harassed by him and they weren't doing much about that."

After reporting the incident to the HR department, this worker "felt like [coworkers who knew of the incident] . . . were making her job harder, like making her feel uncomfortable 'cus they would be mentioning things about him to her and she would just kinda feel really uncomfortable about it." Daniella described the failure of the HR department to sufficiently address a series of sexual harassment complaints against the same person. Instead, they closed the case. Explaining why, she said, "I think it was more favoritism, just because he was really close with our manager. He was kind of like our manager's like right-hand man."

Fear of retaliation against workers who file complaints and the failure of management to adequately address incidents of sexual harassment discourage workers from reporting sexual harassment. For example, Brianna told her interviewer:

> I've been in HR maybe like 5 or 6 times dealing with very prejudiced managers or sexual harassment. I am always the one in the wrong, so I just don't say anything unless it really affects my job, then I will say something. But, so if you don't want to take anything seriously, then I don't want to make it an issue. . . . I literally had a dude rub his boner up against my leg and I went to HR and got written up! . . . I had a manager literally tell me that I was too opinionated and that I better watch out and I was the one who got in trouble! . . . That's why HR at my job is a joke, this is why I see why a lot of people don't take HR seriously because nothing ever gets done."

Because of her frustration with the HR department's inaction and fear of retaliation, Briana no longer makes formal complaints to that department. "Now I just keep quiet, do my job, and go home. . . . I don't wanna lose my job."

The HR problems identified by Briana and other Amazon warehouse workers interviewed for this book echo concerns raised by Amazon's corporate employees in the United States, some of whom have sued or filed legal complaints against their employer for discrimination. Attorneys representing five legal cases of race and/or gender discrimination by US-based Amazon corporate employees, for example, stated to the press:

> Women and employees of color at all levels of Amazon have had their complaints of harassment and discrimination brushed under the rug and met with retaliation for years. . . . Amazon can no longer dismiss abusive behavior

and retaliation by white managers as mere anecdotes. These are systemic problems, entrenched deep within the company and perpetuated by a human resources organization that treats employees who raise concerns as the problem.[10]

The attorneys also claimed that "Amazon's top executives and HR department 'routinely protected and abetted' abusive managers."[11] Amazon Web Services (AWS) employees voiced similar concerns in a petition about the lack of transparency and bias in Amazon's system of investigating discrimination and harassment claims. Signed by 550 employees, the petition claimed that "the system is 'set up to protect the company and the status quo, rather than the employees filing the complaints'" and puts employees filing complaints at risk of retaliation.[12]

In the United Kingdom, the GMB union, representing warehouse workers, lobbied investors to pressure Amazon to improve working conditions in 2019, including taking action to address complaints related to sexual harassment.[13] The following year, several women warehouse workers, employed in a facility at Rugeley Staffordhire, United Kingdom, complained publicly and filed internal complaints about sexual harassment occurring in an Amazon warehouse. They described a "culture of sexual harassment." One claimed that the HR department was unresponsive to her complaints involving a manager. Other incidents involved an instructor and older male coworkers, who were observed harassing younger women.[14]

Along with Amazon, several other US warehouse employers have recently faced highly publicized charges related to sexual harassment, including lawsuits filed by the Equal Employment Opportunity Commission against FYC International in 2014 and an EEOC complaint against Verizon filed by eight female warehouse workers in 2018.[15] In 2019 the Illinois attorney general issued a consent decree with a warehouse company and temporary agency for employment discrimination against women warehouse workers and "pervasive sexual harassment" involving unwelcome advances and sexualized remarks. The company and staffing agency employed women and men for different positions using gendered code words, "lights" and "heavies." Along with a $75,000 fine, the warehouse employer (MTIL Inc.) was required to implement antidiscrimination policies and train workers about these policies. A third-party hotline was set up for workers to report sexual harassment and gender discrimination. This consent decree was issued in response to complaints brought to the attorney general's office in 2016 by Warehouse Workers for Justice, located in Joliet, Illinois.[16]

PREGNANCY-RELATED DISCRIMINATION AND FAILURE TO ACCOMMODATE BREASTFEEDING MOTHERS

Amazon boasts of its family-friendly policies, such as offering relatively generous employment benefits for new parents: twenty weeks of paid leave for parents after childbirth, which can be shared with employees' spouses, and several weeks of reduced and flexible hours after returning to work. Yet Amazon has come under fire for failing to accommodate and firing pregnant warehouse workers in both the United States and other nations. For example, a pregnant Amazon warehouse worker in Great Britain who was surveyed by the GMB union in 2018 described the difficulty of standing for ten hours per shift and being pressured to "work hard" despite her pregnancy. The poor treatment of pregnant Amazon warehouse workers also gained public attention through a series of publicized formal legal complaints. Amazon was charged with violating the federal Pregnancy Discrimination Act, which prohibits employers from discriminating against pregnant women when hiring, firing, or assigning workers to jobs, and the Americans with Disabilities Act (ADA), which prohibits employers from discriminating against disabled workers and requires them to respond to reasonable requests for workplace accommodations. Despite these legal protections, violations of these acts are commonplace in the United States. Between 2010 and 2019, the EEOC received on average 3,520 pregnancy-related charges per year, and that figure excludes many cases that are not reported by women who might lack the time or money needed to pursue a formal complaint, fear employment retaliation for doing so, or might not understand their legal rights.[17]

Between 2011 and 2019 at least seven pregnant women, formerly employed in Amazon warehouses in the United States, sued the corporation for pregnancy discrimination, resulting in at least six settlements out of court by 2019. The women were fired after reporting their pregnancies to management, who also refused their requests for pregnancy-related accommodations, such as longer bathroom breaks and fewer hours spent on their feet. Among the seven women suing Amazon for pregnancy-related discrimination was Beverly Rosales of San Bernardino. Rosales, employed as an Amazon warehouse worker for two years, was fired just a week after Cyber Monday. Managers notified her that she had spent "too much time off task" using the restroom. She was only allowed thirty minutes per day to use the restroom, but that limit was difficult for Rosales to comply with because it took at least ten minutes to walk to and from the restroom from her workstation and she needed to use the bathroom more frequently due to her pregnancy. Although Rosales was still able to make rate, supervisors hassled her for spending too much time using the restroom. Less than two months before being fired, Rosales had notified Amazon of her pregnancy and provided a doctor's note documenting her need to use the restroom more frequently than usual. Amazon refused to provide her with any workplace accommodations. In May 2019 Rosales, whose baby was due the next month, remained unemployed after getting fired by Amazon.[18]

In 2020 Michelle Posey, employed full-time as a stower in Oklahoma City, filed a complaint against Amazon for pregnancy- and disability-related discrimination. According to the complaint, the corporation's handbook does not mention accommodations for pregnancy, and it was unresponsive or slow to respond to requests for a new position. She was pregnant and advised by a doctor to not lift more than fifteen pounds and to work shorter shifts. Posey's job at the time required at least ten hours per shift and lifting up to seventy pounds. Amazon denied her requests, and she took a short unpaid leave of absence. After returning to work several months later, Posey collapsed due to dehydration while working, after which she was granted a short medical leave. During several leaves (one postpartum), and while working shorter shifts after finally being given medical accommodations, points were deducted against Posey's unpaid time off, for not working ten-hour shifts. Even after obtaining medical accommodations, Posey was reassigned to positions requiring her to lift heavy boxes.[19] In support of Posey's EEOC case, six senators sent a letter to the EEOC urging it to investigate Amazon's treatment of pregnant warehouse workers and their failure to provide accommodations to them. "In the 2020 EEOC complaint, the Amazon worker claimed the corporation denied her requests for a job transfer, penalized her for pregnancy-related absences, and 'engaged in unauthorized contact with her doctor in an attempt to change her work restrictions,' according to the letter." They pointed out that this treatment violated both the ADA and the Pregnancy Discrimination Act.[20] Amazon also failed to accommodate the needs of warehouse workers who were breastfeeding mothers, according to Alejandra, who recalled the experience of a breastfeeding mother who needed to lactate but was denied the opportunity to do so.

HETEROSEXISM AND TRANSPHOBIA

Problems of transphobia at Amazon warehouses gained national attention when Allegra Schawe-Lane, a trans woman, and her husband, Dane Lane, two former Amazon warehouse workers, filed legal complaints against the corporation for violating their civil rights, labor rights, and the ADA (because Allegra's transgender status was perceived as a disability). The couple were employed in a warehouse facility in Hebron, Kentucky, in 2014 and 2015, where they experienced multiple acts of gender-based and sexual harassment from coworkers. In one incident, the brake line of their car, parked in a secure parking lot, was cut. The level of workplace hostility they faced surprised them given the lesbian, gay, bisexual, transgender, queer/questioning, intersexed, and asexual/aromatic/agender (LGBTQIA)-friendly reputation of Amazon, whose studios had produced *Transparent*.[21] Amazon also had repeatedly received perfect corporate equality index scores from the Human Rights Campaign (HRC) for its LGBTQ-friendly policies, while Bezos, Amazon's founder and then CEO, received HRC's Equality Award in 2017.[22]

With assistance from the Transgender Legal Defense and Education Fund and before they resigned, the couple filed legal complaints about the discrimination and harassment they had faced with the EEOC, which ruled in their favor. The couple later filed a lawsuit with the US District Court in Covington, Kentucky. Their lawyer claimed that this was not the first court case filed against Amazon involving LGBTQIA rights.[23] Amazon eventually settled out of court with the couple.[24]

Another well-publicized case of transphobic harassment and pregnancy discrimination at Amazon involved a transgender pregnant male warehouse employee, Shaun Simmons. Simmons was employed in a warehouse in Princeton, New Jersey. After he disclosed his pregnancy to his immediate supervisor, the news quickly spread to another supervisor and coworkers. Coworkers then harassed Simmons for his pregnancy and gender identity. For example, when using the men's bathroom, one coworker asked him, "Aren't you pregnant?" The HR department then responded to Simmons's complaint about the harassment by putting him on paid leave. After the paid leave ended, Simmons was demoted to a picker position and asked to lift heavy items, such as large bags of dog food. After he complained of abdominal pain from too much heavy lifting, the HR department put him back on paid leave. After he returned to work, HR staff denied Simmons's request for a workplace accommodation, even though he provided medical documentation of his need to avoid heavy lifting. Amazon also rescinded its earlier offer of a job located at another warehouse so that Simmons could be employed away from his harassers. Simmons sued Amazon for discrimination based on his gender identity and pregnancy, failing to accommodate his disability, and employment retaliation and also named his immediate supervisors in the lawsuit.[25]

There was only one transgender worker in our interview sample, who identified as "gender neutral." They described their experience being falsely categorized in terms of a gender binary. For example, when asked about sexual harassment and discrimination at work, the worker recalled:

> I had like one weird coworker, but I just thought that was part of the warehouse. . . . I am not sure because I am very gender neutral, so I am not sure if he perceived me as a man and talked about women like he does to other men. He generalized . . . but was talking to me. I didn't report him, but I wasn't sure about the situation, so I just kept working.

As this transgender person describes, although they did not like this man's sexist remarks about women, they did not report this incident because they were not sure of the man's motives or which gender the man perceived them to be. That this worker considered this man's remarks to be just "part of the warehouse" suggests just how deeply ingrained sexism and heterosexism are in warehouses.

Several cisgender women interviewed observed or expressed hostility toward transgender workers. For example, describing tensions among supervisors and workers, Alejandra said:

> There was definitely tension, because of their own personal reasons. Some-
> times it was personal reasons or because discrimination against their sex, or
> if they felt like they were a male, but they would consider themself a female,
> or they were a female and they would consider themself a male, for the way
> they would dress or the way they'd speak or anything.

This quote describes employment discrimination against trans workers
by supervisors. Briana, a cisgender worker, described her own discomfort
with trans workers and gender-inclusive restrooms:

> I feel like Amazon is "equal for all" but I feel like they . . . target the like
> transgender and the LGBTQ people more so. . . . Our bathrooms are for all
> genders and I've been there for four years and now any bathroom that you
> go into is all-gender so whatever. So even though they have male and female
> bathrooms they still have transgender people that work at Amazon even
> though they do look like men who are supposed to be like women, they are
> able to use the women's bathroom . . . and a lot of people, women have com-
> plained about that, but that's Amazon policy is "equal opportunity," so what-
> ever they identify as is who they are.

Briana explained that she did not support Amazon's gender-inclusive
bathroom policies and that she was not comfortable sharing the bathroom
with trans workers. Her story reveals how, despite the implementation of
more gender-inclusive policies at Amazon, trans warehouse workers still
face a chilly or unwelcome work climate due to transphobia. Similarly,
Paola recalled, "I had my own problem with some guys that thought it was
interesting to be lesbian," despite policies prohibiting discrimination on
the basis of sexual orientation at Amazon.

RACISM AND XENOPHOBIA

In 2020, in the context of the resurgence of the Black Lives Matter (BLM)
movement and rising public criticism of Amazon's lack of diversity, the
company's (mostly white) executives pledged to "'stand in solidarity with
the Black community—our employees, customers, and partners- in the
fight against systemic racism and injustice.'" That year, Amazon hired
its first Black executive, Alicia Boler Davis, for its top leadership team,
and, under fire from its critics, put a one-year moratorium on its facial

recognition software sold to police because it was found to "dispropor-tionately mis-identify Black people."[26] The corporation also adopted a re-quirement that all employees take diversity and inclusion training, agreed to complete a racial equity evaluation, and stepped up its efforts to recruit professionals of color.[27]

For many Amazon employees, these were token gestures rather than significant strides toward racial equity in a corporation in which the vast majority of Black employees engaged in backbreaking warehouse labor; faced hazardous and precarious employment; earned poverty-level wages; and, like other hourly employees, were given only very limited opportu-nities for upward advancement. According to a *New York Times* exposé, internal records from Amazon's JFK8 warehouse in New York revealed that Black warehouse associates were 50 percent more likely to be fired than their white counterparts.[28]

Along with higher-paid Black corporate employees, Black warehouse workers contested racial discrimination at Amazon by filing a series of legal complaints. For example, in 2019 three Black women warehouse workers employed by Amazon filed federal complaints with the EEOC against Amazon for employment discrimination based on race. These workers were affiliated with the Awood Center, which had been organiz-ing Amazon warehouse workers in the Minneapolis region since 2017. They claim that, compared to white workers, Somali and East African warehouse workers have been given more physically taxing jobs, such as packing heavy items, and have been denied promotions and training opportunities.[29]

Several other racial discrimination lawsuits against Amazon were filed in November 2020, including one by Christian Smalls, a Black Amazon warehouse worker activist who was fired after organizing other warehouse workers around demands for greater protection from COVID-19 in ware-houses in Staten Island, New York, and who became president of Amazon Labor Union in 2022. Smalls's complaint charged Amazon with failing to protect Black, Latino, and immigrant warehouse workers from COVID-19 while providing greater protection for its mostly white male managers. That same month, Denard Norton, a Black Amazon warehouse worker in Essex County, New Jersey, sued Amazon for failing to respond to his multiple complaints about racist comments made by coworkers and his immediate supervisors, promoting a coworker he had reported for saying the N-word, and denying him a promotion based on his race.[30]

Johnnie Corina, a Black warehouse worker who was employed for a year at the Eastvale warehouse in Riverside in 2021, filed another lawsuit, charging that Amazon created a racially hostile workplace. Corina was a community leader. He served as a board member of the Riverside chapter of the National Association for the Advancement of Colored People (NAACP) and as a member of the African American Advisory Committee of the Riverside Unified School District. While employed at the Eastvale warehouse in 2019 and 2020, Mr. Corina and other Black employees were subjected to racist graffiti, which appeared frequently in the employee restroom. The graffiti used the "N-word," referred to white power, and expressed hatred toward and even intentions to kill Black people. Mr. Corina filed multiple complaints about the racist graffiti and filed a complaint when he discovered a rope resembling a noose near a trash compactor. Managers failed to respond effectively to these problems or to identify the culprits. Managers did not even provide any additional sensitivity or diversity training to employees beyond the brief initial training employees had originally received when first becoming employees. They also only reminded employees of Amazon's policies against racist conduct and graffiti through brief and perfunctory reminders; these reminders were included as short entries in building newsletters and a very brief verbal reminder by a general manager during a long speech for about 5,000 warehouse workers that mostly focused on the goals and performance of the Eastvale facility. Although Amazon staff photographed, recorded, and removed the racist graffiti from restroom walls, they did not remove the toilet paper dispenser on which someone had etched the "N-word" until months later, after multiple complaints were filed about it. Meanwhile, Corina suffered from stress, anxiety, and depression from being subjected to these racist actions that became severe and disabling. He eventually went on disability leave from his Amazon job and then found another job. Corina filed his lawsuit after receiving a "right to sue" letter from the Department of Fair Employment and Housing. The lawsuit called upon Amazon to provide a settlement to Corina to pay compensatory and punitive damages and attorney's fees. It also demanded that Amazon expand and improve its employee training related to diversity, cultural sensitivity, and harassment;

provide a more adequate response to racist incidents when they occur; and establish a Black employee network at the facility, similar to other Amazon places of employment, to provide greater support for its Black employees.

Warehouse workers interviewed for this book provided mixed assessments of the racial climate of Amazon warehouses. On the one hand, many interviewees appreciated the racial diversity among Amazon's warehouse employees. As Miguel put it, "You see all types of races there. Hispanic, Latino, white, Indian, Asians. . . . You see everything." Fernando noted, "I think probably one of the pluses of working there was probably the diversity." He enjoyed getting to know immigrant workers from different nations and learning about their cultures. Various workers also perceived that Amazon's initial process of hiring warehouse workers was fair.

On the other hand, some interviewees described various concerns about the racial hierarchy in Amazon's warehouses. As Paola put it, "It was mainly black and brown bodies and the only white people were managers." Similarly, Josh noted, "There's not that many white people. . . . If there are, they're usually higher ups." Like Paola and Josh, various interviewees observed that managers were mostly male and white, while most nonsupervisory warehouse workers were people of color, most commonly Latino, a pattern consistent with workforce data.[31]

When directly asked, nearly 10 percent of workers interviewed reported divisions among workers based on race (see table 5.1). Various interviewees described incidents of differential treatment by race and racialized xenophobia carried out by coworkers, supervisors, or managers. When asked if people were treated differently based on their social background, Daniella responded, "Yes, depending on the supervisor and what their ethnicity is." Similarly, Alejandra claimed that workers "were racially profiled, by upper-higher . . . not all of them, some of them." Alejandra also observed that many associates preferred supervisors and managers of their own race and communicated more openly with them about workplace problems. She also observed racist interactions among coworkers: "I don't want to say this word, but they're very discriminat[ory] towards other associates. Like associates with associates, you know? Because of their background. So like they grew up, their parents taught them this way and whatever, right?" Likewise, Miguel recalled, "There's been a couple of cases of whites and Latinos or white and Black. Sometimes there was a couple [of] people, white people, that would just be rude to these other people so, that's something that was kind of racial."

Some workers described various examples of racialized xenophobia targeting Indian or Latino immigrants. For example, Miguel observed, "There's been a couple of situations, for example, about people from India.... People kinda stay away from [them]." According to Elvia, "They hire the Latinas who don't speak English ... and then they, you pretty much like, 'You gotta be in this Department' and they were supposed to be in a different Department. Stuff of that nature. They are the ones that get picked on." Miguel's and Elvia's observations of hostility and discrimination toward Indian and Spanish-speaking Latina immigrants reveal how groups sometimes faced differential treatment because of intersecting inequalities and a multiply marginalized identity.

Several workers discussed racial discrimination targeting Blacks. For example, Fernando, describing a coworker, reported, "He was African American.... He would get in trouble a lot by the upper management who were white.... It kind of seemed like they were purposely giving him hassle because he was African American." Caryn, a Black warehouse worker, claimed that she did not personally experience racial discrimination at Amazon but heard other workers say, "Amazon doesn't hire Black people."

Workers interviewed also reported various situations in which workers or managers were fired for racist and/or sexist behavior that was reported to the HR department. For example, Miguel reported:

This time . . . it was a white male. . . . They ended up letting him go 'cause he was just being, just throwing sexual jokes or like racist jokes so, the manager said those things. . . . He ended up being fired because he was using too many racist jokes or sexual jokes.

Josh remembered another incident involving racialized and anti-Islamic discrimination that led to a worker being fired:

After the shooting, the San Bernardino shooting . . . I heard that there was people saying like really mean things about . . . Muslims and the people that they thought were Middle Eastern or . . . involved with ISIS. . . . I heard that people were making remarks to them, but literally like the next week the managers addressed that and said there wasn't going to be any tolerance to the person that was making those remarks and they got fired.

Yet Amazon's upper management sometimes responded less forcefully to complaints about racial inequalities in the treatment of workers; they simply transferred the workers rather than firing them. For example, Miguel recalled:

> That manager got moved to a different position. . . . It was because he was being really mean to [my friend] and I think it's 'cus he was white, and she was Hispanic. I think that had a lot to do with it. A lot of people put in a lot of complaints about him too that he was treating people [badly].

Along with racist supervisors and managers, there were also racist co-workers, As Daniella recalled, "We have our racist people. . . . Yes, depending on what your culture is, people will make stereotypical jokes. They will say something that is inappropriate and say they were just kidding and in reality, they are not." Various worker interviews also mentioned that racial and/or ethnic homophily among workers was common, another indicator of the racialized nature of warehouse labor.

Concerns about racial discrimination in the warehouse industry have also been raised about other employers besides Amazon in recent years. For example, various temporary agencies around the nation, which often recruit workers for warehouses, came under fire in the press and through legal complaints for using code words to discriminate against Black job applicants in response to the racial preferences of hiring firms.[32] In 2019 Walmart faced multiple legal complaints claiming that it had practiced racial discrimination against Black warehouse workers in Ellwood, Illinois. Walmart had taken over management of that warehouse, previously operated by Schneider Logistics (a third-party logistics company). As many as 200 of the 589 workers, all of whom were Black and some of whom had worked at the warehouse for years, lost their jobs as a result of Walmart's rules against hiring workers with criminal backgrounds.[33]

AGEISM

Ageism is an age bias that can lead to discrimination against older workers. In 2017 Amazon came under fire for discriminating against older workers when the Communications Workers of America (CWA) and three workers filed a class action lawsuit against Amazon.com, Inc., Cox Communications and

Media Group, T-Mobile US, and hundreds of other large employers and employment agencies. The lawsuit charged Amazon and these other large companies with discriminating against older workers when recruiting for open positions through Facebook. The companies excluded older workers from receiving their job ads, which were only sent to younger workers through Facebook.[34] Amazon sent job recruitment ads to Facebook subscribers between the ages of 22 to 40 or 18 to 50, which attorneys argued violated federal, state, and local laws against employment discrimination against older workers. In 2018 the CWA and workers also filed EEOC charges against Amazon and sixty-five other companies for age discrimination. Although the investigation of the age-discrimination charges against Amazon is still underway, the EEOC ruled in favor of similar complaints against seven other companies in 2019. That same year, Facebook agreed to a historic legal settlement requiring it to change its advertising platforms to prevent future discrimination in the sending of ads related to jobs, housing, and credit.[35]

While these legal complaints involved employment discrimination against older job applicants, age-related discrimination and bias also affected actual Amazon warehouse workers, according to workers interviewed for this book. They reported that ageism intersected with sexism at work in ways that produced discrimination against both older and younger women. For example, Clara recalled that she was often not taken seriously as a lead as a younger woman. In contrast, Fernando observed that older female workers tended to be assigned to be "pickers." Picker positions were commonly perceived to be one of the most difficult and least favorite warehouse jobs, often because workers' productivity was closely monitored and the high work rates expected of pickers put them at risk of termination: "So a lot of the ladies they would send them as pickers. So I realized that if they want people out right away, they're going to send them as pickers and I realized it was a lot of older ladies." Ageism also intersected with class and educational differences to shape workplace relations. For example, Clara also noted that older and more experienced warehouse workers often resented being ordered around by managers who were younger recent college graduates with little if any warehouse work experience.

Intergenerational divisions among workers also emerged on the shop floor due to perceived or actual differences in workers' physical abilities and technical skills. Brenda claimed that sometimes there are tensions between older workers and younger workers because the younger workers have more capability to hit their rate more efficiently. Several workers in their twenties also expressed the opinion that older workers were not as physically capable of performing certain work tasks and should be assigned to less physically strenuous tasks. On the other hand, older and more experienced warehouse workers sometimes viewed younger and less-experienced workers as less capable.

Worker interviews also described various examples of affinity-based divisions, or homophily, by age among workers, which sometimes intersected with other social differences, such as those based on ethnicity or university affiliations. For example, when asked to describe divisions among workers, Anong, a Thai American in his twenties, replied:

> The biggest would be age. People with the same age tend to flop together because they have something to talk about. I wouldn't say race or gender specifically. . . . I guess ethnicity can be one of them; there is a certain group. Like Filipinos from the same department congregate but they are usually around the same age. So I guess there is some ethnic division in the younger age.

Erica recalled her identification with other young student workers enrolled in the same university: "Yeah 'cause there's a lot of people that are like my age that also go to the same school that I go to so I'm like, well that's cool. So it's really cool just like talking to them." Similarly, Maria described a particular clique of older Latina "ladies, senoritas," who often took breaks together. A few older workers also mentioned feeling excluded by younger workers because of their age. Age, sometimes in interaction with other social identities, thus shaped workers' relationships and interactions, in addition to putting older workers at risk of employment discrimination.

WORKPLACE COMPETITION, DISRESPECT, AND CONSTRAINTS ON SOCIALIZING

In addition to problems related to employment discrimination, workplace competition also discouraged the formation of friendly and cooperative relations among workers. Positive working relationships notably contribute to more enjoyable employment experiences; additionally, in many contexts, they increase productivity, revenue streams, and overall corporate success. Yet the Amazon employees we interviewed suggest that the successful e-commerce giant encouraged workplace competition, which sometimes reduced workplace cooperation. As Daniel put it, "Having a rate system in place really made it like, 'Hey I am beating you.' It was more of a toxic environment." Management or supervisors sometimes encouraged competition among workers by praising or giving small rewards for workers or work teams with the best productivity rates. While such workplace competitions and games might have provided extra incentives for workers to work hard and livened up an otherwise dull day at work, they were also a source of stress, resentment, and animosity among workers. Competition among workers over preferred workstations or machines, encouraged by the pressure to meet the productivity standards set by management and the tendency of machinery to malfunction, was also noted. For example, Olivia recalled, "They want certain spots with the machinery they use, so I just see sometimes, people, like, fighting for a spot." Similarly, as discussed in chapter 4, workers also informally competed with one another to get boxes with more items in them because that made it easier to make rate when scanning items. Such types of informal competition strained workplace relationships.

Workers, under pressure to work hard, also sometimes resented workers they believed were not pulling their weight. As Roberto put it, "The thing I dislike most about my job, it's probably that some people get paid the same for doing less work, and other people get paid the same for doing more work." Other workers who were especially fast or productive were expected to help less productive workers to complete tasks. While some workers enjoyed helping one another out, others resented it because it added to their workload and exhaustion. As in many workplaces, workers were also sometimes disrespectful, rude, or unprofessional toward one another or acted in ways that irritated each other.

Workplace rules and the logistical or technical constraints of the job created other workplace constraints that limited workers' ability to socialize and form positive relationships with one another. For example, workers could get into trouble or receive warnings from supervisors for spending too much TOT, including talking with each other, even when they were simply helping to train new workers or collaborating to get their jobs done. For example, Ana said, "Like you can't really be social. . . . Even if you do make friends, and even outside like the warehouse, they have cameras and if you're like sitting next to like your friend, they will flag you so they'll take your picture and then write you up." As workers described, workers' freedom and opportunities to interact with each other varied and depended on their assigned job or rank. For example, Esther observed, "They're all in yellow vests so they all know each other and they all like do their own thing. And like talk to each other. But then us, like the people in the pink, we can't really socialize with each other, we just have to keep working."

According to workers, they often helped each other when loading and unloading trailers and often talked with each other as they worked. Other jobs, such as picking, were more isolating, and workers were sometimes assigned to locations far apart from their coworkers. The impersonal nature of many workplace interactions and managers' heavy reliance on electronic communication also impeded relationship building among workers and shaped how warehouse workers viewed themselves and each other. As Esther put it, "I feel like I'm like a worker bee, like it's just faceless people, like we're just little minions."

Constraints on workplace socializing were further amplified by safety protocols during the COVID-19 pandemic, which further limited workplace interactions. Staggered work shifts and breaks, which aimed to protect workers from exposure to COVID-19, made it difficult for coworkers to socialize and build friendships with one another. Amid the din of loud machinery, face masks and social distancing rules made it even more difficult for workers to hear each other, let alone have meaningful conversations with one another, especially workers who used ear plugs. As Olivia described, "It comes down to us screaming at each other. Sometimes you don't even understand what they're saying." The large size of warehouse facilities and isolating nature of certain tasks, along with high employee turnover and frequent reassignment of workers across departments and tasks, made it difficult for workers to communicate and form social bonds with one another.[36]

FRIENDLY AND HELPFUL COWORKER RELATIONS

Despite workplace discrimination and harassment among coworkers, limited opportunities to interact, and workplace competition, many warehouse workers nevertheless did socialize and collaborate on the job. They helped each other with completing work tasks and learning new skills; they made friends and sometimes even formed tight-knit cliques and long-lasting friendships. Describing the sociality among warehouse workers, Angelo recalled that when "leaving, there'd also be groups huddled outside of the exit," who were talking and socializing after work. The nature of coworker relations varied across facilities. Daniella observed, "Everyone has their little group, their little posse, and every group has a leader." In contrast, Ana observed a general sense of community among workers at her facility and an absence of cliques. Despite such differences, when asked what they liked about their jobs the most, many workers mentioned their coworkers. Erica claimed, "I like my coworkers. If it wasn't for them, I feel like I would dread going there."

As table 5.1 shows, when directly asked during interviews if they had friends at their workplace, fully 75 percent of the Amazon warehouse workers who responded to this question said "yes." Friendships were more prevalent among the prepandemic than the pandemic sample, however; about 83 percent of those interviewed before the pandemic reported having friends at work, compared to only 63 percent of those interviewed during the pandemic. Similarly, 81 percent of those interviewed prior to the pandemic reported positive attitudes toward their coworkers, compared to only 57 percent of those interviewed during the pandemic. It is likely these differences reflect the greater difficulties of interacting with other workers during the pandemic given safety protocols. More of the workers interviewed during the pandemic also had less time on the job on average than those interviewed prior to the pandemic. Indeed, it is striking that about 32 percent of workers interviewed during the pandemic reported neutral or mixed attitudes toward their coworkers, compared to only 11 percent of those interviewed before the pandemic (see table 5.1).

Many workplace relationships were simply friendly acquaintances on the job. Some workers mentioned that packers sometimes fought over workstations because they wanted to work beside and talk to another worker whom they had befriended. Before the pandemic, departments and work shifts often were given the same break times, which facilitated relationship building among coworkers. Some workers had social ties to coworkers or other warehouse workers whom they related to as family members, friends, roommates, or romantic partners off the job. For example, Olivia claimed she had friends employed as packers in other warehouses and that she sometimes hung out with her "super friendly" coworkers after work. Other interviewees had members of their household or family employed in the warehouse industry, sometimes even in the same facility.

Some workplace friendships formed among coworkers around shared social backgrounds, experiences, hobbies, and interests. For example, Julio enjoyed playing golf and discussing that sport with one of his male coworkers. Although workplace friendships often formed around common social identities, such as gender, race, or age, some friendships cut across these social differences. Erica observed, "If you look at some of the friend groups that are in there, you're just like, 'Wow that's really cool!' There's different races, ethnicities, genders. People there aren't very discriminatory."

Coworkers often helped one another to learn their jobs and complete tasks. As workers often noted, the two-day training associates received was often very limited, especially if workers were trained in a large group and had to stand at the back. Ambassadors assigned to train them were also not always very helpful or attentive. As a result, warehouse workers commonly relied upon their coworkers with more experience to give them advice or show them the tricks of the trade that improved their work and helped them to work more efficiently.

Coworkers also helped each other to complete work-related tasks, such as helping to load a trailer. Paola reported that when she was first employed as a picker, "I didn't really have issues reaching [the required work rate], because I had some help from some of my girlfriends who were already working with Amazon two-months before me. They would always throw me the bigger boxes." Although some workers viewed such practices as favoritism, these practices also demonstrated the ways in which workers would help, befriend, and support each other on the job.

Workers routinely provided one another with other sorts of information that went beyond the immediate requirements of their jobs. Frustrated with the lack of information that Amazon would provide about positive COVID-19 cases and worried about exposure to the virus, workers would keep each other informed when they or their fellow workers had been diagnosed with COVID-19. Workers also helped each other navigate Amazon's HR bureaucracy or online system, including completing all of the necessary steps and electronic forms required to gain approval for leaves of absence, transfers, or schedule changes, or to contest an unfair write-up or termination. In addition, workers supported fellow workers who experienced harassment or discrimination, encouraging them to report the incident to HR staff or by reporting what they had observed. They sometimes gave rides to coworkers who needed help with transportation, offered a sympathetic ear, or gave advice to another worker going through a difficult personal situation. Despite workplace inequalities, competition, and constraints on socializing, as well as interpersonal tensions, it is striking that most workers, even during the pandemic when workplace interactions became more difficult, reported friendly relationships with coworkers.

Overall, interviewees recalled negative, positive, and neutral interactions with their coworkers and supervisors. Consequently, coworker relations sometimes reproduced and sometimes counteracted broader systemic inequalities and competitive workplace and production pressures related to capitalism. Along with Amazon's corporate employees, warehouse workers have made numerous complaints about discrimination and harassment, with Amazon's HR department, through legal channels, and in the press. Their efforts have helped bring public attention to problems related to sexism, sexual harassment, racism, heterosexism, transphobia, and ageism at Amazon, as well as to the failures of its understaffed HR department. Such complaints reflect problems arising from systemic inequality not only within Amazon but also in the larger society. These complaints have put both legal and public pressure on Amazon to improve its corporate employment and workplace policies. For example, in 2021 Amazon corporate employees produced a twelve-page internal memo documenting their experiences of race- and/or gender-based discrimination and called on Amazon to make inclusion its fifteenth leadership principle, but they have not yet succeeded.[37] Through his lawsuit, Johnnie Corina from Riverside also called upon Amazon to improve its diversity and sensitivity training and its enforcement of its antidiscrimination and antiharassment policies.

Despite the negative experiences reported, most Amazon warehouse workers interviewed described friendly and supportive relationships with their fellow workers. Such positive relationships and feelings of solidarity among coworkers are an important resource that can facilitate collective action by Amazon warehouse workers, a topic that we explore in chapters 7 and 8. Before turning to public resistance to Amazon in Southern California and beyond, we first examine, in chapter 6, another common source of grievances among warehouse workers besides unfair and discriminatory treatment: the lack of workplace health and safety measures.

6 Boxed and Bruised

WAREHOUSE WORKERS'
INJURIES AND ILLNESSES

"'Nothing is more important than the health and well-being of our employees,'" Bezos told his shareholders in May 2020.[1] Yet Amazon warehouse workers report working long hours, sometimes in deafening spaces, with few breaks from their typically physically grueling, repetitive, and often socially isolating tasks. Together with Amazon's signature employee surveillance systems, designed to ensure workers move quickly while making minimal errors, these conditions take an enormous toll on workers' physical and mental health.

Destiny's experience working at Amazon illustrates some of these health hazards. Destiny worked in an Amazon warehouse in San Bernardino for more than three years between 2014 and 2017 and was age 35 when we spoke. She had applied for the job when she was in the midst of a divorce and needed the income to support her three children. A single mother and domestic violence survivor, Destiny supported two boys (ages 9 and 12) and a 6-year old daughter. At the time of her interview, Destiny was finishing up her associate's degree at a community college and was trained as a pharmacy and EKG technician. She planned to continue her education after graduation so that she could obtain a job in a nonprofit organization or in higher education.

Destiny first worked as a picker and a packer for Amazon, then later helped to train and supervise new employees during the peak season. Previously employed in customer service and as a receptionist, her Amazon job was her first and last job in the warehouse industry. She worked full-time on the night shift, which paid $12.25 per hour, a higher wage than the day shift. Still, her family income was stretched thin, and it was difficult to afford even subsidized childcare for her three children. The working conditions were also very difficult. Describing the job, Destiny said,

> It was stressful. You're not only standing but also doing a lot of physically demanding things. Stressful too because of the rate. So, like even if you go to the restroom really quick, your rate is dropping already. It's a lot. . . . I felt like I was working in a slave factory. But I would always tell myself you're doing this for your kids. And the main benefit [when] I was there: that if you were working for Amazon for a year, they would help pay for your schooling and your education.

Destiny worked four days per week and often worked about twelve hours per shift. She found the work exhausting and struggled to work full-time on the night shift, handle her divorce proceedings, and take care of her children. Destiny and her children often slept in the car in the school parking lot from when she picked them up from day care at 5:30 a.m. until school started at 8:00 a.m. Although she tried to sleep during the day afterward, her neighbors often played music loudly. Severely sleep deprived, Destiny often spent most of her lunch break sleeping rather than eating.

Destiny was injured twice at Amazon. Several other coworkers were "really good friends because we all got injured together. One had a back injury, an ankle injury, and me with my shoulder injury. These all happened at Amazon." Describing the poor treatment that she and her friends experienced while working "light duties" as injured warehouse workers, she said:

> Workers that were not injured thought that those who were injured were receiving "better treatment." And us that were injured felt like we were unworthy or just a bother because we were seen as not being able to do much. I'd have supervisors looking at me and roll their eyes and say, "let me see where to put you."

Destiny's first workplace injury was a permanent injury to her shoulder, which occurred while she was lifting a heavy item:

> I injured myself working in the packing station and at the packing station you have totes. Each tote cannot be more than 35 pounds as far as what the pickers are allowed to put in the tote and what the packers will pack in the boxes. My tote had a battery conserver pack. . . . They're pretty big, probably around 30 to 40 pounds and my tote had three of them. So, I was expecting my tote to be within the range that it was supposed to be in, so when I went to pull the tote off the way they teach us, I pulled, and my shoulder immediately popped off.

Amazon's medical staff at the warehouse could not identify the shoulder injury with their X-rays, so she continued to work. She was given "light duties," such as "sweeping the warehouse, putting stickers on boxes and working in the gift-wrapping department." Although it was lighter than her previous work assignments, the work was very difficult and painful for her because of her injury. Destiny's second injury occurred when she was walking. There were papers on the ground and she slipped on them and fell, injuring her back. "When I injured myself, I will never forget it. My supervisor had like fifty of us all huddled up in our meeting. He says, 'We had fifteen days of no accidents, but now we're back to zero. Because somebody decided to slip and fall on a piece of paper.'" It took a year for doctors affiliated with Kaiser's workers' compensation program to identify Destiny's initial shoulder injury with an MRI. The doctor at Kaiser recommended that she not "lift, push, or pull more than 10 pounds." Afterward, Amazon gave her a stipend to pay for her community college classes and a one-time payment. As she explains, "I signed a release form stating that they paid me for my injury and therefore I would no longer be able to work for any Amazon positions."

When Destiny was interviewed in 2019, she had been unemployed for two years because of her injury, which the doctor said was permanent. Along with her stipend from Amazon, she initially received workers' compensation and later received public assistance while attending school and taking care of her three children.

Destiny's experience is part of a repeated pattern, according to a series of investigations by OSHA of how Amazon's on-site medical staff handled workers' injuries in warehouses. They failed to report injuries to OSHA, discouraged workers from obtaining external medical care, and encouraged injured workers to return to work.[2] Even though problems of underreporting workplace injuries plague OSHA statistics, they still show that the warehouse industry is among the most dangerous industries in the United States in terms of the rates of workplace injuries, including the rates of *serious* injury. They also reveal that the injury rates and rates of serious injuries are significantly higher among Amazon warehouse workers compared to the warehouse industry as a whole.[3] In part, this is because Amazon prides itself on the *speed* of its customer deliveries, which has been key to its growing consumer popularity. Amazon initially offered two-day deliveries to its Prime customers in 2005, then same-day deliveries beginning in 2019. The pressure for Amazon employees to work fast to meet those rapid delivery times has compromised worker safety.[4]

This chapter explores the physical and mental health impacts of working as an Amazon warehouse worker before and during the COVID-19 pandemic. Overall, our findings suggest that Amazon warehouse workers' health concerns are broadly held, multiple in type, and serious in nature. As table 6.1 shows, overall, about 93 percent of those interviewed for this book claimed that they had experienced pain or exhaustion at the end of their work shifts, while about 66 percent of those interviewed did not look forward to coming to work the next day. Overall, about 51 percent of those interviewed expressed concerns with how the job was affecting their physical or mental health, about 51 percent agreed that the job was stressful, nearly half or 48 percent agreed that it was dangerous, and 30 percent of workers expressed concerns about their own physical safety on the job. As one might expect, a greater proportion of Amazon workers interviewed during the pandemic than before it reported that the job was stressful and dangerous, expressed concerns about their own safety, and worried about the impacts of the job on their mental or physical health.

We begin this chapter by exploring workers' health concerns related to physical pain, exhaustion, and workplace injuries. We then discuss interviewees' experiences with mental stress, loneliness, and other negative mental health impacts of their work prior to the pandemic. Many worried about not being able to keep up with Amazon's high productivity quotas; they feared that if they did not make rate, made too many errors, or spent

Table 6.1 Interviewees' Health Concerns

Concern	Prepandemic Sample			Pandemic Sample			Both Samples		
	Frequency	Valid Responses	%	Frequency	Valid Responses	%	Frequency	Valid Responses	%
Has pain/fatigue	40	43	93.02	28	30	93.33	68	73	93.15
Don't look forward to work	28	43	65.12	20	30	66.67	48	73	65.75
Work stress	17	43	39.53	21	31	67.74	38	74	51.35
Job is difficult	13	39	33.33	17	30	56.67	30	69	43.48
Has health concern	16	41	39.02	20	30	66.67	36	71	50.70
Job is dangerous	16	38	42.11	16	29	55.17	32	67	47.76
Has safety concern	8	40	20.00	13	30	43.33	21	70	30.00

too much TOT, they would be disciplined and fired.[5] Next we examine the health risks and stresses related to working during the COVID-19 pandemic in Amazon warehouses, including fears of exposure to this deadly virus. As table 6.1 shows, nearly 67 percent of those employed during the pandemic reported concerns about the impacts of their job on their mental or physical health; specifically, 68 percent described the job as stressful, and 55 percent considered the job to be physically dangerous.

PAIN AND EXHAUSTION

Fully 93 percent of interviewees reported pain and fatigue at the end of their work shifts. Daniel, who mostly worked as a picker and packer, said, "They ask too much [of] you. The job was very exhausting. Everyday I would come home with a new blister." Describing the pain at the end of her work shift, Brianna responded,

> Oh yeah! Your back! Your knees! My feet are always hurting. . . . I think everybody is in pain. . . . I know they give you . . . bio cream and such but the mats we are standing on all day are not cushioned at all so I feel like we're standing on a cement floor all day. This is why my feet always hurt, no matter what kind of shoes you have. It's unbearable.

Likewise, Viviana, who worked in induct, said her body hurt "from just standing in one spot" for hours. Packers described similar pain and exhaustion associated with standing in place at their automated packing stations for ten or more hours while their hands and arms ached from their highly repetitive hand and arm motions.

Many of Amazon's warehouses are voluminous, about the size of "four big-box stores" according to Jimmy. As a result, many workers, especially pickers in warehouses that were not fully automated, spent most of their day walking long distances. Jimmy estimated that he "typically walked four to seven miles within [his] four-hour shift." Ana, who worked full-time (at least ten hours per day) as a picker, said,

> You're walking 16 miles a day, like dead ass 16 miles a day! . . . A lot of people lose weight. . . . Pick was very hard on your body. I would come

home. My back would hurt, my thighs. . . . You're like squatting when you're getting to these items. You're squatting to the lowest line, getting back up, walking real fast.

Kelly, another full-time worker, recalled, "When I worked there as a picker, I lost 20 pounds from walking so much." Both young and middle-aged workers alike complained about foot pain after their shifts. Twenty-one-year-old Jorge described his physical exhaustion from work in this way: "Every day I would come home, and I could barely walk. That was the very first time I ever had to ice my feet." Similarly, Julio confessed that sometimes "my feet actually feel like they have cement in the inside of them."

Clara, who worked for Amazon for four years and was promoted as a process assistant, provided a rich description of the stress and physical exhaustion involved in getting customer orders sent out on time:

> When you're missing an item, you have to go all the way. . . . You had to go literally physically to that item, grab it, and run . . . like power walk to get to where you're at to finish the box. Let's say, for example that I had, it's called CPT [critical push time]. . . . All orders have to get out, like ALL of them . . . like 10,000 orders have to go out. But the last 10 minutes, something goes wrong with the order and someone didn't pack it right. And so it gets shipped out and then it gets to the problem solver. So then . . . someone grabs it and you're like, "Oh my God, we're missing an item!" So we only have 10 minutes to hurry up and fix this order before it's a loss. Because, if we don't ship it out by two o'clock, the customer doesn't get it on time. . . . So we run to the pick mod and the pick mods are huge. And you have to find the location. First you have to search it on the computer. "Oh, here it is. Okay, I'm going to go and see." And then you come back and then you put it in, pack it, and then you put it on the conveyor belt. All within 10 minutes. So you are exhausted.

After completing her work shift, Isabel said, "I would just want to go to sleep and never wake up."

Exhaustion was worsened during peak times when workers were employed overtime. According to Camila,

> Twelve hours for five days a week, that tires out anybody's body, anybody, mentally and physically. You're on your feet for 10 to 12 hours straight. You're

lifting boxes, you're lifting items. You're constantly moving. You're constantly running around. You're moving boxes, you're stacking boxes,
you're . . . pushing totes. It's tiring. And mentally it can be draining, because
they expect so much out of you. . . . They move you from one position to the
next. . . . And at times it can be more stressful on some than others, because
they. . . . They're hard workers, so they take advantage of you.

Olivia's worst days were when she was assigned to work as a water spider, "because it consists of me walking all day for 10 hours." Water spiders
in Amazon warehouses are responsible for making sure workstations are
fully stocked.[6] Describing how the "heavy workload and long hours take
a toll," Veronica described "sore arms and aching feet." Even part-time
workers complained of aches and pains in their backs, hands, or feet by
the end of their five-hour work shifts.

Working long shifts in a warehouse is especially exhausting. As Camila
put it, "You're tired when you wake up. You're tired when you go in, and
you're obviously tired when you come out." Workers' exhaustion was often
worsened by long commutes to and from work. For example, Luis spent
about two to three hours per day commuting to and from work on top of
working full-time with ten- or eleven-hour night shifts as a PA. Although
he asked for a transfer to a warehouse closer to his home, the request
was not granted, so he was considering moving closer to his workplace
at the time of his interview. Although Esther only worked for five hours
per day, she also had to commute for two to three hours per day because
she worked in Riverside but lived in Hemet, where the cost of housing is
more affordable but jobs are scarce. Because heavy traffic is common in
the region, workers often arrive at work early to avoid being penalized
for arriving late. If workers arrive late too many times, they may be fired.
For example, Veronica arrived at 7:00 a.m. and slept or hung out in her
car for thirty minutes until her shift started at 7:30 a.m. Her work shift
usually ended around 6:00 p.m., and it took her another forty minutes to
commute home. She had just enough time to "eat, shower, clean" before
going to sleep at 9:00 p.m. so that she could wake up to start her day
again at 5:30 a.m. As Alejandra observed, some workers also had chronic
illnesses, "and they are still working their butt off over there."

Physical exhaustion and bodily stress can also be worsened by heat.
Although some workers were impressed with the temperature control

inside Amazon facilities compared to other warehouses where they had worked, workers employed in tasks outdoors or near warehouse entrances reported being exposed to too much heat in the summer and fall. Such concerns were especially common among workers assigned to loading or unloading truck trailers, especially when temperatures climbed above 100 or even above 110 degrees F. As Tomas put it, "Yeah, the trailers [are] maybe half an inch thick of metal, so I mean it's gonna be hot in there!" Some workers reported that it becomes hard to breathe when the trailers are hot.

Working in the heat can be dangerous and even fatal. Working in temperatures of 90 degrees or more increases the risk of heat exhaustion and other heat-related illnesses and dehydration. It also increases the risk of other types of workplace accidents among both outdoor and indoor workers, according to a study by researchers at UCLA and Stanford.[7]

Problems related to heat exposure inside warehouses are long-standing in Inland Southern California. For example, a survey of 101 warehouse workers, mostly temporary workers, in Inland Southern California in 2011 found that many complained about working in the heat, many had little or no access to water, and only 63 out of the 361 warehouses in the region had air conditioning.[8] In 2016, after a warehouse worker in an Inland Southern California warehouse was hospitalized for heat exhaustion, warehouse workers and their advocates successfully pushed for the passage of new statewide indoor heat regulations. The new regulations were not expected to go into effect until 2029, however.[9] As of 2021 they were still under review, despite new legal complaints against heat-related illness by warehouse workers.[10]

Along with other warehouse employers, Amazon has come under fire around the nation for its lack of good air conditioning. In 2011, for example, Amazon workers in Breinigsville, Pennsylvania, complained about excessive heat inside the warehouse, which had been built the year before. There the heat index, which measures both heat and humidity, sometimes climbed over 100 degrees on multiple days, and even as high as 110 degrees. Amazon arranged for ambulances to be parked outside the warehouse to help workers suffering from heat stress. Workers' complaints became public through an investigative report and when workers and an emergency room physician filed formal complaints with OSHA. Public complaints and protests about bad working conditions outside Amazon's headquarters in Seattle ensued, as did stories of problems with the temporary air conditioning units it had installed at its Breinigsville facility after it was investigated by OSHA. In response, Amazon built air-conditioned warehouses and invested $52 million in 2012 to install or improve its air conditioning at its older facilities, including the one in Breinigsville.[11] Still, workers have reported that the quality of Amazon's climate control varies across facilities and depends on their job assignments and workstations. Amazon workers' complaints about excessive heat and heat stress have continued to surface across US cities during hot seasons and heat waves nearly a decade later, sometimes becoming focal points for collective actions, news reports, and public testimonies.[12]

INJURIES AND WORKPLACE HAZARDS

Working in warehouses and logistics is physically dangerous. According to the US Bureau of Labor Statistics (BLS), among all industries, the transportation and warehousing industry had the second highest rate of "recordable cases" of nonfatal occupational injuries and illnesses in 2019 (4.4 per 100 full-time workers). Meanwhile, among occupations, the most common warehouse occupation (hand laborers and freight, stock, and material movers) had the third highest rate of nonfatal occupational injuries and illnesses (275.5 per 10,000 full-time workers), while another common warehouse occupation, stockers and order fillers, had the seventh highest rate (176.3 per 10,000 full-time workers).[13] These work injury statistics are based on employer records, which businesses are required by law to submit to OSHA. "Recordable" injuries are those that require medical attention beyond first aid, workers to change jobs or work tasks, or workers to take time off from work to recover.[14] Actual injury rates are likely to be even higher than these official OSHA statistics, however, because they exclude unreported cases. Employers have incentives to underreport injuries because doing so reduces their workers' compensation costs and helps to prevent OSHA inspections. Meanwhile, many workers fail to report injuries, often because they fear losing work or being judged as incompetent or incapable. In some Amazon warehouses, work teams are given pizza parties

if they worked "injury free" for certain periods of time. While such practices might reward workers for working safely, they can also have the un-
intended consequence of pressuring workers to not report their injuries.[15]

Amazon warehouses are especially dangerous. In 2018, 2019, and 2022
Amazon was listed by the National Council of Occupational Safety and
Health (National COSH) among its "dirty dozen" list of US employers that
have been identified as exposing workers to severe and preventable health
and safety risks. Between 2013 and 2018, seven warehouse workers died.
Five of these deaths involved workers being hit or crushed by machinery,
including a truck, a pallet loader, several forklifts, and a conveyor belt.[16]
National COSH listed Amazon again on its "dirty dozen" list in 2019 when
six contract employees died that year, including two killed when a warehouse wall collapsed during a tornado in Baltimore, Maryland. National
COSH also cited news stories of warehouse workers urinating in bottles
and becoming suicidal because of stressful working conditions.[17] In 2020
Amazon was given a "dishonorable mention" by National COSH because
of six deaths from accidents involving delivery drivers, hundreds of warehouse worker injuries, COVID-19 infections in at least seventy-four warehouse and delivery facilities, and at least one COVID-19-related death,
and for firing employee activists who organized for health and safety
improvements.[18] In 2022 Amazon was listed on National COSH's "dirty
dozen" list a third time for multiple reasons: six workers at its Bessemer,
Alabama, facility had died since its opening in 2020 (including two in
2021); the rate of reported workplace injuries among US Amazon warehouse workers was more than double the national rate observed among
other warehouse workers; it was cited four times by the state of Washington for workplace health and safety problems that it failed to adequately
respond to; and it had failed to reinstate Gerald Bryson, a warehouse employee it fired shortly after he lead a protest in Staten Island, New York
(through which participants demanded that Amazon better protect its
workers against COVID-19 exposure).[19]

Severe injuries, heat illnesses, and other types of health and safety complaints filed by Amazon warehouse workers have resulted in a mounting
list of state and federal OSHA investigations over the years and prompted
lawsuits and investigations by attorneys general in multiple states, including California, New York, and Washington. Some of these OSHA

investigations were sparked by tragic reports of work-related deaths. For example, in 2021 six Amazon workers died when a tornado hit a warehouse and it collapsed in Edwardsville, Illinois, leading OSHA to investigate and to recommend that Amazon improve its safety training and workplace protections related to extreme weather incidents.[20] Amazon faced yet another OSHA investigation in 2022 after a warehouse worker died in Cateret, New Jersey, during Prime Day.[21]

Multiple analyses of official OSHA injury data conclude that working in Amazon warehouses is hazardous. OSHA considers occupational injuries to be "serious" if they require workers to spend days off of work to recover or to be reassigned to restricted duties or given job transfers. Will Evans's investigative report, based on an analysis of work-related injury records submitted by twenty-three Amazon FCs to OSHA in 2018, found that overall they had a disproportionately high rate of *serious* occupational injury (9.6 per 100 full-time workers)—about double the rate for the national warehouse industry. While injury rates varied across these FCs, the rate of serious occupational injury at Amazon's Eastvale warehouse, located in Riverside County, was nearly *four* times the average national warehouse industry rate.[22] Evans's subsequent analysis of Amazon's injury records covering 150 Amazon warehouses showed that in 2019 there were 14,000 serious injuries in Amazon FCs (7.7 per 100 full-time workers), which was 33 percent higher than the rate calculated for 2016. Evans reports that despite Amazon's other efforts to increase workplace safety, it failed to reduce its work rate quotas, and even increased them in its newer, more automated warehouses.[23] The Athena Coalition, which includes more than fifty grassroots organizations opposed to Amazon, found that nearly 89 percent of Amazon's injured workers had "serious" injures that caused them to either miss work (5.5 weeks, on average) or be given restricted duties due to their injuries.[24] The most common injuries reported were "sprains, strains, and tears" that involved "workers' backs, shoulders, wrists, knees, ankles, and elbows."[25]

Subsequent reports by the Strategic Organizing Center (SOC), a coalition of labor unions, have examined OSHA data on hundreds of Amazon facilities across the nation.[26] In 2021 the SOC found that between 2017 and 2020, "Amazon's rate of injuries per 100 warehouse workers [was] substantially higher than . . . for non-Amazon employers in the general warehouse industry."[27] They documented that Amazon's injury rate decreased (from 9 to 6.5 per 100 workers) between 2019 and 2020, attributable to the corporation's decision to temporarily suspend the use of their productivity standards between March and October 2020 to discipline workers (a policy adopted in response to public and legal pressure to allow workers more time to follow COVID-19 safety protocols). These researchers also conducted an online national survey of Amazon warehouse workers and delivery drivers regarding workplace health and safety in 2021. A total of 996 Amazon employees from forty-two US states, more than three-quarters of whom were blue-collar warehouse workers, responded.[28] About 42 percent reported experiencing workplace pain or injury that required them to miss work, suggesting that OSHA injury rates, which reflect employer reports, may be underestimating the extent of injuries among Amazon warehouse workers. Among these injured workers, 37 percent reported that Amazon pressured them to return to work before they were ready to do so, and 74 percent experienced pain and additional injury after returning to work.[29]

The SOC's 2022 report indicates that the overall injury rate for Amazon increased by 20 percent between 2020 and 2021, providing further evidence of the corporation's highly dangerous workplace operations.[30] The serious injury rate at Amazon warehouses in 2021 was 6.8 per 100 workers, more than twice the rate in other, non-Amazon warehouses (3.3 per 100 workers). As a result, while Amazon employed 33 percent of all US warehouse workers in 2021, the corporation was responsible for 49 percent of all injuries industry-wide during that year. Amazon warehouse workers who are seriously injured on the job also take longer to recover than their non-Amazon peers do: 62.2 days at Amazon versus 43.5 days at other warehouses.[31] Moreover, the rate of serious injuries is markedly higher at robotic warehouses than at nonrobotic ones. "In 2021, Amazon's sortable facilities with robotic technology had a serious injury rate of 7.3 per 100 workers, 28 percent higher than the rate at non-robotic sortable facilities (5.7 per 100)."[32]

Other analyses similarly conclude that OSHA injury rates among Amazon warehouse workers are higher at more-automated than at less-automated facilities, contrary to Amazon executives' claims that robots help to make warehouse work safer.[33] In more-automated facilities, workers are given even higher work rate quotas than in nonautomated facilities. For example, pickers' scan rates climbed from 100 to 400 items per hour after robots were introduced into some of Amazon's more automated warehouses. As a result, workers at more automated facilities are under tremendous pressure to work at very rapid paces to keep up with robotic machinery and are often required to stand in one place for longer, which is also stressful on the body.[34] Amazon's injury rates also consistently spike in the weeks surrounding Prime Day and Cyber Monday, when consumer demands increase dramatically. During those peak periods, many warehouse employees are under pressure to work more quickly than usual and are exhausted from heavy workloads and working overtime, and there is often an influx of less-experienced temporary workers.[35]

Amazon executives have claimed that their injury rates are higher than the warehouse industry as a whole because they are more diligent in reporting workers' injuries than other employers are. Yet research suggests otherwise. Indeed, a series of OSHA investigations in New Jersey found that Amazon's on-site medical clinics, which examine and treat injured or ill workers, discouraged workers from reporting injuries, from taking time off from work to recover, and from seeking outside medical care and diagnoses when doing so was warranted. Moreover, former medical staff employed by health clinics contracted by Amazon to examine and treat injured workers reported pressure to not recommend remedies that might make workers' injuries "recordable" by OSHA standards.[36] Surveys of Amazon warehouse workers also reveal that at least some do not report their injuries to their employers out of fear of losing work or being judged negatively by managers or supervisors, a finding corroborated by various workers interviewed for this book.[37]

Warehouse labor is dangerous in part because it tends to be physically strenuous, involving heavy lifting, walking long distances, stretching to reach for items, heavy and repetitive lifting, and operating forklifts and working with machines that are sometimes faulty or poorly maintained. Constant electronic monitoring of workers and the pressure to work quickly in order to make rate in Amazon warehouses increases workplace dangers. As Jessica put it, it was "easy to get hurt over rushing to make volume." In her view, Amazon set "unrealistic productivity goals" that endangered workers. Similarly, Jimmy commented, "They had a concern for safety, but were more concerned with speed first."

Results from regional and national surveys suggest that Amazon warehouse workers commonly view their work rate requirements as endangering them. First, 75 percent of the twenty-six Inland Southern California Amazon warehouse workers and delivery drivers surveyed by researchers claimed that Amazon's required work rates were "always" or "often" too high to work safely. Another 75 percent of these workers claimed that they had experienced pain or injured themselves trying to make rate.[38] Second, Amazon's internal safety reports reveal that, when asked, workers often reported that their productivity quotas are too high for them to implement the required safety procedures; if they do so, they often cannot make rate.[39] Finally, a national online survey found that 80 percent of Amazon warehouse workers and delivery drivers who reported having to miss work because of workplace-related pain or injury agreed that their pain or injury was due to the pressure to work fast or other production pressures.[40]

Amazon's initial training for warehouse associates only lasted a few days, which many warehouse workers found inadequate for really learning how to do the job properly. According to Alejandra, employed by Amazon for more than two and a half years before the pandemic, warehouse employees were usually trained in groups of twenty to thirty employees at a time, and sometimes as many as forty at a time, making it difficult for them to hear and see the trainers' presentation. As Viviana explained, "It's dangerous if you don't know what you're doing." When Viviana started her job, she injured herself with a cart: "I think I put the wrong brakes on. . . . I hit like the back of my foot and it hurt really bad. . . . I am not even sure if I was told . . . how to pull the cart." She didn't report her injury because she was new and didn't want her mistake known by managers. Her lower leg and foot were badly bruised and hurt for several weeks. Other interviewees observed workers being injured when they were newly employed or given new work assignments. Brianna, employed as a forklift driver, recalled, "Some lady snapped her leg in 2019 for learning how to drive a forklift. She panicked then she jumped off the forklift while it was moving and it caught her leg . . . and snapped her leg." Many workers reported that inadequate job training contributed to workplace stress and danger.

Interviewees provided rich examples of the hazards of working inside Amazon warehouses. For example, Ana said:

> Any day you don't know what to expect and you could like hurt yourself too. I hurt myself a lot. . . . These aisles are really tall, so like things just fall on you . . . or like sometimes you'd slip. . . . Some things would be really heavy and it would be on a high shelf and then sometimes that would fall. I remember like I almost dropped like a big pot on some dude's head. He was picking right next to me and it just fell. His head was like this far away and I was just like, "I'm so sorry" and he was like "What the fuck?!"

She also noted that when she worked with a conveyor belt, "Sometimes my scanner would get stuck in there [the conveyor belt] and then like drag me." Under pressure to work quickly and make rate, workers would sometimes drop items or leave boxes on the floor, creating hazards for other workers moving about the warehouse. As Diana put it, "People would throw floppies, which were little baggies, everywhere. There was a mess on the floor and people would trip on boxes." Similarly, Alejandra claimed, "Safety wouldn't do their job. . . . [I]f they would see a spill, I would sometimes keep track of it, and they would leave it for like 30 minutes. . . . In those 30 minutes, anything can happen." Some workers, like Alejandra, took the initiative to clean up spills or trash on the floor to prevent workers from falling, but they sometimes received warnings for spending too much TOT. Recalling other workplace hazards, Alejandra reported:

> Sometimes, the people in the processing area would forget to label the things like hazardous or something that contained nuts in it. It would open and the product would open. We'd have someone in the line just bloating up with like . . . hives or rashes . . . or chemicals. A lot of employees are actually allergic to chemicals.

Commenting on the water spider job, Alejandra recalled that "everybody's always getting injured, either their index finger or their thumb finger." Esther claimed that moving heavy items, like "machinery and boxes," was the most dangerous aspect of warehouse work.

According to Robin, "everyone there had some injuries, like back or knee injuries." Several workers reported injuries so severe that they had to stop working. Destiny, featured at the start of this chapter, became permanently disabled by her shoulder injury, while Brenda was on medical leave at the time of her interview because she hurt her back "picking up a heavy tote." Other workers, who were still employed by Amazon at the time of their interviews, reported severe back pain or strained muscles from picking, loading, unloading, or problem solving. Juan, for example, said that "every day after work I feel drained. Usually my shoulder is sore and my back hurts," while Maria strained her muscles while reaching for items placed in "really high bins."

Workers also expressed concerns about dangerous machinery, most commonly conveyor belts. Elvia claimed they moved too quickly, making accidents likely to occur, while Ana described a serious workplace accident involving a conveyor belt. Brianna reported, "Those things are not that sturdy. . . . The rollers fall out of the conveyor belt and I seen them fall on people. Sometimes the conveyors are tipping. I've seen people get their hands caught and I've seen their hair caught in the roller." Esther claimed that the conveyor belts were "too big for one person to reach across," which caused muscle strain. Similarly, Jimmy recalled, "It took me years to recover from all the strain I had to pull. I would pull out my back leaning over the conveyors."

Workers also observed that machinery was not always well maintained, which added to workplace dangers. Julio believed that Amazon took safety more seriously than his previous warehouse employers had done, but still described Amazon warehouses as dangerous: "There's machinery, there's racks, there's tools, there's all kinds of stuff. . . . Anything could go wrong on a daily basis, any hour, any minute." Similarly, Brianna observed, "Every other day, every other hour, something goes wrong. . . . [T]he forklifts are very faulty." She longed for "safe equipment," because "every other machine sometimes breaks down on you. . . . They are a billion dollar company and they're little shitty machines."

Workers described the din of Amazon warehouses, including noisy forklifts, robotic machinery, automated packing machines, and conveyor belts, as well as honking horns from forklift drivers, scanners beeping when workers made mistakes, and loud alarms that sounded when conveyor belts stopped working. Supervisors or safety sabers sometimes screamed instructions in order to be heard by workers. The noise level increased during busy peak seasons. Samuel noted how difficult and stressful it was to work when forklift drivers were "honking their horns all the time." Various workers reported that the lights and sounds of the workplace remained in their heads after work, especially when they tried to go to sleep. Several interviewees experienced permanent hearing loss due to working near noisy machines for long periods of time. Earplugs that they were required to wear during work hours were often under-stocked and unavailable.

Poor responses to workplace emergencies reinforced workers' safety concerns and distrust of Amazon. For example, Robin recalled:

> Someone on the night shift said there was a fire, because when I came into work you could catch the smell. They made people work while the fire was going on, and the alarms were going off. When people were finally evacu-ated, no one knew the evacuation process. . . . It was like 100 workers unac-counted for. There were some that didn't come until the next morning, and then a few managers didn't show up until the next morning. They don't have any fire alarms that you can pull. It's all at the high-end security desk. . . . just so people don't do any pranks. I was bitter about that because they dis-regarded employee safety.

Another alarming incident was a gas leak that occurred in Amazon's East-vale warehouse on New Year's Day in 2019. Managers encouraged Amazon associates to continue working and moved them to other parts of the build-ing while they tried to fix the gas leak, rather than evacuating the building. Workers became dizzy, had headaches, and felt burning sensations in their chests and noses. Some workers vomited in trash cans, and one worker felt so faint that she had to leave the building in a wheelchair. Yet managers informed workers that if they wanted to leave the building, they would have to use their unpaid time off. Only later, after a worker had called 911 about the incident and in response to worker complaints, did Amazon officials agree to not count that time against workers' unpaid time off.[41]

Many interviewees confessed that they had quit their jobs or did not intend to stay long in their jobs, at least in part, because of the negative impacts on their physical or mental health. As Jimmy put it, "It is not something I could do forever because it would kill me physically." Simi-larly, Jorge quit his Amazon job because he was "terrified" about how it was affecting his physical health. As he explained, "I was 20 years old and

I had back problems, like that shouldn't happen." Other workers quit in response to workplace-related stress or depression.

MENTAL STRESS AND FRUSTRATION

The pressure to make rate was perhaps the most common source of stress reported among interviewees. Robin confessed, "I was always scared every day, because I wasn't making rate." Similarly, Jessica said she experienced "mental stress from rushing for 10 hours." Workers failing to make rate were verbally reprimanded or even "yelled at" by supervisors and faced possible termination.

According to Maria, who worked in multiple positions, Amazon keeps raising the productivity standards:

> Through the years, like they've raised our rate a lot. They've dropped the number in our errors. So if we were able to get, let's say five errors we're down and getting two errors before we get like written up for it today.... Yeah, close to perfect. Yeah. And then the same thing for "time off tasks" during the whole day. We used to get like two hours, then one hour, and now we're down to 30 minutes. And anyone over 30 minutes would get a write-up. So I just feel like they've been cutting it, like, down as much as they can and it just continues to get cut.

In addition, Maria found it difficult to make rate consistently when she was rotated across jobs:

> Right now the stress is going from one department to another department because they're short staffed. So my biggest fear is not hitting rate or getting errors. And that's only because if you work, let's say I'm working four days a week or three days a week with my department and they send me for a half day to the pick department. If I get an error there, I'm not able to really make up for that error. So I would end up getting a write-up for that.

Similarly, Samuel recalled:

> I would get transferred to picking, even though it wasn't my position. They cross-trained me in that position and they would get on me for not making picking rate. But when I'm not working there for like weeks at a time, it's

kind of unrealistic to expect me to make rate in a different area that's not mine.

Amazon rotates workers across departments and positions, a practice that helps to cross-train workers so they can fill staffing shortages as needed, and to reduce repetitive motion injuries.[42] Yet the rotation of workers across positions was stressful because workers had to learn new tasks, often with insufficient training, and faced different types of productivity standards and workplace dangers. As Estella recalled, "When switched to docks, [I was] always anxious to go in, afraid of messing up, of getting hurt, not doing a good job. It brought a lot of stress. . . . I felt like I could hurt my back. . . . [D]ocks had me stressed all the time." Elvia, who worked in receiving, also viewed insufficient training as a stressor: "They expect you to get everything at once and then they pretty much throw you out there." Jasmine, employed at Amazon for three and a half years, recalled that the stress of learning new positions caused her nightmares.

Other workers described frustrations related to insufficient staffing and unrealistic goals. For example, Felipe, a young college student who worked the night shift at an Amazon sortation warehouse, recalled:

> What did I hate the most? How they set you up to fail. They set us up to fail all the time. . . . They give us like . . . I think it was like 120 thousand packages and we need like 60 people to do it and they would give us like 30, maybe less.

Many workers also viewed the high work rates and low error rates as unrealistic, resulting in unfair firings. In addition to anxiety, some workers experienced anger and frustration as they tried to achieve goals that seemed almost impossible, especially when faced with unexpected obstacles. As Fernando explained,

> Let's say you're looking for a certain type of shirt if you find the bin that it's in but they are all the same type of shirt but you're looking for a specific barcode. If you're on a time constraint and they're all like medium sized like ironman shirts you're seeing the same shirt but it's not the same barcode that you need. . . . and you have 45 seconds to pick that item. . . . It gets very frustrating, so I would find myself punching the bins, punching the items.

Other workers mentioned the frustration they experienced when machines, such as conveyor belts or tape dispensers, malfunctioned and they were nonetheless still expected to somehow make rate. Workers were sometimes able to explain these problems to their supervisors, who took the negative points or "write-ups" off their work records, but not always. Interviewees described other unreasonable pressures to get deliveries out in time despite a rapid spike in customer demands, insufficient staffing, mechanical problems, or other unexpected backups in the flow of work.

Clara, who worked for Amazon for four years, described the pressures she faced as a PA:

> Because as a supervisor you are under a lot of stress to the point where the managers above you expect you to run your department hitting certain numbers because sometimes it's impossible because a lot of things that go on in one day. So I was constantly having to stress. . . . It was like, "oh my God, if I don't get this done, I'm going to get fired." I had that pressure. . . . My quality of life wasn't good.

For Clara, like many other workers, the everyday work pressures were compounded by long work hours and working overtime, which is very common among supervisors.

ALIENATION, BOREDOM, SOCIAL ISOLATION, AND DEPRESSION

Workers also complained about boredom, alienation, and social isolation at work. As Jose described, "All we do is fold boxes and package all items. All the tasks and the jobs are pretty much dumbed down to where everybody is kind of a cog in this larger system. We don't have any kind of outward stimulation." Similarly, Brenda described her job in induct or as a rebinner as isolating and dull: "You're just there scanning one item at a time for 10 hours. And you're just there by yourself and it's boring."

Angel observed that many Amazon associates seemed depressed, which he attributed to the everyday stress, unfair disciplining, and boredom accompanying the job:

You would walk around the warehouse and see everyone be kind of de-pressed. You would see people just sitting down throughout the warehouse because they didn't want to do their job anymore. It's really simple but it can get really stressful at times because you'd get yelled at for something that's not your fault, like . . . waiting in line at the problem solver because you ac-tually have a question. Or like doing the same thing over and over again everyday, people really get bored of that.

In addition to being repetitive, warehouse labor can often be very iso-lating. For example, Ana, who worked full-time as a picker, remarked: "Honestly, you can just be there and legit cry and like no one would notice or you could just hate your life and no one would notice, like it was just so big and lonely sometimes. It was just like the most isolating feeling like every single day." Adriana also found the long hours of social isolation as a picker very difficult:

In pick you are just at the station by yourself. Sometimes there's someone on the other side but it's so far that what conversation can you really hold with someone? And it's loud, like there's still conveyor belts above . . . and the pods make noise. . . . You are all by yourself. It's depressing and lonely.

Loud machinery and managers' heavy reliance on electronic communi-cation further reduced the opportunities for human interaction. Workers often found it difficult to form meaningful relationships with coworkers, especially in large warehouses that employed hundreds or thousands of people. Along with very high levels of employee turnover, Amazon associ-ates are often rotated across positions frequently, creating other obstacles for developing meaningful workplace relationships.[43]

Workers also experienced impersonal relationships with supervisors and managers. As Mao, a former warehouse associate, observed: "I guess it was pretty hard to keep track of like hundreds or thousands of employees that worked every day. . . . So, unless you're really close to a manager, they probably wouldn't remember your name." Many workers commented that they felt like they were "just a number" to managers and supervisors, who only interacted with them if they failed to make rate, had elevated error rates, or spent too much TOT.

Describing the impersonal and isolating nature of the work environ-ment for pickers, Isabel said: "It felt like I was in solitary confinement for 10 hours walking up and down the aisles . . . and it drove me crazy after a while. . . . [You] felt more like a number than an actual person." For Paola, the combination of impersonal mass production, lack of sunlight, heavy workload, low pay, and the clear injustice of it all was "very depressing."

Some Amazon warehouse workers suffer from severe depression. One journalistic study found that between October 2013 and October 2018 emergency workers were called to Amazon facilities about workers' suicide attempts or ideation or other mental health crises at least 189 times (across forty-six warehouses and seventeen states). While the workers' suicide plans varied, many involved plans to cut their arms with box cutters; some workers even put that plan into action. Like our interviewees, former workers interviewed for that news exposé described their jobs as dehumanizing, stressful, impersonal, isolating, and boring.[44]

FEAR AND ILLNESS DURING THE COVID-19 PANDEMIC

> We are being overworked now that we are on permanent 50- to 60-hour weeks, and the warehouses are not being cleaned and sanitized as the company says they are. The social distancing measures aren't being enforced. And to top it all off we aren't even being offered hand sanitizer. This company is literally going to work some of its employees to death, and I fear for their lives.

So wrote an anonymous worker at Amazon's Eastvale warehouse to the Southern California News Group in March 2020 when the COVID-19 pandemic began to spread across the nation.[45] Many COVID-19–related safety measures, such as the installation of more Plexiglas dividers and more accessibility of hand sanitizers, became more developed over time in the first year of the pandemic, sometimes in response to workers' protests, petitions, and legal complaints in the United States and other nations.[46] For example, Amazon required workers to take temperature checks through thermal cameras before entering the warehouse, to wear face masks, and to remain six feet apart from other workers at all times. Amazon provided face masks to workers who needed them and created a special group of "Safety Sabers" to verbally enforce COVID-19 policies, such as social distancing and other health guidelines like hand washing and sanitizing. Amazon's sanitation team cleaned facilities and work equipment more frequently than before the pandemic. Managers shifted work schedules so that work shifts and breaks were staggered to facilitate social distancing among workers, which sometimes numbered in the thousands at larger warehouses. They also began to train workers in smaller groups and online. Along with members of the safety team, surveillance technology and digital displays monitored workers' compliance with social distancing rules. When workers broke COVID-19 protocols, managers would send employees personal messages. Warehouse workers were also encouraged to report their health and safety concerns through a complaint box to keep management informed.

The physical landscape of warehouse buildings also changed, according to workers. For example, plastic linings or curtains separated workstations, chairs, and tables in break rooms so that only one person could sit in a space at a time. Additional break rooms were created to prevent crowds of workers from congregating. Entrances were reconstructed so that workers managing the arrival and departure of workers, and enforcing social distancing and other safety rules, were protected behind "Plexiglas or plastic." Inside the warehouse, Amazon installed more sanitation stations. Mobile washing stations were initially installed but then later replaced with stations with hand sanitizers and wipes. Aisles were widened, as was the distance between workstations. Colored stickers or tape marked floors exactly where workers were supposed to walk.

Many warehouse workers found Amazon's COVID-19 safety measures to be insufficient, however, and remained deeply concerned about the daily risks of being exposed to this deadly disease. Workers' reports, and other research, suggest that COVID-19 safety rules and practices at Amazon were uneven across facilities, shifts, and over time. They also suggest that COVID-19 safety rules and policies were frequently broken and not consistently enforced in Amazon's warehouses. To the alarm of many workers, various safety measures were rolled back by Amazon in 2021, including mask mandates, Plexiglas dividers, temperature scans, and onsite testing, in facilities around the nation, even though the omicron variant was on the rise and the warehouse workforce had grown amid the holiday peak season.[47]

Broken Safety Rules

Interviewees reported that even basic COVID-19 safety protocols recommended by the Centers for Disease Control and Prevention (CDC) were not always practiced, consistent with survey research findings from Inland Southern California.[48] In some ways, this finding is not surprising given the novelty of these safety rules and the influx of many new workers at that time to meet the surging demand for e-commerce goods, and because of high turnover rates among employees.[49] Research also suggests that too little attention was given to workplace safety in Amazon warehouses during the COVID-19 pandemic. According to workers' interviews and other research, employees received insufficient COVID-19 training, enforcement of safety rules was uneven and insufficient, and pressure to work fast compromised workers' ability to follow COVID-19 protocols.[50]

Interviewees claimed it was common for workers not to maintain proper social distancing at work. As Erica explained, "Going into the facility there is a line wrapped around the corner. I go speak to my supervisor or lead, there's multiple people there. End of shift everyone is cramming for the door. Or break rooms same thing or wash stations. There are multiple exposure points throughout the facility."

Other interviewees observed that despite staggered work shifts, when hundreds of workers entered and exited the building, it was difficult to stay six feet apart. At some warehouses, there could still be as many as 300 workers per shift. As Jose put it, "When there's the shift change, there's no way to not walk by somebody or maintain six feet of social distancing. It [is clear] they tried to organize it, and sometimes it does work, but for the most part, what I've seen consistently is when I clock into work and when I clock out, I am at certain points very frequently within six feet of other people." Angelo also observed that "leaving, there'd also be groups huddled outside of the exit" and socializing after work.

Various workers claimed that it was nearly impossible to work effectively and remain six feet from other workers at all times due to the nature of the job, the physical layout of the facility, and the large number of workers. Angelo said, "When I was close to people, it was because I had to be because of work. They station people close together." Encouraged to work quickly and under pressure to make rate, many workers got within six feet of each other. For example, Stella reported, "If I'm in a rush, I don't want to wait for the person next to me to have to grab their things before I grab mine so I'll grab mine anyways. I know I'm breaking the six-foot rule but, I just, I want to hurry." Humberto said,

> I do worry about possible exposure and I do not feel safe because a lot of the rules are bendable. . . . There can be times when a manager or someone is speaking to you and a lot of times they are very close to you. . . . In certain jobs for example TDR [trailer docking and receiving] you are with a partner and you are right next to each other the entire day. . . . I would say 90% of workers wear their masks properly. . . . The six feet thing is sometimes non-existent. . . . The only time I would get closer than six feet would be in the trailers when someone needs help with loading the trailer and can't keep up with their workload. . . . Most of my time was spent working beside someone else less than six feet apart.

Similarly, Viviana reported,

> If we're really busy . . . we all help out. . . . There was like about four of us. We all came in one spot, so like four of us were within less than six feet of each other and just trying to get the boxes on the pallets. . . . It's frequently happened, happens daily.

Likewise, Esther, who also built pallets, reported, "It's really hard to just have one person there because the flow gets really heavy." Estella said that she was "100 percent worried about exposure. One of the managers had a lot of people in one area if they have a lot of packages. About 20 people would be huddled around. No one would say anything as long as work was getting done." She said she got within six feet of coworkers, "10 times an hour with conveyor belts that had a lot of boxes." She also observed coworkers entering trucks together on the docks despite a rule of one person per truck.

Various workers reported that COVID-19 protocols were not sufficiently enforced by management. For example, Daniel said that managers "weren't monitoring [COVID safety policies] much, they were just monitoring that you got to get the job done." Jose observed that workers favored by managers or Safety Sabers were not reprimanded for failing to maintain proper social distance like other workers were. Various workers also reported that members of the Safety Saber team sometimes violated the COVID-19 safety protocols that they were supposed to enforce.

Workers reported that their managers or supervisors would also sometimes break the safety protocols to communicate with workers. Viviana, for example, said, "[The supervisor] gets really close to tell you and explain your job task and sometimes she does lower her mask to like speak to you, which is very unsafe." Other workers similarly reported that managers, supervisors, and workers would often pull down their masks and get closer than six feet so that they could better hear each other, thereby putting workers at greater risk of infection. Interviewees also claimed that they or fellow workers sometimes lowered their face masks below their chins when working.

Many workers were dissatisfied with the quality of the COVID-19 health training required of warehouse workers, which may have contributed to the frequent breaking of COVID-19 protocols by workers. According to Angelo, this training consisted of online videos, and workers could easily mute the videos and just do something else rather than pay attention to them. Similarly, Elvia claimed that the online training and ongoing COVID-19 safety reminders were very basic and easy to ignore.

According to workers, the extent of sanitation appeared to vary considerably over time and across warehouses and managers. According to Humberto, the frequency and quality of the sanitation often "depends on really who's running the shift." Amazon also relied on workers to sanitize their own equipment, which contributed to inconsistent sanitation. According to Esther, "There's no one there really watching that. You're sanitizing your stuff. It's just up to the workers themselves to make sure that they do it."

The accessibility of hand sanitizers and wipes also appeared to be uneven across warehouses and departments. Esther observed that although hand sanitizers were accessible when entering the warehouse and during breaks, "once you're actually like working on the floor, they're not close by, so they're pretty inaccessible." Under pressure to make rate or face write-ups or being fired, workers often didn't want to use their time to sanitize or wash their hands as frequently as they should. Other research based on surveys of Inland Southern California warehouse workers similarly finds that TOT monitoring discourages workers from washing their hands, and that there are not enough hand-washing stations in Amazon warehouses to make them accessible to workers.[51]

Fears of Exposure to COVID-19

Amazon warehouse workers worried about possible exposure to COVID-19 for themselves and their households, especially when they saw CDC safety protocols being broken. Official notifications of COVID-19 cases by Amazon that were distributed through emails and text messages were regular reminders of the health risks of working during the pandemic. Workers employed at larger warehouses received these notifications weekly or even daily. Due to confidentiality, workers were not notified of who was diagnosed with COVID-19, but they were informed if they might have come into contact with the worker. Many workers wanted additional and more timely information about COVID-19 cases from management, so workers often kept each other informed of confirmed COVID-19 diagnoses through word of mouth.

Workers often worried about being exposed to COVID-19 because of the sheer number of employees at their facilities. As Veronica explained, "There are over 2,000 people per shift in the warehouse, 230 alone in my department." Julio felt "unsafe" at work because "we have like 300 people per shift . . . inside an enclosed facility." In addition to thousands of workers employed at larger warehouses, there was high employee turnover, hundreds of new workers were hired to help with the holiday peak season, and workers were frequently rotated across departments, all of which increased workers' risk of exposure. Viviana summarized many workers' worries and concerns when she said,

> So those notifications [of COVID-19 cases], they kind of scare me because it's like the reality of it, like so many people are getting it in my own warehouse. . . . Being in a warehouse where it's . . . full of people. . . . The reality is, is that it's work. . . . It's like safety is next, you know. We have to get the job done. We have to get those boxes on those pallets and if it's like packed, there's a lot of boxes... It's like more than one person helping in one spot. . . . That is dangerous, I know. You were in a mask, but it's still dangerous to stand so close to people. But you have to get the job done. So I do fear about getting exposed.

Workers often worried that they put the health of their entire households at risk, especially when they lived with very young children or older relatives. For example, Mateo feared being exposed to COVID-19 and putting his 89-year-old grandmother at risk of exposure. Daniella worried that she would expose her 22-year-old daughter and 2-year-old granddaughter to COVID-19, because she often worked in close proximity to other workers and "everybody would be constantly getting COVID at work." Humberto, who was 30 years old, worried about getting COVID-19 at work and then giving it to his 57-year-old mother, who was ill and had a compromised immune system; he observed that "cases just keep happening." Camila worried about getting COVID-19 at work and then infecting her family of seven. As she explained, her three nieces "are still little and my parents are older, so it's a risk factor for all of us." As Jose put it, working at Amazon during the pandemic was not only "physically exhausting, but also really stressful . . . emotionally stressful." Workers sometimes quit their jobs because of fears of being exposed to COVID-19. For many workers, like Daniel, quitting was not an option, however: "It got kind of scary at one point, but at the same time, you gotta make money."

Amazon did occasionally shut down warehouses to sanitize them. According to Esther, "One of the bigger warehouses, a lot of people were getting diagnosed with COVID within a week. I think it was like 10 people in one week, so they shut down the warehouse without paying and they sanitized the whole warehouse." Yet such closures were rare, to the frustration of workers, such as Brianna, who said, "If there's more COVID cases, why are we open?! At least in my building, there has been over 1,500 cases!"

The exact number of COVID-19 cases among Amazon workers is contested. Amazon's records suggest that between March 1 and September 19, 2020, a total of 19,816 out of 1,372,000 US frontline employees of Amazon and Whole Foods (its grocery chain) tested positive for COVID-19. They claim that this COVID-19 rate was less than the rate found in the general population, taking into account workers' age and geographical location.[52] Yet Amazon's records were incomplete because they excluded workers who were never diagnosed or whose illnesses were never recorded because they were fired or quit prior to becoming symptomatic, or who were hired through temporary agencies or subcontractors.

Concerned with the lack of transparency and insufficient information regarding positive COVID-19 cases at Amazon, warehouse workers and their organizations collected and disseminated their own information about COVID-19 cases through social media, the press, protests, and more informal means of communication.[53] Some workers' families and advocates also publicly shared tragic stories of Amazon employees who contracted the illness at work and later died, in an effort to put pressure on the corporation to improve workplace health and safety and provide more support to families when employees got sick or died.[54]

COVID-19 Safety Rules, Stress, and Isolation

While the new safety procedures helped to reduce possible exposures to COVID-19 and worries related to such exposures, the policies themselves created another layer of stress. Describing the role of "social distance champions," Juanita said, "At Amazon, . . . there's always people like telling us, 'six feet distance' and screaming if they see you together."

Olivia described COVID-19 safety rules as adding to workplace stress:

> I get frustrated because I'm having a long day at work and then I still have to like, hear people scream at me when it's not my fault some people behind me may be walking a little [too close] to me. . . . I get really frustrated, because like there's nothing I can do, it's not like I can run away from the person behind me. . . . I don't think it's fair.

Olivia described the Safety Saber team members at her workplace as "really rude" and in need of additional training.

Social distancing rules helped to protect workers from exposure to COVID-19, but they also made it harder to work quickly. Legal records indicate that between March and October 2020, Amazon executives instructed managers to temporarily suspend the disciplining of warehouse workers for failing to maintain productivity standards for work rates and TOT, given the need to keep workers safe from exposure to COVID-19 through social distancing, hand washing, and frequent sanitation. They later reinstated "revised" productivity standards in October 2020.[55] Yet according to *New York Times* reporters, Amazon failed to communicate these policy changes clearly to workers.[56] A national survey of Amazon warehouse and delivery workers found that more than half reported that workers still faced discipline, termination, or the threat of termination for failing to make rate during the pandemic.[57]

Various interviewees, employed by Amazon sometime between March and November 2020, described being pressured to maintain prepandemic productivity standards even though it was more difficult to complete work tasks while also following CDC protocols. For example, Roberto complained, "They want people to do social distancing, so only one person per aisle as well. And they still expect the same workload. . . . It's harder because you have to wait for the person to get out of the aisle." Other research, based on a survey of twenty-six Inland Southern California warehouse workers and delivery drivers, finds that 72 percent of surveyed workers found the pressure to make rate to be more stressful during the COVID-19 pandemic than before it. Various workers also reported that they sometimes faced increased workloads or work quotas during the pandemic due to increases in customer orders and understaffing.[58]

Face masks, COVID-19 safety rules, and staggered shifts protected workers from exposure to the COVID-19 virus but added to feelings of social isolation and stress. Brianna recalled,

> When I get to work everyday I get anxiety. I never had anxiety but now because of COVID, I feel like a lot of us are more depressed and anxiety is up the ass and like I said, if you don't have your mask on and the fact that they can fire you for any little thing now gives me serious anxiety like everyday. . . . If you're caught with [your mask] below your nose for any reason they will give you your final write up. . . . They have them security cameras that will tell you that you're too close to somebody and then they have social distancing police that will go around and make sure that people are six feet apart from each other. . . . So let's say you have a final write up for the mask and let's say you get a write up for your rate, then they will let you go. . . . I am worried about . . . getting laid off.

The constant enforcement of safety rules also made it difficult to relax. As Olivia described, "I come into the break room, and there's just like the people that are enforcing the safety rules. They're, you know, screaming at all these people. . . . That part has affected my break and like how long I can rest." Staggered work breaks were also sometimes not timed well. Olivia was given her first work break only one hour into her shift, and then an hour later she received her lunch break. As a result, she had two three-hour work periods with a break in the middle at the end of the day when she was more tired.

COVID-19–Related Leaves and Unfair Terminations

Amazon provided two weeks of leave for workers who had to quarantine for COVID-19. Workers had to document their diagnosis to receive payment for this leave and had to test negative for the virus before returning to work. Angelo, describing COVID-19 medical leaves at Amazon, said, "They did not make it easy for anyone to do it. . . . It was like a hassle to do it." Camila provided a rich description of the "hassle" she experienced when she sought approval for a COVID-19–related leave of absence. She had come into contact with someone diagnosed with COVID-19 and experienced many of the common symptoms of it, including "chills, headache, throwing up, nausea, soreness."

> So after the two weeks, and instead of trying to deal with my health and just focus on recovering . . . what I was more focused on was, "Am I gonna get fired?" . . . As far as the procedures for having time off, it wasn't easy. I would have to call nurses. I also had to get those papers, those documents I had to send to HR, and I'd constantly have to check in to see if HR had received them, and see if they were processed, if my case manager was on top of it, if I would get a call from them, if I got a date [for COVID-19 test results], if they know that. . . . My testing results weren't going to come in until [a week] after I was expected to come back to work. . . . And I had to wait and I also had to jump through hoops again, to let HR know that, "hey my results aren't in" and I know the procedures that I cannot come back to work unless it shows that I'm negative. After getting this all processed out, finally recovering and showing up to work, they suspended my badge until I had shown documentation, until I was negative. Showed up to work and it was another hoop to jump through to even walk into the building. . . . A person feeling sick, a person feeling all these symptoms, they're worried on top of that, of course they're anxious about if they actually have COVID, or what are they going to do if they do or they don't. All these steps on top of having to jump through all these hoops with HR it's just a lot. There's no reassurance for them, it's just more conflict and more struggles and more difficulties you have to go through.

While Camila successfully navigated all of the steps required of her by Amazon's HR department, she acknowledged that other workers were unable to do so and sometimes faced wrongful termination as a result.

Isabella described her own experience of being unfairly fired for failing to navigate Amazon's complicated process for gaining approval for a

COVID-19–related leave of absence. She got sick and tried unsuccessfully to notify Amazon's HR Department that she was going to get tested for COVID-19. Unfortunately she did not place her information properly in their electronic system, so she was notified that she could no longer come back to work because she had missed too many days of work. As she explained,

> Well, I would go through the app. . . . It didn't help me 'cause I was trying to explain like why I was missing so much. I did have the proof in hand. . . . The HR told me that this is not in the system, they couldn't verify it correctly. . . . What was so crazy 'cause that day I went to work in the morning I didn't see anybody there at HR and I was waiting and then you know, I just got frustrated. . . . They really fired me when I was just trying to work. It was pretty messed up.

A *New York Times* exposé suggests that Isabella's experience was not isolated. Amazon lacked sufficient HR staff to process workers' electronic claims and requests, correct errors in HR records, work through miscommunication, and support workers trying to navigate Amazon's leave and other HR policies, which led to wrongful terminations. Confusion over Amazon's leave policies, which shifted over time and were not clearly communicated, also led to unfair firings.[59]

Various interviewees expressed frustration with the lack of HR staff support and its heavy reliance on online communication through its A to Z app and automated phone systems to carry out HR policies, which were not very easy to understand and navigate. When discussing COVID-19–related leave policies at Amazon, Stella said, "You have to kind of dig for the information a lot and I think it should be a lot more . . . readily available being that it's kind of such a big deal." Viviana recalls her frustration with trying to figure out how to obtain paid time off for COVID-19 while awaiting her test results in this way:

> So I tried calling my Amazon building, going to like [HR] in there, but I couldn't get ahold of any actual person on the phone. . . . I could not figure out what to do and I didn't want to go into the place because I didn't know if I had COVID or not and so we had to wait it out and I took my day unpaid that day. So I just didn't get paid for the day. That's what I had to do because they didn't make it easy on their website to have access to [paid leave].

> They're not very clear with their automated phone calls and policies, not to me at least.

Other workers had difficulty obtaining paid time off, even with positive COVID-19 test results. For example, Brianna told the interviewer about her friend, who was diagnosed with COVID-19 and was promised two weeks of paid leave but was never paid for it.

For many workers, Amazon's retraction of hazard pay and unlimited time off policy in the midst of the pandemic demonstrated just how little the corporation valued them. Between March and May 2020, Amazon paid warehouse workers $2 more per hour as "hazard pay," a temporary wage boost that was portrayed as compensating workers for the risks of COVID-19 exposure they faced while working during the pandemic.[60] At that time, Amazon was in the process of hiring about 100,000 new workers to keep up with the increased demand for home-delivered goods. Hazard pay helped to recruit and retain warehouse workers. Likewise, Amazon's unlimited time off policy also helped Amazon retain workers by preventing them from losing their jobs for COVID-19–related reasons, such as recovery from COVID-19, the need to care for sick relatives, reducing the risks of exposure for immune-compromised relatives, and the need to care for children due to school and childcare closures.[61] Perhaps to reduce labor costs and maintain work discipline, Amazon quickly retracted these policies, even though reported coronavirus cases continued to climb. For workers like Brianna, Amazon's reversal of these policies in the midst of the pandemic was disheartening: "Now that cases are rising we lost our two-dollar [hazard] pay, get no more unlimited time to be with our family so now cases are rising everyday and Amazon does not care. I guess people can be coming up with cases all day long and they don't care." Other interviewees expressed similar frustration with Amazon for its failure to better protect its frontline workers and to maintain its "hazard pay" to compensate them for the additional health risks associated with working during a pandemic.

Workers' stories provide us with a haunting glimpse of the everyday workplace dangers and risks experienced by Amazon warehouse workers that have been documented through national-level surveys and other reports.[62] Amazon workers' concerns about the company's failure to protect them from exposure to COVID-19, including insufficient health training and its failure to enforce social distancing requirements and use of face masks and to install more Plexiglas screens to protect workers, were corroborated by investigations in 2020 and 2021 by Cal/OSHA in response to workers' complaints in three facilities (in Hawthorne, Eastgate, and Rialto). Those investigations resulted in requirements that Amazon pay fines (totaling $42,870) and address the problems.[63] Likewise, employees' concerns about Amazon's negligence in reporting COVID-19 cases were corroborated by a lawsuit filed by the California attorney general's office and findings from related investigations regarding the corporation's failure to comply with the state's "Right to Know" law, adopted in 2021. This lawsuit resulted in an agreement by Amazon to pay a $500,000 fine and to comply with this law, which required employers to notify employees and local health agencies within one day of confirmed COVID-19 cases at their workplaces and to inform them of the total number of such cases at their workplace.[64]

Many interviewees had quit or planned to quit their jobs because of health-related concerns, while others had lost their jobs due to injuries. Such problems contribute to the very high employee turnover rates in Amazon warehouses.[65] Even so, many warehouse workers remained employed by Amazon despite the health risks because their employment options were limited and they needed the money. For example, Mia worried that her job unloading trailers was negatively affecting her physical health, but she kept working at Amazon because it was the only job available to her during the pandemic, and she needed the income.

Given the health risks among Amazon warehouse workers, the absence of health-care benefits for part-time, temporary, and seasonal workers is all the more striking. When asked how the job could be better for workers, Daniel responded:

> Since it's so physically demanding, what I would change or what I would add, is for everyone there, even for temporary or part-time, some form of healthcare because you do get messed up on that job and some people might be too afraid to lose their job to even say like, "Hey I got hurt." I feel like adding some kind of healthcare protection would be very beneficial.

As noted in chapter 3, even full-time Amazon workers sometimes cannot afford Amazon's health-care plan, especially if they support a family.

Fearing for their own health and safety, as well as that of their coworkers and family members, many Amazon warehouse workers, both in Inland Southern California and around the world, engaged in collective action to improve workplace safety. They signed petitions, testified at OSHA hearings, pushed for improvements in health and safety regulations, and even protested and walked off the job. Popular resistance to the negative impacts of the Inland Southern California warehousing industry on workers and communities, including their health, is the focus of the next chapter.

7 Boxing Lessons

COMMUNITY RESISTANCE TO AMAZON AND
WAREHOUSING IN INLAND SOUTHERN CALIFORNIA

Community resistance to Amazon and the expansion of warehousing in Inland Southern California builds upon and revitalizes labor organizing, but also draws on a legacy of grassroots EJ activism in the region.[1] This activism emerged in response to California's most toxic waste site, the Stringfellow Acid Pits (SAP), located at the site of a former Pyrite Canyon rock quarry in Western Riverside County. SAP opened as the Stringfellow Quarry Company in 1956, following lengthy negotiations between Riverside County officials and the quarry's owner, James Stringfellow. State geologist Robert Fox assured Stringfellow that solid bedrock would prevent acids and other toxic materials from leaching into groundwater, and the project was supported by the Santa Ana Regional Water Quality Control Board (RWQCB).[2] In fact, SAP was constructed above an underground alluvial channel running through decomposed granite and fractured bedrock.[3] More than 200 companies, including McDonnel Douglas, Montrose Chemical, General Electric, Hughes Aircraft, Northrop, and Rockwell International, dumped toxic sludge into unlined pits there or sprayed liquid wastes into the surrounding air to improve evaporation.

According to legal scholar and practicing attorney Brian Craig, "There was sulfuric acid, sodium hydroxide, polychlorinated biphenyl (PCB), various pesticides, lead, manganese, and chromium. There were spent acids and caustics, solvents, pesticide byproducts, vapor degreaser waste and paint booth sludge. Sometimes, when organic material got mixed in, the foul brew caught fire."[4] More than thirty-four million gallons of waste were dumped at SAP before the Santa Ana RWQCB closed the site in 1972, in part due to pressure from paleobotanist and community activist Ruth Kirkby and other Parents of Jurupa, Inc. members. Record-breaking rains in winter 1969 caused toxic wastewater reservoirs at SAP to overflow into nearby Glen Avon, a small unincorporated community that is now part of the city of Jurupa Valley.[5] In response, community members lobbied public officials about, and drew media attention to, the consequent threat to local groundwater supplies. Kirkby's scientific background and community presence contributed to her effective opposition to industries responsible for contaminating groundwater and endangering residents' health.[6]

The state and local officials responsible for the contamination "blamed one another," ordered studies, rejected recommended repairs because of the high estimated costs ($410,000 at the time, which would balloon to nearly $250 million), and demanded that Stringfellow help fund the cleanup.[7] Consequently, no essential remediation—that is, encapsulation of hazardous material by filling fissures in the bedrock, installing wells to drain the downstream waste plume, and installing a clay cap—had occurred by the time Southern California was again impacted by colossal rainstorms and flooding, in the winter of 1978. Fearing that the SAP dam, the only barrier between the facility's rapidly overflowing wastewater reservoirs and the residents of Glen Avon, would break, Santa Ana RWQCB officials opted for a series of controlled releases of diluted waste totaling about one million gallons into the Pyrite Creek channel. Glen Avon residents were not informed as the foamy, toxic chemical soup flowed into ditches and culverts; caused sewers to back up; disintegrated shoes and clothing; and contributed to an increasing number and range of health issues, including headaches, dizziness, nausea, asthma, and birth defects.[8]

Local activists sprang into action. Members of community groups— including the Jurupa Women's Club, the Glen Avon Babysitting Cooperative, Glen Avon Crime Watch, Pedley Women's Club, the Glen Avon PTA, and the West Riverside County Businessmen's Association—organized to form Concerned Neighbors in Action (CNA). They demanded that the Environmental Protection Agency (EPA) and state agencies clean up the site and compensate those who had been harmed. Initially, the predominantly female CNA members were roundly denounced by mostly male government agency officials as "hysterical housewives," a pejorative catch-all label for grassroots female activists, particularly those associated with 1970s and 1980s era campaigns to clean up hazardous and toxic waste dumps.[9] Under the leadership of special education teacher and mother Penny Newman, the group responded by shifting from reliance on door-to-door canvassing and newspaper ads to more visible and vocal activism, including protests outside the homes of Riverside County politicians and industrial polluters, and joined forces with national organizations such as the Citizens Clearinghouse for Hazardous Waste, founded by Love Canal's own headline hysterical housewife, Lois Gibbs.

SAP was just one of many "abandoned or uncontrolled hazardous waste sites" in the United States during the 1970s. Some sites, including the Chemical Control Corporation in Elizabeth, New Jersey, and Niagara Falls, New York's, Love Canal neighborhood, were associated with serious public health risks and loss of life, which prompted federal government action.[10] The Comprehensive Environmental Response, Compensation, and Liability Act of 1980 created a "Superfund" to finance cleanups when responsible parties cannot be found. The law requires the parties responsible for intentional, uncontrolled hazardous waste disposal or accidental releases of hazardous substances to carry out the necessary cleanup or reimburse the government for cleanup managed by the EPA. SAP was identified as the most polluted waste site in California and included on the EPA's Superfund National Priorities List in 1983, making funds available for initial remediation: fencing, erosion control, installation of a clay "cap," and disposal of contaminated liquids off-site.[11] That same year, the US government and the state of California sued thirty-one of the companies that had used SAP to cover current and future cleanup reimbursement. Assistant Attorney General Carol Dinkins called it "the largest and most significant hazardous-waste case the U.S. government has ever filed."[12] Glen Avon residents fought to join the suit to ensure the community's engagement in how the cleanup would proceed and who would pay for it.[13] In 1984, CNA also filed a lawsuit against more than 250 corporate dumpers, Riverside County, the state of California, and the US Air Force. At the time, the case was the largest toxic tort in the nation, with personal injury and damage claims made on behalf of 5,000 plaintiffs.

The "ultramarathon" litigation over the SAP cleanup endured more than three decades.[14] In 1989 federal courts found the state of California to be primarily responsible for SAP's contamination of groundwater and floodwaters, which caused physical and emotional harm to thousands of Glen Avon residents.[15] Therefore, in addition to more than $150 million in corporate settlements to cover the costs of cleaning up SAP, California ultimately paid the federal government $99.4 million in 2001.[16] The state pursued cases against insurers of companies that had dumped hazardous wastes at SAP through 2017, a year after the Pyrite Canyon Treatment Facility opened.[17] Meanwhile, at the state level, personal injury settlements in the class action lawsuit brought by 3,800 Glen Avon settlements amounted to nearly $110 million by the end of 1994.[18]

During the preceding year, CNA had changed its name to the Center for Community Action and Environmental Justice (CCAEJ) and broadened its mission to include a range of environmental, health, and social justice issues of particular relevance to Inland Southern California. Within a decade the negative environmental, health, and economic impacts of the logistics industry and warehousing would become central to the work of CCAEJ and its collaborators.[19] CNA's successful resistance to the SAP's contamination illustrates multiple themes that remain relevant to understanding contemporary resistance by CCAEJ and other grassroots organizations to warehousing, especially by Amazon, in this region where politically conservative forces and business interests often prevailed.[20] First, the primary leaders were "weak" in terms of social hierarchy. While both Kirkby (Parents of Jurupa, Inc.) and CNA's Newman were college educated and socioeconomically established members of the community, they were female and political novices with no legal expertise when they took on leadership of their respective organizations. Second, while members of the Parents of Jurupa, Inc. tended to be middle aged, longtime Glen Avon residents who were more scientifically knowledgeable than their neighbors, CNA membership was intentionally inclusive.[21] It organized across racial and economic lines to ensure representation of "everyone who had been exposed to toxins," including the Black, Latino, and immigrant residents who constituted an increasing proportion of Glen Avon and nearby communities by the end of the 1990s.[22] Third, CNA was a coalition of existing community groups and organizations and expanded its mission and capacity for action by joining with other environmental, labor, and geographically based groups. In 1980 CNA collaborated with other neighborhood groups state-wide to establish Communities against Toxic Wastes in Landfills to secure cleanup funding. In 1986 CNA united with more than seventy environmental, labor, and community groups in a coalition called the Toxics Coordinating Project, which sought to reduce toxic air and water pollution in both built and natural environments.[23] Finally, both Parents of Jurupa, Inc. and CNA organized to oppose harm to individual residents and neighborhoods in an unincorporated area, which lacked the political representation and decision-making power enjoyed by municipalities.

Amazon's rise in Inland Southern California coincided with an escalation of this long-standing public resistance to warehousing by community and EJ activists who were concerned about the transportation of goods to and from warehouses, which further exacerbated regional problems with traffic congestion and air pollution and related public health crises, especially the high rate of asthma and other respiratory conditions. Additionally, these activists raised other concerns about broader, negative social impacts of, and potential harms associated with, the growth of warehousing, including reduced green space and opportunities for active transportation; threats to rural and suburban ways of life; the lack of stable, living-wage jobs in the region; the closure of brick and mortar stores and local businesses; insufficient regulation of toxic materials stored or handled in warehouses; and a general worsening of the climate crisis. Consequently, we can understand community and environmental activists' resistance to the rapid expansion of Amazon and warehousing, more broadly, as threat-based mobilization or collective action against actual or perceived threats to groups' "interests, values and, at times, survival."[24]

Labor activists, building on earlier unionization drives among warehouse workers, have similarly protested against Amazon and other warehouse employers in response to perceived threats to workers' rights and labor standards in the warehouse and logistics industries. For example, in response to the growth of Amazon and other nonunion warehouse and logistics companies and their increased reliance on temporary and subcontracted workers in the past decade, labor activists have organized warehouse workers and demanded higher pay and better working conditions, stronger legal protection for these workers, and better enforcement of existing labor laws through collective action, policy advocacy, and litigation.

Over time, community, EJ, and labor activists have been joined by immigrant rights, faith-based, racial justice, and other progressive organizations opposed to Amazon and warehousing, as well as intent on transforming the political balance of power and direction of economic development in the region. The overriding emphasis of these cross-movement alliances and joint actions is to force politicians and policy makers to be more responsive to the needs and demands of the working-class communities of color that they serve and to make the regional economy more equitable, just, and environmentally sustainable.

This chapter provides an overview of the rise and impacts of popular opposition to Amazon and warehousing in Inland Southern California, highlighting the roles of community, EJ, and labor organizations within it. Our narrative focuses on the bridging of these distinct, yet sometimes interrelated, streams of activism, which has distinguished resistance to warehousing in the region and provides lessons for organizing against Amazon elsewhere. We approach this history thematically, focusing on key moments of community, EJ, labor, and collaborative activism, rather than adhering to an overall strict chronological order. We begin by examining efforts by, and impacts of, CCAEJ and other community and EJ organizations to mobilize and resist expansion of warehousing in Inland Southern California. We then discuss labor activists' efforts to organize warehouse workers and improve their working conditions. Next we consider efforts to build cross-movement alliances, including blue-green coalitions among labor and EJ activists, around warehousing and related issues in the region and to engage in joint action against Amazon and the expansion of warehousing. We conclude that growing resistance to warehousing in Inland Southern California, often directed at Amazon, confronts formidable challenges but also reveals the power of multipronged strategies and coalition building for making progress toward more sustainable livelihoods and lives.

ENVIRONMENTAL IMPACTS AND OPPOSITION TO WAREHOUSING

Open land drew late nineteenth-century colonists to establish citrus groves in Riverside. A well-worked quarry nearby a small, census-designated location in Riverside county piqued the interest of local officials looking for a hazardous waste dump site. And "cheap dirt" attracted industrial developers, who, together with representatives of the Long Beach and Los Angeles ports and regional policy makers, promoted a shared vision of logistics as a socially beneficial growth industry.[25] More than 700 warehouses have been constructed in Inland Southern California since the first large, high-tech warehouses were constructed in the 1990s.[26] Through the early 2000s, Riverside and San Bernardino city and county policy makers approved construction of numerous warehouses, arguably without requiring sufficient environmental analysis of their impacts.[27] Fresh from its legal victory over SAP, the newly branded CCAEJ redirected its attention to resisting and mitigating environmental and social justice issues, such as the health threats that diesel exhaust from trucks and trains posed for residents of Mira Loma Village, where $PM_{2.5}$ levels are higher than anywhere else in California.[28]

We begin this section by discussing CCAEJ's pathbreaking legal settlement in partnership with Mira Loma residents that secured environmental and public health mitigations from the developer of a neighboring warehouse complex. Their success was due in part to the establishment of the city of Jurupa Valley, which includes Mira Loma. Grassroots resistance in Inland Southern California has been marked by a persistent lack of representation in warehouse siting decisions by residents of unincorporated communities.[29] We then examine community activism and legal opposition to warehousing, including by Amazon employees, in two representative locations in San Bernardino County: Bloomington, a small (population 24,339 in 2020) census-designated place, and Fontana, a midsize city (population 208,393 in 2020).[30] Both Bloomington and Fontana are young, majority Latino—81 percent and 68 percent, respectively—and working class. In contrast to Bloomington, which is relatively impoverished—median household income was $52,000 in 2019—and, like Glen Avon and Mira Loma until 2011, unincorporated, Fontana is a modern city with a median household income ($73,000 in 2019) commensurate with other Inland Southern California cities.[31] Finally, we address efforts to "green" warehousing and the logistics industry by electrifying warehouses and trucking fleets, including the 40.6-million-square-foot World Logistics Center (WLC) in Moreno Valley and the SCAQMD's Indirect Source Rule (Rule 2305).

CCAEJ and Mira Loma Village

In 2011 CCAEJ escalated its general opposition to traffic congestion and air pollution associated with warehousing, distribution, and transportation—typically expressed through public education initiatives, rallies, protests, and public statements to the press and policy makers—by filing a lawsuit against Riverside County, the City of Jurupa Valley, and developers of a major warehousing project. According to CCAEJ, Riverside County supervisors approved the development, designed to add 1.4 million square feet of storage space adjacent to Mira Loma Village, without a study of the environmental impacts of the project required by the California Environmental Quality Act (CEQA).[32] State Attorney General Kamala Harris joined the suit against the project proposal after visiting Mira Loma Village and witnessing the intense diesel truck traffic passing by the neighborhood. Mira Loma is located downwind from air pollution moving inland from Los Angeles and subject to additional pollution from two major freeways (I-15 and SR 60) and the movement of 15,000 tractor-trailers daily through nearby warehouse complexes.[33] The resulting poor air quality, which CCAEJ members, including local residents, and their allies helped to measure and document, contributes to chronic respiratory disease and other illnesses suffered by the mostly Latino residents of Mira Loma Village, who also endure constant noise and light pollution associated with the warehouses surrounding their neighborhood.[34]

The timing of this legal action is significant because it occurred just over two weeks after the communities of Jurupa Hills, Mira Loma, Glen Avon, Pedley, Indian Hills, Belltown, Sunnyslope, Crestmore Heights, and Rubidoux incorporated as the city of Jurupa Valley, a process that CCAEJ members and their allies had actively promoted through neighborhood outreach and public mobilization.[35] According to former CCAEJ director Penny Newman, residents of the new city expected to have much greater leverage over the land use decisions that affected them than had been true when these decisions were made by distant Riverside County supervisors.[36] Indeed, Riverside County land use planning documents have, since the 1970s, specifically zoned, or considered much of the unincorporated areas of the county open to rezoning, to support expansion of warehousing and logistics. In contrast, Jurupa Valley's General Plans emphasize preservation of the city's "small town character" and "mobility corridors," to facilitate active transportation—pedestrians, cyclists, etc.—and protection of residential areas from industrial land uses, such as warehousing.

CCAEJ won its lawsuit. Although the 2013 settlement did not prevent the project's construction, it did require measures to mitigate the impact of the new warehouses on the residents of Mira Loma Village. A central feature of the settlement is the installation of air filters in every home in Mira Loma Village. CCAEJ partnered with the Swiss technology company IQAir to acquire filters that reduce particulate matter pollution by at least 90 percent. The settlement also mandated Riverside County and the City of Jurupa Valley to add an EJ element to the city's General Plan, develop alternative routes for heavy trucks currently using streets adjacent to Mira Loma Village, institute an air quality monitoring program, develop and implement an anti-idling enforcement program, and create a "Green Project" site.[37] The settlement represents a major victory not only for Mira Loma Village but also for the many often impoverished communities of color located in "diesel death zones" adjacent to freeways connecting the Los Angeles and Long Beach ports through Inland Southern California.[38]

The successful campaign to mitigate the impacts of warehouses in Mira Loma established an initial standard for community demands regarding new warehousing projects in Inland Southern California that constrain Amazon as well. EJ organizations, including CCAEJ, together with other community organizations and sometimes municipalities, have joined in resisting new warehousing developments and logistics centers throughout Riverside and San Bernardino Counties, claiming that they violate environmental laws. Successful settlements and alternative arrangements feature mitigating harm from traffic, air, light, and noise pollutants and from habitat displacement. Community opposition to warehousing in the region continues as many more warehouse projects move forward unabated, despite their increasingly devastating impacts on the natural environment; public health; and rural, small-town, or suburban ways of life.

Challenges to Bloomington's Way of Life

Bloomington is a mostly rural, unincorporated community, where a majority of the residents are Latino and every census tract is low income and in the 90th percentile for ozone pollution.[39] Because Bloomington does not have its own local government, the county makes decisions regarding warehouse developments there. Despite planning documents that specify the community's desire to maintain a rural way of life, by mid-2022 most of the warehouses (four of six) in Bloomington had been constructed near residential areas on land that had formerly been ranches, farms, and nurseries.[40] Bloomington resident Thomas Rocha, who cofounded Concerned Citizens of Bloomington in 2015 and later became a member of the community's municipal advisory council, characterized responsible land use this way: "Put warehouses in commercial areas and leave residential areas alone."[41] Council chair Gary Grossich disagreed entirely at the time. Grossich told news reporters that Bloomington needed the revenue generated from warehousing and logistics, and that he was tired of "watching it go right across . . . the street from our homes and our businesses and our schools and other cities reaping the benefits while we get . . . nothing."[42]

In 2016 CCAEJ joined residents of Bloomington to resist construction of the 344,000-square-foot Slover Distribution Center "so close to homes, schools, and community hubs."[43] They worried that by increasing noise, traffic, and air pollution, the planned DC represented a threat to public health and their historically ranchero way of life. In response to developers' claims that the Slover Distribution Center would generate $6 million for San Bernardino's general fund by 2029 and create 290 jobs, CCAEJ argued that the additional traffic congestion, air pollution, and related impacts on Bloomington residents' health and way of life should not be sacrificed for the county's economic gain. In October 2018 the environmental law firm Earthjustice sued the San Bernardino County Board of Supervisors on behalf of CCAEJ, charging that the project's environmental impact report failed to meet CEQA standards concerning traffic and air pollution impacts. The lawsuit was settled without stopping construction, though the developer agreed to a number of half-hearted mitigation measures, including installation of electric vehicle charging stations.[44]

Concerned Neighbors of Bloomington, often with the support of CCAEJ and other regional EJ organizations, has since mobilized in opposition to warehouses and industrial parks that hinge on the San Bernardino County Board of Supervisors' approval to rezone residential land for commercial

Figure 7.1. Amazon FC, Bloomington, CA. Photo by Parker Allison.

use despite community opposition.[45] In 2018 the San Bernardino County Supervisors approved the 677,000-square-foot Bloomington Commerce Center near Crestmore Elementary School, which required "upzoning" residential areas to more lucrative commercial use.[46] Two years later, the PC4EJ joined the coalition against Howard Industrial Partners' proposed Bloomington Business Park, which would require rezoning twenty-four acres from large acre residential to medium density residential and demolishing more than 200 homes, precipitating the further loss of the "rural, family-oriented" community that more than 70 percent of Bloomington residents favor. According to Howard Industrial Partners in May 2022, eighty homeowners had agreed to sell.[47] By then, Rocha had sold his Bloomington "dream home" and moved to Nevada, in direct response to the opening of an Amazon IXD facility just seventy feet away from a residential community and less than a tenth of a mile from a high school (see figure 7.1).[48]

Reinventing Fontana

Fontana, once an agricultural colony, then a manufacturing center, reinvented itself once again under the leadership of Mayor Acquanetta

Warren, aka "Warehouse Warren." Warren has held onto her office since 2010 with overwhelming voter support, arguably thanks to significant campaign donations from landowners, land speculators, and developers.[49] Developers have bought and torn down hundreds of single-family homes, horse properties, chicken ranches, and small businesses to build "millions of square feet" of warehousing space for e-commerce fulfillment providers, including Amazon, and DCs for many well-known companies, including Coca Cola, FedEx, and Smart & Final.[50] Fontana is home to two Amazon crossdock facilities, both of which opened in 2019 within a mile of local high schools.[51] While neither of these developments provoked community resistance, the city Planning Commission's approval of the West Valley Logistics Center during that same year did. That complex was designed to consume 200 acres and include multiple buildings totaling 3.4 million square feet, just 200 feet from a residential neighborhood. CCAEJ's mobilization of opponents spanned the communities of Bloomington and Jurupa Valley as well as Fontana because polluting emissions from increased truck traffic to and from the proposed project's location would impact the entire air shed, which is already characterized by extremely poor air quality. Additionally, CCAEJ argued that the project would require bulldozing habitat critical for the survival of the coastal California gnatcatcher and destroy a wildlife corridor in the Jurupa Hills and Rattlesnake Mountain. CCAEJ, together with the Sierra Club and the Center for Biological Diversity, sued the City of Fontana, the Fontana City Council, and project developers for acting in violation of CEQA. The lawsuit failed to impede final approval of the West Valley Logistics Center; however, CCAEJ and its coplaintiffs secured a confidential settlement that provides pollution mitigation.[52]

The Fontana Planning Commission did not miss a beat in the wake of this suit and continued to consider and approve warehouse projects, which typically require zoning changes. For example, in 2020 the commission easily agreed to recommend that the City Council change the city's General Plan by rezoning a two-acre parcel from general commercial to light industrial as required to construct a small, 41,000-square-foot DC that was not expected to have a significant effect on the environment.[53] During the following year, the commission responded just as positively to a series of similar zone changes packaged with requests to construct warehouses on the rezoned properties. Despite persistent public opposition from Fontana residents, frequently with the support of local and regional community and EJ organizations, the City Council "steamrolled" over these appeals, allowing warehousing and logistics to further dominate the local and regional economy.

Among these cases is the controversial Slover and Oleander project, in reference to a more than 205,000-square-foot DC and logistics facility that Duke Reality proposed to build on an 8.61-acre property, which required the Planning Commission's approval (given in April 2021) to consolidate seven smaller parcels.[54] Although the Slover and Oleander warehouse and logistics operations could generate up to 200 jobs, the property shares a border with Jurupa Hills High School and is located in one of California's most polluted areas.[55] In 2021 the Fontana City Council denied an appeal by Elizabeth Sena, a Fontana resident, mother, health-care worker, and founding member of the South Fontana Concerned Citizens Coalition. Sena argued that the poor air quality and high incidence of related health issues in Fontana are due to the surge in warehouse development in the city. More than 120 people personally supported Sena's appeal by also speaking or providing letters of support or positive virtual comments. Council member Peter Garcia, also an EPA scientist, countered that the initial environmental study of the project concluded that its impacts on nearby residents and students attending Jurupa Hills High School would not be significant. Mayor Warren and council members John Roberts and Phillip Cothran joined Garcia in denying the appeal. They were supported by members of the Laborers' International Union of North America (LiUNA) 783, which represents construction workers and favored the project because it would create jobs for its members.[56]

In contrast to many other efforts by communities to oppose warehouse developments, this case continued. In July 2021 California attorney general Rob Bonta filed a lawsuit against the City of Fontana, challenging its approval of the project. According to Bonta, CEQA requires the city to implement mitigation measures to reduce air pollution and other harmful impacts that may be associated with warehousing and other logistics operations on the site. Bonta explained: "Plain and simple: Everyone has the right to breathe clean air where they live and where they work. . . . Fontana residents shouldn't have to choose between economic development and clean air. They deserve both."[57]

Piggybacking on the state's initiative, the Sierra Club filed its own law-suit, claiming that the city had failed to conduct the environmental impact analysis CEQA requires.[58] The city and Bonta reached a legally and ethically "innovative" settlement in April 2022 that resolved both cases. The settlement requires Fontana "to adopt the most stringent warehouse ordinance in the state," and the developer, Duke Realty, "to implement new measures to mitigate the Slover and Oleander warehouse project's environmental impacts on the surrounding community."[59]

This settlement arguably establishes new standards for future warehouse developments. Fontana City Council approved a municipal code amendment to include the "Industrial Commerce Centers Sustainability Standards Ordinance," which meets and exceeds all state and federal environmental standards for warehouse and freight operations. The new ordinance covers site designs to divert trucks away from schools and hospitals, promote zero-emission vehicles, increase green space with landscape buffers, and require renewable energy and green building materials. It also includes provisions to promote economic development and protect the health and safety of truckers and construction and warehouse workers.[60] In addition to these new commitments by the city, which will apply to the Slover and Oleander project and *all* future warehouse developments, Duke Realty must implement mitigation measures during and after construction to minimize the impacts of the project on the surrounding community and commit $210,000 to a community benefits fund. From this fund, $160,000 will be earmarked to purchase five years' worth of top-rated air filters for up to 1,750 households located nearest the development. The remaining $50,000 will be used to enhance landscaping buffers along the property line between the warehouse property and the Jurupa Hills High School campus.[61]

Meanwhile, just days before Bonta filed his lawsuit concerning the Slover and Oleander development, the Planning Commission endorsed construction of a 92,433-square-foot warehouse by 9th Street Partners at Valley Boulevard and Catawba Avenue. While the City of Fontana considers the warehouse to be an "in-fill development," which could make it exempt from CEQA, community activists claim that at the least an initial environmental study is still necessary. In 2021 the City Council denied resident Janet Meza's appeal, which underscores the proposed project's proximity to a residential area, where she and her family live, and Poplar Elementary School. The South Fontana Concerned Citizens Coalition and CCAEJ both supported Meza's appeal; still, the council was swayed by countervailing support for the project by LiUNA members and students, who sought potential jobs associated with the development.[62]

Resisting Amazon, Moreno Valley's World Logistics Center

EJ activists have also publicly opposed Amazon's overwhelming presence in the region, which renders it complicit in decimating Inland Southern California neighborhoods as well as harming the physical and emotional health of the region's residents. According to a report by the PC4EJ in collaboration with researchers from the University of Redlands, the simple presence of more warehouses in Inland Southern California has increased the number of tractor-trailers rolling in and out of the predominantly low-income communities of color where warehousing, transportation, and delivery facilities are located. That is, warehouses are "indirect sources" of the polluting emissions that impact the region's lower-income communities of color that have been most affected by asthma, bronchitis, and other respiratory health issues as well as a number of cancers.[63] The situation has become so perilous that even Amazon employees are sounding the alarm. Emily Cunningham, a founding member of Amazon Employees for Climate Justice, told NBC News that families in the region "are being treated like sacrifices. . . . It's as if their lives don't matter as much, and that's wrong."[64]

Cunningham's assessment is eerily similar to Inland Southern California EJ organizer Anthony Victoria's claim that "our communities of color have become the sacrifice for one of the biggest, wealthiest companies in the world."[65] While Amazon is not, of course, the only e-commerce or warehousing company in Inland Southern California, it is the most prominent. In fact, the region is recognized for having the third largest concentration of Amazon warehouses in the United States.[66] Amazon's warehousing and delivery facilities in Inland Southern California occupy a total of more than fifteen million square feet, or nearly half the size of the proposed World Logistics Center (WLC), a massive complex approved for development by the Moreno Valley City Council in 2015 despite concerted community opposition to it.[67]

Until very recently, construction of the WLC was delayed by court proceedings associated with the environmental impacts of 68,712 daily motor
vehicle trips that analysts expect it to generate, nearly a quarter of which
will be made by diesel-fueled trucks.[68] A coalition of environmental and
social justice groups represented by Earthjustice sued the City of Moreno
Valley three times for its failure to comply with CEQA, demanding a detailed and accurate analysis of the WLC's environmental impacts. In April
2021 Earthjustice reached a $47 million settlement with WLC's devel-
oper, Iddo Benzeevi, which effectively recognizes that the WLC will be
an indirect source of the air pollution that threatens the health of nearby
residents and the region as a whole. The settlement requires Benzeevi to
invest in electric vehicles (EVs) and EV charging stations; electrification
of trucks, forklifts, and other logistics equipment; rooftop solar sufficient
to power 50 percent of each warehouse's demand; air filtration, noise
mitigation, and other physical solutions to impacted residences located
nearest the complex; and provision of $4 million to protect wildlife in the
San Jacinto Wildlife Area.[69] This landmark settlement ups the ante with
respect to what communities can demand from Amazon and other warehousing, transportation, and distribution companies in the future.

Regulating Indirect Sources in Southern California

In hindsight, the WLC settlement signaled the future direction of goods
movement, which emphasizes the transport and storage elements of logistics, by showing "what can and must be done to reduce the adverse
health and air pollution impacts" of warehouses.[70] Indeed, the SCAQMD
adopted Rule 2305, which is expected to reduce nitrogen oxides (NO_x)
and PM produced mainly by diesel trucks and tractor-trailers traveling
to and from warehouses by regulating the owners and operators of *warehouse facilities*, which are regarded to be indirect sources of NO_x and PM
emissions.[71] Rule 2305 implements SCAQMD's Warehouse Actions and
Investments to Reduce Emissions (WAIRE) Program, which applies to
owners and operators of the approximately 3,000 existing and new large
warehouses (100,000 square feet or more) who conduct warehousing activities in at least 50,000 of those square feet and are located in the South
Coast Air Basin, which includes most of LA and Orange Counties and

Riverside and San Bernardino Counties. Warehouse owners and operators earn WAIRE points by implementing emissions-reducing activities—
specifically, investing in zero emissions and net zero emissions vehicles
and supporting technologies—or paying fines to offset the number of truck
trips associated with their facilities. The rule notably applies to every one
of Amazon's FCs in Inland Southern California.

    This achievement reflects years of activism and calls for greater air qual-
ity regulation, which has helped to bring attention to the environmental and
spatial justice implications of warehousing, distribution, and transportation.
The entire South Coast Air Basin experiences some of the nation's worst air
quality, largely (75 percent) due to stationary sources and related activities,
including warehouses and goods movement.[72] Because most warehouses
are located in less affluent, and often also more socially diverse, locations far
from the richer consumers who purchase the goods stored and processed in
them, those who suffer the most negative health impacts from diesel truck,
tractor-trailer, and rail traffic typically gain least from e-commerce. Consequently, community and EJ organizations throughout the South Coast
Air Basin have lobbied the SCAQMD to regulate "warehouse" emissions for
decades. In Inland Southern California, these organizations have included
CCAEJ, the Sierra Club My Generation Campaign, Partnership for Working
Families, and more recently, PC4EJ. In fact, in 2014 CCAEJ was arguably
the first Southland organization to articulate the idea of demanding that
local air quality regulators use the federal Clean Air Act's "indirect source
review" provisions, though their initial focus was railyards.[73]

    Regulatory activity related to controlling the indirect sources of emis-
sions from warehousing and goods movement began with discussions
among California state elected officials and SCAQMD Governing Board
members in 2007.[74] The 2008 Sustainable Communities & Climate Protection Act (SB 375) provided a partial response to the problem by requiring regional transportation plans and transit projects to be consistent
with the sustainable communities or other strategies for reducing green-
house gas emissions adopted by metropolitan planning organizations
(MPOs).[75] Had it been adopted, SCAQMD's Proposed Rule 2301 (2009)
for controlling emissions from new or redevelopment projects would have
included warehouses; however, forward movement on the current indirect
source regulation began with the SCAQMD Governing Board's adoption

of the district's 2016 Air Quality Management Plan, which included five facility-based mobile source measures (FBMSM) covering warehouses and DCs, commercial airports, new or redevelopment projects, commercial marine ports, and railyard and intermodal facilities. The process for developing and implementing these voluntary and regulatory measures included extensive public input.

In the case of Rule 2305 pursuant to FBMSM for warehouses and DCs, input included statements from numerous Southland community organizations as well as from warehousing, transportation, and other regulated companies and other stakeholders, such as real estate brokerages. While most activists were strongly in favor of Rule 2305, some criticized the financial incentives to be funded by taxpayers, including residents of communities that are heavily impacted by air pollution from truck and train transport. To the extent that the costs of regulation cannot be passed along to consumers via higher prices for goods, warehousing and distribution businesses opposed the anticipated expenses and related reporting associated with Rule 2305.[76]

These divisions shaped the legal battle that emerged within weeks of the rule's adoption. Specifically, the California Trucking Association sued SCAQMD; then Airlines for America and the state of California, on behalf of the California Air Resources Board (CARB), filed motions to intervene as plaintiff and defendant, respectively.[77] The outcome of such challenges to the new rule will contribute to existing precedent established in 2005 by San Joaquin Valley Air Pollution Control District's (APCD's) Indirect Source Review rule (Rule 9510), which focuses on construction and development projects.[78] The suit did not impede the beginning of the compliance period for Rule 2305 on January 1, 2022.

MOBILIZING WORKERS AND IMPROVING LABOR PRACTICES

Another stream of regional resistance to Amazon and the warehouse industry emerged from labor activists, who viewed the rapid expansion of nonunionized warehouses as a threat to workers' rights and labor standards in the logistics industry. Along with the WWRC, regional, national, and international unions sought to improve labor practices in the warehouse industry and to recruit new members, expand their presence in the region, and block the growth of Amazon, a corporation publicly opposed to unionization efforts and whose growth threatened to displace unionized workers in logistics and the grocery industry. As early as the late nineteenth century workers in Inland Southern California had formed unions.[79] Early labor activists sometimes engaged in militant actions, such as the 1917 and 1919 packinghouse and orange pickers' strikes.[80] Efforts to unionize warehouse workers in the region and to strengthen their organizing capacity through ongoing membership drives and merging preexisting union locals are fairly recent, occurring mostly after 1970 as the industry expanded. Today, unionized warehouse workers in Inland Southern California are most often represented by the International Brotherhood of Teamsters Local 63, which represents workers in Central and Southern California as well as Arizona and Nevada. This local, initially based in Los Angeles and formed in 1975, expanded and gained a presence in Inland Southern California in part through the merger of several smaller Teamsters locals that represented warehouse workers and truck drivers as well as workers employed in agriculture, groceries, and other industries.[81] Local 63 has won some impressive union contracts for warehouse workers, including those employed by United Parcel Service and various food suppliers providing groceries; these union contracts provide members with living wages, seniority pay, and access to good pensions, health insurance, and paid vacations.[82]

Union organizing failed to keep pace with the rapid growth of warehousing in the region, however, and changes in the industry, especially increased reliance on third-party logistics (3PL), temporary employment agencies, and seasonal workers presented new challenges for union organizing. Big box retailers increasingly used warehousing and 3PL companies—which handle inventory management, warehousing, and fulfillment services— some of which proved to be irresponsible "fly-by-night" operations that generated complex and shifting subcontracting arrangements that were difficult for workers and activists to identify and navigate. These arrangements also created separations in legal responsibility between those who directly employed warehouse workers and the retail companies that benefited from their labor and set the terms of their employment contracts, making it difficult to pressure powerful retail companies to improve their working conditions. Warehouse employers, in turn, increasingly relied on temporary employment agencies, which presented both legal and practical challenges for traditional union organizing strategies. As elsewhere in the nation, union failures to invest more resources in organizing new workers in the region, and to embrace nontraditional organizing strategies, were obstacles to organizing warehouse workers. As a result, much of the rapidly expanding warehouse industry that prevailed in the early 2000s was not unionized.[83]

Renewed efforts to organize warehouse workers emerged through Change to Win's (CTW's) Warehouse Workers United (WWU) campaign, which became public in 2008. The CTW labor federation, later renamed the Strategic Organizing Center (SOC), was initially formed in 2005 by seven unions that broke away from the American Federation of Labor and Congress of Industrial Organizations (AFL-CIO) in an effort to revitalize and grow the labor movement through an emphasis on organizing, recruiting, and mobilizing workers, especially those at workplaces that are not yet unionized.[84] Initially, the WWU campaign focused on organizing temporary warehouse workers, many of whom were immigrant Latino workers. Given the vulnerability of low-wage, temporary, and immigrant workers, and adopting an industry-wide strategy, organizing took place mainly in the community rather than at workplaces. Like subsequent worker organizing efforts, worker organizing engaged, and was sometimes led by, formerly as well as currently employed warehouse workers; this approach was adopted in response to many warehouse workers' status as temporary workers, high rates of worker turnover and unemployment in the industry, and widespread employer retaliation against worker activists.[85]

Through a series of well-publicized and conspicuous public protests, warehouse workers and their allies, including labor, environmental, faith-based, student, and other community activists, brought public and media attention to the terrible working conditions and low pay endured by temporary warehouse workers and the need for national labor law reforms. Protests in WWU's early years initially targeted temporary employment agencies and 3PL companies, as well as warehouse employers. These protests included noisy pickets outside warehouses, unfurling banners across buildings, and even civil disobedience at times. Perhaps the most dramatic of these protests occurred in Mira Loma, California, in May 2009. Ten protesters stopped traffic by handcuffing themselves to a forklift in the middle of a major intersection that was commonly used by trucks coming and going from a major warehouse hub. Hundreds of workers and community supporters rallied around the courageous protesters, who were eventually arrested for the action.[86]

These protest actions helped to expand and solidify community support for warehouse workers and brought considerable media and political attention to the need for national labor law reform and other initiatives to improve labor conditions in the warehouse industry. Yet because the WWU campaign failed to organize warehouse workers into a union, the Teamsters and CTW reduced their funding for WWU in 2010 and eventually withdrew funds from the campaign entirely in 2013. In part, this outcome reflected the serious challenges of organizing workers in this sector, especially in the context of weak US labor laws, strong employer hostility to unions, and the rising use of subcontracted and temporary work arrangements. Yet it also reflected internal union politics, including shifts within the CTW federation and its leadership, and the lack of strong support for long-term investments in worker organizing and nontraditional models of organizing.[87]

Although this loss of funding immediately reduced WWU staffing and slowed efforts to organize warehouse workers, the few remaining WWU staff members eventually forged alternative organizing partnerships and expanded WWRC with funding from grants and donations. Formed in 2011, WWRC is a nonprofit workers' center for warehouse workers, which provides legal assistance, education, health care, and other services for warehouse workers. Initially an offshoot of WWU that carried out a few projects, WWRC eventually became the main advocacy organization for warehouse workers in the region.

The Making Change at Walmart Campaign

In 2010 WWRC shifted its strategy by targeting Walmart, a major corporation with significant power and influence in the warehouse industry, and joining a new transnational campaign, Making Change at Walmart (MCAW). The United Food and Commercial Workers Union (UFCW, an international union that represents about 1.3 million workers, including grocery, food processing, health care, meat packing, and retail workers) created the MCAW campaign in 2010, in collaboration with UniGlobal, a global union representing workers from over 150 countries, the CTW union federation, the Teamsters, and other labor unions and organizations. These organizations represented, or sought to organize, workers employed by Walmart or by companies and temporary agencies that were part of the corporation's transnational supply chain, which produced, stored, assembled, or transported its products. The UFCW, which also sought to unionize Walmart's retail employees, provided most of the funding for the MCAW campaign and usually dominated decision-making. In addition to WWRC, the MCAW campaign included Warehouse Workers for Justice in Chicago and New Labor in New Jersey, both of which were also organizing warehouse workers.[88]

The MCAW campaign increased media attention and political support for warehouse workers in Inland Southern California. Many of the warehouse workers who stored and handled Walmart products were temporary, subcontracted, and immigrant workers who often faced labor law violations, including unsafe working conditions, insufficient work breaks, and wage theft. Combining direct action, negative publicity, and legal complaints, WWRC and its allies pressured Walmart, its contractors, and their temporary agencies to improve labor conditions in the warehouses that served Walmart.

Given the challenges of making gains locally in a Republican-dominated region, WWRC focused instead on appealing to state policy makers, working in collaboration with lawyers, unions, and other labor experts and advocacy organizations. WWRC appealed to state regulatory agencies to better enforce labor laws and to California legislators to develop new protective legislation. With assistance from WWRC and its allies, warehouse workers filed a series of successful complaints about labor law violations, putting legal pressure on Walmart, its contractors, and temporary agencies to improve their labor practices. Warehouse workers won a series of favorable rulings from both the California Labor Commission and Cal/OSHA in response to their complaints about labor law violations, including violations in wage and hour and health and safety laws.

Warehouse workers won legal settlements too, including a $4.7 million legal settlement from Schneider Logistics, a Walmart contractor, in 2013.

The case involved 568 workers employed by a DC in Mira Loma who were not fully paid for their work, including unpaid overtime, and were denied required work breaks. Another lawsuit charged a subsidiary of Schneider Logistics for similar kinds of wage and hour violations and for employer retaliation for their complaints; this case ended with a $21 million legal settlement in 2014 before a formal ruling was made. Significantly, Walmart was named as a codefendant in this case, suggesting that retailers could potentially be held liable for the practices of their contractors.[89] Along with collective action, successful legal complaints put media pressure on Walmart and its contracted warehouses to improve working conditions and employment security for thousands of warehouse workers in the region.

Another legal case, focusing on the dangers of working in extreme heat, increased political support for a new state law to better protect workers from indoor heat. After working inside a metal freight container at 110 degrees, Domingo Blancas had heat stroke and was hospitalized for three days in 2011. Blancas and his coworkers filed a legal complaint about the unsafe working conditions they faced; the complaint named a warehouse operator (National Distribution Center) as well as its temporary staffing agency (Tri-State Staffing), which served Walmart and other big box retailers. Four years later, Cal/OSHA ruled in favor of the workers, setting a legal precedent for multiemployer responsibility for protecting workers from illness, if health hazards are known. Cal/OSHA's ruling, and the media publicity surrounding this case, helped to gain support among legislators for passage of a new state law in 2016, which required Cal/OSHA to propose new regulations by 2019 to better protect indoor workers from heat-related illnesses and injuries, the first legislation of its kind in the nation. Subsequently, WWRC and its members provided input on the development of new statewide regulations that aim to prevent heat illness among indoor workers.[90]

In conjunction with these legal cases and related workers' grievances, warehouse workers and their supporters carried out dramatic protests, including rallies, civil disobedience, unfair labor practice (ULP) strikes; circulated petitions; and held press conferences. Like the legal complaints, these actions usually targeted Walmart-contracted warehouse operators and temporary agencies. Such actions brought additional media attention to unjust treatment of warehouse workers and sometimes protected workers against employer retaliation. This activism also demonstrated that warehouse workers had gained broad community support, including support from unions, students, faith-based organizations, immigrant rights, and other community groups. Meanwhile, a series of reports documented bad labor conditions in the industry, including low wages, insecure employment, lack of benefits, and unsafe working conditions. In these ways, WWRC and its supporters put increased public and media pressure on warehouse operators to improve their labor practices.

The most dramatic action in this campaign was the 2012 "Walmarch," a fifty-mile, public march by warehouse workers and community supporters that began at WWRC's office in Ontario and ended at Los Angeles City Hall. Participants marched and rallied in various cities along the way. Meanwhile, warehouse workers engaged in a ULP strike that lasted fifteen days. Workers involved were employed at two Walmart contractors, Swift Transportation and Warestaff, a temporary agency.[91] Walmarch participants publicized workers' concerns, which helped to gain greater support for state legislation to improve regulation of the warehouse industry. By the end of the march, Governor Jerry Brown agreed to sign a bill into law requiring firms and temporary agencies to guarantee that they had sufficient funds for workers' wages and to comply with existing labor laws.

During the MCAW campaign, eight major Walmart warehouses in the region agreed to hire thousands of workers, previously employed by temporary agencies, as direct employees. This change helped workers to gain greater employment security, living wages, and employment benefits. Yet the campaign failed to unionize warehouse workers, prompting UFCW leaders to withdraw funding from this warehouse worker organizing campaign as well as union organizing drives among Walmart associates. Much like the earlier decision by CTW and the Teamsters to disinvest from organizing warehouse workers in the region, the withdrawal of UFCW support for this campaign reflected both the serious challenges associated with organizing within this sector in the contemporary United States and internal union politics and shifts in union leadership, which limited the support for long-term and deep investments in worker organizing and union membership engagement.[92] Arguably, these latter factors contributed to limits on the MCAW campaign itself, including organizers' heavy reliance on low-participation tactics, such as media and online campaigns, and the failure to build a strong base of support for this campaign among UFCW members and leaders.[93]

Despite this setback, WWRC staff continued to engage with warehouse workers in the broader Southern California region with the financial support of grants and donations. For several years they collaborated with the Teamsters on a campaign targeting California Cartage, a prominent warehousing and storage corporation, that eventually resulted in the unionization of warehouse workers employed in a facility located at the Port of Long Beach-Los Angeles. In 2019 WWRC returned its attention to Inland Southern California, this time with a new target: Amazon.[94]

The Amazon Campaign

By 2018 Amazon had become the region's largest private-sector employer.[95] Targeting Amazon was important not only because it employed tens of thousands of warehouse workers but also because other employers viewed Amazon as a trendsetter. Amazon's growth, which increasingly relied on nonunion, third-party delivery service providers in addition to building up its own transportation and delivery services, also threatened the jobs of truckers and other delivery drivers, many of whom were unionized through the Teamsters. In response, the Teamsters began to mobilize their rank-and-file members, workers, and the community to oppose the expansion of Amazon and to support efforts to organize Amazon warehouse workers as early as 2016 in Inland Southern California and various other US regions; these early campaigns targeting Amazon, including those described later in this chapter, sowed the seeds for even broader efforts by the Teamsters to confront Amazon (described more fully in chapter 8).[96]

To challenge Amazon's expansion in Inland Southern California and advocate on behalf of Amazon's rapidly growing warehouse workforce, WWRC and the Teamsters formed regional, statewide, national, and transnational partnerships. Regionally, WWRC and the Teamsters joined together with EJ organizations and other community organizations to advocate for local moratoria on warehouse developments, as well as more community benefits, improved environmental protection, and greater regulatory oversight of approved warehousing and logistics projects. WWRC and the Teamsters also benefited from statewide coalitions, including the California Federation of Labor. Both nationally and internationally, Teamsters' international and national leaders and staff coordinated their resistance to Amazon. Meanwhile, WWRC helped to build the Athena coalition in 2019. Athena is a national alliance of nearly fifty labor and community organizations that have united to challenge Amazon's rising influence in communities. It includes other worker centers besides WWRC, such as the Awood Center in Minnesota and Warehouse Workers for Justice in Illinois, focused on Amazon warehouse workers. Other partner organizations focus on EJ, local democracy, immigrant rights, racial justice, and opposing Amazon's monopoly practices that negatively affect small businesses.

While giving its partner organizations considerable autonomy, Athena affiliates share some resources and coordinate days of action nationally. In 2019 WWRC engaged in three nationally coordinated days of action with other organizations in the Athena coalition. For example, on Cyber Monday WWRC and its regional allies, including EJ organizations and the Teamsters, organized a protest outside an Amazon warehouse that called for a CBA for "good jobs and clean air" as part of a larger campaign targeting a proposed air cargo facility at the San Bernardino International Airport (discussed more fully later). The Teamsters, WWRC, and immigrant rights, EJ, and other activists in the region also held a demonstration on "Prime Day" to protest Amazon's role in providing technology to the US Immigration and Customs Enforcement (ICE).[97] WWRC, CCAEJ, and other regional allies also participated in the Global Climate Strike with a march and rally involving close to one hundred community activists and residents, including many Latino high school students. Speakers at the rally publicly criticized local politicians for approving warehousing and logistics developments, such as new Amazon facilities, with little regard for the negative impacts on air pollution, climate change, and residents' health.

During the COVID-19 pandemic, Amazon warehouses expanded rapidly, and the corporation's growing workforce risked exposure to COVID-19 along with other safety issues, such as injuries. More than half of the Amazon facilities operating in Inland Southern California in 2022 had opened since 2020; Amazon hired nearly 4,000 people in the region during 2020, contributing to an increase of 36,500 warehouse and transportation workers between the beginning of the pandemic and the end of 2021.[98] In response to Amazon warehouse workers' health and safety concerns, WWRC filed health and safety complaints with Cal/OSHA and several county departments of public health. The complaints were filed on behalf of Amazon warehouse workers employed in facilities located in Hawthorne (Los Angeles County) and Eastvale (Riverside County). Among other concerns, the complaint letters documented the failure to shut down and properly sanitize facilities where there was a confirmed case of COVID-19 and to provide several weeks of paid leave for workers who might have been exposed to the virus. The Eastvale complaint letter, filed in April 2020, was a petition signed by over 500 Amazon employees demanding that Eastvale managers improve their efforts to prevent the spread of COVID-19 among workers (see figure 7.2).[99] To further publicize the concerns of Amazon warehouse workers and other frontline retail and ecommerce workers, WWRC members and supporters engaged in a car caravan action outside of Amazon's delivery station in the California South Bay city of Hawthorne, the same day that they filed the Hawthorne warehouse workers' legal complaints. This action was part of a national day of protest in 2020 that included walkouts by workers and consumer boycotts that targeted Amazon and Whole Foods (owned by Amazon) as well as Shipt, Instacart, and Target.[100] Later that year, WWRC affiliates and their allies engaged in a candlelight vigil and rally during Prime Day outside of Bezos's mansion in Beverly Hills to protest ongoing health and safety problems and low pay at Amazon warehouses. The event also helped to publicize Cal/OSHA's citations of Amazon for failing to adequately train and protect warehouse workers from COVID-19. Former Amazon warehouse workers, along with other activists, spoke at the event.[101]

Also in 2020, Amazon warehouse workers and labor activists formed a new grassroots organization called IE Amazonians Unite. Concerned about workers' exposure to COVID-19, Amazon warehouse workers tracked and disseminated information about positive COVID-19 cases among Amazon warehouses in the region through the IE Amazonians Unite Facebook page. They also conducted an online survey of 373 Amazon warehouse workers in the region about their health and safety concerns. The survey results revealed that most respondents did not think Amazon was doing enough to keep workers safe and had concerns about their inability to wash hands and maintain social distance due to working conditions and their inability to self-isolate due to the need for a

Figure 7.2. Semi-truck traffic at automated Amazon FC, Eastvale, CA. Photo by Parker Allison.

paycheck. Nearly half of survey respondents observed insufficient supplies of hand sanitizers and masks.[102]

While efforts to organize Amazon warehouse workers in the region, including worker-led efforts, emerged and spread during the COVID-19 pandemic, WWRC, the Teamsters, and their allies in the state and regional labor movement successfully pursued the passage of a new state law to regulate work pace, which previous chapters noted contributes to high levels of stress, turnover, and risk of injuries among warehouse workers, especially those at Amazon facilities. Since 2019, WWRC, the Teamsters, and their allies have documented the need for this legislation through research reports and testimonies by warehouse workers and experts during public hearings and rallies.[103] Former Amazon warehouse workers even disrupted a conference in Inland Southern California, where an Amazon official was speaking about workplace health and safety and technology, to bring attention to their safety concerns.[104] State Assembly member Lorena Gonzalez, who represents southern San Diego, responded to warehouse workers' complaints about dangerous working conditions by introducing AB 701, which was signed into law in September 2021 (see figures 7.3 and 7.4). AB 701 protects warehouse workers

Figure 7.3. Press conference and rally to support AB 701 (the Warehouse Quotas law), September 7, 2021, San Bernardino, CA. Left to right: Atlas Pyke, Bennie Tinson (WWRC), and Arun Ramakrishna. Photo by Ellen Reese.

Figure 7.4. Public march to support AB 701 (the Warehouse Quotas law), September 7, 2021, San Bernardino, CA. Donavan Caver, community and labor activist and WWRC board member. Photo by Ellen Reese.

from work rates and standards that "prevent compliance with meal or rest periods, use of bathroom facilities, including reasonable travel time to and from bathroom facilities, or occupational health and safety laws."[105] The law also requires employers to provide information about required work rates and protects the rights of workers to ask questions about or complain about work rates that contribute to violations in state or federal labor laws, including workplace health and safety laws. Finally, the law requires the California labor commissioner to collaborate with other stakeholders to educate workers and employers about AB 701 and to be notified when warehouse employers have an injury rate 1.5 times the average rate for the warehouse industry as a whole, which was true of Amazon at the time this law was passed.[106]

Building Regional Alliances for a More Sustainable Economy

The growth of warehousing and Amazon's proliferation in the region have provided opportunities for intentional, strategic collaborations among community organizations responding to the socioeconomic, environmental, labor, and broader political and structural impacts of Amazon's dominance among warehousing, transportation, and distribution services. The most recent of these joint campaigns focused on opposing the proposed project to expand the Eastgate Air Cargo Logistics Center at the San Bernardino International Airport (see figure 7.5). Collaborating organizations called upon local policy makers and the developer to adopt a legally enforceable CBA for the project to ensure that it would create jobs with good pay and benefits and protect surrounding communities from traffic congestion and air and noise pollution.[107]

Collaborations among labor and EJ activists, in particular, were forged slowly at first, given the need to build good working relationships and overcome distrust stemming from differences in their organizational missions. Whereas EJ activists often seek to curb economic development projects to protect the environment, labor activists typically seek to expand and improve job opportunities for workers, sometimes in ways that negatively affect the environment.[108] Beginning in 2008, staff and members of WWU/WWRC, CCAEJ, the Teamsters, and other activist organizations, including those focused on immigrant rights and racial justice,

Figure 7.5. Amazon Prime semi-truck at regional air hub at San Bernardino International Airport. Photo by Parker Allison.

participated in deep discussions over their concerns about and hopes for the regional economy. These dialogues contributed to building trust and a *common* vision for the region. Initially, the staff of these organizations practiced collaborating through small projects, such as public events and "toxic tours" to educate their members and the public about the region's logistics industry. Along with other organizations, they also organized "know your rights" workshops for immigrants.[109] Through such small steps, working relationships between members of WWU/WWRC; CCAEJ; the Teamsters; and other environmental, labor, and social justice organizations grew and deepened into more transformative partnerships and joint projects that often involved other local organizations. Some of these projects focused on civic participation initiatives that sought to shift the local balance of political power in the region, establish Jurupa Valley as a city, and strengthen immigrant rights; more recently, a joint campaign has sought to establish a CBA for "Eastgate," referring to Amazon's air cargo facility at San Bernardino International Airport.

The Eastgate Air Cargo Logistics Center is a warehousing and distribution facility, about 700,000 square feet, adjacent to the San Bernardino International Airport. The Eastgate project, approved in 2019, entails a thirty-five-year lease between the developer—Hillwood Enterprises—and its tenant, later disclosed to be Amazon.[110] Those promoting this project promised it would create as many as 4,000 new jobs, in exchange for at least twenty-six additional flights daily—and considerable airport-related traffic, air pollution, and noise.[111] According to the American Lung Association's 2021 report, among US counties, San Bernardino County has the worst ozone levels in the nation and the sixth highest level of year-round particle pollution, which is related to the logistics industry, especially the many diesel trucks, trains, air freight, and delivery vehicles it brings into and out of the region.[112] Environmental, labor, and other community activists were concerned that the project would further expose local residents, especially children and the elderly, to air pollution and related health problems such as lung disease and asthma by adding up to 500 truck trips to overcrowded freeways and streets, increasing the number of early morning and night time flights and making it difficult for local residents to sleep. In addition, the current plan lacked any labor standards to ensure that the warehouse jobs created would be well-paid, safe jobs, with benefits. Activists feared the project would simply create more low-paying, "dead end" jobs at yet another Amazon warehouse facility.[113]

To oppose the project plan, various community organizations formed the SBAC coalition in 2019. Along with interested community members, the SBAC includes labor organizations (Teamsters Local 1932, Service Employees International Union Local 2015, the Inland Empire Central Labor Council, and Warehouse Workers Resource Center), EJ organizations (including the Sierra Club My Gen Campaign, CCAEJ, and later PC4EJ), the Inland Congregations United for Change (ICUC, a faith-based organization affiliated with PICO), and Inland Coalition for Immigrant Justice (ICIJ). Many members of ICUC and ICIJ are people of color, who are disproportionately employed in or living near warehouses in the region.[114]

In response to the proposed Eastgate plan, SBAC and its supporters demanded the establishment of a legally binding CBA, or a contract between SBAC, the San Bernardino International Airport Authority, and

Hillwood Enterprises. The purpose of the CBA was to ensure mitigation of harm to nearby residents and businesses and benefits for the project for the community, especially those living nearest Eastgate as well as in San Bernardino County more generally. Specifically, the group demanded that the following measures be included in a CBA for this project. First, they sought measures to reduce air pollution associated with Eastgate, including requirements that Hillwood use zero-emissions technology, monitor air quality, and distribute air filters to residents living nearest the center and airport to protect their health. They also insisted that the developer and its tenant (Amazon) provide funding for soundproofing to mitigate noise pollution and for maintaining local roads affected by the increased traffic congestion created by the project. Finally, they demanded that the tenant (Amazon) provide living wages, benefits, and employment security to its employees and agree to limit the hiring of temporary workers, create job training funds, and hire local residents.[115] SBAC's demands grew out of a shared regional vision that included "clean air and good jobs" and greater community voice and influence on economic development policies in San Bernardino. This vision and SBAC's specific demands drew on a series of discussions among its member organizations and local residents about the interconnections between racial, immigrant, environmental, and economic justice.

As part of the process of developing and communicating their common vision for the region and specific demands, SBAC engaged in community outreach, visiting residents at their homes in the areas surrounding the airport in 2019. They also attended community meetings and other gatherings to listen to residents' concerns and encourage them to attend a community workshop to learn more about and discuss the Eastgate proposal. About seventy people, including former and current Amazon warehouse workers and local residents, attended SBAC's first community workshop, where pledge cards to act were collected. Although racially diverse, most attendees, like the residents of the San Bernardino community, were working-class Latinos; a small majority were women, and simultaneous Spanish translation was provided to ensure equitable opportunities for participation. During the workshop, SBAC emphasized the importance of community solidarity around a shared agenda for both EJ and good jobs, rather than viewing these as contradictory goals.

Two months later, hundreds of people, mostly affiliated with SBAC, attended a public hearing to discuss the Eastgate project. By then SBAC had collected about 600 pledge cards from community members interested in the issue. Community residents and warehouse workers expressed their concerns about the Eastgate project proposal. Speakers demanded a comprehensive environmental impact report before the project was approved, along with the development of a CBA for the project. Community speakers explained how the proposed project would disproportionately harm Black and Latino residents, increase traffic congestion, and add more air pollution to the area, and that it did not guarantee local residents would be hired to work at the facility or be offered competitive wages and benefits. Some community members did express support for the proposed project, including members of LiUNA, who viewed the proposed air cargo facility as a way to generate construction jobs for their members.[116]

Despite heated community opposition to the Eastgate project and demands for a more accurate and comprehensive environmental impact report for it, the Federal Aviation Administration as well as the San Bernardino International Airport Authority approved the plan in December 2019. Hillwood Enterprises was granted a thirty-five-year lease for the project with up to fourteen years of extensions on that lease.[117] In opposition to this decision, hundreds of community residents participated in a series of protests and rallies organized by SBAC. One of these protests, held outside an Amazon warehouse, occurred on Cyber Monday. Another protest occurred inside Hillwood Enterprise's office. In addition, CCAEJ, the Sierra Club, and Teamsters Local 1932 (three member organizations of SBAC) filed a legal complaint, and the state filed a second legal complaint against the approval of the project; these complaints claimed that the approved project violated the National Environmental Protection Act (NEPA).[118] The Ninth Circuit Court of Appeals ruled against these complaints, but a dissenting judge disagreed, claiming that "this case wreaks of environmental racism."[119] Both the plaintiffs and the California attorney general responded to the decision by filing for a rehearing of the case, arguing that the decision violated earlier legal precedents established for NEPA.[120]

Despite the initial setbacks—a failed CBA campaign and an unfavorable court ruling upholding the legality of the Eastgate project—SBAC continued to organize workers and community residents for joint action to challenge Amazon's advance in the region and to promote a more just and environmentally sustainable economy. As part of building political support for that effort, organizations and individuals affiliated with SBAC actively supported the successful campaign and voted for Ben Reynoso, an economic organizer for ICUC and active member of SBAC, to represent the fifth ward on the San Bernardino City Council. Once in office in 2021, Reynoso advocated for a policy to create a temporary, forty-five-day moratorium on the construction of new warehouse developments in the city of San Bernardino in order to study their impacts on the city and the need for stricter standards and new regulations for warehouse developments. If adopted, the moratorium could be extended up to two years, a measure that SBAC and its member organizations, now including PC4EJ, actively supported. Between 2015 and 2021, the city approved twenty-six warehouse projects, adding 9.6 million square feet more of warehousing to the city's expansive warehouse industry. Five out of the seven San Bernardino City Council representatives voted in favor of the proposed moratorium, which left it one vote shy of the four-fifths majority required to pass.[121]

Although the City of San Bernardino did not approve a temporary moratorium on new warehouse development, many of the community and EJ activists involved in that campaign were successful in winning approval for temporary warehouse moratoria in other nearby cities, including Chino, Colton, Jurupa Valley, Pomona, Perris, Norco, Redlands, Riverside, and San Bernardino.[122] Undeterred, SBAC activists and their allies have continued to engage in public outreach and present their demands to politicians in San Bernardino. For example, SBAC activists appeared before San Bernardino City Council members at their December 2021 meeting; many held signs calling for "clean air and good jobs." Cheered on by the group, various members, including local residents and representatives of Teamsters Local 1932, WWRC, and PC4EJ, made public comments to support a city-wide moratorium on warehouse developments and a comprehensive environmental assessment and CBA for the Eastgate project. Speakers also vowed to support the election of new political leaders if those currently in office continued to block their demands.[123] These and other community and labor activists have also formed new coalitions, participated in discussions of San Bernardino's new General Plan, gained support for a CBA for the redevelopment of the Carousel Mall, mobilized voters, and worked with local residents to develop and put into motion a "people's plan" to transform the local economy.[124]

These community-labor alliances in San Bernardino helped to provide strong community support for Amazon workers at the Eastgate air cargo facility when more than 150 of them, affiliated with an independent worker-led organization, the Inland Empire Amazon Workers United, engaged in a walkout on August 15, 2022. The workers demanded a $5 an hour raise, pointing out that their current wages, which ranged from $17 to $19.25 per hour at that facility, were insufficient given the rising cost of living. They also demanded an end to employment retaliation against worker organizing by Amazon and improvements in workplace health and safety policies related to heat. Workers loading and unloading cargo from airplanes outdoors often did so in temperatures above 100 degrees in summer months, putting them at risk of heat illness.[125]

After walking off the job, workers joined community supporters for a lively rally at a neighborhood church in San Bernardino. Community activists, including members and affiliates of SBAC, PC4EJ, WWRC, and various local unions, including several Teamsters locals, cheered on the Amazon worker activists as they entered the church. Inside, worker activists described their walkout and organizing efforts. Community activists offered them words of encouragement and support and drew connections between workers' action and community resistance to Amazon and warehousing. [126] Through this action, and news coverage of it, workers made public their efforts to organize at the Eastgate facility. There, workers have organized fellow workers during breaks at work and in the community since at least 2021. Initially, workers circulated and signed a petition that demanded changes to Amazon's holiday closures and scheduling that had reduced workers' income, then later focused on other concerns, such as those related to their low wages and workplace health and safety.[127]

On September 9, 2022, less than a month after the walkout by Eastgate Amazon workers, Amazon workers at ONT8 in Moreno Valley held a press conference at which they publicly announced their efforts to form a new union through Amazon Labor Union (ALU), an independent worker-led union that had won a union election earlier that year in Staten Island, New York. At this press conference, ONT8 worker activists involved in collecting ALU union authorization cards were joined by ALU's president,

Chris Smalls, as well as community and EJ activists affiliated with CCAEJ. This grassroots unionization drive is led by grassroots Amazon warehouse worker activists, such as Nannette Plascencia, who had worked at ONT8 for nearly eight years. During the pandemic, Plascencia helped to establish the United 4 Change Coalition ONT8 to help push for better wages and more workplace safety.[128] In late 2022, both this ALU unionization campaign and workplace organizing by members of the Inland Empire Amazon Workers United were still underway and continuing to assist and express and provide hope to Amazon warehouse workers' desire for better pay and working conditions and a greater voice at work, both within the region and beyond it.

MOBILIZING AND UNITING REGIONAL RESISTANCE TO THE WAREHOUSE INDUSTRY

Perhaps the most important lesson to be learned from the history of the growth of resistance to the warehouse industry in Inland Southern California is the power of grassroots organizing and coalition building to make gains in economic, social, and environmental justice. Resistance to the warehouse industry emerged from two relatively distinct streams of community-based activism. The first activist stream focused on self-governance and EJ and emerged in response to threats posed by the expansion of warehousing and logistics to the natural environment, public health, and the quality of community life. Community and EJ activists in the region, mostly white working-class women in the 1970s, became more diverse over time in terms of their gender, racial, and ethnic makeup. The other activist stream emerged from the labor movement and focused on organizing warehouse workers and their supporters in response to workplace grievances and threats to workers' rights and working conditions associated with the rapid rise of nonunion warehouse facilities in the region.

Contemporary collaboration among environmental, social justice, labor, and other community activists, including those focusing on faith-based organizing, racial justice, civic engagement, and immigrant rights, grew over time through dialogue, mutual support for one another's campaigns, and joint public education and civic engagement projects. Over time, blue-green coalitions and other regional alliances deepened and became more transformative, providing the foundation for establishing SBAC and articulating the group's demand for "clean air and good jobs." So far, activists have not yet won their main demands for a warehouse moratorium in the city of San Bernardino and a CBA for the air cargo facility at the San Bernardino airport, but they have achieved local warehouse moratoria in other cities. Perhaps most important, activists have helped to set into motion ongoing efforts to mobilize, organize, and forge deep alliances among warehouse workers, other workers, community residents, and a broad range of organizations in the region.

Most of the organized resistance to warehousing, including recent campaigns directed at Amazon, has concerned specific facilities, proposed projects, or offenses, as well as mitigating the environmental and health impacts on local residents. Yet regional activists have made impressive gains by scaling up their demands and alliances to address regional and statewide policies. For example, legal complaints by warehouse workers affiliated with WWRC yielded favorable rulings from the California Labor Commission and Cal/OSHA concerning labor law violations, sending a strong message to the warehouse industry to comply with the law. Protests and policy advocacy also led to the passage of new state laws that provide warehouse workers with new rights, including new health and safety protections related to indoor heat and work pace.[129] Similarly, Inland Southern California residents—individually as well as under the auspices of EJ organizations such as CCAEJ and PC4EJ—have contributed to significant improvements in regional environmental regulation. In response to the organizing efforts of these individuals and organizations as well as their counterparts throughout Southern California, SCAQMD adopted pathbreaking regulations in 2021 that seek to reduce hazardous emissions from indirect sources, including in particular Amazon's "megawarehouses" located throughout Riverside and San Bernardino Counties. Rule 2305 requires warehouses and other facilities that attract sources of high levels of hazardous emissions into the region to either implement measures to reduce these emissions and their local impacts or pay fees.[130]

Collectively, regional resistance to Amazon, warehousing, and the logistics industry has yielded substantive changes, including the rise of exciting new organizing campaigns by local residents and workers, the forging of cross-movement alliances among activists, and new regulatory tools and legal precedents for protecting air quality and workers' rights, all of which pave the way for future organizing and additional victories. In the next chapter we discuss the rise of popular resistance to the expansion of warehousing and Amazon beyond Inland Southern California. There we explore how regional organizing is contributing to broader waves of national and transnational organizing against Amazon by workers and communities.

8 Beyond the Box

CONFRONTING AMAZON AND THE POLITICS
OF EXPLOITATION AND INEQUALITY

The impacts of Amazon's expansion on workers, communities, and natural landscapes in Inland Southern California—one of the nation's largest logistics clusters—represent a microcosm of the far-reaching, and often complex, ways the neoliberal global political economy jeopardizes lives and livelihoods. Many of the issues Amazon and other warehouse workers in Inland Southern California, and the communities where warehouses are located, face are national, even global in scope. Increased traffic congestion, air and noise pollution, and respiratory illness and death due to breathing toxic air, along with the overall squandering of human and natural resources, are global hallmarks of the environmental impacts of the rapid, rampant growth of Amazon and warehousing.[1] Low pay, insufficient employment benefits, electronic surveillance, "algocratic management," precarious employment, lack of workplace health and safety, employment discrimination, and harassment affect not just Amazon warehouse workers but also many other types of workers around the world today.[2]

How can we respond to such threats and hold corporations, particularly Amazon, and policy makers accountable to workers and their communities? Warehouse workers and their allies have organized to form unions and other associations and have won important improvements in their jobs through collective and legal action. They have also begun to win important policy changes, including state-level restrictions on the use of quota requirements in California and New York, to better protect workplace health and safety and prevent employer retaliation against workers who make complaints about dangerous work paces. How can additional warehouse workers, as well as delivery drivers and other logistics workers, environmental and social justice activists, and community members be organized and empowered to expect corporations and policy makers to guarantee living wages, provide safe workplaces, protect and increase green spaces, and support healthy communities? What organizational, institutional, or legal tools and strategies are available to these activists? Legal settlements, like the 2021 agreement that required significant energy, air quality, and conservation mitigations as conditions for development of the WLC in Riverside County to proceed, should be applauded. But they consume time the region—indeed, the planet—does not have to waste. The WLC debacle took nearly a decade to resolve, during which Amazon constructed more than fifty facilities in the region, where an increasingly working-class, especially Latino, population grew by one million, who experienced the region's hottest temperatures and suffered the most during the COVID-19 pandemic. How can workers and residents of Inland Southern California and other major logistics hubs, who have been especially affected socioeconomically and ecologically by the rise of Amazon, warehousing, and the logistics industry, claim their right to standards of living and working that are socially, economically, and environmentally sustainable?

We begin this chapter by arguing that collective action by both warehouse workers and their communities has been necessary to challenge Amazon's exploitative labor practices, employment discrimination in the corporation, and unrestrained build-out of warehousing facilities. Here we review the variety of ways that Amazon workers and their communities, in Europe, the United States, and lower-income nations, have organized and fought back to hold Amazon accountable. Their actions include workplace petitions and actions, union organizing drives, legal complaints, community protests, and policy advocacy, as well as engaging in local, regional, national, and transnational resistance campaigns targeting Amazon. These activists face enormous challenges confronting not only

Amazon but also the broader neoliberal global order underlying its ascendancy. Yet their efforts provide positive examples of how building power from below, through grassroots organizing, collective action, and coalition building, has helped to improve the lives of workers and their communities and to broaden support for a more just, equitable, and sustainable economy. We then discuss how neoliberal policies have enabled Amazon and other warehousing, distribution, and transportation corporations to take advantage of workers, communities, and natural resources in Inland Southern California and elsewhere.[3] We argue that new policies, in addition to changes in the warehousing and logistics industries, are needed. Our discussion highlights how other nations provide policy models that would help to strengthen US workers' rights.

WORKERS AND COMMUNITIES MOBILIZE AGAINST AMAZON

Community, environmental, and labor activists have mobilized throughout Inland Southern California in response to myriad threats posed by the expansion of Amazon and the warehousing and logistics industry more generally to the natural environment, workers, and communities. Popular opposition to Amazon's environmentally and socially harmful practices has also spread widely across the United States, in Europe, and elsewhere internationally. Activists participating in these campaigns regard Amazon, the exemplary warehousing enterprise, as an existential threat.[4] They have sometimes gained support from politicians, even conservative ones. For instance, in 2017 Republican Riverside County supervisor Kevin Jeffries alone voted against a warehousing project in the historically rural San Gorgonio Pass, arguing, "Just because a warehouse can be built, it doesn't mean that it should be. . . . The location for this warehouse is today a very beautiful area, and it will never be recaptured or recover after this [is built.]"[5] Jeffries's opposition is reminiscent of Paris mayor Anne Hidalgo's declaration that Amazon's Prime one-hour delivery service threatened the city's "laid back" way of life.[6] She also recognized that the new service could increase traffic congestion and pollution in the city and imperil local businesses.[7]

These campaigns have been significantly shaped, if not also fueled, by a particular historical context that is still unfolding—one that is marked by the deepening climate crisis, the global COVID-19 pandemic, and a wave of social justice activism that includes rising militancy and popularity among organized labor and the BLM movement.[8] Taken together, climate change, the coronavirus, and protests and actions associated with BLM and other movements have raised deep concerns among the public at large about systemic inequalities and sustainable livelihoods that have, more broadly, shaped and animated workers' and communities' responses to Amazon.

The recent sharp uptick in activism directed against Amazon in the United States was ushered in by the COVID-19 pandemic, which significantly reshaped labor markets and working conditions. Although this pandemic created novel challenges for workers and activists alike, it also presented new opportunities for organizing both inside Amazon warehouses and in the communities where they are located. Consumer demand for home delivery during the COVID-19 pandemic fueled an unprecedented growth in Amazon's workforce, which swelled by more than 175,000 new employees, who were urged to meet increasingly high levels of productivity while facing unprecedented workplace health hazards.[9] The pressure-cooker environment that emerged served as a catalyst to organize, and sometimes unionize, Amazon workers, despite social distancing rules and myriad other pandemic-related challenges associated with a global pandemic. Simultaneously, Amazon's need to recruit and retain tens of thousands of new workers in tight labor market conditions, along with public and media pressure, may have contributed to managers' willingness to offer concessions in response to workers' demands and collective action, even in the absence of unionization. Amazon workers' success combined with corporate concessions inspired new efforts to organize and unionization drives. Finally, the specter of industry-wide job losses and deteriorating working conditions due to market competition from Amazon, a largely nonunion corporation, may have increased union leaders' motivations to invest in organizing Amazon warehouse workers despite the obvious challenges of doing so.

Community-based opposition to Amazon also increased during the COVID-19 pandemic, which aroused widespread public consciousness of social and environmental justice. From the first months of the pandemic, Geoffrey Pleyers argues, social justice activists worldwide participated in protests (when released from lockdowns), defended workers' rights, provided mutual aid and solidarity across a range of issue areas, monitored policy makers, and contributed to public education campaigns.[10] Support for Amazon unionization to secure higher wages and better working conditions actually extended beyond activist communities. A recent poll found that 77 percent of Americans supported the Amazon workers' Bessemer unionization drive.[11] Concern for the environmental and public health effects of warehousing, not limited to Amazon, also included activist as well as broader communities. As noted in chapter 2, local officials in Inland Southern California consistently approve warehouses for construction in poor locations that are already burdened by air pollution.[12] A Consumer Reports analysis found that nationwide, Amazon warehouses are disproportionately located in poor communities of color whose residents are systematically "sacrificed in the name of economic development," according to Chicago-based activist José Acosta-Córdova.[13]

In the following discussion we briefly review the rise and impacts of recent campaigns targeting Amazon and protests spearheaded by organized labor and community activists, first in Europe, where they have been on the rise since 2013; then in the United States; and finally in other parts of the world. Consistent with our community case study of Inland Southern California, we focus mainly on community, EJ, and labor organizing and protest; however, Amazon has also faced other significant challenges to its practices, including news and research exposés; legal complaints in various nations charging Amazon with violating antitrust, trade, labor, data privacy, tax, and equal rights laws; shareholder proposals; and a wide range of policy campaigns that aim to better regulate employers' practices, the environment, and the economy.

In assessing outcomes, it is important to consider that many of these campaigns are relatively new and still unfolding. Activist workers, along with community and EJ activists, often organize under distinct and variable political, legal, social, and shop floor conditions that complicate direct comparisons. They also frequently organize in the face of serious obstacles, including electronic surveillance by Amazon and investigation by anti-union Pinkerton spies, a tactic harking back to the nineteenth century. And their organizing occurs in the context of very high levels of worker turnover, abundant temporary and seasonal workers, and an employer that is absolutely opposed to unionization and apt to retaliate by resorting to targeted discipline, illegal termination of activist workers, and any number of other anti-union tactics.[14] Differences across context and the lack of hindsight about ongoing struggles make it difficult to draw general or definitive lessons. Nevertheless, we anticipate that this review will reveal the ways that organizing and collective action by workers and communities, even where successful formal unionization of Amazon warehouse workers has not yet occurred, has contributed to expanding grassroots power and improving people's lives.

European and Transnational Resistance to Amazon

Shortly after Amazon opened its first warehouse in San Bernardino in 2012, and years before public unionization drives emerged in the United States, Amazon warehouse workers in Europe had already begun organizing strikes and various other bold actions for better wages and working conditions through unions and other types of organizations. Amazon workers have formed unions in various European nations, including Germany, France, Italy, and the Czech Republic.[15] Unionization of Amazon workers in these nations has been facilitated by a legal and political context that generally favors workers' rights to unionize and bargain collectively. Even so, Amazon warehouse workers have confronted considerable resistance to their demands and efforts to negotiate union contracts and sectoral bargaining agreements. Multiple unions representing Amazon warehouse workers have formed in many of these nations, sometimes even within the same facility, which is allowable under some national labor laws in Europe. This organizational diversity, along with linguistic, ideological, strategic, and tactical differences among activists, has complicated efforts to collaborate. Activists have nonetheless organized and executed a number of impressive, coordinated national and transnational strikes and protests.[16]

In 2013, 1,100 Amazon warehouse workers in Bad Hersfeld, Germany, engaged in the first work stoppage strike in the corporation's history. German Amazon workers, organized through the Ver.di union, have since engaged in a series of actions and strikes demanding that Amazon improve working conditions and sign a bargaining contract with them. In 2022, for example, Ver.di organized a strike on Prime Day involving workers at seven FCs to pressure Amazon to accept its sectoral bargaining agreement, which had not been accepted at the time of this writing. Nevertheless, Amazon has already responded to union demands and pressure by increasing workers' pay and adopting additional workplace improvements.[17]

Workers and activists have also organized Amazon warehouse workers in other European nations. In 2014 about 400 Amazon workers in Poland joined a grassroots union led by rank-and-file worker volunteers. Their action included participation in a work slowdown in support of striking Amazon workers in Germany.[18] Unionization campaigns later succeeded in the Czech Republic, another Eastern European nation, where Amazon located to serve German consumers while avoiding German unions and thereby saving on labor costs, a strategy we discuss more fully later.[19] Also in 2014, three major French unions organized actions against Amazon, calling for greater respect for unionization efforts as well as improvements in wages and working conditions.[20] For years French, Spanish, and Italian unions have also organized Amazon warehouse workers and engaged in strikes and protests, sometimes winning wage gains and better working conditions. During 2020 Amazon's warehouse workers in Italy, Spain, Poland, and France organized a series of strikes related to insufficient workplace protections against exposure to COVID-19, which put pressure on Amazon to improve its health and safety practices.[21]

The outcomes of efforts in European nations to organize Amazon warehouse workers have varied, depending in part on the strength of workers' rights. For example, attempts to unionize Amazon warehouse workers in Great Britain, underway since 2013, have faced an uphill battle amid weak national labor laws and active corporate resistance. So far the General, Municipal, Boilermakers and Allied Trade Union's (GMB's) long-standing efforts to recruit and unionize workers have been stymied by the corporation's union busting efforts.[22] Meanwhile, GMB has organized protests to publicize poor working conditions, with specific emphasis on fair compensation, workplace safety, and security, and has pressed Amazon to mitigate the mental and physical health impacts associated with Amazon's work-rate requirements in highly automated warehouses.[23]

Italian unions and their supporters have been particularly effective in making gains for Amazon workers, in part because of their militancy and strong national labor laws that allow for sectoral bargaining. In 2018 Amazon workers in Italy won a historic workplace collective agreement that regulated work on the weekend at the Piacenza FC.[24] That same year, Italian unions organized a strike among Amazon's outsourced delivery drivers that resulted in negotiations over their working conditions.[25] In 2021 Italian workers engaged in a national strike against Amazon and its use of algorithms that involved temporary, subcontracted, and direct employees.[26] Later that year, Italian unions signed a series of related national sectoral bargaining agreements with Amazon covering both warehouse workers and last-mile delivery drivers, including temporary and subcontracted workers.[27]

In addition to engaging in nation-based organizing, Amazon warehouse workers and labor activists have formed transnational alliances to improve their capacity to challenge Amazon's exploitative labor practices through coordinated actions. Initially these transnational alliances were formed across Europe, but they were subsequently expanded to include workers and other labor activists from the United States and other nations. Direct communication among Amazon warehouse workers that focuses on shared concerns and their common target has helped labor activists to overcome their organizational, ideological, linguistic, and national differences.[28] Many of these transnational actions have targeted Amazon facilities on major consumer holidays, including Black Friday, Cyber Monday, and Prime Day. In 2018, for example, UNI Global Union and other unions organized work stoppages and other protest actions on Black Friday that involved thousands of European workers in Germany, Italy, the United Kingdom, Poland, and Spain, proclaiming, "We are not robots!"[29] Transnational Social Strike, which seeks to unite and build solidarity among Amazon workers across Europe and other nations, including the United States, has also organized transnational meetings and actions by workers, including a series of strikes in 2019. Another major transnational coalition targeting Amazon was the Make Amazon Pay coalition, formed in 2020 by UniGlobal, Progressive International; Amazon Workers International; and a broad array of labor and community organizations, networks, and coalitions based in the global North and South;

its actions seek to challenge Amazon's environmental, labor, monopolistic, and tax practices. This developing trend in transnational collaborations provided the foundation for another series of strikes and protests targeting Amazon on Black Friday, which involved activists in at least sixteen nations in 2020 and twenty nations in 2021.[30]

Along with labor activists, environmental and other community activists have also engaged in various national and transnational protests against Amazon in Europe. Opposition to Amazon has been especially broad based and vehement in France, where Amazon faced opposition from the Yellow Vest Movement, which has shifted from an anti-tax movement to a broader revolt against neoliberalism and rising wealth inequality.[31] In 2021 EJ, labor, anti-capitalist, and other community activists engaged in an impressive day of protests and actions involving multiple French towns. Participants expressed a broad range of concerns with Amazon and its plans to build more warehouses in France, where there were eight at the time. At one such protest, a crowd of about 800 to 1,400 people rallied and planted shrubs to demonstrate how the open land could be used to promote life rather than filling it with concrete to build warehouses. At a smaller protest in Ensisheim, participants opposed the plan to build a warehouse on former farmland. An environmental activist, Isabelle Schaeffer, proclaimed: "'Today, we condemn an economic system that is at the end of its rope and which is using the planet.'"[32] Amazon has also faced the ire of transnational climate activists during climate strikes and other transnational protests. For example, in 2021 the Extinction Rebellion targeted more than a dozen Amazon FCs in Germany, Great Britain, and the Netherlands on Black Friday in order to raise public awareness about "Amazon's exploitative and environmentally destructive business practices, disregard for workers' rights in the name of company profits, as well as the wastefulness of Black Friday."[33] Through actions such as these, community activists have helped to put pressure on Amazon to improve its environmental and other business practices.

Worker and Community Resistance in the United States

The rise in grassroots community, EJ, and labor activism directed at warehouses and DCs serving Amazon and other major companies in Inland

Southern California since the mid- to late 1990s was part of a broader national trend, especially in major logistics clusters. Besides occasional protests involving Amazon warehouse workers, such as in Seattle in 2012, organized warehouse worker resistance to Amazon, in particular, did not become publicly visible in the United States until about 2018.[34] Over the next few years, especially amid the COVID-19 pandemic, it spread quickly nationwide, involving worker centers, worker-led independent organizations and unions, such as Amazonians United and ALU, as well as more traditional and well-established unions. Black and Latino workers, including women of color and immigrants, have played leading roles in many of these campaigns.[35] Along with current warehouse workers, former warehouse workers, some of whom, like Chris Smalls, were fired by the corporation after organizing protests, have played important roles in organizing Amazon warehouse workers, as did salts, or activists who intentionally take jobs to help other workers to organize.[36]

US activists engaged in organizing Amazon warehouse workers are divided ideologically as well as organizationally; they have mainly included liberals and leftists, including democratic socialists, anarchists, and communists. Like the situation in Europe, the organizational and ideological diversity among Amazon workers and their supporters has sometimes complicated efforts to collaborate. Yet this diversity has also enabled new and diverse grassroots leaders to emerge, and activists to experiment with different tactics and styles of organizing under disparate and challenging organizing conditions.

The Awood Center, a nonprofit worker center based in Minneapolis, Minnesota, carried out some of the earliest protests by Amazon warehouse workers in the United States. Many of Amazon's warehouse workers in that region were Somali Muslim immigrants, who viewed the high productivity rates required of them as a threat to their ability to pray, as well as to take bathroom breaks when needed. In December 2018 about 250 Amazon warehouse workers and supporters marched to and then protested outside an Amazon FC in Shakopee, Minnesota. In addition to prayer and bathroom breaks, participants demanded other improvements in their working conditions, racial justice, and independent review boards to process workers' complaints instead of Amazon's HR department. In March 2019, and in response to a work speed-up, Amazon warehouse workers in Shakopee organized a work stoppage involving about half of the sixty night-shift stowers working that night. Participants voted on a list of demands, including more reasonable work rates, greater accommodations for workers' prayer and bathroom breaks, an end to the use of temporary workers, and improvements in machinery to better safeguard workers against injuries. Awood members also engaged in collective actions, including a walkout at an Eagan facility over parking-related issues. In response, managers provided them with payments for towed vehicles and the right to clock in from the parking lot. Three women affiliated with Awood later filed federal complaints against Amazon for discriminating against Muslim Somali and East African warehouse workers in terms of work assignments and training and promotion opportunities.[37]

Amazon warehouse workers also organized in other cities, such as Robinson, New Jersey, and in Staten Island, New York. In Robinson in 2018, Amazon workers who were affiliated with Warehouse Workers Stand Up, an organization formed by a coalition of unions and other labor and community organizations, protested with their supporters for safer and more humane working conditions, including improvements in pay and access to paid sick days. The protest was called in response to a workplace accident in which a warehouse robot broke a can of bear repellent and exposed at least seventy-eight workers to toxic gas, an incident that highlighted the threats to workers' health that workplace automation at Amazon presented.[38] The Retail, Wholesale and Department Store Union (RWDSU, affiliated with the United Food and Commercial Workers union since 1993) engaged in early efforts to organize Amazon warehouse workers on Staten Island, New York. In 2019 these workers and RWDSU members protested Amazon's stringent work rate requirements.[39]

Other early worker organizing campaigns were carried out by Amazonians United, an independent organization led by rank-and-file workers, many of whom are Black or Latino. By 2021 Amazonians United had formed chapters in various cities, including Chicago, New York, Sacramento, and Upper Marlboro, Maryland.[40] Members of Amazonians United have demanded, and won, various improvements for workers through collective actions that have included petitions, protests, and walkouts, targeting Amazon managers. The Chicago-based chapter, formed in 2019, has been particularly active and effective. Members have used collective action and escalating tactics to gain better access to clean drinking water; more respectful treatment from certain managers; the right to be paid when workers are required to leave work because of heat, lack of electricity, or lack of work; improvements in workplace safety; and increased pay.[41]

The ongoing proliferation of local actions by Amazon workers across US cities and transnationally coordinated protests targeting Amazon, as well as increased worker activism more generally since 2019, helped to encourage further activism by Amazon warehouse workers in response COVID-19–related health and safety issues. In the United States, organizations supporting Amazon warehouse workers demanded that Amazon do more to protect its employees from exposure to COVID-19 while they are working in its vast DCs and other facilities. One of the most well publicized actions occurred in March 2020, when Smalls, an activist worker employed at the JFK8 facility in Staten Island, New York, helped to organize a walkout, demanding that Amazon do more to protect workers from COVID-19. Smalls, along with other worker-activists like Gerald Bryson, were subsequently fired, which many viewed as employer retaliation for their organizing (Amazon was subsequently required to reinstate Bryson under court order). Undeterred, Smalls formed a new organization, The Congress of Essential Workers (TCOEW), which organized a series of protests at Bezos's mansions in the United States, calling for better wages and working conditions for US workers at Amazon and beyond.[42] He later helped to lead a successful unionization drive at JFK8 (described more fully later).

Members of DCH1 Amazonians United in Chicago also organized a particularly bold strike in 2020, involving as many as eighty workers and calling for greater health and safety measures to limit the spread of COVID-19 in the workplace. They won improved access to masks and cleaning supplies; however, managers also responded by writing up the strike leaders for violating social distancing rules and other failures to comply with corporate policies.[43] Workers then filed a complaint with the National Labor Relations Board (NLRB) charging management with violating their right to organize. The NLRB ruled in the workers' favor. Under the leadership of women of color, this chapter of Amazonians United also demanded and eventually won paid time off for part-time warehouse workers, enabling them to quarantine if needed.[44]

In addition to increased activism by Amazon warehouse workers, union organizing at US Amazon facilities also gained new ground during the COVID-19 pandemic. As mentioned previously, the magnitude of threats to union workers' jobs and labor standards associated with the expansion of Amazon, along with the sheer size and rising numbers of Amazon's warehouse workers whose bad working conditions had become widely publicized, prompted major unions, including the RWDSU and the Teamsters, to invest additional resources to confront Amazon and organize these warehouse workers.[45]

In 2021 nearly 6,000 eligible employees, most of whom were Black workers, at a Bessemer, Alabama, warehouse gained national attention when they were asked to cast votes on whether to join the RWDSU. The unionization bid failed amid a barrage of anti-union propaganda and various intimidating actions by Amazon. RWDSU filed complaints with the NLRB, charging that Amazon's efforts to undermine the election, including setting up a ballot box in its parking lot with surveillance cameras, violated national labor laws. In December 2021, in response to RWDSU's complaints, the NLRB ordered that a new union election take place.[46] The second RWDSU union election in 2022 yielded more than 400 challenged ballots, 993 "no" votes, and 875 "yes" votes. Although the union gained more support than it had during its first union election, it did not clearly win a majority of "yes" votes among eligible votes cast; because the results were too close to call, a hearing was scheduled to discuss the status of the challenged ballots.[47] The RWDSU union also filed twenty-one objections that Amazon had once again violated labor laws during the election, including threatening to close the warehouse, firing a pro-union worker, and suspending another pro-union worker.[48]

Years after efforts to organize Amazon warehouse workers at the JFK8 facility in Staten Island, New York, began (including an earlier failed unionization drive by the RWDSU), the Amazon Labor Union (ALU) made history at that facility on April 1, 2022; it won the very first successful union election among Amazon warehouse workers in the United States.[49] A total of 2,654 (nearly 32 percent of the 8,325 eligible workers) voted in favor of the ALU, while 2,131 (25.5 percent) voted against unionization.[50] The ALU's success surprised many, especially because it is an independent labor union composed of volunteers and financed through donations, rather than a mainstream union. Its organizing committee included current Amazon warehouse workers, some of whom were salts, as well as former workers, including its cofounder and president, Smalls, whose status as a celebrity activist surged to new heights.

Pro-union Amazon workers were led by an ALU organizing committee that was racially and ethnically diverse and included many immigrants and women, much like the workforce they sought to organize. ALU organizers talked with their fellow workers during their lunch and other breaks, sharing meals and water with them, and as they entered or left the facility. They also communicated with them by phone and social media in multiple languages during off-duty hours. As union supporters gained influence at JFK8, they wore ALU T-shirts at work to express their solidarity and make their growing support visible. Union activists also attended mandatory work meetings where Amazon representatives criticized the union, vocally countering those arguments.[51]

Hoping to build on the momentum from its first election victory and support from various major unions, the ALU carried out a second union election in a nearby smaller facility in Staten Island (LDJ5). Unable to successfully counter Amazon's persistent anti-union communications among most of the warehouse workers at LDJ5, the ALU lost this second election. Compared to JFK8, more workers at LDJ5 were part-time employees, fewer organizers were employed there, and union organizers had spent less time building strong relationships with the workers. Out of 1,600 eligible workers, 380 workers (24 percent) voted for the union, and 618 (39 percent) voted against it.[52] The ALU faced another major setback: Amazon's legal challenge to their union victory, a move that delayed, and threatened to block, progress on union contract negotiations. Rather than recognizing ALU's victory, Amazon contested it by filing twenty-five objections about the election process with the NLRB. Amazon charged the ALU with violating national labor laws and claimed that the regional NLRB office in Brooklyn provided undue favor to the union.[53] Amazon also fired several ALU organizers; the union views these terminations, like earlier firings of Amazon worker activists, as employer retaliation, and has demanded their reinstatement.[54] Despite these series of setbacks at the end of 2022, ALU leaders and organizers are preparing for their first union contract negotiations with Amazon, which will include their demand for $30 per hour for Amazon warehouse workers. They have also promised to actively support additional unionization drives at other Amazon warehouses; within months, Amazon warehouse workers, inspired by the ALU, formed ALU chapters in other Amazon facilities, including in Campbellsville, Kentucky, and Albany, New York, and Amazon workers in other cities and states have visited with, or been in communication with, ALU organizers.[55]

Along with other major unions, the Teamsters and their members, many of whom are employed in warehousing and delivery services, have supported independent organizing efforts among Amazon warehouse workers, including those by the ALU. At their annual convention in 2021, the Teamsters passed a special resolution to create a new Amazon division to oversee their efforts, underway since at least 2016, to oppose Amazon's expansion and to support efforts to organize and unionize Amazon workers. As their resolution states, the Teamsters support "building genuine worker power at Amazon" through "shop-floor militancy by Amazon workers" and "unquestioned solidarity from warehousing and delivery Teamsters."[56] The Teamsters have worked to educate their rank-and-file members, including unionized United Parcel Service drivers, about Amazon. They have also mobilized their members to talk informally to nonunion Amazon warehouse workers and drivers they personally know about unionization and encourage them to organize and act at their workplaces with their fellow workers.[57] Teamsters' leaders and members have also supported Amazon workers when they have engaged in workplace actions or carried out unionization campaigns, viewing these as critical parts of the broader struggle to improve wages and working conditions in the warehousing and logistics industries. They hope that Amazon workers and supporters will in turn actively support Teamsters' union contract negotiations with United Parcel Service in 2023, the largest private sector union bargaining agreement in North America.[58]

Even in the absence of formal unionization, worker organizing, along with growing public criticism of Amazon articulated by politicians, journalists, and other groups, has led to notable gains for US Amazon warehouse workers, including increased wages, greater workplace safety, and other improvements in working conditions.[59] In 2021 and 2022 Amazon warehouse workers continued to press for additional pay increases and various other demands through collective action in multiple states and cities. For example, walkouts by Amazon warehouse workers were organized in 2022 by Amazonians United in Chicago, New York City, and Upper Marlboro, Maryland; by the Awood Center in Shakopee, Minnesota; and in Doraville, Georgia.[60]

Amazon is also facing organized resistance from other parts of its workforce besides warehouse workers, including ongoing efforts to organize and unionize Whole Foods workers, delivery drivers, and high-tech workers. The latter have pressured the corporation to improve various other aspects of its business practices. For example, in 2019 high-tech workers organized through Amazon Employees for Climate Justice wrote and circulated an open letter to Bezos, the corporation's CEO at the time, demanding that Amazon adopt a comprehensive climate action plan. Some 8,000 Amazon employees, including many high-tech workers, signed this letter.[61] The global climate strike attracted participation from about 1,000 Amazon employees in Seattle, many of whom were high-tech workers. In response, Amazon pledged to become carbon neutral by 2040 and to purchase electric vehicles, a promise that many climate justice activists are using to hold Amazon accountable.[62] High-tech Amazon workers, along with other community and labor activists, also protested Amazon's development and sale of surveillance equipment, which has been used by local police as well as immigration enforcement agents. Some of these actions were coordinated by Athena, a national network of over forty community and labor organizations formed in 2019 in response to growing concerns about Amazon.[63] In 2022 almost thirty Amazon employees, who call themselves No Hate at Amazon, held a protest (die-in) in Seattle during a Pride Month celebration organized by the company. They called upon the company to stop selling books with content promoting hate against transgender people.[64]

In addition to warehouse workers, other Amazon employees have joined together to confront persistent problems with employment discrimination and harassment within the corporation. In 2021, 550 Amazon Web Services (AWS) employees signed a petition calling on Amazon's leaders to do more to stop employment discrimination and harassment based on gender, race, and sexuality at the corporation.[65] This petition—as well as journalistic exposés, leaked internal records, and a series of highly publicized lawsuits and legal complaints against employment discrimination by Amazon employees, including high-level managerial and corporate employees, many of whom were women of color—have increased pressure on the corporation to treat its workers more equitably.[66]

Of course Amazon was not alone in facing rising numbers of legal complaints and other actions related to employment discrimination on the basis of race, gender, sexuality, and/or other identities; the rise of the BLM and #metoo movements and increasing activism among workers, queer, and other communities have inspired many workers to use the law to seek greater workplace equity. A report by Good Jobs First released in 2020 revealed that in the United States, "since 2000, 99 percent of Fortune 500 companies have paid settlements in at least one discrimination or sexual harassment lawsuit . . . and that's not including the cases without a public record or incidents victims didn't report."[67] And in 2019 alone, the EEOC received 7,500 sexual harassment complaints.[68]

Community as well as labor resistance to the development of new Amazon FCs or other logistics facilities has also emerged in many US cities, perhaps most dramatically in Long Island, New York. At the end of a highly publicized bidding war involving 238 US, Canadian, and Mexican cities, Amazon decided in 2019 to build its second headquarters (HQ2) in Long Island, New York. Amazon faced heated resistance from a broad range of workers and community residents, activists, and leaders, who engaged in protests and made public statements against the plan. They claimed it lacked sufficient community benefits and protections for workers and local residents and included $3 billion in government incentives for Amazon, which could be better spent meeting other public needs. Amazon responded by canceling its initial second headquarters (HQ2) plans and moving the project to Arlington, Virginia. Virginia Educators United then protested lawmakers' decision to offer Amazon generous tax breaks rather than raise revenue for public education.[69]

The Teamsters have been particularly active in building community-based opposition to the establishment of new Amazon facilities in various US cities. From the perspective of the Teamsters and their allies, the growth of these nonunion facilities threatens unionized workers' jobs and the labor standards they have secured in the logistics industry, in addition to the quality of life in the community. Like the campaign against the expansion of the Eastgate Airport in San Bernardino to serve Amazon detailed in chapter 7, these local campaigns have often involved coalitions among EJ, labor, and other community organizations; mobilizing the Teamsters' own members, other workers, and community members; and targeting local politicians to press their demands.[70] As a result, Teamsters locals and their allies have gained the support of local policy makers from coast to coast for their demands that aimed to stop Amazon's unfettered growth. For example, in 2021 a total of twelve Boston-area municipalities adopted nonbinding resolutions that call upon Amazon to protect labor standards and to meet with community and labor groups if and when it expands. That same year, local politicians in Arvada, Colorado, San Jose, California, and Oceanside, California, rejected proposals for new Amazon facilities. The Teamsters and their allies also gained support for temporary moratoria on FCs and delivery stations in Contra Costa County, California, and delivery stations in San Francisco, similar to the warehouse moratoria adopted by various cities in Inland Southern California.[71]

When local politicians have approved new Amazon facilities despite public opposition to them, the Teamsters and their allies have opposed their construction through lawsuits. For example, several Teamsters locals joined with local residents, PC4EJ, and West Covina Alliance for Responsible Development to file a CEQA lawsuit against the developer and the city of West Covina, California, to halt construction of a newly approved 177,240-square-foot Amazon facility, estimated to generate over 900 additional unmitigated vehicle trips. They charged that the city and developer failed to adequately assess and minimize the environmental impacts.[72] In the settlement of this lawsuit, the developer agreed to use more renewable energy sources and carry out various measures to reduce the impacts of increased traffic, noise, and sound pollution related to the new facility. Afterward, and likely in response to this, Amazon withdrew from the site.[73]

Community activists have also promoted local policy changes affecting Amazon and demanded other improvements in the corporation's business practices. For example, community activists have used petitions, statements, and protest rallies to publicly criticize lawmakers' proclivity to provide corporate welfare and tax giveaways to Amazon, and sometimes have even persuaded local policy makers to reject such proposals, as occurred in Fort Wayne, Indiana, in 2021.[74] In Seattle, community activists protested Amazon's failure to pay its fair share of taxes and successfully mobilized support for a new business tax in 2020 that will help to pay for more affordable housing, environmental projects, and union jobs.[75] In 2022, Seattle Pride barred Amazon from sponsoring its annual Pride Day parade because the company engaged in various actions that were seen as harmful to the LGBTQIA community, including financially supporting politicians who support anti-LGBTQIA legislation and allowing anti-LGBTQIA groups to raise money through its Amazon Smile program.[76] Examples such as these show how resistance to Amazon is growing in communities as well as among workers in the United States.

Resistance to Amazon Outside of North America and Europe

Amazon's presence and resistance to it have been growing rapidly in other nations outside of Europe and the United States. As of 2021, Amazon had warehouse facilities in at least twenty-four nations, including Australia, Canada, Japan, Singapore, India, United Arab Emirates, Egypt, Kuwait, Saudi Arabia, and was constructing facilities in additional nations, including South Africa.[77] Resistance to Amazon has already begun to emerge in these nations, including lower-income nations, as the cases of India and South Africa demonstrate.

Indeed, when Bezos toured India in 2020, protests erupted across the nation. The Confederation of All-India Traders, which speaks for seventy million traders and 40,000 trade associations, organized about 300 actions, including protests and rallies. In New Delhi, protesters charged Bezos with being an "economic terrorist," criticizing the use of online discounts and other exclusive and predatory pricing practices by Amazon and Walmart's Flipkart that threaten local businesses.[78] India's antitrust regulator also began formal investigations of legal complaints against Amazon and Flipkart, claiming that their pricing practices violate Indian trade laws, including "neutral marketplace" requirements that apply to e-commerce businesses.[79]

Amazon has also faced vocal opposition in South Africa, where indigenous leaders and groups protested the construction of a headquarters facility in River Club, Cape Town. Participants expressed ecological and heritage-based concerns about the project because it was located in a floodplain region where important indigenous battles against Portuguese settlers occurred.[80] Another protest there was organized on Black Friday in 2021 by various indigenous organizations and their allies, in coordination with other protests occurring that day around the world, such as those organized by other Make Amazon Pay affiliates. At the Cape Town march and rally, activists presented a petition signed by 57,600 people opposing the development of the headquarters on the land.[81]

These protests in India and South Africa demonstrate how anti-monopoly, environmental, and community opposition to Amazon is rising in lower-income nations. Worker protests against Amazon are spreading there as well. Black Friday protests against Amazon in 2020, for example, included worker actions all across Amazon's global supply chain, involving warehouse workers in Mexico, garment workers in Bangladesh, and Amazon Ring call center workers in the Philippines.[82] While growing opposition to Amazon in the world's lower-income nations is very similar to, and connected with, anti-Amazon activism in wealthier nations, activists in some of these nations have linked their struggles to anti-imperialist and indigenous movements, which tend to be more widespread outside of North America and Europe.

Reversing the Neoliberal Policy Agenda

The activists and allies who have mobilized throughout Inland Southern California, in the United States, across Europe, and worldwide in response to the threats Amazon poses to individual workers, their families, natural landscapes, communities, and entire ways of life should be commended. Not only have they mobilized and empowered people, they have also helped to expose the ways in which Amazon's business practices and global expansion have been facilitated by neoliberal policies. As noted in chapter 1, neoliberal policies, on the rise around the world since the late 1970s and increasingly entrenched in the United States, tend to uphold business interests in the economy. They include provision of corporate subsidies, elimination of price controls, deregulation of capital and labor markets, lowering trade barriers, reduction of business taxes, and rollbacks in government protection for the environment and workers' rights.[83] By minimizing corporations' labor and social costs, such measures enable employment discrimination and the generally exploitative business and employment practices embraced by Amazon and other low-wage employers. Reversing this neoliberal policy agenda is therefore essential to improving workers' rights, supporting communities, and protecting the natural environments that surround them. Perhaps some of the most obvious examples that help to illustrate this point relate to workers' rights and their ongoing struggles with Amazon.

Amazon warehouse workers' struggles to unionize and bargain with the corporation have helped to expose the need to strengthen all workers' rights to form unions and bargain with their employers. Common examples of how weak labor rights have failed to protect workers from exploitative corporations are found in collective bargaining. Workers' rights to form unions have long been far more limited in the United States than in European nations, where workers can engage in sectoral bargaining to uplift working conditions in entire industries and can form unions even in the absence of majority support of other workers.[84] US workers' right to form unions and bargain collectively are also weakly enforced, and corporations usually face relatively small penalties for violating them, which has facilitated the rise of illegal "union busting" practices, including illegal firing of worker activists, over time. Although workers' rights have been under attack and union membership has also been declining in Europe, still over half of the continents' employees are covered by collective bargaining agreements, compared to 10.3 percent in the United States in 2021.[85] Collective bargaining laws and other labor laws, including those related to employee classification, also need to be revised to better protect workers' rights given the rise of temporary employment, independent contracting, and subcontracting.

Strengthening laws mandating minimum or living wages would help to raise the wage floor for workers. Minimum wage laws are especially lax in the United States in comparison to European nations.[86] The US federal minimum wage (currently $7.25) has not been increased since 2009. That said, many states, including California, have raised the minimum wage in response to demands for a living wage and Fight for $15 movements.[87] Still, minimum wage levels remain grossly insufficient for meeting the rising costs of living, including the high cost of housing, especially in California, northeastern US states, and many large cities and coastal areas throughout the United States.[88]

In the current neoliberal political economy, low-income workers and communities, often further marginalized in terms of race/ethnicity and immigration status, have often faced the brunt of the proliferation of bad jobs, air pollution, and environmental degradation associated with the growth of warehousing and logistics. Research consistently demonstrates that most Amazon warehouses in the United States are located in neighborhoods where a greater share of low-income individuals and people of color live than is the case for typical, or median, neighborhoods in the same metropolitan areas.[89] Partly as a result of this situation, most warehouse workers nationally are Black, including those employed by Amazon, although in some regions, such as Inland Southern California, Latinos predominate.[90] According to Alessandro Delfanti, Amazon intentionally recruits socially marginalized workers elsewhere in the world as well, often immigrants and refugees, who are unlikely to have meaningful alternatives to warehouse employment.[91] While Delfanti provides examples from Western Europe, the situation is also evident in poorer nations and communities in Eastern Europe, such as Poland and the Czech Republic.[92] Similarly, in India many Amazon workers are Dalits or members of other low castes, who face socially sanctioned workplace and wage discrimination, when they are fortunate enough to gain employment at all.[93]

At every spatial level of aggregation, Amazon profits by exploiting workers in lower-wage regions to serve customers in higher-wage and -income regions, often by allying with local and regional policy makers.[94] This spatial injustice is manifest among Amazon workers in Inland Southern California who fulfill Prime, two-day delivery orders that originate outside of the region—in wealthier Orange and San Diego Counties, for instance. Regional and local policy makers colluded with professional business associations—including the Distribution Management Association (DMA) of Southern California and affiliated both with the Los Angeles and Long Beach ports, and the Inland Empire Economic Partnership (IEEP), which manages collaborations among the region's developers, real estate brokers, logistics professionals, and workforce development services—and responded to these job losses by actively promoting warehouse development and logistics.[95] This strategy capitalized on the neoliberal turn in the United States toward inexpensive offshore manufacturing paired with intermodal freight transportation, and the

rapid rise in "on-demand" big box retail and container shipping, to generate jobs for residents of Inland Southern California. Instead of requiring
employers to generate good jobs and to provide other community benefits
and protections, local policy makers competed with one another by offering industrial developers and corporations cash subsidies, tax breaks,
infrastructure and transportation investments, and other incentives to
build warehouses and, later, more complex DCs, in the region—initially
requiring little more than the promise of jobs.[96]

Similar to what has occurred in Inland Southern California, state and
local politicians in many locations across the United States frequently have
welcomed warehouse developments and other logistics facilities into their
communities as a way to boost lagging employment. Like their Inland
Southern California counterparts, they have routinely offered companies,
especially Amazon, generous subsidies, tax breaks, and other incentives,
with at best limited environmental mitigations, community benefits, or
protections for workers.[97] Yet increases in Amazon jobs have contributed
to reductions in other forms of employment. This socioeconomically costly
situation has been particularly evident when considering rising closures
of small businesses and other brick-and-mortar retail stores, a trend that
was already on the rise even before the onset of COVID-19 pandemic-
related business closures. According to Alec MacGillis, the rapid growth
of Amazon and e-commerce in recent decades, in addition to the broader
decline in the middle class, has put many brick-and-mortar retail stores
out of business. As MacGillis writes, "By late 2018, mall vacancies would
reach their highest level since the Great Recession."[98]

When deciding where to site its warehouses, Amazon has frequently
followed the well-worn path of generations of major corporations and
taken advantage of global as well as regional inequalities in labor costs
and weak laws governing environmental, labor, and trade protection. For
example, in North America many US-based corporations, including Amazon and other e-commerce enterprises, increasingly locate warehouses in
Mexico, where labor costs are lower and environmental regulations are
less stringent. National trade policies have encouraged this trend. A US
customs exemption (Section 321) effectively allows companies to benefit
from relatively low Mexican wages to ship items worth less than $800
duty-free to the United States.[99]

Likewise, in Europe Amazon has often located its warehouses in nations where workers have fewer rights and are less unionized. Workers in relatively impoverished Eastern European nations mostly process orders for wealthier German consumers, an arrangement made possible due to Amazon's strategic siting of FCs near highways entering Germany along the Czech Republic's northern border with that nation. In this case, differences in labor costs are due to German workers' rights—including maximum hours, paid sick leave, and extensive limits on termination—and unionization of Amazon warehouse workers. Characteristic of the political-economic race to the bottom, when Amazon quickly found it difficult to recruit, even in the Czech Republic, the corporation bussed in workers from poorer, further outlying communities, where unemployment rates were high and wages for manual labor remained lower than what Amazon pays.[100]

Amazon has also taken advantage of comparative differences in national laws that allow corporations to pay part-time, seasonal, temporary agency, and outsourced employees less and provide them with fewer employment benefits than regular employees. Amazon's practice of relying heavily on seasonal workers in the United States is recent and contrasts with practices in other nations. Previously Amazon, like many other warehouse employers in the United States, relied more heavily on temporary agency workers, who were denied employment benefits and paid lower wages than direct hires. This shift in employment practices in Amazon's US FCs and other facilities—from temps to an increasing reliance on seasonal workers—is likely to be related to recent court cases decided against temporary agencies. Costly litigation against these agencies' labor practices yielded a series of legal rulings in favor of joint employer responsibility for working conditions and encouraged reliance on cost-cutting innovations related to the use of electronic technologies and applications to recruit, screen, on-board, and train employees.[101] In other nations, such as the Czech Republic, Italy, and Mexico, Amazon has continued to rely heavily on temporary staffing agencies to hire warehouse workers, hindering unionization and workers' ability to claim labor rights and protections.[102] The outsourcing of Amazon delivery drivers, many of whom have been hired as independent contractors rather than as direct employees, has similarly denied many of these underpaid drivers basic labor rights, including collective bargaining rights.[103]

Reversing the neoliberal policy agenda by strengthening labor laws and improving their enforcement to better protect workers in response to, and to curb, the growth of nontraditional employment arrangements is a tall order, but some nations provide positive examples worth following. For example, a law passed in Mexico in 2021 banning companies from hiring through subcontracted third-party agencies for nonspecialized services could limit that practice in Mexico, at least.[104] The exception for specialized service workers included in this law limits its reach. Still, passage of this law represents an important step forward for many workers and their allies, who encouraged the Mexican government to do more to resist employers' heavy reliance on subcontracted workers, including temporary agency workers.[105] Within months of the passage of this law, 2.3 million previously outsourced workers were hired directly, providing many of these workers, including Amazon warehouse workers, with better wages and more employment benefits.[106] Lawsuits challenging problems of employee misclassification and policies designed to strengthen gig workers' rights in various US states and nations could also help to provide many Amazon employees, including delivery drivers, with additional labor rights, including collective bargaining rights.[107]

Banning or strictly limiting the use of noncompete agreements would help to further protect workers' rights. In 2015 news stories began surfacing about Amazon's eighteen-month noncompete agreements in their US employment contracts, which were used even when hiring temporary and seasonal warehouse workers.[108] Noncompete agreements require that workers not accept employment in jobs supporting goods or services that might compete with a particular company, and tend to put downward pressure on workers' wages.[109] Amazon's noncompete agreement was notably very broad in scope, given that Amazon is a transnational corporation that has become "the everything store," selling an enormous variety of products. Amazon's employment contract also required workers to agree to provide copies of their signed contracts, including the noncompete agreements, to prospective employers. When Amazon closed its warehouse in Coffeyville, Kansas, it even required laid-off warehouse workers to sign an agreement that made them "'fully comply'" with the noncompete clauses of their employment contracts in order to receive their severance pay.[110]

While California and some other US states ban or greatly limit non-compete agreements, national laws in the United States, like various other nations, do not prohibit them. Many US states condone noncompete agreements, with varying restrictions on their use, sometimes explicitly barring their use among low-income workers. Traditionally, employers have used noncompete clauses in high-skilled occupations to retain talent, but they have spread widely across many industries and occupations to include many low-wage positions. A 2014 nationally representative survey of 11,505 workers, for example, found that about 38 percent of all US workers, including 35 percent of workers without bachelor's degrees, have signed a noncompete agreement at some point in their lives, and about 18 percent of all US workers were working under one at the time they were surveyed. About 12 percent of surveyed workers in transportation and material moving occupations had signed a noncompete agreement.[111]

Improving regulations related to work pace and the collection and use of employees' productivity data would help to protect Amazon and other workers whose productivity is increasingly being surveilled electronically by their employers and who are subjected to algocratic management techniques.[112] As discussed in chapter 7, California AB 701 prohibits warehouse employers from requiring work quotas that prevent workers from taking breaks or using the restroom when needed, and that otherwise jeopardize their health and safety. This new law also requires employers to disclose quota requirements and protects workers from employer retaliation when exercising their rights to obtain information and file complaints about quotas. This new law only applies to workers in California, however. New York state adopted a similar law, the Warehouse Worker Protection Act (WWPA), in 2022, and similar bills are being advanced in other US states.[113]

Laws protecting workers, including data privacy policies, have also helped to counter the spread of algocratic forms of management and the electronic surveillance of workers' productivity. For example, in the European Union workers enjoy data privacy rights under the General Data Protection Regulation (GDPR), and national laws in Europe also regulate the conditions under which workers can be fired. In 2019 and 2020, Inicjatywa Pracownicza (IP), a Polish trade union, won a legal case contesting the firing of an Amazon warehouse worker based on his productivity data as violating Polish labor laws. Since then Amazon warehouse workers in Poland with "permanent contracts" cannot be fired for failing to make rate or meet the corporation's other productivity standards. Unfortunately, only about 25 percent of warehouse workers there have permanent contracts, pointing to the need for more regulation over the use and rights of temporary workers. IP has also filed a legal complaint against Amazon's use of employee productivity data as a violation of GDPR that is still under review by the Warsaw data protection authority. A favorable ruling in this GDPR case could provide additional limits to the use of algorithmic management and electronic surveillance by Amazon, as well as other employers in Poland, and could pave the way for similar legal cases across Europe.[114]

Strengthening other government regulations related to workplace health and safety and improving their enforcement is also necessary to reduce dangerous working conditions. As discussed in chapter 6, Amazon warehouse workers in Inland Southern California and elsewhere beyond the region report numerous health and safety concerns, including the lack of enforcement of COVID-19 safety protocols; high levels of mental stress; and high rates of serious workplace injuries, even higher than the industry average.[115] Existing health and safety regulations provide important legal avenues for holding Amazon accountable for such problems. In the United States and Europe, Amazon warehouse workers have filed legal complaints and lawsuits about workplace dangers related to COVID-19, some of which have resulted in various improvements in workplace safety at Amazon.[116] In California, New York, and Washington, attorneys general even pursued legal cases to force Amazon to do more to protect warehouse workers from COVID-19, which resulted in Amazon agreeing to provide greater transparency about diagnosed cases.[117] In France, where workers have greater rights than in the United States, Amazon warehouses were closed for an entire month in 2020 when workers' legal complaints about their lack of safety from COVID-19 resulted in several favorable rulings.[118]

In the United States, workplace health and safety, much like equity-related and many other rights, are generally compromised by lax regulations and inadequate funds for their enforcement. Funding for OSHA has not kept pace with the increase in the number of workers for decades.[119] Between 2009 and 2019 this trend continued, leading to declines in the overall number of workplace health and safety inspections, especially routine inspections, both nationally and among the twenty-six states that have state-level OSHA affiliates.[120] Low and declining unionization rates in the United States further reduce workers' access to organizational resources for protecting workplace safety.[121]

Transforming a corporate giant like Amazon and reversing the politics that gives rise to the exploitation of workers and their communities is a tall order. Yet as the historian Nelson Lichtenstein reminds us: "It has happened before. Dominant corporations have been forced to radically transform their business practices, sometimes prodded by public sentiment and customer preference, at other moments by an activist government and the unions it helped to empower."[122]

Strengthening government policies regarding workers' rights to organize, form unions, and engage in sectoral bargaining; banning noncompete agreements; placing restrictions on the use of subcontracted, seasonal, gig, and temporary agency workers; strengthening regulations regarding work pace and workplace surveillance; and strengthening workplace health and safety laws and states' capacity to enforce them are just a few examples of how workers and their supporters can fight back against neoliberal policies that expose workers around the world to dangerous and exploitative working conditions.

Many activists targeting Amazon worldwide understand that it is necessary to hold politicians accountable for their complicity with corporations and that organizing is often necessary for winning new rights, regulations, and other policy changes to reverse the neoliberal policy agenda. Policy wins, in turn, often help to fuel further organizing both in and beyond workplaces by helping to create positive momentum; expanding rights and protections for activists, workers, and other vulnerable and marginalized groups; and providing additional tools for industry and social change.

Breaking Out of the Box

Marginally regulated, global "one-click" capitalism, compliments of Amazon, immiserates workers who serve the corporation's millions of customers, and sometimes even kills them through workplace accidents, the impacts of mental stress, and exposure to COVID-19 and too much heat.

It also wrecks the communities where its facilities are located, while its enormous carbon footprint and environmental practices contribute to the destruction of the entire planet. As detailed throughout this book, Amazon warehouse workers endure highly stressful and physically dangerous working conditions. In addition, Don MacKenzie, director of the Sustainable Transportation Lab, explains that "on an item-by-item basis, whether home delivery is greener depends on how many items you buy per trip. We don't replace one shopping trip with one online delivery. We replace it with four or five or six home deliveries."[123] The combined effect of all those orders, shipped separately, some of which are returned, is tons of CO_2, particulates, and other air pollutants from trucks, trains, and planes. These emissions put—in the United States, typically Black and Latino, and/or working-class—residents of communities near Amazon facilities and other warehouses at risk of cardiac disease and respiratory illness. They also contribute to the global climate crisis and threaten many species, including our own, with extinction.

The immediate threats that motivate workers, residents of communities where Amazon operates, and their allies might sometimes appear far less dire, but that is not always so. As a community member told the Banning Planning Commission prior to its vote in favor of a warehouse project adjacent to an active senior (age 55 or older) community and across the street from residential neighborhoods in Beaumont, "You will have blood on your hands."[124] Banning and Beaumont (see figure 8.1) are small suburban cities (30,276 and 48,272, respectively, in 2020) located in the San Gorgonio Mountains pass between the more urban San Bernardino and the desert cities. Like the residents of Bloomington, many people who live in Banning and Beaumont opted out of city life in favor of open space—in this case, desert landscapes and views of mountain peaks reaching 11,503 feet. Additionally, they reside thirty miles farther east, are a little older on average (37 compared to 33 in Bloomington), and are much less likely to be Latino (43 percent compared to 81 percent) than white (38 percent compared to 14 percent).[125] Yet their experiences are sufficient to unite them in mounting persistent, strong resistance, individually and as members of community organizations—for example, Concerned Citizens of Bloomington and No Way Gateway—and in coalition with environmental and labor organizations.[126] This chapter's discussion

Figure 8.1. Amazon FC in Beaumont "area of interest," Riverside County, CA. Photo by Parker Allison.

of how workers and communities mobilize against Amazon illustrates the dynamics of how building relationships and solidarity locally can scale up regionally, nationally, and transnationally.

Confronting Amazon and the politics of exploitation and inequality is an epic battle, the outcome of which will define the nature of work and the quality of community life in the future. In a very real sense, it will also determine the fate of our planet. Most importantly, this confrontation with Amazon (and all that it represents and embodies) provides an opportunity for us—workers, activists, residents, and consumers—to define *who* we are in relationship to one another, the places where we live and work, and the natural environments that nourish us. Activists, in particular, face a corporation that is openly hostile to unions, spies on them, retaliates against them, and even illegally fires those it employs.[127] Yet they persevere, organizing and empowering workers and members of communities near Amazon facilities; building solidarity; and winning immediate improvements, including higher wages, safer working conditions, greater respect at the workplace, improved environmental practices and policies, new worker rights, and new business taxes. The various activists and groups involved in these struggles sometimes work, or appear to work, at cross-purposes or apart from one another, but many nonetheless take action, collaborate, and support one another. These efforts, still relatively new and unfolding, are worthy of our support. Already they are inspiring another generation of activists, who bring new ideas to the table and are developing and enacting novel strategies for mobilizing people and broadening support—across social movements, workers, groups, communities, and nations—for a more just, equitable, and environmentally sustainable way of life.

Methodological Appendix

AMAZON WAREHOUSE WORKER INTERVIEWS

Our data on warehouse workers' experiences draws heavily from eighty-two in-depth interviews of former and current Amazon warehouse workers employed in Riverside and San Bernardino Counties. As we discuss in chapter 1, recruiting workers in low-wage jobs, who are vulnerable to employment retaliation by current or future employers, and asking them to share their views and experiences at work is often challenging, even if they are promised confidentiality. In light of this situation, and following the methods used by other researchers studying low-wage workers, we relied heavily on workers' personal networks to recruit respondents.[1] Finding Amazon warehouse workers and people who knew them was not difficult because Amazon relies so heavily on the labor of our students and their friends and families. We recruited a team of student research assistants who were enrolled in the University of California, Riverside. These research assistants were trained and were offered course credit to help us recruit, collect, and transcribe interviews with Amazon warehouse workers. Participants, who were given gift cards for their interviews, were mainly recruited through the research team's personal network of friends and acquaintances, family members, and coworkers; through email using an undergraduate student listserv; and by snowball sampling from respondents' own networks. To our knowledge, none of the interviewees were involved in efforts to organize Amazon warehouse workers or actively resist Amazon, although one participated in various actions and meetings organized by the WWU and WWRC before the organization focused on Amazon.

These interviews were collected in several waves. The first wave of interviews was collected between 2018 and 2019. Altogether forty-seven former and current Amazon warehouse workers participated in these interviews. Interviews mainly focused on respondents' personal experiences as Amazon employees and their work histories and included gathering information about their social characteristics. In the second wave of interviews, collected in the fall of 2020 in the midst of the COVID-19 pandemic, respondents were asked many of the same questions as the first wave of respondents. In addition, they were asked a new set of questions regarding their work experiences, many of which related to workplace health and safety related to COVID-19. Altogether, we collected thirty-five interviews with former or current blue-collar warehouse workers in this second wave of interviews.

The workers interviewed for this book were current and former warehouse workers who were employed in a variety of jobs. Following Juan De Lara, who has extensively researched blue-collar warehouse workers in Inland Southern California, the five most common nonmanagerial, "blue-collar" warehouse occupations are industrial truck and tractor operators (forklift drivers); laborers and material movers; packers and packagers; shipping, receiving, and traffic clerks; and stock clerks and order fillers.[2] These occupations reflect BLS categories, though, rather than the specific job titles used by Amazon or by the workers themselves. What follows is a full list of the various blue-collar jobs held by the workers interviewed for this book. These job titles were based on BLS categories or, more commonly, those named by our interviewees and their descriptions of their daily work tasks.

Interviewees' Jobs (*Indicates management-related position)

Amazon Safety Committee member

area manager (in training)*

auditor

bin builder

case receiver

driver assist ("under the roof" and "on the road")

fluid load associate

forklift driver

inbound associate

incoming count quality assurance (ICQA) associate

inventory associate or inventory counter

learning ambassador or specialist

loader, reloader, unloader (aka package handler)

outbound associate (or outbound dock)

package handler

packer (or packing, including gift wrap)

palletizer (manual)

picker (or multipicker)

problem solver

process assistant

receiver

scanner

seasonal human resource specialist*

ship dock

sorter

splitter

stower

technician (who built storage units or pods)

temperature checker

traffic clerk

training ambassador

trailer docking and releasing (TDR) associate

water spider

Most of the workers interviewed identified as "warehouse associates." Warehouse associates are employed in a variety of tasks and roles, most commonly in picking, packing, loading, stowing, or unloading. Over time they are usually cross-trained to work in various roles and departments so that they can be used as needed. While most of these workers were employed in entry-level, or tier 1, jobs, some of them held tier 2 or 3 jobs that required more skill and experience, including process assistants, auditors, and traffic clerks. More experienced and well-performing warehouse associates were sometimes employed as "learning ambassadors," helping to train and coach new workers as they learned how to carry out their jobs and to work more quickly. Process assistants have low-level supervisory roles. For these responsibilities, they are paid a few more dollars per hour and are often asked to work overtime. Yet they generally work alongside other warehouse associates, are directed to help out wherever is needed in the warehouse, and follow the orders of higher-level managers. For these reasons, we consider process associates to be employed in nonmanagerial, blue-collar jobs even if they had some low-level supervisory responsibilities. Two of the workers interviewed were initially hired as warehouse associates but were later promoted to managerial roles (one as a seasonal HR representative and the other as an area manager in training; their job titles are indicated in the list by asterisks).[3]

Table A.1 shows the social or demographic characteristics of the interview respondents and table A.2 shows the characteristics of interviewees' jobs and their work experience at Amazon and in the warehouse industry. Both tables provide information about the respondents in the first (prepandemic) and the second (pandemic) interview waves and then for all respondents (combining information for both samples).

As table A.1 shows, the typical Amazon warehouse worker in our interview sample was a native-born Latino in their early twenties who was single, had no children, lived with their parents, and had some college education. Compared to Amazon warehouse workers in the region, young and student workers appeared to be overrepresented in both interview samples. Most of those interviewed in both interview waves were below the age of twenty-five, which is not surprising given that we recruited workers through university students' personal networks. Most interviewees were also women. While this result may have been an artifact of the largely female interview teams, some workers employed during the pandemic reported that about half or most of the workers at their facility were women. Like most warehouse workers in the region, most of those interviewed in both waves were Latino, although our interview samples included white, Black, Asian, and mixed race workers. Most interviewed workers were native born, although a significant minority were immigrants, who made up nearly one out of four of those interviewed during the pandemic but only 13 percent of the earlier sample. Most interviewees were single, although working parents made up about one-third of the prepandemic sample and about 14 percent of the pandemic sample.[4]

Although most interviewees in our sample were full-time employees who were directly hired by Amazon, there were other notable differences in the job characteristics of our two interview samples. As table A.2 shows, most of those interviewed prior to the pandemic (in wave 1) were former employees and employed in Riverside County, while most of those interviewed during the pandemic (in wave 2) were current employees and employed in San Bernardino County. Among those interviewed before the pandemic, 51 percent had first been hired within a few years of the time of their interview (between 2016 and 2019), while 49 percent had been hired in earlier years, between 2012 and 2015. Full-time workers hired directly by Amazon made up the bulk of both samples. Combining both samples, only 14 percent of those interviewed were hired through temporary agencies, a practice that Amazon phased out in later years. Among those interviewed during the pandemic, nearly 56 percent were new hires who were first hired in 2020, while the other 44 percent had been hired in previous years. The median length of employment at Amazon was about 7.5 months in the prepandemic sample and 9.5 months in the pandemic sample. Among all respondents, the length of employment at Amazon ranged between one and eighty-four months; about 28 percent of all respondents were employed for at least two years, although not always consecutively. Overall, the median length of time employed in the warehouse or logistics industry was about eighteen months for all respondents, and this experience ranged between one month and ten years. Although our interview samples lacked older workers, who were likely to have had more work experience than most of those interviewed and had other specific features that made them not fully representative of all Amazon warehouse workers in the region, we believe these interviews have nonetheless yielded important insights into workers' experiences.

Table A.1 Interviewees' Social Characteristics

Variable	Prepandemic Sample (N = 47)		Pandemic Sample (N = 35)		Both Samples (N = 82)	
	Frequency	% of Sample*	Frequency	% of Sample*	Frequency	% of all Respondents*
Gender						
Female	25	53.19	21	60.00	46	56.10
Male	21	44.68	14	40.00	35	42.68
Queer/nonbinary	1	2.13	0	0.00	1	1.22
Total valid responses	*47*		*35*		*82*	
Latino (all races)	31	67.39	27	77.14	58	71.60
Total valid responses	*46*		*35*		*81*	
Race/ethnicity						
Latinx	27	58.70	25	71.43	52	64.20
Non-Hispanic white	7	15.22	1	2.86	8	9.88
Mixed race	7	15.22	4	11.43	11	13.58
Asian/Pacific Islander	3	6.52	3	8.57	6	7.41
Black	2	4.35	2	5.71	4	4.94
Total valid responses	*46*		*35*		*81*	
Foreign-born	6	13.04	8	24.24	14	17.72
Total valid responses	*46*		*33*		*79*	
Age when hired						
18–24	25	60.98	22	64.71	47	62.67
25–29	11	26.83	6	17.65	17	22.67

30–39	5	12.20	4	11.76	9	12.00
40 and older	0	0.00	2	5.88	2	2.67
Total valid responses	*41*		*34*		*75*	
Educational attainment						
High school or GED	8	17.39	10	29.41	18	22.50
Technical/professional license	4	8.70	1	2.94	5	6.25
Some college	26	56.52	19	55.88	45	56.25
Bachelor's and up	8	17.39	4	11.76	12	15.00
Total valid responses	*46*		*34*		*80*	
Marital status						
Single/never married	38	82.61	29	85.29	67	83.75
Married/domestic partnership	7	15.22	3	8.82	10	12.50
Separated/divorced	1	2.17	2	5.88	3	3.75
Total valid responses	*46*		*34*		*80*	
Living w/ parent(s)	24	52.17	23	65.71	47	58.02
Total valid responses	*46*		*35*		*81*	
Parents of minors	15	34.09	5	14.29	20	25.32
Total valid responses	*44*		*35*		*79*	
Average household size	4.53		4.09		4.34	

NOTE: Data on the social characteristics of interviewees in our prepandemic sample are also reported in table 5.1 in Reese and Struna (2020).

* All percentages shown are for valid responses (omitting unclear or no answers).

Table A.2 Interviewees' Job Characteristics

Variable	Prepandemic Sample (N = 47)		Pandemic Sample (N = 35)		Both Samples (N = 82)	
	Frequency	% of Sample*	Frequency	% of Sample*	Frequency	% of all Respondents*
County						
Riverside County	28	60.87	15	44.12	43	53.75
SB County	18	39.13	19	55.88	37	46.25
Total valid responses	46		34		80	
Employment status						
Former Employee	33	70.21	9	25.71	42	51.22
Current Employee	14	29.79	26	74.29	40	48.78
Total valid responses	47		35		82	
Employed two or more times	5	12.50	6	17.14	11	14.67
Total valid responses	40		35		75	
Start year						
2012–2015	19	48.72	2	5.88	21	28.77
2016–2019	20	51.28	13	38.24	33	45.21
2020	0	0.00	19	55.88	19	26.03
Total valid responses	39		34		73	
Work schedule						
Part-time	13	29.55	6	18.75	19	25.00
Full-time	31	70.45	26	81.25	57	75.00
Total valid responses	44		32		76	

Hiring pathway					
Temp agency	10	22.22	1	2.94	11	13.92
Direct hire	35	77.78	33	97.06	68	86.08
Total valid responses	*45*		*34*		*79*	
Amazon experience (median months)	9.5		7.5		9.0	
Warehouse experience (median months)	24.0		9.5		18.0	

NOTE: Data on the job characteristics of interviewees in our prepandemic sample are also reported in table 5.2 in Reese and Struna (2020).

* All percentages shown are for valid responses (omitting unclear or no answers).

Notes

1. OPENING THE BOX: AMAZON'S IMPACT ON WAREHOUSING, WORKERS, AND COMMUNITIES

1. Fieldnotes, September 7, 2021. The press conference and rally demanded passage of AB 701, which was later enacted and is described more fully in chapter 7. It prohibited employers from setting work quotas so high that they compromised workplace safety or interfered with warehouse workers' ability to use the restroom or take their required work breaks and provided workers' with new rights to obtain information and file complaints about their required work quotas without employer retaliation.

2. Fieldnotes, September 7, 2021.

3. Knoblauch (2021).

4. Isidore (2021).

5. DCs are specialized warehouses that serve as hubs for retail outlets.

6. Isidore (2021).

7. Quaker (2022).

8. IsIdore (2021).

9. According to Forbes's annual midyear list of the world's wealthiest people, Jeff Bezos held the number one position for four years before being overtaken by Elon Musk in 2022, although their real-time wealth and relative status fluctuated somewhat within these years (Perry 2022).

10. Pitcher (2020); Stoller (2020).

11. *CNN* (2020).

12. Jacob and Paynter (2021).

13. By April 2022 the combined effects of waning online sales and poor investment performance reduced his net wealth to under $150 billion (Vannucci, Shah, and Bloomberg 2022). Bloomberg Billionaires Index (2022).

14. Glassdoor (2020).

15. Data USA (2020)—income is the average of reported median for east and west public use mircrodata areas (PUMAs); Glasmeier (2020).

16. Hamilton (2020).

17. Data USA (2020); Gupta (2020).

18. Stone (2013).

19. Brandt (2011); Marcus (2011); Spector (2000); Stone (2013).

20. Alimahomed-Wilson, Allison, and Reese (2020).

21. Here we draw loosely upon traditional Marxist notions of labor exploitation under capitalism through which corporate profits are derived from a process of surplus appropriation in which wage workers are paid wages below the value of the labor they help to produce for their employers. We also draw upon Dunaway's (2014) insight that in order to minimize production costs, capitalism tends to depend upon unpaid household labor, often disproportionately performed by women, and to generate external costs that are born by communities, such as air pollution and road damage on heavily trafficked delivery routes.

22. Sheffi (2012); Katzanek (2018).

23. Alimahomed-Wilson et al. (2020).

24. Glaser (2021).

25. Ballou (2004); Chua et al. (2018).

26. Alimahomed-Wilson (2011, 2016); Bonacich and Wilson (2008); Chua et al. (2018); Cowen (2014).

27. Chua et al. (2018:622); Peano (2021).

28. Hill Collins and Bilge (2016).

29. For example, see Emmons Allison et al. (2018); Ducre (2018); Hopkins and Noble (2018); Hopkins (2019); Joassart-Marcelli (2009); McDowell (2008); Peano (2021); Rodó-de-Zárate and Baylina (2018); Valentine (2007).

30. Alimahomed-Wilson (2016); Emmons Allison et al. (2018).

31. Marcuse (2009).

32. Gurusami (2017:5).

33. Rubin (2012); Emmons Allison et al. (2018); see also Economic Policy Institute (2019); Oh (2017).

34. Browne and Askew (2005); Browne and Misra (2003); Catanzarite (2000).

35. Bishop (2021); Duhigg (2019).

36. Amazon Staff (2021).

37. Kantor, Weise, and Ashford (2021).

38. These figures are for 2017 (Flaming and Burns 2019:34)

39. Gutelis and Theodore (2019:24).

40. Emmons Allison et al. (2018); Gonos and Martino (2011); Moody (2017); Warehouse Workers for Justice (2017).

41. Emmons Allison et al. (2018). These findings are consistent with prior research documenting the complex interactions between social inequalities and inequalities based on employment status in other settings (Chang and England 2010; Fuller and Vosko 2008; Vallas and Cummins 2014).

42. Center for Social Innovation (2018).

43. De Lara (2019).

44. Day and Soper (2020).

45. Jones and Zipperer (2018).

46. Shearer, Shah, and Gootman (2019).

47. Smith (2020); Shearer et al. (2019).

48. Tung and Berkowitz (2020); Del Rey (2022).

49. Ducre (2018).

50. Here we build upon insights from other critical logistics scholars (Chua et al. 2018; De Lara 2018; Gilmore 2002).

51. Dunaway (2014:63).

52. Ballou (2004); Chua et al. (2018).

53. Center for Social Innovation (2018, 2019); Nakano Glenn (2012); Petrongolo and Ronchi (2020); Wakabayashi and Donato (2005).

54. Amazon Employees for Climate Justice (2020).

55. Yuan (2018a, 2018b).

56. Moody (2017); Yuan (2018a).

57. Yuan (2018b).

58. Fielding (2018).

59. Author's calculations; see chapter 2 for details.

60. Finn (2016).

61. Los Angeles Economic Development Corporation (2017).

62. De Lara (2018); Los Angeles Economic Development Corporation (2017).

63. Patterson (2015).

64. Yuan (2018a, 2018b).

65. Bonacich and Wilson (2008); Finn (2016); Jaller and Pineda (2017); Sheffi (2012); Yuan (2018a, 2018b).

66. De Lara (2018); Baldassare et al. (2020).

67. Patterson (2015); De Lara (2018).

68. Emmons Allison, Cline, and Reese (2017); De Lara (2018); Patterson (2015).

69. Lifsher (2019).

70. De Lara (2018); Patterson (2015).

71. Cited in Amazon (2018).

72. Good Jobs First (2020).

73. Kalleberg (2011); Luce (2014).

74. Alimahomed-Wilson et al. (2020).

75. Buck (2018).

76. Our methodological approach is guided by Schrock (2013) and consistent with Valentine's (2007) intersectional, feminist geographic study of a deaf, working-class, lesbian mother. See also Brown (2012); Hopkins (2018, 2019); Rodo-de-Zarate and Baylina (2018).

77. Center for Social Innovation (2018).

78. Milkman, Gonzalez, and Narro (2010).

79. See Flaming and Burns (2019:34).

80. Almaguer ([1994] 2009); Patterson (2015).

81. Aneesh (2009); Delfanti (2021).

82. Tung and Berkowitz (2020).

83. Athena Coalition (2019); Evans (2019a, 2020); Strategic Organizing Center (2021, 2022).

84. Center for Biological Diversity (2019); Sisson (2019).

85. Woodcraft, Boyer, and Victoria (2021).

86. MacGillis (2021a).

2. BOXING IN OUR COMMUNITY: AMAZON EXPANDS INLAND SOUTHERN CALIFORNIA'S WAREHOUSE EMPIRE

1. Winther (1963).

2. City of Riverside Planning Department (n.d.).

3. Jenkins (2016:3).

4. Editors (1895).

5. Daniel (1982).

6. Jenkins (2016); Patterson (2015); Sackman (2000).

7. Olmstead and Rhodes (2017:1).

8. Harris (2019).

9. Pike Bond (2019); UCR School of Business Center for Economic Forecasting and Development (2019).

10. Hayasaki (2021); Reese and Scott (2019); Levin (2021).

11. De Lara (2018); Patterson (2015).

12. CCAEJ (2020).

13. Long (2021).

14. MacGillis (2021a:266).

15. Gonzales (2014).

16. Robinson (1957); Robinson and McGurk (2013).

17. Scharf (1978).

18. Caragozian (2021).

19. Pursuant to the Mexican Secularization Act of 1833.

20. Haas (1995); Lothrop (1994); Robinson (1957); Robinson and McGurk (2013).

21. Monroy (1997); Robinson (1957); Robinson and McGurk (2013).

22. The Treaty of Cahuenga, 1847, ended the conquest of California. Under the Treaty of Guadalupe Hidalgo, 1848, Mexico ceded Alta California and other territories to the United States and agreed to establish the Texas border at the Rio Grande.

23. History (2010).

24. The Compromise of 1850 consisted of five bills, under which (1) California would be admitted to the union as a free state; (2) the remainder of the Mexican cession was divided into the Utah and New Mexico territories; (3) the union paid Texas $10 million to renounce its claim to part of New Mexico; (4) the Fugitive Slave Act was passed; and (5) the buying and selling of slaves was abolished in Washington, D.C.

25. United States Census Bureau (1852). The census did not include most Native Californians and inhabitants of Colusa, Marin, and Sutter Counties.

26. United States Census Bureau (1852).

27. Hurtado (1999).

28. Hurtado (1999); Taniguchi (2000).

29. Suarez (2019).

30. Suarez (2019).

31. The California Land Act of 1851 required holders of Spanish and Mexican land grants to present their titles for confirmation by the three-person Board of Land Commissioners, appointed by the US president, which was in direct violation of Article VIII of the Treaty of Guadalupe Hidalgo; Articles IX and X extend property rights to all Mexican nationals.

32. Breschini, Haversat, and Hampson (1983).

33. Guinn (1890).

34. Street (1979).

35. Because they are seedless, navel orange trees are propagated from grafted cuttings. Navel orange trees were brought to the United States from Bahia, Brazil, by the US Department of Agriculture in 1870 and propagated on sweet orange seedlings. Riverside's parent tree is one of these trees.

36. Patterson (2015); Sackman (2000).

37. Patterson (2015).

38. Giovannini (1985).

39. The Chinese Exclusion Act of 1882 restricted immigration from China. Almaguer ([1994] 2009); Carpio (2019); Patterson (2015).

40 California law banned "aliens" from citizenship and leasing land.

41. Carpio (2019); Patterson (2015); Maier (n.d.).

42. Gonzalez (1994).

43. O'Brien (2018).

44. Verge (1994); Patterson (2015).

45. Rivas-Rodriguez and Olguin (2014).
46. Center for Social Innovation (2018); Patterson (2015).
47. Rivas-Rodriguez and Olguín (2014).
48. Patterson (2015); Davis ([1990] 2006).
49. The Bracero program refers to agreements between the US and Mexican governments, codified in 1942 by executive order and the bilateral Mexican Farm Labor Act, that allowed male, Mexican workers to fill seasonal jobs on US farms.
50. Roberts (1972).
51. South Coast AQMD (1997).
52. Pope, Bates, and Raizenne (1995).
53. Roberts (1972).
54. The US federal government enacted the Clean Air Act in 1963; California adopted auto emissions standards in 1966 and statewide Ambient Air Quality Standards in 1969.
55. Bachus (1981); Riverside Agricultural Commission (2018).
56. We borrow the phrase "warehouse empire" from Patterson (2015). Hayasaki (2021).
57. De Lara (2018).
58. De Lara (2013a:81).
59. De Lara (2018); Patterson (2015). On the significance of conservative Democrats in Riverside and San Bernardino Counties, see McGhee and Krimm (2012).
60. Gibson and Jung (2005); United States Census Bureau (2010).
61. De Lara (2018).
62. De Lara (2018:55). Although air quality in Inland Southern California has improved by as much as 50 percent since the 1970s, the region still experiences the nation's highest ozone and $PM_{2.5}$ levels (Roach 2020).
63. Cuevas (2012).
64. Shane (2013); De Lara (2018); Larsen (2022).
65. Baldassare et al. (2020); see also McGhee (2020).
66. Base Realignment and Closure is a congressionally authorized process the DoD used to support US forces, increase operational readiness, and facilitate new ways of doing business more efficiently and effectively between 1988 and 2005.
67. De Lara (2018); Patterson (2015); Center for Social Innovation (2019).
68. The great inflation (1965–1984) spanned the end of the global monetary system established during World War II, four economic recessions, two energy shortages, and peacetime implementation of wage and price controls. Strochak et al. (2019); Urban Institute (2021).
69. United States Census Bureau (1977).
70. Prop 13 limits property taxes to no more than 1 percent of assessed value, plus any locally approved rates; caps annual increases in assessed property values to the lower of 2 percent or the percentage growth in the state's Consumer

Price Index (CPI); and shifts public school funding from property taxes to the state's general funds.

71. Patterson (2015); Sanders et al. (1984).

72. Patterson (2015); Trombley (1985).

73. De Lara (2018:43).

74. Patterson (2015).

75. Levine (1990).

76. *Los Angeles Times* (1985).

77. Bonacich and Wilson (2008).

78. Bonacich and Wilson (2008); Patterson (2015).

79. Emmons Allison (2020).

80. Center for Social Innovation (2019); Lee (1998).

81. Manning (1997).

82. Center for Social Innovation (2019); De Lara (2018).

83. Allen (2010).

84. De Lara (2018); United States Bureau of Labor Statistics (2019).

85. Mordechay (2019).

86. Woodhouse (2011).

87. Do et al. (2021).

88. Sasser et al. (2021).

89. Mora and Davila (2018); Tessum et al. (2019).

90. United States Bureau of Labor Statistics (2013).

91. Husing (2018); United States Bureau of Labor Statistics (2019).

92. Waddell (2021).

93. California collects a 1 percent local sales tax as part of the larger sales and use tax levied on most items for sale. The revenue generated is returned to the local government where the sale occurred. See Lewis and Barbour (1999).

94. Emmons Allison et al. (2018).

95. See Chittum (2012) on the San Bernardino deal and Lifsher (2012) on the state sales tax issue.

96. Cafcas and LeRoy (2016).

97. Delivery stations are excluded from map 2.1 to constrain the geographic space and clarify information included in the image.

98. De Lara (2018:67).

99. Alimahomed-Wilson (2020).

100. These counts are based on locations; there may be multiple facilities at a single address.

101. Alimahomed-Wilson, Allison, and Reese (2020); DePillis and Sarlin (2018).

102. CBRE (2017).

103. Sohaib (2022).

104. Emmons Allison (2020).

105. *Daily News* (2021).
106. Horseman (2021); Smith (2015).
107. Los Angeles County Economic Development Corporation (2017).
108. Weise (2021a).
109. Droesch (2021); Weise (2021b).
110. De Lara (2018); Pierson and Khouri (2016).
111. Biro (2015); Manuel (2016).
112. De Lara (2018:2).
113. Kohl (2019).
114. De Lara (2018).
115. De Lara (2018); see also Kohl (2019).
116. Smith (2015).
117. De Lara (2018); Emmons Allison (2020); Torres, Victoria, and Klooster (2021); Yuan (2018a).
118. Torres et al. (2021).
119. MacGillis (2021a); see also Houde, Newberry, and Seim (2021).
120. Waddell (2021).
121. Amazon Employees for Climate Justice (2020).
122. American Lung Association (2019).
123. Nakano Glenn (2012).
124. Emmons Allison (2020).
125. Yuan (2018b).
126. Yuan (2018a, 2018b).
127. MacGillis (2021a, 2021b); Waddell (2021).
128. Kaveh et al. (2021).
129. Yuan (2018b, 2019).
130. Sisson (2017).
131. Larsen (2022); Guilhem (2015).
132. Dobard et al. (2016).
133. Sisson (2017); Yuan (2018a).
134. Yuan (2018b).
135. Stroik and Finseth (2021).
136. Stroik and Finseth (2021).
137. Kirkendall (2016); see also Newman (2012).
138. Nakano Glenn (2012).
139. Palmer (2021b).
140. Hanley (2018).
141. Hanley (2018). Amazon is Rivian's largest investor. McCabe and Weiss (2019); Peters (2019).
142. Sisson (2021).
143. Mayo (2021).
144. Meisenzhal (2021).

145. Jones and Zipperer (2018).

146. Jones and Zipperer (2018).

147. Husing (2019); ZipRecruiter (2021).

148. Glasmeier (2019).

149 De Lara (2013b).

150. DeVries (2019); Stone (2013).

151. Allison, Herrera, and Reese (2015); De Lara (2013b, 2018); Alimahomed-Wilson et al. (2020).

152. Matsakis (2018).

153. Gershgorn (2017).

154. Katzanek (2012).

155. McCrea (2019).

156. DePillis and Sarlin (2018); Emmons Allison (2020).

157. Corkery (2018).

158. Lawson (2019); Katzanek (2019).

3. BEHIND THE BOX: EXPLOITATIVE CONDITIONS IN AMAZON'S WAREHOUSES

1. Kimball (2021); Phillips (2021).

2. Browne and Misra (2003); Emmons Allison et al. (2018). For a general review of intersectional feminist theory and/or scholarship upon which we are building, see Crenshaw (1989), Hill Collins and Bilge (2016), and Ducre (2018).

3. Flaming and Burns (2019).

4. Amazon Staff (2021).

5. This phrase was introduced to us by Veronica Alvarado, deputy director of WWRC.

6. Whitehead (2019).

7. Tanzi (2021).

8. Flaming and Burns (2019).

9. We excluded the two workers most recently employed in managerial occupations from this calculation.

10. Human Impact Partners and Warehouse Workers Resource Center (2021).

11. Human Impact Partners and Warehouse Workers Resource Center (2021).

12. These are valid percentages, omitting respondents who did not respond to these questions.

13. For the age compositions of interviewees and Amazon warehouse workers in Southern California, see the appendix and Flaming and Burns (2019) respectively.

14. Snider and Weise (2018); Matsakis (2018).

15. Weise (2018).

16. Baker (2018).

17. Hamilton (2020).

18. Kantor, Weise, and Ashford (2021).

19. Kinder and Stateler (2020).

20. Faulkner (2021).

21. Howley (2021).

22. Jackson (2021).

23. Center for Social Innovation (2018).

24. Specifically, in December 2022 the average base salary was $17.32 (city of Riverside)/$17.43 (city of San Bernardino) for food service associate and $18.80 (city of Riverside)/$18.93 (city of San Bernardino) for retail associate (Indeed 2022); Gatta (2019); Walters and Misra (2015); Rolf (2016).

25. This is a valid percentage, excluding workers who did not respond to these questions.

26. Center for Social Innovation (2018).

27. Allison, Herrera, and Reese (2015); De Lara (2013b); Gutelis and Theodore (2019).

28. Day and Soper (2020). Mitchell and LaVecchia (2016) surveyed 1,300 wage postings in Glassdoor.com and found that Amazon warehouse wages were about 9 percent less than the industry average, and the percentage was even less in certain metro areas.

29. This interview, conducted by Reese, is featured in Center for Social Innovation (2018).

30. Del Rey (2022).

31. Day and Soper (2020).

32. Hurdle (2021). Confounding explanations for flat and falling wages in the wake of Amazon's arrival in an area include low market concentration of comparable employment opportunities, Amazon's strategic provision of benefits to permanent employees to offset low hourly wages, and the corporation's reliance on unskilled and young workers with limited employment options (*The Economist* 2018).

33. Glasmeier (2020).

34. Aurand et al. (2020).

35. Flaming and Burns (2019:45).

36. Berentz (2017).

37. Government Accounting Office (2020).

38. Flaming and Burns (2019:38).

39. Gatta (2019).

40. Grusky et al. (2021).

41. Enzinna (2022).

42. On divergent uses of the slave metaphor by particular and divergent social groups and activists in different time periods in the United States, see Boris (1998) and Dorsey (2009).

43. Perry (2022).

44. Mitchell and LaVecchia (2016).

45. Because "staffing services" is considered a distinct industry in government statistics, estimates of the percentage of blue-collar warehouse workers that are employed as temps are rough and can vary across sources (Emmons Allison et al. 2018).

46. Among warehouse workers in Inland Southern California, only about one out of five temporary warehouse workers, compared to 54 percent of direct hires, had employer-provided health insurance. On average, direct hires earned about $21,444 per year and $11.33 per hour, while temps earned $10,034 per year and $9.42 per hour. Overall, according to the 2009–2013 American Community Survey (ACS), blue-collar warehouse workers earn an average annual income of only $16,800 (Allison et al. 2015). De Lara (2013b), using ACS data, found that about 70 percent of all temporary blue-collar warehouse workers in Inland Southern were employed less than ten months per year, which also kept their annual incomes significantly lower on average than directly employed warehouse workers.

47. Mitchell and LaVecchia (2016).

48. Smith (2017).

49. Kauffman Borgeest and Ryan LLP (2017).

50. Kantor et al. (2021).

51. We draw upon ideas and interviews cited in Reese (2020) in this section.

52. Hanani (2020).

53. *Washington Post* (2019).

54. Warehouse Workers for Justice (2017); see also chapter 4 for more evidence of this from various legal cases.

55. Flaming and Burns (2019:38).

56. Dunaway (2014).

57. Flaming and Burns (2019).

58. This section builds upon on ideas from, and interviews cited in, Reese and Scott (2019). Among those interviewed during the pandemic, mostly current workers, 51.42 percent indicated that they were enrolled in college at the time of their interviews. We did not directly ask interviewees if they were enrolled in school when they worked at Amazon in the first wave, although many of them indicated this was the case during their interviews.

59. Since interviews were conducted between 2018 and 2020, statistics for enrolled UCR students for fall 2019 were used in these comparisons (UCR Institutional Research 2022).

60. The percent of interviewees raised in the region is a valid percentage, omitting three respondents who did not respond to this question. This percentage might be even higher since respondents who claimed they were raised in the United States, California, or Southern California were coded as being raised outside of the region. The percentage of UCR students that are international is for fall 2019 (UCR Institutional Research 2022).

61. Fifteen expressed interest in careers in education or social services, eight participants wanted to become business owners or work in business administration, six desired careers in health care, five in the arts, five in the government or public service, three in journalism, and three in biology or veterinary science; two had dreams of becoming lawyers, and one person wanted to work in a restaurant.

62. Ten wanted careers in education or social services, four participants wanted to work in business administration, two desired careers in health care, and one sought to help to improve the environment or work with animals.

63. Sixty-two interviewees were below the age of 30, nineteen were age 30 or more, and one participant did not indicate their age. Some of these participants expressed interest in more than one type of career. Eight interviewees, all below the age of 30, were not asked or did not respond to this question about their dream jobs.

4. BOXED IN: DISCIPLINE, CONTROL, AND MECHANISMS OF EXPLOITATION IN AMAZON WAREHOUSES

This chapter draws on ideas presented, and interviews cited, in Alimahomed-Wilson and Reese (2021), Reese and Scott (2019), and Reese and Struna (2020).

1. Delfanti (2021).

2. Aneesh (2009).

3. Taylor (2014).

4. Tung and Berkowitz (2020); see also Del Rey (2022).

5. Lecher (2019).

6. Reese and Struna (2020); Human Impact Partners and Warehouse Worker Resource Center (2021).

7. Kantor, Weise, and Ashford (2021); Public Justice and Make the Road New York (2020).

8. Human Impact Partners and Warehouse Worker Resource Center (2021).

9. Evans (2020); Strategic Organizing Center (2021).

10. This was published in Bloodworth (2019) and also publicized through news interviews.

11. Organise (2018).

12. Human Impact Partners and Warehouse Workers Resource Center (2021); Organise (2018).

13. Gurley (2021a).

14. Hautala (2021); Lecher (2019); Public Justice and Make the Road New York (2020).

15. Semuels (2018).

16. Semuels (2018).

17. Tung and Berkowitz (2020).

18. Kantor et al. (2021); see also Del Rey (2022).

19. Industry estimates were based on BLS estimates, cited in Del Rey (2022). In some facilities, Amazon's turnover rates were as high as 150 percent even before the pandemic, according to internal corporate records (Kantor et al. 2021).

20. Kantor et al. (2021).

21. Del Rey (2022).

22. Taylor (2014).

23. Kantor et al. (2021).

24. Del Rey (2022).

25. De Lara (2013b, 2018); Center for Social Innovation (2018); Tung and Berkowitz (2020).

5. MOVING BOXES TOGETHER: INEQUALITIES AND SOCIAL RELATIONS AMONG WAREHOUSE WORKERS

Parts of this chapter, including some quotes from interviewees, are reprinted from Reese (2020); it also builds upon some ideas presented in Reese and Scott (2019).

1. These figures are for 2017 in the four-county region of Los Angeles, Orange, Riverside, and San Bernardino Counties (Flaming and Burns 2019:34).

2. For these and other percentages reported in chapter 4, we excluded those not responding to the question at hand and the responses of the HR representative who responded to these questions in terms of her current managerial job, rather than her former experience as a warehouse associate.

3. Emmons Allison et al. (2018); Evans (2016b); Peck and Theodore (2001); Warehouse Workers for Justice (2017).

4. Allison et al. (2018).

5. Evans (2016b); Peck and Theodore (2001).

6. Warehouse Workers for Justice (2017).

7. Emmons Allison et al. (2018).

8. A greater percentage of those employed as managers and senior leaders within Amazon (About Amazon Staff 2021) is likely a microcosm of larger patterns found in the broader warehouse industry and consistent with male domination within managerial occupations more generally.

9. Alimahomed-Wilson (2016); Warehouse Workers for Justice (2017).

10. Sonnemaker (2021b).

11. Sonnemaker (2021b).

12. Greene (2021).

13. Farrell (2019).

14. Tanno (2020).

15. States News Service (2014); Peck (2018).

16. Targeted News Service (2019); see also Warehouse Workers for Justice (2017).

17. Ng and Rubin (2019).

18. Ng and Rubin (2019).

19. Frison (2020).

20. Palmer (2021a).

21. Bonazzo (2017); Crary (2017).

22. Avery (2020).

23. Bonazzo (2017); Crary (2017).

24. Avery (2020).

25. Avery (2020).

26. Associated Press (2021).

27. Del Rey (2021).

28. Kantor, Weise, and Ashford (2021).

29. *Washington Post* (2019).

30. Panico (2020); Sonnemaker (2021a).

31. Flaming and Burns (2019).

32. Evans (2016a, 2016b).

33. Gibson (2019).

34. An investigation by the news organization ProPublica found that Facebook's platform made it possible to discriminate against Blacks, Latinos, and Asian Americans by excluding them from receiving ads for various economic opportunities, including housing and employment ads (Angwin and Parris Jr. 2016). Related legal complaints charged other companies with gender- and age-based discrimination, such as targeting Facebook job ads to younger men (American Civil Liberties Unions 2019; Cohen 2019; Communication Workers of America 2017; Mulvaney 2020).

35. American Civil Liberties Unions (2019); Cohen (2019); Communication Workers of America (2017); Mulvaney (2020).

36. Stuart (2021); on employee turnover rates, see Tung and Berkowitz (2020) and Del Rey (2022).

37. Del Rey (2021).

6. BOXED AND BRUISED: WAREHOUSE WORKERS' INJURIES AND ILLNESSES

This chapter draws on ideas presented, and interviews cited, in Alimahomed-Wilson and Reese (2021), Reese and Scott (2019), and Reese and Struna (2020).

1. Cited in Evans (2020).

2. Evans (2020); see also Strategic Organizing Center (2021).

3. These studies and their methodology are discussed more fully later in the chapter (Athena Coalition 2019; Evans 2019a, 2020; Human Impact Partners and Warehouse Workers Resource Center 2021; Strategic Organizing Center 2021, 2022).

4. Strategic Organizing Center (2021); Evans (2020).

5. Selyukh (2021).

6. The "water spider" concept and personnel position in lean production processes is inspired by the whirligig beetle, which can appear to hang between the water and the air while quickly going from place to place, keeping both the environments in its sight simultaneously. The water spider's responsibilities revolve around reducing wasted resources, including time, by enabling others to focus on their assigned roles in the process.

7. Park, Pankratz, and Behrer (2021).

8. The survey was conducted by UCLA researchers and the Warehouse Workers Resource Center (Kimball 2021).

9. SB 1167 directs Cal/OSHA to draft and propose heat illness and injury prevention standards for indoor worksites by January 1, 2019.

10. Phillips (2021).

11. Soper (2012).

12. Kimball (2021); Phillips (2021).

13. United States Bureau of Labor Statistics (2020).

14. Evans (2020).

15. Evans (2020).

16. National COSH (2018).

17. National COSH (2019); WJZ-CBS Baltimore (2019). On suicide calls, see Zahn and Paget (2019).

18. National COSH (2020).

19. National COSH (2022).

20. Occupational Safety and Health Administration (2022).

21. Rosenberg (2022).

22. Evans (2019b).

23. Evans (2020).

24. This study examined Amazon's records of occupational injuries at twenty-eight facilities in sixteen states between 2014 and 2019 and found that the total rate of recordable injuries (10.76 per 100 full-time workers) was more than twice that rate for the general warehouse industry, and more than three times the rate for all private sector employers (Athena Coalition 2019).

25. (Athena Coalition 2019:3).

26. The SOC coalition includes the Service Employees International Union (SEIU), the International Brotherhood of Teamsters (IBT), Communications Workers of America (CWA), and United Farmworkers of America (UFA).

27. Strategic Organizing Center (2021:3).

28. Among survey respondents, 52 percent worked in fulfillment centers, 9 percent worked in delivery stations, and 8 percent worked in sortation centers. The remaining 24 percent were last mile delivery drivers (Strategic Organizing Center 2021).

29. Between 2018 and 2020, Amazon introduced a new "light duty" policy that increased the number of injured workers assigned to "light duty"rather than given days off of work; this policy helps to reduce the cost of workers' compensation (Strategic Organizing Center 2021).

30. Strategic Organizing Center (2022).

31. Strategic Organizing Center (2022).

32. Strategic Organizing Center (2022:9).

33. Evans (2019a, 2020); Strategic Organizing Center (2021:1).

34. Evans (2020).

35. Evans (2019a, 2020).

36. Evans (2020).

37. Human Impact Partners and Warehouse Workers Resource Center (2021).

38. Human Impact Partners and Warehouse Workers Resource Center (2021).

39. Evans (2020).

40. Strategic Organizing Center (2020).

41. Evans (2019b).

42. Evans (2019b).

43. Stuart (2021); Tung and Berkowitz (2020).

44. Zahn and Paget (2019).

45. Katzanek (2020).

46. Amazon provides detailed information on its efforts over time to keep employees and the community safe from COVID-19 (Amazon Staff 2022); Alimahomed-Wilson and Reese (2020a, 2020b).

47. Kerr and Varner (2021).

48. Human Impact Partners and Warehouse Worker Resource Center (2021).

49. Tanzi (2021); Tung and Berkowitz (2020); Del Rey (2022).

50. Human Impact Partners and Warehouse Workers Resource Center (2021); Kantor, Weise, and Ashford (2021); Strategic Organizing Center (2021).

51. Human Impact Partners and Warehouse Workers Resource Center (2021).

52. Alimahomed-Wilson and Reese (2020); Hussain (2021).

53. See Alimahomed-Wilson and Reese (2020a), especially chapters 15 and 17. Nonactivist workers interviewed for this book also reported sharing information about COVID-19 cases with their coworkers.

54. For example, see Dean (2020), Kantor et al. (2021), and National COSH (2020).

55. Strategic Organizing Center (2021).

56. Kantor et al. (2021).

57. Strategic Organizing Center (2021).

58. Human Impact Partners and Warehouse Worker Resource Center (2021).

59. Initially, Amazon provided workers with unlimited time off during the pandemic and then later documentation and approvals for extended leaves (Kantor et al. 2021).

60. Hamilton (2020).

61. Kantor et al. (2021).

62. Athena Coalition (2019); Evans (2019a, 2019b, 2020); Strategic Organizing Center (2021, 2022).

63. Hussain (2021a).

64. Hussain (2021b).

65. Del Rey (2022); Tung and Berkowitz (2020).

7. BOXING LESSONS: COMMUNITY RESISTANCE TO AMAZON AND WAREHOUSING IN INLAND SOUTHERN CALIFORNIA

1. Sarathy (2013).

2. Lawton (2020).

3. Craig (2020).

4. Quoted in Lawton (2020:59).

5. Rantz (1970).

6. Bennett (1992); Foehringer Merchant (2014).

7. Lawton (2020:60); Craig (2020); Gold (2001); McNary (1992).

8. Craig (2020); Lawton (2020).

9. Foehringer Merchant (2014); Seager (1993).

10. The Chemical Control Corporation operated as a hazardous waste disposal plant from 1972 until it was condemned in 1979; more than 50,000 drums of hazardous chemicals remained on the property when a fire erupted on April 21, 1980, leading to a major hazardous materials emergency. Love Canal, near Niagara Falls, New York, was long used as a municipal and industrial chemical dumpsite. In 1953 Hooker Chemical Company filled the canal with dirt and sold it to the city for $1.00. By the end of that decade, one hundred homes and a school had been built on the property; twenty years, a record rainfall, and mounting miscarriages and birth defects in the area later, the state's Department of Health and the US EPA had both initiated investigations.

11. Environmental Protection Agency (2016).

12. Thornton (1983).

13. Associated Press (1986); Mydans (1991). Residents were initially barred from participating, with the exception of CNA and its leader, Penny Newman; that decision was overturned by the 9th U.S. Circuit Court of Appeals and upheld by the Supreme Court. The final settlement included more than 3,800 Glen Avon residents.

14. Craig (2020).

15. Gormond (1993).

16. Craig (2020); Gold (2001); Gormond (1993).

17. This facility replaced the aging Pre-Treatment Plant and is operated by the state Department of Toxic Substances Control. The SAP cleanup is expected to take 500 years.

18. Craig (2020).

19. Sarathy (2013).

20. On regional politics, see De Lara (2018); McGhee (2020).

21. American Management Systems (1981).

22. Sarathy (2013:260).

23. Coalition partners included the League of Conservation Voters, California Public Interest Research Group, California Rural Legal Assistance, Campaign for Economic Democracy, Citizens for a Better Environment, Coalition for Clean Air, Environmental Defense Fund, Environmental Health Coalition of San Diego, Greenpeace, United Farmworkers of America, and Federated Firefighters of California, AFL-CIO. The group's more specific aims were to (1) prevent toxic pollution before it occurs, (2) expand the right to know laws, (3) facilitate greater citizen involvement in environmental policy making, and (4) pass a bill of rights for those injured by toxic chemicals that includes holding polluters liable.

24. Tarrow (1998:86). On the importance of various types of perceived threats in motivating protest and for excellent reviews of this theme within social movement literature generally and political process models in particular, and which build upon Tilly's (1978) initial insights, see also Almeida (2003, 2008, 2015, 2019); McKane and McCammon (2018); and Meyer (2004).

25. De Lara (2018).

26. CBRE (2020).

27. De Lara (2018).

28. Barboza (2015).

29. De Lara (2018); Larsen (2022). See Guilhem (2015) on the Mira Loma case.

30. Data USA (2020).

31. Data USA (2020).

32. *Grist* (2020).

33. IQ Air (2022).

34. Danelski (2013).

35. Jurupa Valley was incorporated on July 1, 2011; the lawsuit was filed on July 18, 2011.

36. Penny Newman, interview by Emmons Allison, August 13, 2015.

37. Green Project site elements include a 100kW capacity solar array, vehicle charging stations, setbacks with landscaping buffer elements, and LEED (Leadership in Energy and Environmental Design) silver certification for buildings over 100,000 square feet. See *Fontana Herald News* 2014).

38. See Waddell (2021).

39. Data USA (2022); Mayorquin (2022). Low income census tracts are those with median household incomes at or below 80 percent of the statewide median income or with median household incomes below the threshold designated as low income by the Department of Housing and Urban Development's Low Income Limits. Designation in the 90th percentile for ozone pollution means that ozone pollution is worse than at least 90 percent of census tracts in California.

40. County of San Bernardino (2007, 2019).

41. Mayorquin (2022).

42. Mayorquin (2022).

43. Molina (2018).

44. Sisson (2019).

45. Steinberg (2017).

46. Mayorquin (2022); Victoria (2017).

47. Sandoval (2021); Sisson (2019).

48. Mayorquin (2022).

49. Venturi (2021).

50. Esquivel (2019).

51. As of 2022, Amazon's other Fontana locations were in industrial areas of the city.

52. Center for Biological Diversity (2019); Sisson (2019).

53. City of Fontana (2020).

54. City of Fontana (2021).

55. Ingold (2020).

56. Ingold (2021).

57. Venturi (2021).

58. Whitehead (2022).

59. Bonta (2022).

60. Bonta (2022); Fontana City Council (2022).

61. Bonta (2022).

62. Fontana City Council (2022).

63. Torres, Victoria, and Klooster (2021).

64. Solon and Glaser (2021).

65. Singh (2021).

66. Singh (2021).

67. Sarathy (2021); Singh (2021).

68. Ghori (2016).

69. Woodcraft (2021).

70. Comment by Joe Lyou to Earthjustice (Woodcraft 2021).

71. South Coast AQMD (2021b).

72. South Coast AQMD (2022).

73. Morton (2015).

74. Lyou (2021).

75. MPOs are federally mandated and funded local transportation policy-making bodies that represent all urbanized areas in the United States.

76. See South Coast AQMD (2021a).

77. Latham & Watkins LLP (2021).

78. San Joaquin Valley APCD (2017).

79. The Carpenters Union Local 235, for example, was founded in 1886. The Riverside County Labor Council was formed through a charter of the American Federation of Labor in 1912 by five local unions representing construction workers, typographers, tobacco workers, painters, and barbers (Phillips 1972).

80. For a good overview of these strikes, see Garcia (2001), Patterson (2015), and Van Valen (1953).

81. See Teamsters Local 63 (n.d.).

82. For details on the UPS agreement see, for example, see Teamsters Local 63 (2018).

83. De Lara, Reese, and Struna (2016).

84. The CTW federation was formed by seven unions: Teamsters, SEIU, UNITE-HERE, UFCW, Laborers, Carpenters, and the UFW; most of these unions later left it to rejoin the AFL-CIO. As of 2022, the SOC includes the Teamsters, SEIU, and the CWA.

85. De Lara et al. (2016).

86. De Lara et al. (2016).

87. De Lara et al. (2016).

88. De Lara et al. (2016).

89. De Lara et al. (2016).

90. Reese and Bielitz (2021).

91. De Lara et al. (2016).

92. Reese and Bielitz (2021); De Lara et al. (2016); Olney and Rand (2020).

93. Olney and Rand (2020).

94. Reese and Bielitz (2021); De Lara et al. (2016).

95. Katzanek (2018).

96. Alimahomed-Wilson and Reese (forthcoming).

97. Reese and Bielitz (2021).

98. Berger (2021); Whitehead (2021b).

99. Reese and Bielitz (2021).

100. Reese and Bielitz (2021).

101. Fieldnotes, October 13, 2020.

102. Vazquez and Conrow (2021).

103. Fieldnotes, Assembly Labor and Committee Hearing in Riverside, California on March 6, 2020; Athena Coalition (2019); Strategic Organizing Center (2021, 2022); Tung and Berkowitz (2020).

104. Gurley (2020a).

105. California Legislative Information (2021).

106. California Legislative Information (2021); Alimahomed-Wilson and Reese (2022); Strategic Organizing Center (2021).

107. Reese and Bielitz (2021).

108. Rose (2000).

109. De Lara et al. (2016).

110. Brown (2013); Warehouse Workers Resource Center (2019).

111. Sandoval (2019).

112. American Lung Association (2021).

113. Vasquez and Conrow (2021).

114. Reese and Bielitz (2021).

115. Reese and Bielitz (2021).

116. Reese and Bielitz (2021).

117. Whitehead (2019).

118. Whitehead (2020).

119. See "Opinion" in the case documents for CCAEJ vs. Federal Aviation Authority, Ninth Circuit Court of Appeals, Case No. 20-70272. Retrieved January 19, 2022 (http://climatecasechart.com/climate-change-litigation/case/center-for-community-action-environmental-justice-v-federal-aviation-administration/).

120. Case documents for CCAEJ vs. Federal Aviation Authority, see "petitions for rehearing."

121. Whitehead (2021a). On Chino, see Scauzillo (2021).

122. Guilhem (2022); Hager Pacific (2021).

123. Fieldnotes, December 16, 2021.

124. Fieldnotes, April 28, May 1, and July 14, 2022; see also https://justsb.org/.

125. Fieldnotes, August 15, 2022; Gurley and O'Donovan (2022).

126. Fieldnotes, August 15, 2022.

127. Gurley and O'Donovan (2022).

128. Ding and Hussain (2022); United 4 Change ONT8 and Amazon Labor Union (2022).

129. Reese and Bielitz (2021).

130. Woodcraft, Boyer, and Victoria (2021).

8. BEYOND THE BOX: CONFRONTING AMAZON AND THE POLITICS OF EXPLOITATION AND INEQUALITY

1. Amjed and Harrison (2013); deSouza, Ballare, and Niemeier (2022).

2. Aneesh (2009); Delfanti (2021).

3. In Emmons Allison et al. (2018), we refer to this complex of systemic relations as a "matrix of exploitation," building on Hill Collins's concept of a "matrix of domination" (Hill Collins [1990] 2022).

4. This mobilization can thus be understood as an example of threat-based mobilization, following the insights of social movement scholars such as Almeida (2003, 2008, 2015, 2019), McKane and McCammon (2018), Meyer (2004), Tarrow (1998), and Tilly (1978).

5. Schiavone (2017).

6. Kosoff (2016).

7. Willsher (2016).

8. Pleyers (2020).

9. Weise (2020).

10. Pleyers (2020).

11. Jaffe (2021).

12. Torres, Victoria, and Klooster (2021).

13. Waddell (2021).

14. Alimahomed-Wilson and Reese (2021); Tung and Berkowitz (2020); Del Rey (2022); Gurley (2020b); Solon and Glaser (2021); Weise (2021c).

15. Votavova (2020).

16. Alimahomed-Wilson and Reese (2020a, 2020b; Boewe and Schulten (2020).

17. Boewe and Schulten (2020); Reuters (2022b).

18. Amazon Workers and Supporters (2018); Boewe and Schulten (2020).

19. Votanova (2020).

20. Boewe and Schulten (2020).

21. Boewe and Schulten (2020); Alimahomed-Wilson and Reese (2020a, 2020b).

22. Boewe and Schulten (2020).

23. GMB Union (2022).

24. Transnational Social Strike Platform (2019).

25. Alimahomed-Wilson and Reese (2020b); Massimo (2020).

26. Precarious Connections (Italy) (2021).

27. Gius (2022).

28. Gius (2022); Transnational Social Strike Platform (2019).

29. Alimahomed-Wilson and Reese (2020b).

30. Uniglobal (2021).

31. Alimahomed-Wilson and Reese (2020b).

32. The Local (2021).

33. Quoted in Chan (2021).

34. In 2012, public and legal complaints by US Amazon warehouse workers about bad working conditions, including being required to work in 115 degree F temperatures in Pennsylvania, began to surface in the news, and a few former Pennsylvania warehouse workers spoke at a small protest of about thirty-five union and labor activists outside of Amazon's headquarters in Seattle that year (Parkhurst 2012).

35. Alimahomed-Wilson and Reese (2021).

36. Olney and Wilson (2022).

37. Alimahomed-Wilson and Reese (2021); DeManuelle-Hall (2019).

38. Chen (2019); Warehouse Workers Stand Up is a coalition of prolabor organizations calling for a code of conduct for warehouse workers in New Jersey and New York, including the Retail Wholesale and Department Store Union.

39. Alimahomed-Wilson and Reese (2020b, 2021); Weise (2021d).

40. Alimahomed-Wilson and Reese (2022).

41. Alimahomed-Wilson and Reese (2022); DCH1 Amazonians United (2020); Gibson (2021).

42. Alimahomed-Wilson and Reese (2020b, 2021).

43. DCH1 Amazonians United (2020).

44. Alimahomed-Wilson and Reese (2021); DCH1 Amazonians United (2020).

45. Alimahomed-Wilson (2020); Alimahomed-Wilson and Reese (2020b, 2022).

46. Scheiber (2021).

47. Hsu (2022a).

48. Palmer (2022a, 2022b).

49. Blanc (2022a, 2022b).

50. Leon (2022a).

51. Blanc (2022a, 2022b); Enzinna (2022).

52. Leon (2022b); Weise, Scheiber, and Marcos (2022).

53. Hsu (2022b).

54. Leon (2022b).

55. Enzinna (2022); Leon (2022b); Weise, Scheiber, and Marcos (2022).

56. Teamsters (2021a).

57. Gurley (2021b).

58. Alimahomed-Wilson and Reese (2022).

59. Alimahomed-Wilson and Reese (2020b); DeManuelle-Hall (2019); Transnational Social Strike Platform (2019).

60. Clark (2022); Gibson (2021); Reilly (2022); WSB-TV News Staff (2022).

61. Alimahomed-Wilson and Reese (2020b).

62. DeManuelle-Hall (2019).

63. Alimahomed-Wilson and Reese (2020b).

64. Long (2022).

65. Milmo (2021); Greene (2021).

66. See Del Rey (2021); Burke (2020); *Business Insider* (2021); Associated Press (2021); Sonnemaker (2021a, 2021b); Waltemath (2021).

67. Sonnemaker (2021a).

68. Sonnemaker (2021a).

69. Alimahomed-Wilson and Reese (2020a).

70. Alimahomed-Wilson and Reese (2022).

71. Alimahomed-Wilson and Reese (2022); Teamsters (2021b); Real Deal Staff (2022).

72. Alvarez (2021); Morales (2022).

73. Alimahomed-Wilson and Reese (2022); Morales (2022).

74. Alimahomed-Wilson and Reese (2020b, 2022).

75. Rosenblum (2020).

76. According to the Merriam-Webster online dictionary (2022), LGBTQIA refers to lesbian, gay, bisexual, transgender, queer/questioning, intersexed, and asexual/aromatic/agender, but the meaning of LGBTQIA is dynamic and varies among those using the term. Long (2022).

77. Wulfraat (2021).

78. Wulfraat (2021).

79. Wulfraat (2021).

80. Wilson and Prinsloo (2021).

81. Staff writer (2021).

82. Gurley (2020c).

83. Kalleberg (2011).

84. Gius (2022).

85. Kalleberg (2011); Luce (2014); United States Bureau of Labor Statistics (2022).

86. The European Union recently reached agreement on common rules establishing minimum wages across the twenty-seven member nations that are sufficient to ensure a decent standard of living, as well as a corresponding enforcement system (Reuters 2022a).

87. Almeida (2019:75–79); Rolf (2016).

88. Aurand et al. (2020).

89. Waddell (2021).

90. Kantor, Weise, and Ashford (2021); Alimahomed-Wilson and Reese (2021).

91. Delfanti (2021).

92. Kafkadesk Prague Office (2021); Votavova (2020).

93. Sprague and Sathi (2020); Coffey et al. (2018).

94. Alimahomed and Reese (2020b); Kantor et al. (2021).

95. De Lara (2018).

96. De Lara (2018).

97. For numerous examples of this trend across US cities, see Good Jobs First (2022); MacGillis (2021a); Mitchell and LaVecchia (2016).

98. MacGillis (2021a:268); see also Mitchell and LaVecchia (2016).

99. Elliott and Matsakis (2021).

100. "Race to the bottom" refers to competitive situations, often between companies or nations, in which one "actor" gains a contract or increases sales by undercutting their adversary's prices by reducing quality, relaxing environmental and/or workplace standards, or cutting labor costs in terms of wages or workers. Votavova (2020); Kafkadesk Prague Office (2021).

101. For example, see Kauffman Borgeest and Ryan LLP (2017) and other cases pursued by WWRC and its members, discussed in chapter 7.

102. Kafkadesk Prague Office (2021); Precarious Connections (Italy) (2021); Murray and Asher-Schapiro (2021).

103. Alimahomed-Wilson (2020).

104. Murray and Asher-Schapiro (2021).

105. Gonzalez Jimenez (2021).

106. Murray (2021).

107. For a good overview of policies related to gig workers' rights across nations and US states, see Ets Hokin (2022).

108. Woodman (2015).

109. Starr, Prescott, and Bishara (2021).

110. Woodman (2015).

111. Starr, Prescott, and Bishara (2021).

112. Aneesh (2009).

113. Roth (2022).

114. Although Amazon requires its employees to sign a "privacy notice," regarding the collection of their productivity data by managers, employees are required to sign this notice in order to be hired, making "employee consent" relatively meaningless, at least according to the European Data Protection Board (Kafkadesk Prague Office 2021).

115. Athena Coalition (2019); Evans (2019a); Human Impact Partners and Warehouse Workers Resource Center (2021); Strategic Organizing Center (2021).

116. Alimahomed-Wilson and Reese (2020b, 2021).

117. California Attorney General Press Office (2021); New York Attorney General Press Office (2021).

118. Walt (2020).

119. Kalleberg (2011).

120. Burke (2021).

121. Luce (2014).

122. Lichtenstein (2009:258).

123. Nguyen (2018).

124. McAllister (2021).

125. Data USA (2020).

126. Schiavone (2017).

127. Alimahomed-Wilson and Reese (2021); Gurley (2020a); Solon and Glaser (2021); Weise (2021c).

METHODOLOGICAL APPENDIX: AMAZON WAREHOUSE WORKER INTERVIEWS

1. Milkman, Gonzalez, and Narro (2010).

2. De Lara (2013b); see also De Lara (2018).

3. One worker was employed on the Transportation Operations Management (TOM) team but not in a managerial role; he reported directly to a manager and was employed in a part-time tier 3 position. His work resembled that of a traffic clerk and auditor, involving a lot of scanning and routine paperwork. The worker who became an area manager in training resigned before becoming a manager and discussed their experiences as an associate or process associate at length in the interview. The third worker employed as an HR representative mainly focused on their experience in that position rather than as an associate in the interview.

4. Flaming and Burns (2019) provide useful information on the characteristics of Amazon warehouse workers in Southern California in 2017, which we summarize in chapter 1.

References

Alimahomed-Wilson, Jake. 2011. "Men Along the Shore: Working Class Masculinities in Crisis." *Norma* 6(1):22–44.

Alimahomed-Wilson, Jake. 2016. *Solidarity Forever? Race, Class, Gender and Unionism in the Ports of Southern California.* Minneapolis, MN: Lexington Books.

Alimahomed-Wilson, Jake. 2020. "The Amazonification of Logistics: E-Commerce, Labor, and Exploitation in the Last Mile." Pp. 69–84 in *The Cost of Free Shipping: Amazon in the Global Economy*, edited by Jake Alimahomed-Wilson and Ellen Reese. London: Pluto Press.

Alimahomed-Wilson, Jake, Juliann Allison, and Ellen Reese. 2020. "Introduction: Amazon Capitalism." Pp. 1–34 in *The Cost of Free Shipping: Amazon in the Global Economy*, edited by Jake Alimahomed-Wilson and Ellen Reese. London: Pluto Press.

Alimahomed-Wilson, Jake and Ellen Reese, eds. 2020a. *The Cost of Free Shipping: Amazon in the Global Economy.* London: Pluto Press.

Alimahomed-Wilson, Jake and Ellen Reese. 2020b. "Conclusion: Resisting Amazon Capitalism." Pp. 275–84 in *The Cost of Free Shipping: Amazon in the Global Economy*, edited by Alimahomed-Wilson and Ellen Reese. London: Pluto Press.

Alimahomed-Wilson, Jake and Ellen Reese. 2021. "Surveilling Amazon's Warehouse Workers: Racism, Retaliation and Worker Resistance Amid the Pandemic." *Work in the Global Economy* 1(1–2): 55–73.

Alimahomed-Wilson, Jake and Ellen Reese. 2022. "Teamsters Confront Amazon: An Early Assessment." *New Labor Forum* 31(3):43–51 (https://doi .org/10.1177/10957960221116835).

Allen, Nicholas. 2010. "Exploring the Inland Empire: Life, Work, and Injustice in Southern California's Retail Fortress." *New Labor Forum* 19(2): 37–43.

Allison, Juliann, Joel Herrera, and Ellen Reese. 2015. "Why the City of Ontario Needs to Raise the Minimum Wage: Earnings among Warehouse Workers in Inland Southern California." UCLA Institute for Research on Labor and Employment. *Research & Policy Brief* 36:1–10. Retrieved December 16, 2021 (http://www.irle.ucla.edu/publications/documents/ResearchBrief_Reese36.pdf).

Almaguer, Tomas. [1994] 2009. *Racial Fault Lines: The Historical Origins of White Supremacy in California*. Berkeley: University of California Press.

Almeida, Paul. 2003. "Opportunity, Organizations, and Threat-Induced Contention: Protest Waves in Authoritarian Settings." *American Journal of Sociology* 109(2): 345–400.

Almeida, Paul. 2008. *Waves of Protest: Popular Struggle in El Salvador, 1925–2005*. Minneapolis: University of Minnesota Press.

Almeida, Paul. 2015. "The Role of Threats in Popular Mobilization in Central America." Pp. 105–25 in *Social Movement Dynamics: New Perspectives on Theory and Research*, edited by Federico M. Rossi and Marisa Von Bulow. Surrey, UK and Burlington, VT: Ashgate.

Almeida, Paul. 2019. *Social Movements: The Structure of Collective Mobilization*. Oakland: University of California Press.

Alvarez, Adan. 2021. "Community Members and Activists Demand Halting Proposed Amazon Facility Bringing Traffic and Low-Paying Jobs into the City." International Brotherhood of Teamsters Press Release, December 8. Retrieved January 26, 2022 (https://teamster.org/2021/12/west-covina -residents-hold-picket-line-and-file-ceqa-lawsuit-to-halt-amazon -development/).

Amazon. 2018. "Amazon's Impact in Southern California." Retrieved December 27, 2020 (https://blog.aboutamazon.com/job-creation-and-investment /amazons-impact-in-southern-california).

Amazon Employees for Climate Justice. 2020. "How Amazon Emissions Are Hurting Communities of Color." Retrieved December 16, 2021 (https:// amazonemployees4climatejustice.medium.com/environmental-justice-and -amazons-carbon-footprint-9e10fab21138).

Amazon Staff. 2021. "Our Workforce Data." Retrieved December 20, 2021 (https://www.aboutamazon.com/news/workplace/our-workforce-data).

Amazon Staff. 2022. "Workplace Safety: Keeping Employees Safe." Retrieved December 7, 2022 (https://www.aboutamazon.com/workplace/safety).

Amazon Workers and Supporters. 2018. "'Stop Treating Us Like Dogs!' Workers Organizing Resistance at Amazon in Poland." Pp. 96–100 in *Choke Points:*

Logistics Workers and Solidarity Movements Disrupting the Global Capitalist Supply Chain, edited by Jake Alimahomed-Wilson and Emmanuel Ness. London: Pluto Press.

American Civil Liberties Union. 2019. "In Historic Decision on Digital Bias, EEOC Finds Employers Violated Federal Law When They Excluded Women and Older Workers from Facebook Job Ads." ACLU Media. Retrieved December 20, 2021 (https://www.aclu.org/press-releases/historic-decision -digital-bias-eeoc-finds-employers-violated-federal-law-when-they).

American Lung Association. 2019. "State of the Air." Retrieved December 16, 2021 (https://www.lung.org/research/sota).

American Lung Association. 2021. "Most Polluted Places to Live." Retrieved January 15, 2022 (https://www.lung.org/research/sota/key-findings/most -polluted-places).

American Management Systems. 1981. *Analysis of Community Involvement in Hazardous Waste Site Problems*. Report to the U.S. Environmental Protection Agency.

Amjed, Tayyab Waqas and Norma J. Harrison. 2013. "A Model for Sustainable Warehousing: From Theory to Best Practices. Pp. 1–28 in *Proceedings of the International Decision Sciences Institute and Asia Pacific DSI Conference*. Houston, TX: Decision Sciences Institute.

Aneesh, Aneesh. 2009. "Global Labor: Algocratic Modes of Organization." *Sociological Theory* 27(4): 347–70.

Angwin, Julia and Terry Parris Jr. 2016. "Facebook Lets Advertisers Exclude Users by Race." *Propublica*, October 28. Retrieved September 13, 2022 (https://www.propublica.org/article/facebook-lets-advertisers-exclude-users -by-race).

Associated Press. 1986. "Court to Consider Barring Residents from Acid Pit Suit." June 2. Retrieved January 25, 2021 (https://apnews.com/article /6f0bcae6b75d7c8ddd38311241aa7c75).

Associated Press. 2021. "Amazon Sued over Discrimination, Sexual Harassment Claims." Associated Press State & Local, March 3. Retrieved December 20, 2021 (https://apnews.com/article/technology-amazoncom-inc-race-and -ethnicity-discrimination-lawsuits-276d320ed730d184d79c61f6e3d98e86).

Athena Coalition. 2019. "Packaging Pain: Workplace Injuries in Amazon's Empire." Retrieved December 20, 2021 (https://s27147.pcdn.co/wp-content /uploads/NELP-Report-Amazon-Packaging-Pain.pdf).

Aurand, Andrew, Dan Emmanuel, Dan Threet, Ikra Rafi, and Diane Yentel. 2020. "Out of Reach: The High Cost of Housing." National Low Income Housing Coalition. Retrieved December 20, 2021 (https://reports.nlihc.org /oor/2020).

Avery, Dan. 2020. "Transgender Man Files Pregnancy Discrimination Suit against Amazon." *NBC News*, October 6. Retrieved December 20, 2021

(https://www.nbcnews.com/feature/nbc-out/transgender-man-files
-pregnancy-discrimination-suit-against-amazon-n1242324).

Bachus, Edward J. 1981. "Who Took the Oranges Out of Orange County? The
Southern California Citrus Industry in Transition." *Southern California
Quarterly* 63(2):157–73.

Baker, Dean. 2018. "Amazon's $15 an Hour Minimum Wage and the Federal
Reserve Board." Truthout, October 8. Retrieved December 20, 2021 (https://
truthout.org/articles/amazons-15-an-hour-minimum-wage-and-the-federal
-reserve-board/).

Baldassare, Mark, Dean Bonner, Alyssa Dykman, and Rachel Lawler. 2020.
"California's Electorate: A New Look and Why It Matters." Public Policy
Institute of California. Retrieved July 20, 2022 (https://www.ppic.org
/publication/californias-exclusive-electorate-a-new-look-at-who-votes-and
-why-it-matters/).

Ballou, Ronald H. 2004. *Business Logistics/Supply Chain Management.* 5th ed.
Upper Saddle River, NJ: Prentice Hall.

Barboza, Tony. 2015. "People Living Near 60 Freeway in Ontario Breathe the
Worst Air in the Southland." *Los Angeles Times*, September 9. Retrieved
January 25, 2021 (https://www.latimes.com/science/la-me-freeway-soot
-20150909-story.html).

Bennett, Peter. 1992. "Down to Earth: Jurupa Mountains Cultural Center's
Directors Teach Visitors the Love of Nature." *Los Angeles Times*, February 16.
Retrieved January 25, 2021 (https://www.latimes.com/archives/la-xpm-1992
-02-16-vw-4246-story.html).

Berentz, Lauren. 2017. "As Rents Rise, More Renters Turn to Doubling Up."
Zillow, December 14. Retrieved December 20, 2021 (https://www.zillow.com
/research/rising-rents-more-roommates-17618/).

Berger, Paul. 2021. "Logistics Hiring Surge in California's Inland Empire Can't
Satisfy Demand." *Wall Street Journal*, December 22. Retrieved January 25,
2022 (https://www.wsj.com/articles/logistics-hiring-surge-in-californias
-inland-empire-cant-satisfy-demand-11640205600).

Biro, Andrew. 2015. "Spaces of Environmental Justice." *Contemporary Political
Theory* 14(4):45–47.

Bishop, Todd. 2021. "Amazon Elevates Two More Execs to Its Senior Leadership
Team under New CEO Andy Jassy." *Geek Wire*, July 7. Retrieved December 20, 2021 (https://www.geekwire.com/2021/amazon-elevates-two-execs
-senior-leadership-team-new-ceo-andy-jassy/).

Blanc, Eric. 2022a. "Here's How We Beat Amazon: An Interview with Angelika
Maldonado." *Jacobin*, April 2. Retrieved June 21, 2022 (https://www.jacobin
mag.com/2022/04/amazon-labor-union-alu-staten-island-organizing).

Blanc, Eric. 2022b. "How Amazon's Immigrant Workers Organized to Win a
Union on Staten Island: An Interview with Brima Sylla." *Jacobin*, April 4.

Retrieved June 21, 2022 (https://www.jacobinmag.com/2022/04/amazon
-warehouse-alu-staten-island-immigrant-workers).

Bley, Kenneth and Lisa Patricio. 2017. "The Initiative and CEQA." *Lay of the Land: Exploring State and Federal Regulation of Land Use and Development in California*, February 13. Retrieved January 25, 2021 (https://landuse .coxcastle.com/the-initiative-and-ceqa/).

Bloodworth, James. 2019. *Hired: Six Months Undercover in Low-Wage Britain*. London: Atlantic Books.

Bloomberg Billionaires Index. 2022. "#2. Jeff Bezos. $135B." Retrieved July 11, 2022 (https://www.bloomberg.com/billionaires/profiles/jeffrey-p-bezos/).

Boewe, Jörn and Johannes Schulten. 2020. "Amazon Strikes in Europe: Seven Years of Industrial Action, Challenges, and Strategies." Pp. 209–24 in *The Cost of Free Shipping: Amazon in the Global Economy*, edited by Jake Alimahomed-Wilson and Ellen Reese. London: Pluto Press.

Bonacich, Edna and Jake B. Wilson. 2008. *Getting the Goods: Ports, Labor, and the Logistics Revolution*. Ithaca, NY: Cornell University Press.

Bonazzo, John. 2017. "Trans Woman, Husband Sue Amazon over Workplace Discrimination and Sexual Harassment." *New York Observer*, August 9. Retrieved December 20, 2021 (https://observer.com/2017/08/amazon -transgender-workplace-discrimination-bias/).

Bonta, Rob. 2022. "Attorney General Bonta Announces Innovative Settlement with City of Fontana to Address Environmental Injustices in Warehouse Development." Retrieved June 26, 2022 (https://oag.ca.gov/news/press-releases/attorney -general-bonta-announces-innovative-settlement-city-fontana-address).

Boris, Eileen. 1998. "When Work Is Slavery." *Social Justice* 25(1):28–46.

Brandt, Richard L. 2011. *One Click: Jeff Bezos and the Rise of Amazon.com*. London: Penguin Random House.

Breschini, Gary, Trudy Haversat, and Paul Hampson. 1983. "A Cultural Resources Overview of the Coast and Coast Valley Study Areas." Report on file at Cabrillo College, Aptos.

Brown, Michael. 2012. "Gender and Sexuality I: Intersectional Anxieties." *Progress in Human Geography* 36(4):541–50.

Brown, Steve. 2013. "New Amazon Warehouses Are Big Projects for Developer Hillwood." *Dallas Daily News*, January 31. Retrieved January 25, 2021 (https://www.dallasnews.com/business/2013/01/31/new-amazon-warehouses -are-big-projects-for-developer-hillwood/).

Browne, Irene and Rachel Askew. 2005. "Race, Ethnicity, and Wage Inequality Among Women." *American Behavioral Scientist* 48(9):1275–92.

Browne, Irene and Joya Misra. 2003. "The Intersection of Gender and Race in the Labor Market." *Annual Review of Sociology* 29:487–513.

Buck, Fielding. 2018. "Why Amazon Already Has a Strong Presence in Southern California." *The Sun* (San Bernardino), January 18. Retrieved December 27,

2020 (https://www.sbsun.com/2018/01/18/why-amazon-already-has-a
-strong-presence-in-southern-california/).

Burke, Henry. 2021. "Biden's Budget Must Strengthen OSHA" (blog), April 2.
Revolving Door Project. Retrieved January 22, 2022 (https://
therevolvingdoorproject.org/bidens-budget-must-strengthen-osha/).

Burke, Minyvonne. 2020. "Ex-Amazon Manager Says She Scoured Applicants'
Social Media to Determine Race, Gender." *NBC News*, February 26.
Retrieved December 20, 2021 (https://www.nbcnews.com/news/us-news/ex
-amazon-manager-says-she-scoured-applicants-social-media-determine
-n1143441).

Business Insider. 2021. "Insiders Reveal What Its Really Like Working at
Amazon When It Comes to Hiring, Firing, Performance Reviews and More."
August 27. Retrieved December 20, 2021 (https://businessinsider.mx/work
-at-amazon-jobs-performance-reviews-hiring-firing-interviews-warehouses
-delivery-drivers/?r=US&IR=T).

Cafcas, Thomas and Greg LeRoy. 2016. "Will Amazon Fool Us Twice? Why State
and Local Governments Should Stop Subsidizing the Online Giant's Growing Distribution Network." Good Jobs First. Retrieved January 11, 2022
(https://www.goodjobsfirst.org/sites/default/files/docs/pdf/amazon
-subsidies.pdf).

California Attorney General Press Office. 2021. "In Nationwide First, Attorney
General Judgment Requiring Amazon 'Right to Know' Law to Help Protect
Workers against COVID-19." Retrieved January 26, 2022 (https://oag.ca.gov
/news/press-releases/nationwide-first-attorney-general-bonta-secures
-judgment-requiring-amazon-comply).

California Legislative Information. 2021. "AB-701: Warehouse Distribution
Centers." Retrieved January 25, 2021 (https://leginfo.legislature.ca.gov/faces
/billNavClient.xhtml?bill_id=202120220AB701).

Caragozian, John S. 2021. "Few Heroes: California Mission Secularization."
Retrieved December 4, 2022 (https://www.cschs.org/wp-content/uploads/2021
/12/History-Resources-Caragozian-Mission-Secularization-11-29-21.pdf).

Carpio, Genevieve. 2019. *Collisions at the Crossroads: How Place and Mobility
Make Race*. Oakland: University of California Press.

Catanzarite, Lisa. 2000. "Brown-Collar Jobs: Occupational Segregation and
Earnings of Recent-Immigrant Latinos." *Sociological Perspectives*
43(1):45–75.

CBRE. 2017. "Average Size of Newly Built Warehouses Swells Due to
E-Commerce." Commercial Real Estate Services. Retrieved December 16,
2021 (https://www.cbre.us/about/media-center/average-size-of-newly-built
-us-warehouses-swells-due-to-ecommerce).

CBRE. 2020. "North American Big Box Review and Outlook, Inland Empire."
Retrieved January 25, 2021 (https://www.cbre.com/insights/local-response
/industrial-big-box-report-inland-empire).

Center for Biological Diversity. 2019. "Lawsuit Challenges Massive Southern California Warehouse Project." Retrieved January 25, 2021 (https://www .biologicaldiversity.org/news/press_releases/2019/west-valley-logistics -center-04-12-2019.php).

Center for Community Action and Environmental Justice (CCAEJ). 2020. "Billions off Our Backs." Retrieved December 30, 2020 (https://storymaps .arcgis.com/stories/5d2ba8cbcd1d412897549b9d5d13e548).

Center for Social Innovation (with Ellen Reese, Saman Banafti, Michael Bates, Marlenee Blas-Pedral, Renan Cortes, Mirella Deniz-Zaragoza, Luis Higinio, Elijah Knapp, Karthick Ramakrishnan, Sono Shah, and Yiming Shao). 2018. "The State of Work in the Inland Empire." UC Riverside: Center for Social Innovation. Retrieved December 17, 2021 (https://socialinnovation.ucr.edu /research/work/).

Center for Social Innovation (with Tina Aoun, Paola Avendano, Elizabeth Ayala, Marlenee Blas-Pedral, Denise Davis, Stephanie DeMora, Dr. Jennifer Merolla, Dr. Karthick Ramakrishnan, Dalia Valdez Renteria, Gary Rettberg, Sono Shah, Yiming Shao, Bia Vieira, and Esau Casimiro Vieyra). 2019. "The State of Women in the Inland Empire." UC Riverside: Center for Social Innovation. Retrieved December 17, 2021 (file:///Users/juliannallison/ Downloads/state-of-women-ie-web.pdf).

Chan, Kelvin. 2021. "Activists Block Amazon Warehouses in Black Friday." *U.S. News & World Reports*, November 26. Retrieved January 21, 2022 (https:// www.usnews.com/news/business/articles/2021-11-26/climate-activists-block -amazon-uk-warehouses-on-black-friday).

Chang, Chen Fen and Paula England. 2010. "Gender Inequality in Earnings in Industrialized East Asia." *Social Science Research* 40:1–14.

Chen, Michelle. 2019. "Is This the Turning Point in the Fight against Amazon?" *The Nation*, December 21. Retrieved January 29, 2022 (https://www.the nation.com/article/amazon-workers-labor-prime/).

Chittum, Ryan. 2012. "Squeeze: A WSJ Follow Story Waters Down and LAT Scoop from Two Weeks Ago." Retrieved July 20, 2022 (https://archives.cjr .org/the_audit/amazons_california_tax_squeeze.php).

Chua, Charmaine, Martin Danyluk, Deborah Cowen, and Laleh Khalili. 2018. "Introduction: Turbulent Circulation: Building a Critical Engagement with Logistics." *Environment and Planning D: Society and Space* 36(4):617–29.

City of Fontana. 2020. Regular Planning Commission Meeting, October 6 (Recording). Retrieved January 25, 2021 (https://fontanaca.swagit.com/play /10072020-514).

City of Fontana. 2021. Regular Planning Commission Meeting, April 20 (Recording). Retrieved January 25, 2021 (https://fontanaca.swagit.com/play/04212021-1031).

City of Riverside Planning Department. n.d. "Cultural Resources Design Applications." Retrieved December 16, 2021 (https://www.riversideca.gov /historic/pdf/CR_Designation_Applications.pdf).

Clark, Mitchell. 2022. "Amazon Workers in New York and Maryland Are Protesting for Better Wages." *The Verge*, March 16. Retrieved July 26, 2022 (https://www.theverge.com/2022/3/16/22981230/amazonians-united-warehouse-walkouts-3-raise-breaks).

CNN. 2020. "Jeff Bezos Is Now Worth a Whopping $200 Billion." August 27. Retrieved September 1, 2020 (https://www.cnn.com/2020/08/27/tech/jeff-bezos-net-worth-200-billion-intl-hnk/index.html).

Coffey, Diane, Payal Hathi, Nidhi Khurana, and Amit Thorat. 2018. "Explicit Prejudice: Evidence from a New Survey." *Economic & Political Weekly* 53(1). Retrieved December 4, 2022 (https://www.epw.in/journal/2018/1/special-articles/explicit-prejudice.html).

Cohen, Patricia. 2019. "Nice Résumé: Wait, You're How Old?" *New York Times*, June 8. Retrieved December 20, 2021 (https://www.nytimes.com/2019/06/07/business/economy/age-discrimination-jobs-hiring.html).

Communication Workers of America. 2017. "Class Action Law Suit Hits T-Mobile, Amazon, Cox and Hundreds of Large Employers for Allegedly Using Facebook to Exclude Millions of Older Americans from Job Ads in Violation of Age Discrimination Laws." Retrieved December 20, 2021 (https://cwa-union.org/news/releases/class-action-lawsuit-hits-tmobile-amazon-cox-for-alleged-age-discrimination).

Corkery, Michael. 2018. "Hard Lessons (Thanks to Amazon) Breathe New Life into Retail Stores." *New York Times*, September 3. Retrieved December 16, 2021 (https://www.nytimes.com/2018/09/03/business/retail-walmart-amazon-economy.html).

County of San Bernardino. 2007. Bloomington Community Plan. Retrieved June 15, 2022 (http://www.sbcounty.gov/uploads/lus/communityplans/bloomingtoncp.pdf).

County of San Bernardino. 2019. Bloomington Community Action Guide. Retrieved June 15, 2022 (https://countywideplan.com/wp-content/uploads/sites/68/2020/07/00_Bloomington_CAG_2019DRAFT_compressed.pdf).

Cowen, Deborah. 2014. *The Deadly Life of Logistics: Mapping Violence in Global Trade.* Minneapolis: University of Minnesota Press.

Craig, Brian. 2020. *Stringfellow Acid Pits: The Toxic and Legal Legacy.* Ann Arbor: University of Michigan Press.

Crary, David. 2017. "Kentucky Man, Transgender Wife Sue Amazon for Workplace Bias." *Associated Press*, August 9. Retrieved December 20, 2021 (https://apnews.com/article/9e977003405a4a2f8060f211bc578c45).

Crenshaw, Kimberle. 1989. "Demarginalizing the Intersection of Race and Sex: A Black Feminist Critique of Antidiscrimination Doctrine, Feminist Theory, and Antiracist Politics." *University of Chicago Legal Forum* 1:139–67.

Cuevas, Steven. 2012. "Amazon Holds Grand Opening for San Bernardino Mega Warehouse." KPCC, October 18. Retrieved December 27, 2020 (https://www

.scpr.org/news/2012/10/18/34677/amazon-holds-grand-opening-san-bernardino
-mega-war/).

Daily News. 2021. "Amazon Triples Its 'Last Mile' Delivery Network in Southern
California." Retrieved January 25, 2022 (https://us.newschant.com/us-news
/los-angeles/amazon-triples-its-last-mile-delivery-network-in-southern
-california-daily-news/).

Danelski, David. 2013. "Air Pollution: Battle Still on for Clean Air." *Press-
Enterprise*, September 5. Retrieved January 25, 2021 (https://centerforhealth
journalism.org/fellowships/projects/air-pollution-battle-still-clean-air).

Daniel, Cletus. 1982. *Bitter Harvest: A History of California Farmworkers,
1870–1941.* Berkeley: University of California Press.

Data USA. 2019. "California." Retrieved December 17, 2021 (https://datausa.io
/profile/geo/california).

Data USA. 2020. "Riverside, CA." Retrieved December 17, 2021 (https://datausa
.io/profile/geo/riverside-ca/#:~:text=In%202018%2C%20Riverside%2C
%20CA%20had,%2467%2C850%2C%20a%201.38%25%20increase).

Data USA. 2022. "Bloomington, CA." Retrieved June 26 (https://datausa.io
/profile/geo/bloomington-ca#:~:text=About,%2452%2C085%2C%20a%200
.643%25%20increase).

Davis, Mike. [1990] 2006. *City of Quartz: Excavating the Future in Los Angeles.*
New York: Verso Books.

Day, Matt and Spencer Soper. 2020. "Amazon Has Turned a Middle-Class
Warehouse Career into a McJob." Bloomberg, December 17. Retrieved
December 21, 2020 (https://www.bloomberg.com/news/features/2020-12
-17/amazon-amzn-job-pay-rate-leaves-some-warehouse-employees
-homeless).

DCH1 Amazonians United. 2020. "Amazonians United! An Interview with
DCH1 (Chicago) Amazonians United." Pp. 265–74 in *The Cost of Free
Shipping: Amazon in the Global Economy*, edited by Jake Alimahomed-
Wilson and Ellen Reese. London: Pluto Press.

Dean, Sam. 2020. "He Was Part of Amazon's Coronavirus Hiring Spree: Two
Weeks Later He Was Dead." *Los Angeles Times*, May 27. Retrieved December 20, 2021 (https://www.latimes.com/business/technology/story/2020-05
-27/la-fi-tn-amazon-worker-dead-hiring-wave).

De Lara, Juan. 2013a. "Goods Movement and Metropolitan Inequality: Global
Restructuring, Commodity Flows, and Metropolitan Development."
Pp. 75–92 in *Cities, Regions, and Flows*, edited by Peter V. Hall and Markus
Hesse. New York: Routledge.

De Lara, Juan. 2013b. "Warehouse Work: Path to the Middle Class or Road to
Economic Insecurity?" USC Program for Environmental and Regional
Equity (PERE). Retrieved October 1, 2013 (https://dornsifecms.usc.edu
/assets/sites/242/docs/WarehouseWorkerPay_web.pdf).

De Lara, Juan. 2018. *Inland Shift: Race, Space and Capital in Southern California*. Oakland: University of California Press.

De Lara, Juan. 2019. "Working Harder for Less Money in Inland Southern California." October 23. Retrieved December 27, 2020 (https://www.juan delara.com/blog/2019/10/23/working-hard-for-less-money).

De Lara, Juan, Ellen Reese, and Jason Struna. 2016. "Organizing Temporary, Subcontracted, and Immigrant Workers: Lessons from Change to Win's Warehouse Worker United Campaign." *Labor Studies* 41(4):309–32.

Delfanti, Alessandro. 2021. *The Warehouse: Workers and Robots at Amazon*. London: Pluto Press.

Del Rey, Jason. 2021. "Bias, Disrespect, and Demotions: Black Employees Say Amazon Has a Race Problem." Vox Recode, February 26. Retrieved December 20, 2021 (https://www.vox.com/recode/2021/2/26/22297554/amazon-race -black-diversity-inclusion).

Del Rey, Jason. 2022. "Leaked Amazon Memo Warns the Company Is Running Out of People to Hire." Vox, June 17. Retrieved August 1, 2022 (https://www .vox.com/recode/23170900/leaked-amazon-memo-warehouses-hiring -shortage).

DeManuelle-Hall, Joe. 2019. "The Hard Fight at Amazon." *Labor Notes*, November 27. Retrieved on July 30, 2022 (https://labornotes.org/blogs/2019 /11/hard-fight-amazon).

DePillis, Lydia and Jon Sarlin. 2018. "It's Amazon's World; We Just Live in It." *CNN Business*, October 4. Retrieved December 17, 2021 (https://www.cnn .com/2018/10/03/tech/amazon-effect-us-economy/index.html).

deSouza, Priyanka N., Sudheer Ballare, and Deb A. Niemeier. 2022. "The Environmental and Traffic Impacts of Warehouses in Southern California." *Journal of Transport Geography* 104 (https://doi.org/10.1016/j.jtrangeo.2022 .103440).

DeVries, Mark. 2019. "Is It Possible to Get Hired at Amazon Corporate without a Degree?" *Quora*, March 19. Retrieved December 17, 2021 (https://www.quora .com/Is-it-possible-to-get-hired-at-Amazon-corporate-without-a-degree).

Ding, Jaime and Suhauna Hussain. 2022. "Amazon Workers in Fulfillment Center at Moreno Valley Announce Union Drive." *Los Angeles Times*, September 9. Retrieved September 13, 2022 (https://www.yahoo.com/video /amazon-workers-fulfillment-center-moreno-013135653.html).

Do, Khanh, Haofei Yu, Jasmine Velasquezz, Marilyn Grell-Brisk, Heather Smith, and Desunica E. Ivey. 2021. "A Data-driven Approach for Characterizing Community Scale Air Pollution Exposure Disparities in Inland Southern California." *Journal of Aerosol* 152:1–11 (https://doi.org/10.1016/j .jaerosci.2020.105704).

Dobard, John, Kim Engie, Karthick Ramakrishnan, and Sono Shah. 2016. "Unequal Voices: California's Racial Disparities in Political Participation."

UC Riverside School of Public Policy. Retrieved December 17, 2021 (https://www.advancementprojectca.org/wp-content/uploads/2016/07/Unequal-Voices-Single-Page-Low-Res-7-1-16.pdf).

Dorsey, Peter A. 2009. *Common Bondage: Slavery as Metaphor in Revolutionary America*. Knoxville: University of Tennessee Press.

Droesch, Blake. 2021. "Amazon Dominates UC Ecommerce, though Its Market Share Varies by Category." *Insider Intelligence*, April 21. Retrieved December 17, 2021 (https://www.emarketer.com/content/amazon-dominates-us-ecommerce-though-its-market-share-varies-by-category).

Ducre, Kishi Animashaun. 2018. "The Black Feminist Spatial Imagination and an Intersectional Environmental Justice." *Environmental Sociology* 4(1):22–35.

Duhigg, Charles. 2019. "Is Amazon Unstoppable?" *New Yorker*, October 10. Retrieved December 20, 2021 (https://www.newyorker.com/magazine/2019/10/21/is-amazon-unstoppable).

Dunaway, Wilma A. 2014. "Through the Portal of the Household: Conceptualizing Women's Subsidies to Commodity Chains." Pp. 55–71 in *Gendered Commodity Chains*, edited by Wilma A. Dunaway. Stanford, CA: Stanford University Press.

Economic Policy Institute. 2019. "Median/average Hourly Wages." State of Working America Data Library. Retrieved December 6, 2020 (https://www.epi.org/data/#?subject=wage-avg).

The Economist. 2018. "Unfulfillment Centers: What Amazon Does to Jobs." January 20. Retrieved December 27, 2020 (https://www.economist.com/united-states/2018/01/20/what-amazon-does-to-wages).

Editors. 1895. "Statistics of Riverside County." *Los Angeles Herald* 43 (82). Retrieved January 25, 2022 (https://cdnc.ucr.edu/?a=d&d=LAH18950101.2.78&e=-------en--20--1--txt-txIN-------1).

Elliott, Vittorria and Louise Matsakis. 2021. "Why Amazon Really Built a Warehouse on the U.S.-Mexico Border." *Rest of World*, September 10. Retrieved January 21, 2022 (https://restofworld.org/2021/amazon-warehouse-tijuana/).

Emmons Allison, Juliann. 2020. "What Happens When Amazon Comes to Town? Environmental Impacts, Local Economies, and Resistance in Inland Southern California." Pp. 1176–93 in *The Cost of Free Shipping: Amazon in the Global Economy*, edited by Jake Alimahomed-Wilson and Ellen Reese. London: Pluto Press.

Emmons Allison, Juliann, Nathaniel Cline, and Ellen Reese. 2017. "The Need for a Better Deal for Workers and Residents in Inland Southern California." UCLA Institute for Research on Labor and Employment. Retrieved December 17, 2021 (https://irle.ucla.edu/wp-content/uploads/2018/02/IRLE-Research-and-Policy-Brief-40_-Final-PDF.pdf).

Emmons Allison, Juliann, Joel S. Herrera, Jason Struna, and Ellen Reese. 2018. "The Matrix of Exploitation and Temporary Employment: Earning Inequality among Inland Southern California's Blue Collar Warehouse Workers." *Journal of Labor and Society* 21(4):533–60.

Environmental Protection Agency (EPA). 2016. "Stringfellow Superfund Site Community Involvement Plan." Retrieved January 25, 2022 (https://www.jurupavalley.org/DocumentCenter/View/587/US-EPA-Community-Involvement-Plan-Stringfellow-Superfund-Site-PDF).

Enzinna, Wes. 2022. "What Will Chris Smalls Do Next? He Did the Impossible: Unionize an Amazon Warehouse; Then the Hard Part Began." *Intelligencer*, July 21. Retrieved July 26, 2022 (https://nymag.com/intelligencer/article/chris-smalls-amazon-profile.html).

Esquivel, Paloma. 2019. "When Your House Is Surrounded by Massive Warehouses." *Los Angeles Times*, October 27. Retrieved January 25, 2022 (https://www.latimes.com/california/story/2019-10-27/fontana-california-warehouses-inland-empire-pollution).

Ets-Hokin, Gabe. 2022. "What to Expect with Coming Independent Contractor Legislation." Retrieved July 31, 2022 (https://therideshareguy.com/pro-act-state-legislation/).

Evans, Will. 2016a. "When Companies Hire Temp Workers by Race, Black Workers Lose Out." *Reveal News*, January 6. Retrieved December 29, 2021 (https://revealnews.org/article/when-companies-hire-temp-workers-by-race-black-applicants-lose-out/).

Evans, Will. 2016b. "Growing Temp Industry Shuts out Black Workers, Exploits Latinos," *Chicago Reporter*, June 8. Retrieved December 20, 2021 (http://chicagoreporter.com/growing-temp-industry-shuts-out-black-workers-exploits-latinos/).

Evans, Will. 2019a. "Crippled Backs, a Crushing Death: Investigation Reveals Cost of Amazon Prime for Workers." *The Register-Guard*, December 2. Retrieved December 20, 2021 (https://www.indystar.com/story/news/investigations/2019/11/25/amazon-fulfillment-centers-worker-safety-investigation/4283245002/).

Evans, Will. 2019b. "Behind the Smiles: Amazon's Internal Injury Records Expose the True Toll of Its Relentless Drive for Speed." Reveal, November 25. Retrieved December 27, 2020 (https://www.revealnews.org/article/behind-the-smiles/).

Evans, Will. 2020. "How Amazon Hid Its Safety Crisis." Reveal, September 29. Retrieved December 20, 2021 (https://revealnews.org/article/how-amazon-hid-its-safety-crisis/).

Farrell, Sean. 2019. "Unions Lobby Investors to Press Amazon over UK Working Conditions." *The Guardian*, May 20. Retrieved December 20, 2021 (https://www.theguardian.com/technology/2019/may/20/unions-lobby-investors-to-press-amazon-over-uk-working-conditions).

Faulkner, Cameron. 2021. "Amazon's Pay Raise for Over 500,000 Workers Comes at an Interesting Time." *The Verge*, April 28. Retrieved December 20, 2021 (https://www.theverge.com/2021/4/28/22408440/amazon-hourly-wage -increase-2021-factory-delivery-workers).

Fielding, Buck. 2018. "Why Amazon Already Has a Strong Presence in Southern California." *The Sun*, January 18. Retrieved December 27, 2020 (https://www .sbsun.com/2018/01/18/why-amazon-already-has-a-strong-presence-in -southern-california/).

Finn, Tyler. 2016. "Inland Empire Outlook: Logistics Flies High." Rose Institute of State and Local Government, Claremont McKenna College, March 4. Retrieved November 2019 (http://roseinstitute.org/inland-empire-outlook -logistics-flies-high/).

Flaming, Daniel and Patrick Burns. 2019. "Too Big to Govern: Public Balance Sheet for the World's Largest Store." Economic Roundtable. Retrieved December 20, 2021 (https://economicrt.org/publication/too-big-to-govern/).

Foehringer Merchant, E. 2014. "Radical Housewife Activism: Subverting the Toxic Public/Private Binary." Senior thesis, Pomona College. Retrieved January 25, 2022 (https://scholarship.claremont.edu/pomona_theses/101/).

Fontana City Council. 2022. Ordinance No. 1891. Retrieved June 26, 2022 (https:// www.fontana.org/DocumentCenter/View/38188/Full-Approved-Ordinance).

Fontana Herald News. 2014. "Settlement Is Announced in Lawsuit Challenging Approval of Industrial Project in Mira Loma Village." April 30. Retrieved December 5, 2022 (https://www.fontanaheraldnews.com/news/settlement-is -announced-in-lawsuit-challenging-approval-of-industrial-project-in-mira -loma-village-located/article_95302678-1570-52bf-b279-547cc9423958.html).

Frison, Allison. 2020. "Evil Company Alert: Amazon Accused of Pregnancy and Disability Discrimination by Warehouse Worker." Working Solutions NYC, December 20. Retrieved December 20, 2021 (https://www.workingsolutions nyc.com/evil-company-alert-amazon-accused-of-pregnancy-and-disability -discrimination-by-warehouse-worker/).

Fuller, Sylvia and Leah Vosko. 2008. "Temporary Employment and Social Inequality in Canada: Exploring Intersections of Gender, Race, and Immi- gration Status." *Social Indicators Research* 88(1):31–50.

Garcia, Matt., 2001. *A World of Its Own: Race, Labor, and Citrus in the Making of Greater Los Angeles, 1900–1970*. Chapel Hill: University of North Carolina Press.

Gatta, Mary. 2019. *Waiting on Retirement: Aging and Economic Insecurity in Low-Wage Work*. Stanford, CA: Stanford University Press.

Gershgorn, Dave. 2017. "An Amazon Competitor Is Showing That Automation Doesn't Have to Mean the End of Human Jobs." *Quartz*, April 27. Retrieved December 4, 2022 (https://qz.com/970332/an-amazon-competitor-is -showing-that-automation-doesnt-have-to-mean-the-end-of-human-jobs).

Ghori, Imran. 2016. "Judge Sides with Moreno Valley in Challenge against World Logistics Center." *Press Enterprise*, August 22. Retrieved January 25, 2022 (http://www.pe.com/articles/environmental-810973-city-state.html).

Gibson, Kate. 2019. "Walmart Accused of Racial Discrimination by Warehouse Workers with Records." *CBS News*, April 23. Retrieved December 29, 2021 (https://www.cbsnews.com/news/walmart-discrimination-complaint-african-american-warehouse-workers-with-records-lose-jobs/).

Gibson, Kate. 2021. "Amazon Workers in Chicago Stage Walkout to Demand Better Pay and Working Conditions." *CBS News*, December 22. Retrieved July 26, 2022 (https://www.cbsnews.com/news/amazon-workers-walkout-pay-working-conditions/).

Gibson, Campbell and Kay Jung. 2005. "Historical Census Statistics on Population Totals by Race, 1790–1990, and by Hispanic Origin, 1970–1990, for Large Cities and Other Urban Places in the United States." United States Census Bureau. 2010. Retrieved December 17, 2021 (https://web.archive.org/web/20120812191959/http://www.census.gov/population/www/documentation/twps0076/twps0076.html).

Gilmore, Ruth W. 2002. "Fatal Couplings of Power and Difference: Notes on Racism and Geography." *The Professional Geographer* 54(1):15–24.

Giovannini, Joseph. 1985. "An Inland Empire Built on Oranges." *New York Times*, July 7. Retrieved December 17, 2021 (https://www.nytimes.com/1985/07/07/travel/an-inland-empire-built-on-oranges.html).

Gius, Isabelle. 2022. "Thinking Sectorally." *American Prospect*, July 27. Retrieved July 31, 2022 (https://prospect.org/labor/thinking-sectorally-labor-bargaining/).Glaser, April. 2021. "Amazon Now Employs Almost 1 Million People in the U.S.—or 1 in Every 169 Workers." *NBC Business New*, July 30, Retrieved August 1, 2022 (https://www.nbcnews.com/business/business-news/amazon-now-employs-almost-1-million-people-u-s-or-n1275539).

Glasmeier, Amy. 2019. "Living Wage Calculator." Massachusetts Institute of Technology. Retrieved December 17, 2021 (https://livingwage.mit.edu/).

Glasmeier, Amy K. 2020. "Living Wage Calculation for San Bernardino County, California." Massachusetts Institute of Technology. Retrieved January 1, 2021 (https://livingwage.mit.edu/counties/06071).

Glassdoor. 2020. "Amazon Warehouse Worker Hourly Pay." Updated December 14, 2020. Retrieved December 27, 2020 (www.glassdoor.com/Hourly-Pay/Amazon-Amazon-Warehouse-Worker-Hourly-Pay-E6036_D_KO7,30.htm).

GMB Union. 2022. "Your Union in Amazon." Retrieved August 5, 2022 (https://www.gmb.org.uk/amazon).

Gold, Scott. 2001. "State to Pay $114.5 Million for Cleanup of Toxic Dumps." *Los Angeles Times*, May 1. Retrieved January 25, 2022 (https://www.latimes.com/archives/la-xpm-2001-may-01-me-57923-story.html).

Gonos, George and Carmen Martino. 2011. "Temp Agency Workers in New Jersey's Logistics Hub: The Case for a Union Hiring Hall." *WorkingUSA: The Journal of Labour and Society* 14(4):499–525.

Gonzales, Alfonso. 2014. *Reform without Justice: Latino Migrant Politics and the Homeland Security State*. Oxford: Oxford University Press.

Gonzalez, Gilbert G. 1994. *Labor and Community: Mexican Citrus Worker Villages in a Southern California County, 1900–1950*. Champaign: University of Illinois Press.

Gonzalez Jimenez, Alejandra. 2021. "Mexico Labor Reform May Not Be Enough for Auto Logistics Workers." NACLA, July 1 (https://nacla.org/mexico-labor -reform-outsourcing-autoworkers).

Good Jobs First. 2020. "Amazon: Taxpayer Subsidies Help Build Its Monopoly." Retrieved December 28, 2020 (https://www.goodjobsfirst.org/amazon).

Good Jobs First. 2022. "Amazon Tracker." Retrieved July 31, 2022 (https:// goodjobsfirst.org/amazon-tracker/).

Gormond, Tom. 1993. "State Found Liable for Acid Pits Leakage: But the Jury Awards Less Than $160,000, Saying Plaintiffs Exaggerated Injury Claims in Seeking Damages of $3.1 Million." *Los Angeles Times*, September 16. Retrieved January 25, 2022 (https://www.latimes.com/archives/la-xpm-1993 -09-16-mn-35825-story.html).

Government Accounting Office. 2020. "Federal Social Safety Net Programs: Millions of Full-time Workers Rely on Federal Health Care and Food Assistance." GAO-21-45. Retrieved December 20, 2021 (https://www.gao.gov /assets/gao-21-45.pdf).

Greene, Jay. 2021. "Amazon Opens Discrimination Investigation after Internal Petition Wins Backing of Hundreds of Employees." *Washington Post*, July 23. Retrieved December 8, 2022 (https://www.washingtonpost.com/technology /2021/07/23/amazon-gender-discrimination-investigation/).

Grist. 2020. "Seeking Environmental Justice in California's Diesel Death Zones." Retrieved January 25, 2022 (https://grist.org/Array/seeking-environmental -justice-in-californias-diesel-death-zones/).

Grusky, David B., Ann Carpenter, Erin Graves, Anna Kallschmidt, Pablo Mitnik, Bethany Nichols, and Matthew C. Snipp. 2021. "The Rise of the Noxious Contract." Stanford Center on Poverty and Inequality. Retrieved December 20, 2021 (https://inequality.stanford.edu/covid/noxious-contract).

Guilhem, Matt. 2015. "How the Inland Empire Became Home to Massive Ware-houses." KCRW, August 18. Retrieved December 17, 2021 (https://www.kcrw.com /news/articles/how-the-inland-empire-became-home-to-massive-warehouses).

Guilhem, Matt. 2022. "Inland Empire as Warehouse Hub: Is the Era Ending?" KCRW, September 22. Retrieved December 5, 2022 (https://www.kcrw.com /news/shows/greater-la/logistics-industry-missing-women-fine-dining /inland-empire-warehouses-amazon).

Guinn, J. T. 1890. "Exceptional Years: A History of California Floods and Drought." *Historical Society of Southern California, Los Angeles* 1(5):33–39.

Gupta, Ruchi. 2020. "How Much Does Jeff Bezos make a Second?" *Market Realist*, August 13. Retrieved December 31, 2020 (https://marketrealist.com /p/how-much-does-jeff-bezos-make-a-second/#:~:text=Breaking%20the %20amount%20down%20more,achieved%20on%20July%202020%2C %202020).

Gurley, Lauren Kaori. 2020a. "Amazon Warehouse Workers and Abandoning Their Jobs in Droves and Amazon is Encouraging It." *Motherboard Tech by Vice*, March 6. Retrieved September 5, 2022 (https://www.vice.com/en /article/pkexdb/amazon-warehouse-workers-are-abandoning-their-jobs-in -droves).

Gurley, Lauren Kaori. 2020b. "Secret Amazon Reports Expose the Company's Surveillance of Labor and Environmental Groups." *Motherboard Tech by Vice*, November 23. Retrieved January 24, 2022 (https://www.vice.com/en /article/5dp3yn/amazon-leaked-reports-expose-spying-warehouse-workers -labor-union-environmental-groups-social-movements).

Gurley, Lauren Kaori. 2020c. "Amazon Workers to Stage Black Friday Protests in 15 Countries." *Vice*, November 27. Retrieved January 21, 2021 (https:// portside.org/2020-11-27/amazon-workers-stage-coordinated-black-friday -protests-15-countries).

Gurley, Lauren Kaori. 2021a. "Amazon Denies Workers Pee in Bottles: Here Are the Bottles." *Motherboard: Tech by Vice*, March 25. Retrieved December 20, 2021 (https://www.vice.com/en/article/k7amyn/amazon-denies-workers-pee -in-bottles-here-are-the-pee-bottles).

Gurley, Lauren Kaori. 2021b. "The Teamsters Announce Coordinated Nation-wide Project to Unionize Amazon," *Motherboard*, June 22. Retrieved June 20, 2022 (https://portside.org/node/26033/printable/print).

Gurley, Lauren Kaori and Caroline O'Donovan. 2022. "Amazon Workers Walk Off Job at Major West Coast Air Hub." *Washington Post*, August 15 (https:// www.adn.com/nation-world/2022/08/15/amazon-workers-walk-off-job-at -major-west-coast-air-hub/).

Gurusami, Susila. 2017. "Working for Redemption: Formerly Incarcerated Black Women and Punishment in the Labor Market." *Gender & Society* 31(4):433–56.

Gutelis, Beth and Nik Theodore. 2019. "The Future of Warehouse Work: Technological Change in the U.S. Logistics Industry." UC Berkeley Labor Center and Working Partnerships USA. Retrieved December 20, 2021 (http://laborcenter.berkeley.edu/pdf/2019/Future-of-Warehouse -Work.pdf).

Haas, Lisbeth. 1995. *Conquests and Historical Identities in California, 1769–1936.* Berkeley: University of California Press.

Hager Pacific. 2021. "Change Happen Gradually and Then All at Once," November 17. Retrieved June 20, 2022 (https://www.hagerpacific.com/post /change-happens-gradually-and-then-all-at-once).

Hamilton, Isobel A. 2020. "Amazon Drops $2 Coronavirus Pay Rise for Warehouse Workers as CEO Jeff Bezos' Fortune Nears $150 Billion." *Business Insider*, June 3. Retrieved September 3, 2020 (https://www.businessinsider .com/amazon-cuts-2-dollar-hazard-pay-bezos-150-billion-2020-6).

Hanani, Zakiyah. 2020. "Amazon's Warehouse Workers Get Same Parental Leave as Corporate Employees." Workstream. Retrieved December 20, 2021 (https://www.workstream.us/blog/amazons-hourly-warehouse-workers-get -same-parental-leave-as-corporate-employees).

Hanley, Steve. 2018. "Amazon Thumbs Its Nose at Sustainability, Orders 20,000 Conventional Mercedes Sprinter Vans." *Clean Technica*, September 10. Retrieved December 17, 2021 (https://cleantechnica.com/2018/09/10/amazon -thumbs-its-nose-at-sustainability-orders-20000-conventional-mercedes -sprinter-vans/).

Harris, Charlie. 2019. "Amazon in the Inland Empire." *Inland Empire Outlook*. Rose Institute. Retrieved December 17, 2021 (http://roseinstitute.org/wp -content/uploads/2018/04/Spring2018_Amazon-in-the-IE.pdf).

Hautala, Laura. 2021. "Amazon Adjusts 'Time off Task' Policy That Critics Said Limited Bathroom Breaks." *CNet*, June 2. Retrieved December 20, 2021 (https://www.cnet.com/news/amazon-adjusts-time-off-task-policy-that -critics-said-limited-bathroom-breaks/).

Hayasaki, Erika. 2021. "Amazon's Great Labor Awakening." *New York Times*, February 18. Retrieved December 17, 2021 (https://www.nytimes.com/2021 /02/18/magazine/amazon-workers-employees-covid-19.html).

Hill Collins, Patricia. [1990] 2022. *Black Feminist Thought: Knowledge, Consciousness, and the Politics of Empowerment, 30th Anniversary Edition*. New York: Routledge.

Hill Collins, Patricia and Sirma Bilge. 2016. *Intersectionality*. Boston: Polity Press.

History, ed. 2010. "California Gold Rush." April 6. Retrieved December 17, 2021 (https://www.history.com/topics/westward-expansion/gold-rush-of-1849).

Hopkins, Peter. 2019. "Social Geography I: Intersectionality." *Progress in Human Geography* 43(5):937–47.

Hopkins, Peter and Greg Noble. 2018. "Feminist Geographies and Intersectionality." *Gender, Place & Culture* 25(4):585–90.

Horseman, Jeff. 2021. "Inland Empire Is Warehouse Central, but How Did It Happen?" *The press Enterprise*, September 29. Retrieved December 17, 2021 (https://www.pe.com/2021/09/29/inland-empire-is-warehouse-central-but -how-did-it-happen/).

Houde, Jean-François, Peter Newberry, and Katja Seim. 2021. "Economies of Density in E-Commerce: A Study of Amazon's Fulfillment Center Network."

National Bureau of Economic Research. Retrieved December 17, 2021 (https://www.nber.org/papers/w23361).

Howley, Daniel. 2021. "Amazon Looks to Hire 75,000, Offers $17 an Hour and $1K Sign-On Bonus." *Yahoo! Finance*, May 13. Retrieved December 20, 2021 (https://finance.yahoo.com/news/amazon-hiring-75000-workers-offers-17-per-hour-142506984.html).

Hsu, Andrea. 2022a. "Do-over Election at Amazon's Bessemer Warehouse Is Too Close to Call." National Public Radio, March 31. Retrieved June 21, 2022 (https://www.npr.org/2022/03/31/1090123017/do-over-union-election-at-amazons-bessemer-warehouse-is-too-close-to-call).

Hsu, Andrea. 2022b. "Amazon Seeks to Overturn Historic Staten Island Union Victory at Labor Hearing." National Public Radio, June 13. Retrieved June 21, 2022 (https://www.npr.org/2022/06/13/1104549165/amazon-labor-union-election-hearing-staten-island-objection-nlrb-warehouse).

Human Impact Partners and Warehouse Workers Resource Center. 2021. "The Public Health Crisis Hidden in Amazon Warehouses." Human Impact Partners. Retrieved December 20, 2021 (https://humanimpact.org/wp-content/uploads/2021/01/The-Public-Health-Crisis-Hidden-In-Amazon-Warehouses-HIP-WWRC-01-21.pdf).

Hurdle, Jon. 2021. "Another Warehouse Project Faces Legal Fight." *NJ Spotlight News*, June 23. Retrieved December 20, 2021 (https://www.njspotlightnews.org/2021/06/robbinsville-mercer-county-nj-lawsuit-challenges-approval-two-warehouses-zoning-board-rushed-intimidated-environmental-wildlife/).

Hurtado, Albert L. 1999. "Sex, Gender, Culture, and a Great Event: The California Gold Rush." *Pacific Historical Review* 68(1):1–19.

Husing, John. 2018. *Quarterly Economic Report* 30(2). Retrieved December 17, 2021 (http://www.johnhusing.com/QER%20Reports/QER%20April%202018%20web.pdf).

Husing, John. 2019. *Quarterly Economic Report* 31(2). Retrieved December 17, 2021 (http://johnhusing.com/QER%20Reports/QER%20April%202019%20web.pdf).

Hussain, Suhauna. 2021a. "Amazon Warehouse in Rialto Fined $41,000 for Coronavirus Safety Violations." *Los Angeles Times*, May 4. Retrieved December 20, 2021 (https://www.latimes.com/business/story/2021-05-04/amazon-warehouse-rialto-fined-covid-safety-violations).

Hussain, Suhauna. 2021b. "Amazon to Pay California $500,000 for 'Concealing' COVID Cases among Workers." *Los Angeles Times*, November 15. Retrieved July 31, 2022 (https://www.latimes.com/business/story/2021-11-15/amazon-covid-outbreak-workplace-safety-right-to-know-penalty).

Indeed. 2022. "Browse Top Paying Jobs by Industry." Retrieved December 12, 2022 (https://www.indeed.com/career/salaries).

Ingold, Russell. 2020. "Fontana City Council Approves More Warehouses." *Fontana Herald News*, November 23. Retrieved December 5, 2022 (https://www.fontanaheraldnews.com/news/fontana-city-council-approves-more-warehouse-projects/article_5d1dbc40-2878-11eb-9c70-7bf3f81728cc.html).

Ingold, Russell. 2021. "Fontana City Council Denies Appeal of Planning Commission's Vote in Favor of Another Warehouse." *Fontana Herald New*, November 3. Retrieved December 5, 2022 (https://www.fontanaheraldnews.com/news/fontana-city-council-denies-appeal-of-planning-commissions-vote-in-favor-of-another-warehouse-project/article_7362692e-384e-11ec-8026-77dc6746ebf1.html).

Isidore, Chris. 2021. "Labor Group Says Amazon Massively Underreported Covid Cases Contracted at Work." *CNN*, November 30. Retrieved July 19, 2022 (https://www.cnn.com/2021/11/30/business/amazon-covid-cases/index.html).

IQ Air. 2022. "Taking Action for Clean Air in Mira Loma." Retrieved December 5, 2022 (https://www.iqair.com/us/newsroom/taking-action-clean-air-mira-loma).

Jackson, Shirley. 2021. "Amazon Is Offering up to $3,000 Signing as It Tries to Hire 150,000 Seasonal Workers." *Business Insider*, October 19. Retrieved December 20, 2021 (https://www.businessinsider.com/amazon-giving-3000-signing-bonuses-to-hire-150000-seasonal-workers-2021-10).

Jacob, Mary K. and Sarah Paynter. 2021. "Jeff Bezos' $500M Real Estate Portfolio: See All His Luxury Houses." *New York Post*, July 6. Retrieved July 19, 2022 (https://nypost.com/article/jeff-bezos-houses-real-estate-portfolio/).

Jaffe, Sarah. 2021. "It'll Take a Movement: Organizing at Amazon after Bessemer." *New Labor Forum* 30(3):30–37.

Jaller, Miguel and Leticia Pineda. 2017. "Warehousing and Distribution Center Facilities in Southern California: The Use of the Commodity Flow Survey Data to Identify Logistics Sprawl and Freight Generation Patterns." University of California-Davis. Retrieved November 2019 (https://escholarship.org/uc/item/5dz0j1gg).

Jenkins, Benjamin Thomas. 2016. "The Octopus's Garden: Railroads, Citrus Agriculture, and the Emergence of Southern California." Dissertation, University of California, Riverside.

Joassart-Marcelli, Pascale. 2009. "The Spatial Determinants of Wage Inequality: Evidence from Recent Latina Immigrants in Southern California." *Feminist Economics* 15(2):33–72.

Jones, Janelle and Ben Zipperer. 2018. "Unfulfilled Promises: Amazon Fulfillment Centers Do Not Generate Broad-based Employment Growth." Economic Policy Institute, February 1. Retrieved December 21, 2020 (https://www.epi.org/publication/unfulfilled-promises-amazon-warehouses-do-not-generate-broad-based-employment-growth/).

Kafkadesk Prague Office. 2021. "In Central Europe, Concern over Toll, Fairness of Amazon's Algorithms." September 16. Retrieved January 21, 2022 (https://kafkadesk.org/2021/09/16/in-central-europe-concern-over-toll-fairness-of-amazon-algorithms/).

Kalleberg, Arne L. 2011. *Good Jobs, Bad Jobs*. New York: Russell Sage Foundation.

Kane, Joseph W. and Adie Tomer. 2017. "Amazon's Recent Hiring Spree Puts New Focus on Warehouse Jobs and Worker Needs." *The Avenue*, September 12. Brookings. Retrieved December 17, 2021 (https://www.brookings.edu/blog/the-avenue/2017/09/12/amazons-recent-hiring-spree-puts-new-focus-on-warehouse-jobs-and-worker-needs/).

Kantor, Jodi, Karen Weise, and Grace Ashford. 2021. "Inside Amazon's Employment Machine: The Amazon That Customers Don't See." *New York Times*, June 15. Retrieved December 20, 2021 (https://www.nytimes.com/interactive/2021/06/15/us/amazon-workers.html).

Katzanek, Jack. 2012. "Moreno Valley Skechers Warehouse Has Caused Net Job Loss." *Press Enterprise*, February 1. Retrieved December 17, 2021 (https://www.pe.com/2012/02/01/moreno-valley-skechers8217-warehouse-has-caused-net-job-loss/).

Katzanek, Jack. 2018. "Amazon Grows Its Inland Empire Stake with New Center Coming to Beaumont." *Press Enterprise*, November 2. Retrieved January 1, 2021 (https://www.pe.com/2018/11/02/amazon-building-new-distribution-facility-in-beaumont-will-hire-1000/).

Katzanek, Jack. 2019. "Inland Empire's Retail Vacancies Are Highest in the Nation: Was it E-Commerce or Overbuilding?" *The Press-Enterprise*, July 15. Retrieved December 16, 2022 (https://progressiverep.com/inland-empires-retail-vacancies-are-highest-in-the-nation-was-it-e-commerce-or-overbuilding-the-press-enterprise/).

Katzanek, Jack. 2020. "Amazon Fallout: Eastvale Worker Says Company 'Ho-hum' on Worker Safety." *Press Enterprise*, March 30. Retrieved December 27, 2020 (https://www.pe.com/2020/03/30/amazon-fallout-eastvale-staff-say-company-ignoring-coronavirus-safety/).

Kauffman Borgeest & Ryan LLP. 2017. "Wage and Hour Liability: Sample Verdicts and Reported Settlements in Excess of $2 Million, October 2012–October 2017." Retrieved December 20, 2021 (http://eperils.com/wp-content/uploads/2017/10/W&H-LossTableOct2012-2017.pdf).

Kerr, Dara and Maddy Varner. 2021. "Amazon Is Rolling Back COVID Protocols in Its Warehouses: Workers Say It's Premature." *The Markup*, December 21. Retrieved January 27, 2022 (https://themarkup.org/working-for-an-algorithm/2021/12/21/amazon-is-rolling-back-covid-protocols-in-its-warehouses-workers-say-its-premature).

Kimball, Whitney. 2021. "Amazon's New Safety Crisis Could be Heat Waves." *Gizmodo*, June 29. Retrieved December 20, 2021 (https://gizmodo.com/amazons-new-safety-crisis-could-be-heat-waves-1847188930).

Kinder, Molly and Laura Stateler. 2020. "Amazon and Walmart Have Raked in Billions in Additional Profits During the Pandemic, and Shared Almost None of It with Their Workers." Brookings. Retrieved December 20, 2021 (https://www.brookings.edu/blog/the-avenue/2020/12/22/amazon-and-walmart-have-raked-in-billions-in-additional-profits-during-the-pandemic-and-shared-almost-none-of-it-with-their-workers/).

Kirkendall, Eric. 2016. "Environmental & Community Groups File Suit to Prevent More Diesel Exhaust Pollution in Inland Empire." Moving Forward Network. Retrieved December 17, 2021 (http://www.movingforwardnetwork.com/2016/06/environmental-community-groups-file-suit-to-prevent-more-diesel-exhaust-pollution-in-inland-empire/).

Knoblauch, Jessica. 2021. "What It's Like to Be Boxed in by Amazon." *Lit: Stories from the Frontlines of Climate Justice* (blog). EarthJustice. May 24. Retrieved July 11, 2022 (https://earthjustice.org/blog/2020-april/amazon-inland-empire-workers-covid-19).

Kohl, Ellen. 2019. "'When I Take Off My EPA Hat': Using Intersectional Theories to Examine Environmental Justice Governance." *Professional Geographer* 71(4):645–53.

Kosoff, Maya. 2016. "Mon Dieu: Paris Declares Amazon a Threat to the French Way of Life." *Vanity Fair*, June 22. Retrieved July 31, 2022 (https://www.vanityfair.com/news/2016/06/paris-is-going-to-war-with-amazon-prime).

Larsen, Tatum. 2022. "ACLU Files Lawsuit against Riverside County's Redistricting Map on Behalf of Latino Voters." News Channel 3, June 15. Retrieved July 26, 2022 (https://kesq.com/news/2022/06/15/aclu-files-lawsuit-against-riverside-countys-redistricting-map-on-behalf-of-latino-voters/).

Latham & Watkins LLP. 2021. "California and Key Stakeholders Join Warehouse Regulation Lawsuit." *Latham's Clean Energy Report*, November 8. Retrieved January 25, 2022 (https://www.cleanenergylawreport.com/california/california-and-key-stakeholders-join-warehouse-regulation-lawsuit/).

Lawson, Richard. 2019. "Here Are the 10 Retail Markets with the Highest Vacancy Rates." LoopNet, July 3. Retrieved December 16, 2021 (https://www.loopnet.com/learn/here-are-the-10-retail-markets-with-the-highest-vacancy-rates/2007158871/).

Lawton, Dan. 2020. "Stringfellow Acid Pits: The Toxic Legacy by Brian Craig." *California Litigation* 33(2):58–63.

Lecher, Colin. 2019. "How Amazon Automatically Tracks and Fires Warehouse Workers for 'Productivity.'" *The Verge*, April 25. Retrieved December 8, 2020 (https://www.theverge.com/2019/4/25/18516004/amazon-warehouse-fulfillment-centers-productivity-firing-terminations).

Lee, Don. 1998. "The First Taste of Good Life in Inland Empire: Growth." *Los Angeles Times*, April 6. Retrieved December 16, 2021 (https://www.latimes.com/archives/la-xpm-1998-apr-06-mn-36584-story.html).

Leon, Luis Feliz. 2022a. "Amazon Workers in Staten Island Clinch a Historic Victory," *Labor Notes*, April 1. Retrieved June 21, 2022 (https://labornotes .org/2022/04/amazon-workers-staten-island-clinch-historic-victory).

Leon, Luis Feliz. 2022b. "Amazon Bites Back in Vote at Second New York Warehouse." *Labor Notes*, May 13. Retrieved June 22, 2022 (https://www .labornotes.org/blogs/2022/05/amazon-bites-back-vote-second-new-york -warehouse).

Levin, Sam T. 2021. "Amazon's Warehouse Boom Linked to Health Hazards in America's Most Polluted Region." *The Guardian*, April 15. Retrieved December 17, 2021 (https://www.theguardian.com/technology/2021/apr/15/amazon -warehouse-boom-inland-empire-pollution).

Levine, Richard. 1990. "New York Port Loses Top Spot to Los Angeles." *New York Times*, June 12. Retrieved December 17, 2021 (https://www.nytimes.com/1990 /06/12/nyregion/new-york-port-loses-top-spot-to-los-angeles.html).

Lewis, Paul G. and Elisa Barbour. 1999. "California Cities and the Local Sales Tax." Public Policy Institute of California (PPIC). Retrieved January 11, 2022 (https://www.ppic.org/wp-content/uploads/content/pubs/report/R_799 PLR.pdf).

Lichtenstein, Nelson. 2009. *The Retail Revolution: How Wal-Mart Created a Brave New World of Business*. New York: Metropolitan Books.

Lifsher, Marc. 2012. "Amazon Poised to Get a Cut of California Sales Tax." *Los Angeles Times*, May 19. Retrieved January 11, 2022 (https://www.latimes .com/business/la-xpm-2012-may-19-la-fi-amazon-sales-taxes-20120520 -story.html).

The Local. 2021. "Hundreds Protested Plans to Expand Amazon in France." January 30. Retrieved July 31, 2022 (https://www.thelocal.fr/20210131 /hundreds-protest-amazon-expansion-in-france/).

Long, Katherine A. 2021. "New Amazon Data Shows Black, Latino and Female Employees Are Underrepresented in Best-paid Jobs." *Seattle Times*, April 14. Retrieved December 16, 2021 (https://www.seattletimes.com/business /amazon/new-amazon-data-shows-black-latino-and-female-employees-are -underrepresented-in-best-paid-jobs/).

Long, Katherine A. 2022. "Amazon Employees Storm a Company Pride Month Celebration, Protesting the Sale of Transphobic Content." *BusinessInsider*, June 1. Retrieved July 26, 2022 (https://www.businessinsider.com/amazon -employees-protest-transphobic-books-2022-6).

Los Angeles Economic Development Corporation. 2017 "Goods on the Move: Trade and Logistics in So. California." Institute for Applied Economics. Retrieved November 2019 (https://laedc.org/wp-content/uploads/2017/06 /TL_20170515_Final.pdf).

Los Angeles Times. 1985. "By Comparison, Land in the Inland Empire is Dirt Cheap." August 13, p. A16.

Lothrop, Gloria R. 1994. "Rancheras and the Land: Women and Property Rights in Hispanic California." *Historical Society of Southern California* 76(1):59–84.

Loudenback, Tanza and Skye Gould. 2018. "Jeff Bezos Is So Rich That Spending $1 to the Average Person Is Like $88,000 to Him—Here's What Spending Looks Like When You're a Billionaire." *Business Insider*, May 1. Retrieved March 21, 2019 (https://www.businessinsider.com/jeff-bezos-worlds-richest -person-views-spending-money-2018-5).

Luce, Stephanie. 2014. *Labor Movements: Global Perspectives*. Malden, MA: Polity.

Lyou, Joe. 2021. "Coalition for Clean Air's Joe Lyou on SCAQMD's Indirect Source Rule Vote May 7th." *The Planning Report: Insider's Guide to Planning and Infrastructure*, May 5. Retrieved January 25, 2022 (https://www .planningreport.com/2021/05/05/coalition-clean-air-s-joe-lyou-scaqmd-s -indirect-source-rule-vote-may-7th).

MacGillis, Alec. 2021a. *Fulfillment: Winning and Losing in One-Click America*. New York: Farrar, Strous and Giroux.

MacGillis, Alec. 2021b. "The Union Battle at Amazon Is Far from Over." *New Yorker*, April 13. Retrieved December 16, 2021 (https://www.newyorker.com /news/news-desk/the-union-battle-at-amazon-is-far-from-over).

Maier, Audrey. n.d. "A Woman's World: A History of Female Labor in Citrus Packinghouses." Retrieved December 17, 2021 (http://sweet-sour-citrus.org /essays/women-in-the-packing-houses/).

Manning, Sue. 1997. "California Mall a 'Mighty' Big Draw." AP, November 26. Retrieved December 16, 2021 (https://apnews.com/article /7ba848128f3328bc6395b107169d38e3).

Manuel, Jennifer. 2016. "Social and Spatial Justice: Grassroots Community Action." Newcastle University. Retrieved December 17, 2021 (http://depts .washington.edu/tatlab/socialjustice/wp-content/uploads/2016/02/Manuel -Social-and-Spatial-Justice-Supporting-Grassroots-Community-Action.pdf).

Marcus, James. 2011. *Amazonia: Five Years at the Epicenter of the Dot.com Juggernaut*. New York: The New Press.

Marcuse, Peter. 2009. "Spatial Justice: Derivative but Causal of Social Injustice." *Spatial Justice* 1(4):1–6.

Massimo, Francesco. 2020. "A Struggle for Bodies and Souls: Amazon Management and Union Strategies in France and Italy." Pp. 129–44 in *The Cost of Free Shipping: Amazon in the Global Economy*, edited by Jake Alimahomed-Wilson and Ellen Reese. London: Pluto Press.

Matsakis, Louise. 2018. "Why Amazon Really Raised Its Minimum Wage to $15." *Wired*, October 2. Retrieved December 17, 2021 (https://www.wired .com/story/why-amazon-really-raised-minimum-wage/).

Mayo, Aleeya. 2021. "Amazon's Carbon Emissions Rose 19% Last Year, Showing Just How Far It Has to Go to Reach Its Net-zero Carbon Pledge." *Business

Insider, July 1. Retrieved December 17, 2021 (https://www.businessinsider
.com/jeff-bezos-amazon-carbon-emissions-rose-in-2020-2021-7).

Mayorquin, Orlando. 2022. "When Residential Neighborhoods Are Rezoned for
Warehouses." KCET, May 2. Retrieved June 15, 2022 (https://www.kcet.org
/shows/earth-focus/when-residential-neighborhoods-are-rezoned-for
-warehouses).

McAllister, Toni. 2021. "Large Warehouse-Retail Project Gets OK in Banning."
Patch, December 1. Retrieved July 31, 2021 (https://patch.com/california
/banning-beaumont/large-scale-banning-warehouse-retail-project-gets
-commission-ok).

McCabe, David and Karen Weiss. 2019. "Amazon Accelerates Efforts to Fight Climate
Change." *New York Times*, September 19. Retrieved December 17, 2021 (https://
www.nytimes.com/2019/09/19/technology/amazon-carbon-neutral.html).

McCrea, Bridget. 2019. "Annual Warehouse and Distribution Center Automation
Survey: More Automation, Please." Modern Materials Handling. Retrieved
December 17, 2021 (https://www.mmh.com/article/annual_warehouse_and
_distribution_center_automation_survey_more_automation).

McDowell, Linda. 2008. "Thinking through Work: Complex Inequalities,
Constructions of Difference, and Trans-national Migrants." *Progress in
Human Geography* 32(4):491–507.

McGhee, Eric. 2020. "California's Political Geography 2020." Sacramento and
San Francisco: Public Policy Institute. Retrieved July 19, 2022 (file:///Users
/ellen/Downloads/californias-political-geography-2020.pdf).

McGhee, Eric and Daniel Krimm. 2012. "California's Political Geography."
Public Policy Institute of California. Retrieved July 3, 2022 (https://www
.ppic.org/wp-content/uploads/content/pubs/report/R_212EMR.pdf).

McKane, Rachel G. and Holly J. McCammon. 2018. "Why We March: The Role
of Grievances, Threats, and Movement Organizational Resources in the 2017
Women's Marches." *Mobilization: An International Quarterly* 23(4):401–24.

McNary, Dave. 1992. "Companies Agree to $150 Million Acid-Pit Clean Up."
United Press International, July 30. Retrieved December 5, 2022 (https://
www.upi.com/Archives/1992/07/30/Companies-agree-to-150-million-acid-pit
-clean-up/2931712468800/).

Meisenzahl, Mary. 2021. "The Pandemic Boosted US E-commerce Spending by
$183 billion—Equivalent to an Extra Holiday Season." *Business Insider*,
March 15. Retrieved December 17, 2021 (https://www.businessinsider.com
/covid-19-e-commerce-spending-increased-183-billion-2021-3).

Merriam-Webster. 2022. "LGBTQIA." Retrieved August 1, 2022 (https://www
.merriam-webster.com/dictionary/LGBTQIA).

Meyer, David S. 2004. "Protest and Political Opportunities." *American Sociological Review* 30:125–45.

Milkman, Ruth, Ana L. Gonzalez, and Victor Narro (with Bernhardt, Annette,
Theodore, Nik, Heckathorn, Douglas, Auer, Mirabai, DeFilippis, James,

Perelshteyn, Jason, Polson, Diana, & Spiller, Michael). 2010. *Wage Theft and Workplace Violations in Los Angeles: The Failure of Employment and Labor Law for Low-wage Workers*. University of California, Los Angeles: Institute for Research on Labor and Employment. Retrieved December 17, 2021 (https://www.labor.ucla.edu/wp-content/uploads/2018/06/LAwagetheft.pdf).

Milmo, Dan. 2021. "Jeff Bezos' Space Flight Firm 'Rife with Sexism,' Employees' Letter Claims." *The Guardian*, October 1. Retrieved December 20, 2021 (https://www.theguardian.com/technology/2021/oct/01/jeff-bezos-space-flight-firm-rife-with-sexism-letter-employees-claims).

Mitchell, Stacy and Olivia LaVecchia. 2016. "Amazon's Stranglehold: How the Company's Tightening Grip Is Stifling Competition, Eroding Jobs, and Threatening Communities." ILSR. Retrieved July 31, 2022 (https://ilsr.org/wpcontent/uploads/2020/04/ILSR_AmazonReport_final.pdf).

Molina, Alejandra. 2018. "Enough with the Warehouses." *Next City*, August 10. Retrieved November 2019 (https://nextcity.org/urbanist-news/this-inland-empire-community-says-enough-with-the-warehouses).

Monroy, Douglas. 1997. "The Creation and Re-creation of Californio Society." *California History* 76(2/3):173–95.

Moody, Kim. 2017. *On New Terrain: How Capital Is Reshaping the Battleground of Class War*. Chicago: Haymarket Books.

Mora, Marie T. and Alberto Davila. 2018. "The Hispanic–White Wage Gap Has Remained Wide and Relatively Steady: Examining Hispanic–White Gaps in Wages, Unemployment, Labor Force Participation, and Education by Gender, Immigrant Status, and Other Subpopulations." Economic Policy Institute, July 2. Retrieved December 17, 2021 (https://www.epi.org/publication/the-hispanic-white-wage-gap-has-remained-wide-and-relatively-steady-examining-hispanic-white-gaps-in-wages-unemployment-labor-force-participation-and-education-by-gender-immigrant/).

Morales, Robert. 2022. "Amazon Has Pulled Out of West Covina Delivery Station Project." *San Gabriel Valley Tribune*, March 11. Retrieved December 8, 2022 (https://www.sgvtribune.com/2022/03/11/amazon-has-pulled-out-of-west-covina-delivery-station-project/).

Mordechay, Kfir. 2019. "Inland Boom and Bust: Race, Place, and the Lasting Consequences of the Southern California Housing Bubble." Blueprint for Belonging Project, Othering and Belonging Institute, UC Berkeley. Retrieved December 17, 2021 (https://belonging.berkeley.edu/sites/default/files/inland_boom_and_bust-_race_place_and_the_lasting_consequences_of_the_southern_california_housing_bubble.pdf).

Morton, Alekzandir. 2015. "Harping on Harmonics: Strategy and Advocacy in Center for Community Action & Environmental Justice v. BNSF Railway." *Ecology LQ* 42:557–64.

Mulvaney, Erin. 2020. "Amazon, T-Mobile Targeted Job-Ads Ruling Could Affect Bias Cases." *Bloomberg Law*, March 16. Retrieved December 20, 2021

(https://news.bloomberglaw.com/daily-labor-report/amazon-t-mobile
-targeted-job-ads-ruling-could-affect-bias-cases).

Murray, Christine. 2021. "Analysis-Mexico's Ban on Subcontracting Aimed to
Help Workers: Is It Succeeding?" *Reuters*, July 28 (https://www.reuters.com
/article/idUSL8N2OV5FU).

Murray, Christine and Avi Asher-Schapiro. 2021. "Inside Amazon's Shadow
Workforce in Mexico." Thomas Reuters Foundation Long Reads, April 28.
Retrieved January 21, 2022 (https://longreads.trust.org/item/Inside
-Amazon-shadow-workforce-Mexico).

Mydans, Seth. 1991. "Settlements Reached on Toxic Dump in California." *New
York Times*, December 24. Retrieved December 5, 2022 (https://www.nytimes
.com/1991/12/24/us/settlements-reached-on-toxic-dump-in-california.html).

Nakano Glenn, Evelyn. 2012. *Forced to Care: Coercion and Caregiving in
America*. Cambridge, MA: Harvard University Press.

National Council for Occupational Safety and Health (COSH). 2018. "The Dirty
Dozen 2018: Employers Who Put Workers and Communities at Risk."
Retrieved December 20, 2021 (https://coshnetwork.org/sites/default/files
/Dirty%20Dozen%202018,%204-25-18+FINAL(1).pdf).

National Council for Occupational Safety and Health (COSH). 2019. "The Dirty
Dozen 2019." National COSH. Retrieved December 20, 2021 (https://
nationalcosh.org/sites/default/files/uploads/2019_Dirty_Dozen.pdf).

National Council for Occupational Safety and Health (COSH). 2020. "Dirty
Dozen: Special Coronavirus Edition." Retrieved December 20, 2021 (https://
nationalcosh.org/sites/default/files/2020%20Dirty%20Dozen%20Report.pdf).

National Council for Occupational Safety and Health (COSH). 2022. "Dirty
Dozen, 2022." Retrieved July 26, 2022 (https://nationalcosh.org/sites/default
/files/uploads/2022_Dirty_Dozen.pdf).

Newman, Penny. 2012. "Inland Ports of Southern California–Warehouses,
Distribution Centers, Intermodal Facilities Impacts, Costs and Trends."
Center for Community Action and Environmental Justice. Retrieved
January 25, 2022 (http://docplayer.net/92362053-Inland-ports-of-southern
-california-warehouses-distribution-centers-intermodal-facilities-impacts
-costs-and-trends.html).

New York Attorney General Press Office. 2021. "Attorney General James Seeks
Emergency Relief to Protect Rights and Safety of Amazon Workers." Press
Release, November 30, 2021. Retrieved January 26, 2022 (https://ag.ny.gov
/press-release/2021/attorney-general-james-seeks-emergency-relief-protect
-rights-and-safety-amazon).

Ng, Alfred and Ben Fox Rubin. 2019. "Amazon Fired These 7 Pregnant Workers:
Then Came the Lawsuits." CNET, May 6. Retrieved December 20, 2021
(https://www.cnet.com/features/amazon-fired-these-7-pregnant-workers
-then-came-the-lawsuits/).

Nguyen, Nicole. 2018. "The Hidden Environmental Cost of Amazon Prime's Free, Fast Shipping." *Buzz Feed News*, July 21. Retrieved July 31, 2018 (https://www.buzzfeednews.com/article/nicolenguyen/environmental-impact-of-amazon-prime).

O'Brien, Bobby. 2018. "Florida Orange Juice Has Roots in WWII Military." *WUSF Public Media*, November 16. Retrieved December 17, 2021 (https://www.wlrn.org/2018-11-16/florida-orange-juice-has-roots-in-world-war-ii-military).

Occupational Safety and Health Administration. 2022. "OSHA News Release—Region 5." April 26. Retrieved July 31, 2022 (https://www.osha.gov/news/newsreleases/region5/04262022).

Oh, Soo. 2017. "The Gender and Racial Wage Gap: On Equal Pay Day, the Wage Gap Is Narrowing, but Not Quickly Enough." *Vox*, April 4. Retrieved on December 27, 2020 (https://www.vox.com/identities/2017/4/4/15179156/equal-pay-day-race-gender-wage-gap).

Olmstead, Alan L. and Paul W. Rhode. 2017. "A History of California Agriculture." University of California Agriculture and Natural Resources. Retrieved December 17, 2021 (https://s.giannini.ucop.edu/uploads/giannini_public/19/41/194166a6-cfde-4013-ae55-3e8df86d44d0/a_history_of_california_agriculture.pdf).

Olney, Peter and Rand Wilson. 2020. "Think Big: Organizing a Successful Amazon Workers' Movement in the United States by Combining the Strengths of the Left and Organized Labor." Pp. 250–64 in *The Cost of Free Shipping: Amazon in the Global Economy*, edited by Jake Alimahomed-Wilson and Ellen Reese. London: Pluto Press.

Olney, Peter and Rand Wilson. 2022. "It's Time for Salting to Make a Comeback." *Jacobin*, July 26 (https://jacobin.com/2022/07/union-organizing-salt-salting-starbucks-amazon-ups).

Organise. 2018. "Amazon: What's It Like Where You Work?" Retrieved December 20, 2021 (https://static1.squarespace.com/static/5a3af3e22aeba594ad56d8cb/t/5ad098b3562fa7b8c90d5e1b/1523620020369/Amazon+Warehouse+Staff+Survey+Results.pdf).

Palmer, Annie. 2021a. "Senators Urge Investigation into Amazon over Alleged Discrimination against Pregnant Warehouse Workers." CNBC, September 10. Retrieved December 20, 2021 (https://www.cnbc.com/2021/09/10/senators-call-for-amazon-investigation-over-alleged-pregnancy-discrimination.html).

Palmer, Annie. 2021b. "Amazon Poised to Pass UPS and FedEx to Become Largest U.S. Delivery Service by Early 2022, Exec Says." *NBC Tech News*, November 29. Accessed December 5 2022 (https://www.cnbc.com/2021/11/29/amazon-on-track-to-be-largest-us-delivery-service-by-2022-exec-says.html).

Palmer, Annie. 2022a. "Amazon Illegally Interfered in Amazon Warehouse Vote, Union Alleges." CNBC, April 8. Retrieved June 21, 2022 (https://www

.cnbc.com/2022/04/07/amazon-illegally-interfered-in-alabama-warehouse
-vote-union-alleges.html).

Palmer, Annie. 2022b. "Amazon Must Reinstate Fired Worker Who Led Protest
over Working Conditions, Judge Rules." CNBC, April 19. Retrieved August 1,
2022 (https://www.cnbc.com/2022/04/19/amazon-must-reinstate-fired
-warehouse-worker-judge-rules.html).

Panico, Rebecca. 2020. "Black Warehouse Worker's Lawsuit Says Managers
Used N-word, Denied Him Promotions." NJ.com, November 18. Retrieved
December 21, 2021 (https://www.nj.com/essex/2020/11/black-amazon
-warehouse-workers-lawsuit-says-managers-used-n-word-denied-him
-promotions.html).

Park, R. Jisung, Nora Pankratz, and A. Patrick Behrer. 2021. "Temperature,
Workplace Safety, and Labor Market Inequality." Institute of Labor
Economics Discussion Paper No. 14560. Retrieved December 21, 2021
(https://ftp.iza.org/dp14560.pdf).

Parkhurst, Emily. 2012. "Workers, Unions Protest Amazon Working Conditions."
Puget Sound Business Journal, May 10. Retrieved January 21, 2021 (https://
www.bizjournals.com/seattle/blog/techflash/2012/05/workers-protest
-amazon-warehouse.html).

Patterson, Thomas. 2015. *From Acorns to Warehouses: Historical Political
Economy of Southern California's Inland Empire*. Walnut Creek, CA: Left
Coast Press.

Peano, Irene. 2021. "Gendering Logistics: Subjectivities, Biopolitics and Extraction
in Supply Chains." Pp. 16–27 in *Gendering Logistics: Feminist Approaches for
the Analysis of Supply-Chain Capitalism*, edited by Carlotton Benvegnù,
Niccolò Cuppini, Mattia Frapporti, Evelina Gambino, Floriano Milesi, Irene
Peano, and Maurilio Pirone. Bologna: University of Bologna Press.

Peck, Emily. 2018. "Women Describe Rampant Groping, Sexual Harassment at
Verizon-Contracted Warehouse." *Huffington Post*, May 2. Retrieved December 21, 2021 (https://www.huffpost.com/entry/sexual-harassment-complaint
-contract-warehouse_n_5ae9cb66e4b06748dc8e802b).

Peck, Jamie and Nik Theodore. 2001. "Contingent Chicago: Restructuring the
Spaces of Temporary Labor." *International Journal of Urban and Regional
Research* 25(3):471–96.

Perry, Daryl. 2022. "Who Is the Richest Person in the World? It's Not Jeff Bezos
Anymore." *USA Today*, June 20. Retrieved July 19, 2022 (https://www.usa
today.com/story/money/2022/06/20/richest-person-in-the-world/76647
86001/).

Peters, Adele. 2019. "How Amazon Plans to Make Half of Its Shipments Carbon
Neutral by 2013." *Fast Company*, February 21. Retrieved December 17, 2021
(https://www.fastcompany.com/90309906/how-amazon-plans-to-make-half
-of-its-shipments-carbon-neutral-by-2030).

Peters, Alan and Peter Fisher. 2004. "The Failures of Economic Development Incentives." *Journal of the American Planning Association* 70(1):27–37.

Petrongolo, Barbara and Maddalena Ronchi. 2020. "Gender Gaps and the Structure of Local Labor Markets." *Labour Economics* 64:101819 (https://doi.org/10.1016/j.labeco.2020.101819).

Phillips, Anna. 2021. "More Warehouse Workers Toiling in Extreme Heat: Temperatures at Facilities Can Hover above 90 Degrees for Hours; State Officials Have Not Yet Finalized Regulations." *Los Angeles Times*, October 12. Retrieved December 21, 2021 (https://www.pressreader.com/usa/los-angeles-times/20211012/281535114171177).

Phillips, Burnell W., ed. 1972. *Riverside County Labor (with References to San Bernardino County)*. Riverside, CA: Riverside County Labor Federation.

Pierson, David and Andrew Khouri. 2016. "Amazon Plans Fifth Warehouse in the Inland Empire." *Los Angeles Times*, March 31. Retrieved December 17, 2021 (https://www.latimes.com/business/la-fi-amazon-center-20160401-story.html).

Pike Bond, Victoria. 2019. "Inland Empire Business Activity Jumps Following First Quarter Slowdown: New Analysis Reveals Region's Most and Least Competitive Industries." *UC Riverside News*, August 8. Retrieved December 17, 2021 (https://news.ucr.edu/articles/2019/08/08/inland-empire-business-activity-jumps-following-first-quarter-slowdown).

Pitcher, Jack. 2020. "Jeff Bezos Adds Record $13 Billion in a Single Day." *Bloomberg News*, July 20. Retrieved September 2, 2020 (https://www.bloomberg.com/news/articles/2020-07-20/jeff-bezos-adds-record-13-billion-in-single-day-to-his-fortune).

Pleyers, Geoffrey. 2020. "The Pandemic Is a Battlefield: Social Movements in the COVID-19 Lockdown." *Journal of Civil Society* 16(4):295–312.

Pope, Arden, III, David V. Bates, and Mark E. Raizenne. 1995. "Health Effects of Particulate Air Pollution: Time for Reassessment?" *Environmental Health Perspectives* 103(5):472–80.

Precarious Connections (Italy). 2021. "The National Strike against Amazon and Its Exploitative Algorithm in Italy." *Logistics of Exploitation*, March 22. Retrieved January 21, 2022 (https://www.transnational-strike.info/2021/03/22/the-national-strike-against-amazon-and-its-exploitative-algorithm-in-italy/).

Press, Alex. 2018. "No Space to Be Human." *The Nation*, December 20. Retrieved December 17, 2021 (https://www.thenation.com/article/heike-geissler-seasonal-associate-amazon/).

Public Justice and Make the Road New York. 2020. "Amazon Warehouse Associates: Know Your Rights!" Public Justice. Retrieved December 21, 2021 (https://www.publicjustice.net/awa-know-your-rights/).

Quaker, Daisy. 2022. "Amazon Stats: Growth, Sales and More." *Grow Your Business* (blog), Amazon, March 31. Retrieved July 11, 2022 (https://sell.amazon.com/blog/grow-your-business/amazon-stats-growth-and-sales).

Rantz, S. E. 1970. *Urban Sprawl and Flooding in Southern California*. U.S. Geological Survey.

Real Deal Staff. 2022. "Amazon Halts Work on SF Warehouse after Delivery Center Moratorium." *The Real Deal*, March 23. Retrieved June 20, 2022 (https://therealdeal.com/sanfrancisco/2022/03/23/amazon-halts-work-on-sf -warehouse-after-delivery-center-moratorium/).

Reese, Ellen. 2020. "Gender, Race, and Warehouse Labor in the United States." Pp. 102–15 in *The Cost of Free Shipping: Amazon in the Global Economy*, edited by Alimahomed-Wilson and Ellen Reese. London: Pluto Press.

Reese, Ellen and Rudolph Bielitz. 2021. "The Warehouse Worker Resource Center in Southern California." Pp. 294–311 in *Inciting Justice and Progressive Power—The Partnership for Working Families Cities*, edited by David B. Reynolds and Louise Simmons. New York: Routledge.

Reese, Ellen and Alexander Scott. 2019. "Warehouse Employment as a Driver of Inequality in the Inland Empire: The Experiences of Young Amazon Workers." Othering and Belonging Institute, UC Berkeley. Retrieved December 17, 2021 (https://belonging.berkeley.edu/warehouse-employment -driver-inequality-inland-empire-experiences-young-amazon-warehouse -workers).

Reese, Ellen and Jason Struna. 2020. "Automation and the Surveillance-Driven Warehouse in Inland Southern California." Pp. 85–101 in *The Cost of Free Shipping: Amazon in the Global Economy*, edited by Alimahomed-Wilson and Ellen Reese. London: Pluto Press.

Reilly, Mark. 2022. "Amazon Workers in Shakopee Protest over Pay, Time Off for Eid Holiday." *Minneapolis/St. Paul Business Journal*, May 2. Retrieved July 26, 2022 (https://www.bizjournals.com/twincities/news/2022/05/02 /amazon-workers-in-shakopee-protest-eid-holiday.html).

Reuters. 2022a. "Draft Law on Joint Standards for Minimum Wages in EU Passes Crucial hurdle." June 7. Retrieved July 23, 2022 (https://www.reuters .com/business/sustainable-business/draft-law-joint-standards-minimum -wages-eu-passes-crucial-hurdle-2022-06-07/).

Reuters. 2022b. "German Union Verdi Calls for 'Prime Day' Strike by Amazon Workers." July 10. Retrieved July 27, 2022 (https://www.reuters.com /business/german-union-verdi-calls-prime-day-strike-by-amazon-workers -2022-07-10/).

Rivas-Rodriguez, Maggie and B. V. Olguín. 2014. *Latina/os and World War II: Mobility, Agency, and Ideology*. Austin: University of Texas Press.

Riverside Agricultural Commission. 2018. "Riverside Agricultural Production Report 2018." Retrieved December 17, 2021 (https://storymaps.arcgis.com /stories/c0748c117e374c32983e0b590c73fe80).

Roach, Caillie. 2020. "Air Pollution in the Inland Empire." Retrieved December 17, 2021 (https://storymaps.arcgis.com/stories/fe2811197ce1427db17a808593f1526e).

Roberts, Steven V. 1972. "Heavy Smog Blights Life in Riverside, Calif." *New York Times*, August 3. Retrieved December 17, 2021 (https://www.nytimes.com /1972/08/03/archives/heavy-smog-blights-life-in-riverside-calif-angry -citizens-urge.html).

Robinson, William Wilcox. 1957. *The Story of Riverside County*. Riverside, CA: Title Insurance and Trust Company.

Robinson, William Wilcox and Allen C. McGurk. 2013. *The Story of San Bernardino County*. Whitefish, MT: Literary Licensing.

Rodó-de-Zárate, Maria and Mireia Baylina. 2018. "Intersectionality in Feminist Geographies." *Gender, Place & Culture* 25(4):547–53.

Rolf, David. 2016. *The Fight for $15: The Right Wage for a Working America*. New York: The New Press.

Rosalsky, Greg. 2019. "When Computers Collude." NPR, April 2. Retrieved December 27, 2020 (https://www.npr.org/sections/money/2019/04/02 /708876202/when-computers-collude).

Rose, Fred. 2000. *Coalitions across the Class Divide: Lessons from the Labor, Peace, and Environmental Movements*. Ithaca, NY: Cornell University Press.

Rosenberg, Eli M. 2022. "Amazon Workers Demand Details in Warehouse Workers' Death." *NBC News*, July 22. Retrieved July 26, 2022 (https://www .nbcnews.com/business/business-news/amazon-worker-death-prime-day -new-jersey-rcna39534).

Rosenblum, Jonathan. 2020. "Lessons from the Amazon Tax Victory in Seattle." *Labor Notes*, July 23. Retrieved January 23, 2022 (https://labornotes.org /2020/07/lessons-amazon-tax-victory-seattle).

Roth, Emma. 2022. "New York Gets Closer to Cracking Down on Amazon's Warehouse Production Quotas." *The Verge*, June 4. Retrieved July 23 (https://www.theverge.com/2022/6/4/23154379/new-york-cracking-down -amazon-warehouse-production-quotas-warehouse-worker-protection-act).

Rubin, Beth A. 2012. "Shifting Social Contracts and the Sociological Imagina-tion." *Social Forces* 91(2):327–46.

Sackman, Douglas C. 2000. "'Nature's Workshop': The Work Environment and Workers' Bodies in California's Citrus Industry, 1900–1940." *Environmental History* 5(1):27–53.

San Bernardino Airport Communities (SBAC). 2019. "Who Are the San Bernar-dino Airport Communities?" Retrieved December 5, 2022 (https:// sbairportcommunities.org/home).

Sanders, Welford, Judith Getzels, David Mosena, and JoAnn Butler. 1984. *Affordable Single-family Housing: A Review of Development Standards*. Chicago: American Planning Association.

Sandoval, Manny B. 2019. "Hundreds of San Bernardino Residents Speak Out at FAA Hearing on Eastgate Air-cargo Logistics Project." *Inland Empire Community News*, August 13. Retrieved January 25, 2022 (http://iecn.com

/hundreds-of-san-bernardino-residents-speak-out-at-faa-hearing-on-air
-cargo-logistics-project-eastgate/).

Sandoval, Manny B. 2021. "Concerned Neighbors of Bloomington Fight for
Quality of Life, Oppose Warehouse Saturation." *Inland Empire Community
News*, February 3. Retrieved January 25, 2022 (http://iecn.com/concerned
-neighbors-of-bloomington-fight-for-their-livelihood-amid-warehouse
-oversaturation/).

San Joaquin Valley Air Pollution Control District (APCD). 2017. "Indirect
Source Review Rule." Retrieved December 5, 2022 (https://ww2.valleyair.org
/permitting/indirect-source-review-rule-overview/).

Sarathy, Brinda. 2013. "Legacies of Environmental Justice in Inland Southern
California." *Race, Gender, and Class* 20(3–4): 254–68.

Sarathy, Brinda. 2021. "Before Amazon: Land, Labor, and Logistics in the
Inland Empire of WWII." *Boom California*, September 22. Retrieved
January 25, 2022 (https://boomcalifornia.org/2021/09/22/before-amazon
-land-labor-and-logistics-in-the-inland-empire-of-wwii/).

Sasser, Jade, Bronwyn Leebaw, Cesunica Ivey, Brandon Brown, Chikako
Takeshita, and Alexander Nguyen. 2021. "Commentary: Intersectional
Perspectives on COVID-19 Exposure." *Journal of Exposure Science &
Environmental Epidemiology* 31:401–3.

Scauzillo, Steve. 2021. "Chino Enacted 45-day Moratorium on Warehouses."
Daily Bulletin, October 27. Retrieved January 19, 2022 (https://www.daily
bulletin.com/2021/10/27/chino-enacts-moratorium-on-warehouses/).

Scharf, Thomas L. 1978. "Impact of Colonization on the Native California
Societies." *San Diego Historical Quarterly* 24(1). Retrieved December 17,
2021 (https://sandiegohistory.org/journal/1978/january/impact/).

Scheiber, Noam. 2021. "Union Vote at Amazon Warehouse in Alabama Is
Overturned by Regional Labor Office." *New York Times*, November 29.
Retrieved January 24, 2022 (https://www.nytimes.com/2021/11/29/business
/amazon-bessemer-alabama-election.html).

Schiavone, Renee. 2017. "Board Backs Massive Warehouse Project in Cherry
Valley Despite Community Objections" *Patch*, October 17. Retrieved July 30
(https://patch.com/california/banning-beaumont/massive-warehouse
-project-approved-cherry-valley-despite-community).

Schrock, Richelle D. 2013. "The Methodological Imperatives of Feminist
Ethnography." *Journal of Feminist Scholarship* 5(Fall):54–60.

Seager, Joni. 1993. *Earth Follies: Feminism, Politics and the Environment*. New
York: Routledge.

Selyukh, Alina. 2021. "California Bill Passes, Giving Amazon Warehouse Workers
Power to Fight Speed Quotas." *NPR News*, September 8. Retrieved December 7, 2022 (https://www.kpcc.org/npr-news/2021-09-08/california-law-passes
-giving-amazon-warehouse-workers-power-to-fight-speed-quotas).

Semuels, Alana. 2018. "What Amazon Does to Poor Cities." *The Atlantic*, February 1. Retrieved December 21, 2021 (https://www.theatlantic.com /business/archive/2018/02/amazon-warehouses-poor-cities/552020/).

Shane, Daniel. 2013. "A Revobluetion: The Inland Empire's New Political Geography." The Rose Institute of State and Local Government, Claremont McKenna College. Retrieved July 3, 2022 (https://roseinstitute.org/a -revobluetion-the-inland-empires-new-political-geography/).

Shearer, Chad, Isha Shah, and Marek Gootman. 2019. "Advancing Opportunity in California's Inland Empire." Brookings Metropolitan Program, February. Retrieved December 27, 2020 (https://www.brookings.edu/wp-content /uploads/2019/02/Full-Report_Opportunity-Industries_Inland-California _Final_Shearer-Shah-Gootman.pdf).

Sheffi, Yossi. 2012. *Logistics Clusters: Delivering Value and Driving Growth*. Cambridge, MA: MIT Press.

Singh, Maanvi. 2021. "Pollution Is Everywhere: How One-click Shopping Is Creating Amazon Warehouse Towns." *The Guardian*, December 11. Retrieved January 25, 2021 (https://www.theguardian.com/us-news/2021 /dec/11/how-one-click-shopping-is-creating-amazon-warehouse-towns-were -disposable-humans).

Sisson, Patrick. 2017. "How Amazon's 'Invisible' Hand Can Shape Your City." *Curbed*, May 2. Retrieved December 17, 2021 (https://www.curbed.com/2017 /5/2/15509316/amazon-prime-retail-urban-planning).

Sisson, Patrick. 2019. "Your Cyber Monday Shopping Is Polluting This Small Town." *Curbed*, December 2. Retrieved January 25, 2021 (https://archive .curbed.com/2018/11/20/18104847/cyber-monday-warehouse-real-estate -pollution-amazon).

Sisson, Patrick. 2021. "The Quest to Green an Empire of Mega-Warehouses." *Citylab*, June 14. Retrieved December 17, 2021 (https://www.bloomberg.com /news/articles/2021-06-14/california-launches-new-war-on-warehouse -pollution).

Smith, Kevin. 2020. "Amazon Looking to Hire 4,900 in Inland Empire." *Press Enterprise*, September 14. Retrieved November 30, 2020 (https://www.pe .com/2020/09/14/amazon-looking-to-hire-4900-in-the-inland-empire /?clearUserState=true).

Smith, Noah. 2015. "In California's Inland Empire, Economic Recovery Brimming with Industrial Complexes." *New York Times*, April 4. Retrieved December 17, 2021 (https://www.nytimes.com/2015/08/05/realestate /commercial/an-economic-recovery-brimming-with-industrial-complexes -in-southern-california.html).

Smith, Sandy. 2017. "Two Worker Deaths in September at Different Amazon Warehouses Spawn Concern from Worker Advocates." *EHS Today*, October 5. Retrieved December 21, 2021 (https://www.ehstoday.com/safety

/article/21919294/two-worker-deaths-in-september-at-different-amazon
-warehouses-spawn-concern-from-worker-advocates).

Snider, Mike and Elizabeth Weise. 2018. "Amazon Ups Minimum Wage to $15 for All Full, Part-Time, and Seasonal Employees." *USA Today*, October 2. Retrieved December 21, 2021 (https://www.usatoday.com/story/money /business/2018/10/02/amazon-minimum-wage-increase-15-all-its-employees /1495473002/).

Sohaib, Sharjeel. 2022. "Inland Empire to House Amazon's Largest Warehouse: Bigger Than Disney California Adventure Park." Startempire Wire, June 17. Retrieved July 29, 2022 (https://startempirewire.com/inland-empire -amazons-largest-warehouse/#:~:text=In%20the%20Inland%20Empire%2C %20Amazon,over%204%20million%20square%20feet).

Solon, Olivia and April Glaser. 2021. "'Treated Like Sacrifices': Families Breathe Toxic Fumes from California's Warehouse Hub." *NBC News*, April 27. Retrieved January 25, 2022 (https://www.nbcnews.com/tech/tech-news /treated-sacrifices-families-breathe-toxic-fumes-california-s-warehouse -hub-n1265420).

Sonnemaker, Tyler. 2021a. "2020 Brought a Wave of Discrimination and Harassment Allegations against Major Companies Like Amazon, McDonald's, and Pinterest: These Are Some of the Year's High-Profile Legal Battles." *Business Insider*, January 1. Retrieved December 21, 2021 (https:// www.businessinsider.com/every-company-that-was-sued-discrimination -and-harassment-lawsuits-2020-2021-1?r=MX&IR=T).

Sonnemaker, Tyler. 2021b. "Amazon hit with 5 lawsuits from warehouse and corporate employees alleging discrimination and retaliation." *Business Insider*, May 19. Retrieved December 21, 2021 (https://www.businessinsider .com/amazon-five-discrimination-retaliation-lawsuits-warehouse-corporate -employees-2021-5).

Soper, Spencer. 2012. "Amazon Workers Cool after Company Took Heat for Warehouses." *Seattle Times*, June 12. Retrieved December 21, 2021 (https:// www.seattletimes.com/business/amazon-workers-cool-after-company-took -heat-for-hot-warehouses/).

South Coast AQMD. 1997. "The Southland's War on Smog: 50 Years of Progress toward Clean Air." Retrieved December 17, 2021 (https://www.aqmd.gov /home/research/publications/50-years-of-progress).

South Coast AQMD. 2021a. "Re: Opposition to Proposed Rule 2305." Retrieved January 25, 2022 (http://www.aqmd.gov/docs/default-source/planning /fbmsm-docs/pr-2305-comments-vol-4.pdf?sfvrsn=33).

South Coast AQMD. 2021b. "Rule 2305: Warehouse Indirect Source Rule— Warehouse Actions and Investments to Reduce Emissions (WAIRE) Program." Retrieved January 24, 2022 (http://www.aqmd.gov/docs/default -source/rule-book/reg-xxiii/r2305.pdf?sfvrsn=15).

South Coast AQMD. 2022. "About." Retrieved January 24, 2022 (https://www
.aqmd.gov/nav/about#:~:text=About%2025%25%20of%20this%20area's,%2C
%20ships%2C%20trains%20and%20airplanes).

Spector, Robert. 2000. *Amazon.com: Get Big Fast; Inside the Revolutionary
Business Model That Changed the World*. New York: Random House
Business.

Sprague, Jeb and Sreerekha Sathi. 2020. "Transnational Amazon: Labor
Exploitation and the Rise of E-commerce in South Asia." Pp. 50–65 in *The
Cost of Free Shipping: Amazon in the Global Economy*, edited by Jake
Alimahomed-Wilson and Ellen Reese. London: Pluto Press.

Staff Writer. 2021. "Amazon Faces Black Friday Protest March in South Africa."
BusinessTech, November 24. Retrieved January 14, 2022 (https://
businesstech.co.za/news/technology/541072/amazon-faces-black-friday
-protest-march-in-south-africa/).

Starr, Evan, J. J. Prescott, and Norman Bishara. 2021. "Noncompete Agreements in the U.S. Labor Force." *Journal of Law and Economics* 64(1):53–84.

States News Service. 2014. "EEOC Sues FYC International for Sexual Harassment." *States News Service*, September 26. Retrieved December 21, 2021
(https://www.eeoc.gov/newsroom/eeoc-sues-fyc-international-inc-sexual
-harassment).

Steinberg, Jim. 2017. "Why These Bloomington Residents Want to Keep Warehouses Out." *The Sun*, June 23. Retrieved January 24, 2022 (https://www
.sbsun.com/2017/06/23/why-these-bloomington-residents-want-to-keep
-warehouses-out/).

Stoller, Kristin. 2020. "The Top 10 Richest Women in the World." *Forbes*, April 7.
Retrieved September 2, 2020 (https://www.forbes.com/stories/the-10-richest
-women-in-the-world-2020/).

Stone, Brad. 2013. *The Everything Store: Jeff Bezos and the Age of Amazon*. New
York: Random House.

Strategic Organizing Center. 2021. "Primed for Pain: Amazon's Epidemic of
Workplace Injuries." Retrieved December 21, 2021 (https://thesoc.org
/amazon-primed-for-pain/).

Strategic Organizing Center. 2022. "The Injury Machine: How Amazon's
Production System Hurts Workers." Retrieved June 30, 2022 (https://thesoc
.org/wp-content/uploads/2022/04/The-Injury-Machine_How-Amazons
-Production-System-Hurts-Workers).

Street, Richard S. 1979. "Marketing California Crops at the Turn of the Century."
Southern California Quarterly 6(3):239–53.

Strochak, Sarah, Dailin Young, and Alanna McCargo. 2019. "Mapping the
Hispanic Homeownership Gap." Urban Institute. Retrieved December 17,
2021 (https://www.urban.org/urban-wire/mapping-hispanic-home
ownership-gap).

Stroik, Paul and Ryan Finseth. 2021. "Second Draft Socioeconomic Impact Assessment for Proposed Rule 2305—Warehouse Indirect Source Rule—Warehouse Actions and Investments to Reduce Emissions (WAIRE) Program and Proposed Rule 316—Fees for Rule 2305." South Coast Air Quality Management District (AQMD). Retrieved December 17, 2021 (https://www .aqmd.gov/docs/default-source/planning/fbmsm-docs/pr-2305_sia_2nd -draft_4-7-21.pdf?sfvrsn=8).

Stuart, Freddie. 2021. "My Life as an Amazon Warehouse Worker." *Jacobin*, August 2. Retrieved December 21, 2021 (https://www.jacobinmag.com/2021 /08/my-life-as-an-amazon-warehouse-worker).

Suárez, Camille A. 2019. "How California Was Won: Race, Citizenship, and the Colonial Roots of California, 1846–1879." Dissertation, University of Pennsylvania. Retrieved December 17, 2021 (https://repository.upenn.edu /dissertations/AAI13901759).

Taniguchi, Nancy J. 2000. "Weaving a Different World: Women and the California Gold Rush." *California History* 79(2):141–68.

Tanno, Sophie. 2020. "Personal Trainer, 38, Who Worked in Amazon Warehouse during Lockdown 'Was Sexually Harassed by Sleazy, Vile Boss Who Scrolled through Her Facebook Photos Saying How Sexy She Was.'" *Mail Online*, July 5. Retrieved December 21, 2021 (https://www.dailymail.co.uk/news /article-8491245/Employees-claim-suffered-sexual-harassment-Amazon -warehouse.html).

Tanzi, Alexandre. 2021. "Amazon Boosted Workforce by 75% during Covid—And It's Still Hiring." *Bloomberg*, October 29. Retrieved December 21, 2021 (https://www.bloomberg.com/news/articles/2021-10-29/amazon-boosted -workforce-by-75-during-covid-and-is-still-hiring).

Taylor, Bill. 2014. "Why Amazon Is Copying Zappos and Paying Employees to Quit." *Harvard Business Review*, April 14. Retrieved December 21, 2021 (https://hbr .org/2014/04/why-amazon-is-copying-zappos-and-paying-employees-to-quit).

Targeted News Service LLC. 2019. "Attorney General Raoul Announces Settlement with Bolinbrook Warehouse over Claims of Sexual Harassment and Discrimination." Targeted News Service LLC, U.S. State News, May 13. Retrieved from Nexis Uni database September 23, 2021.

Tarrow, Sidney. 1998. *Power in Movement: Social Movements and Contentious Politics*. Cambridge: Cambridge University Press.

Teamsters. 2021a. "Special Resolution: Building Worker Power at Amazon." June 24. Retrieved June 20, 2022 (https://teamster.org/wp-content/uploads /2021/06/62421CONVENTIONRESOLUTIONAMAZON.pdf).

Teamsters. 2021b. "After Sustained Push from Local 414, Fort Wayne, Indiana City Council Nixes Amazon Tax Abatement." Retrieved January 23, 2022 (https://teamster.org/2021/07/after-sustained-push-from-local-414-fort -wayne-city-council-nixes-amazon-tax-abatement/).

Teamsters Local 63. 2018. "UPS and UPS Freight Agreements, 2018–2023."
Retrieved January 18, 2022 (http://www.teamsters63.org/index.php/benefits
/ups-and-ups-freight-agreements-2018-2023).

Teamsters Local 63. n.d. "About Us." Retrieved January 18, 2022 (http://www
.teamsters63.org/index.php/about-us-2).

Tessum, Christopher W., Joshua S. Apte, Andrew L. Goodkind, Nicholas Z.
Muller, Kimberley A. Mullins, David A. Paolella, Stephen Polasky,
Nathaniel P. Springer, Sumil K. Thakrar, Julian D. Marshall, and Jason D.
Hill. 2019. "Inequity in Consumption of Goods and Services Adds to Racial-
Ethnic Disparities in Air Pollution Exposure." *Proceedings of the National
Academy of Sciences* (PNAS) 116(13):6001–6.

Thornton, Mary. 1983. "Lawsuit Is Filed for Cleanup of Stringfellow Acid Pit."
Washington Post, April 22. Retrieved January 24, 2022 (https://www
.washingtonpost.com/archive/politics/1983/04/22/lawsuit-is-filed-for
-cleanup-of-stringfellow-pit/45caba2d-8bd5-454e-a624-9d8447b89dd6/).

Tilly, Charles. 1978. *From Mobilization to Revolution*. Reading, MA: Addison-
Wesley.

Torres, Ivette, Anthony Victoria, and Dan Klooster. 2021. "Warehouses,
Pollution, and Social Disparities." Earthjustice. Retrieved December 17, 2021
(https://earthjustice.org/sites/default/files/files/warehouse_research_report
_4.15.2021.pdf).

Transnational Social Strike Platform. 2019. *Strike the Giant! Transnational
Organization Against Amazon* (Fall). Retrieved July 31, 2022 (https://www
.transnational-strike.info/app/uploads/2019/11/Strike-the-Giant_TSS
-Journal.pdf).

Trombley, William. 1985. "Affordable Housing Fuels Boom." *Los Angeles Times*,
August 11. Retrieved January 25, 2022 (https://www.latimes.com/archives/la
-xpm-1985-08-11-mn-3212-story.html).

Tung, Irene and Deborah Berkowitz. 2020. "Disposable Workers: High Injury
and Turnover Rates at Fulfillment Centers in California." National Employment Law Project. Retrieved December 21, 2021 (https://www.nelp.org
/publication/amazons-disposable-workers-high-injury-turnover-rates
-fulfillment-centers-california/).

UCR Institutional Research. 2022. "Enrollments: Demographic." Retrieved
July 11, 2022 (https://ir.ucr.edu/stats/enroll/demographic).

UCR School of Business Center for Economic Forecasting and Development.
2019. "Inland Empire Business Activity Index." UC Riverside. Retrieved
December 17, 2021 (https://ucreconomicforecast.org/wp-content/uploads
/2019/08/Business_Activity_Index_Q2_2019.pdf).

Uniglobal. 2021. "Make Amazon Pay Coalition Announces Global Programme
of Strikes and Protests in at Least 20 Countries on Black Friday." Retrieved
January 14, 2021 (https://uniglobalunion.org/MAP2021).

United 4 Change ONT8 and Amazon Labor Union. 2022. "Media Advisory for September 9, 2022." Retrieved on September 13, 2022 (https://m.facebook .com/CCAEJ/?locale=en_GB).

United States Bureau of Labor Statistics (BLS). 2013. "Metropolitan Area Employment and Unemployment—December 2012." BLS. Retrieved December 17, 2021 (https://www.bls.gov/news.release/archives/metro _01302013.pdf).

United States Bureau of Labor Statistics (BLS). 2019. "Metropolitan and Nonmetropolitan Area Occupational Employment and Wage Estimates: Riverside-San Bernardino-Ontario, CA." Retrieved December 17, 2021 (https://www.bls.gov/oes/2019/may/oes_40140.htm).

United States Bureau of Labor Statistics (BLS). 2020. "News Release: Employer-Reported Workplace Injuries and Illnesses-2019." Retrieved December 20, 2021 (https://www.bls.gov/news.release/pdf/osh.pdf).

United States Bureau of Labor Statistics (BLS). 2022. "Economic News Release: Union Members Summary." Retrieved July 31, 2022 (https://www.bls.gov /news.release/union2.nro.htm).

United States Census Bureau. 1852. "Population and Industry of California, by the State Census for the Year 1852."Retrieved December 17, 2021 (https:// www2.census.gov/library/publications/decennial/1850/1850a/1850a-47.pdf).

United States Census Bureau. 1977. *Money Income in 1975 or Families of Persons in the United States*. Report Number P60-105.

United States Census Bureau. 2010. "QuickFacts." Retrieved December 17, 2021 (https://www.census.gov/quickfacts/fact/table/US/PST045219).

United States Court of Appeals for the Ninth Circuit. 2021. Case number 20-70272. Retrieved January 19, 2022 (http://climatecasechart.com/climate -change-litigation/wp-content/uploads/sites/16/case-documents/2021 /20211118_docket-20-70272_opinion.pdf).

Urban Institute. 2021. "Reducing the Racial Homeownership Gap." Retrieved December 17, 2021 (https://www.urban.org/policy-centers/housing-finance -policy-center/projects/reducing-racial-homeownership-gap).

Valentine, Gill. 2007. "Theorizing and Researching Intersectionality: A Challenge for Feminist Geography." *Professional Geographer* 59(1):10–21.

Vallas, Steven P. and Emily Cummins. 2014. "Relational Models of Organizational Inequalities: Emerging Approaches and Conceptual Dilemmas." *American Behavioral Scientist* 58(2):228–65.

Vannucci, Cecile, Jill R. Shah, and Bloomberg. 2022. "Jeff Bezos Loses $20 Billion in Hours as Amazon Shares Slump." *Fortune*, April 29. Retrieved July 1, 2022 (https://fortune.com/2022/04/29/jeff-bezos-loses-20-billion-amazon -shares-slump/).

Van Valen, Nelson. 1953. "The Bolsheviki and the Orange Growers." *Pacific Historical Review* 22(1):39–50.

Vasquez, Mario and Teresa Conrow (Teamsters Local 1932). 2021. "Amazon Organizing Strategy." Guest presentation for Sociology of Work class at UC-Riverside (via Zoom), October 14.

Venturi. 2021. "Fontana Council Steamrolls over Appeal of Another Warehouse OK." *San Bernardino County Sentinel*, October 1. Retrieved January 24, 2022 (https://sbcsentinel.com/2021/10/fontana-council-steamrolls-over-appeal-of-another-warehouse-approval/).

Verge, Arthur C. 1994. "The Impact of the Second World War on Los Angeles." *Pacific Historical Review* 63(3):289–314.

Victoria, Anthony. 2017. "Bloomington Residents Continue to Speak against Warehouse Development." *Inland Empire Community News*, August 21. Retrieved January 25, 2022 (http://iecn.com/bloomington-residents-continue-speak-warehouse-development/).

Victoria, Anthony. 2022. "Can Banning New Warehouses Improve Air Quality in the Inland Empire?" KCET, March 10. Retrieved December 5, 2022 (https://www.kcet.org/news-community/can-banning-new-warehouses-improve-air-quality-in-the-inland-empire).

Votavova, Klara. 2020. "Czechs Don't Use Amazon, but Amazon Does Use Czechs." *Jacobin*, December 26. Retrieved January 21, 2022 (https://www.jacobinmag.com/2020/12/amazon-czech-republic-germany-unions).

Waddell, Kaveh. 2021. "When Amazon Expands, These Communities Pay the Price." *Consumer Reports*, December 9. Retrieved December 17, 2021 (https://www.consumerreports.org/corporate-accountability/when-amazon-expands-these-communities-pay-the-price-a2554249208/).

Wakabayashi, Chizuko and Katharine M. Donato. 2005. "The Consequences of Caregiving: Effects on Women's Employment and Earnings." *Population Research and Policy Review* 24(5):467–88.

Walt, Vivienne. 2020. "France Is the One Place Where Amazon Workers are Winning." *Fortune*, May 13. Retrieved January 26, 2022 (https://fortune.com/2020/05/13/amazon-workers-coronavirus-shutdown-france-labor-rights/).

Waltemath, Joy. 2021. "Amazon Facing Five New Lawsuits Alleging Race and Sex Discrimination, Sexual Harassment, Retaliation." *CCH Work Day*, May 25.

Walters, Kyla and Joya Misra. 2015. "Hours as Punishment and Rewards: Scheduling Practices in Retail Clothing. *Work in Progress*. Retrieved August 1, 2022 (https://workinprogress.oowsection.org/2015/12/03/hours-as-rewards-punishment-scheduling-practices-in-clothing-retail/).

Warehouse Workers for Justice. 2017. "Boxed In: Gender Discrimination in Illinois Warehouses." Retrieved September 1, 2019 (http://www.ww4j.org/uploads/7/0/0/6/70064813/boxed_in_small.pdf).

Warehouse Workers Resource Center. 2019. "Holding San Bernardino to a Higher Standard." Retrieved January 25, 2022 (http://www.warehouseworkers.org/holding-san-bernardino-to-a-higher-standard/).

Washington Post. 2019. "Muslim Workers Accuse Amazon of Discrimination at Shakopee Warehouse." May 14. Retrieved December 21, 2021 (https://www .twincities.com/2019/05/14/3-muslim-workers-accuse-amazon-of -discrimination-at-shakopee-warehouse/).

Waters, Michael. 2021. "Amazon Now Ships More Parcels Than FedEx." *The Amazon Effect*, September 17. Retrieved December 17, 2021 (https://www .modernretail.co/platforms/amazon-now-ships-more-parcels-than-fedex/).

Weise, Elizabeth. 2018. "Amazon Upping Wages to $15 per Hour but Cuts Stock Awards, Incentive Pay." *USA Today*, October 3. Retrieved December 21, 2021 (https://www.usatoday.com/story/tech/2018/10/03/amazon-ups-wages-15 -hour-but-cuts-stock-awards-incentive-pay/1515113002/).

Weise, Karen. 2020. "Amazon Angles to Grab Back Customers." *New York Times,* May 22. Retrieved January 24, 2022 (https://www.nytimes.com/2020 /05/22/technology/amazon-coronavirus-target-walmart.html).

Weise, Karen. 2021a. "Amazon's Profit Soars 220 Percent as Pandemic Drives Shopping Online." *New York Times*, May 12. Retrieved December 17, 2021 (https://www.nytimes.com/2021/04/29/technology/amazons-profits-triple .html).

Weise, Karen. 2021b. "How Amazon Managed to Dethrone Walmart." *New York Times*, August 20. Retrieved January 29, 2022 (https://www.nytimes.com /interactive/2021/08/20/technology/how-amazon-beat-walmart.html).

Weise, Karen. 2021c. "Amazon illegally Fired Activist Workers, Labor Board Finds." *New York Times*, April 5. Retrieved January 24, 2022 (https://www .nytimes.com/2021/04/05/technology/amazon-nlrb-activist-workers.html).

Weise, Karen. 2021d. "Labor Organizers at Amazon's Staten Island Warehouse Refile Petion for a Union Election." *New York Times*, December 22. Retrieved January 24, 2022 (https://www.nytimes.com/2021/12/22/business/amazon -union-staten-island.html).

Weise, Karen, Noam Scheiber, and Coral Murray Marcos. 2022. "Amazon Labor Union Loses Its Vote at Second Warehouse on Staten Island." *New York Times*, May 3. Retrieved June 22, 2022 (https://www.nytimes.com/2022/05 /02/technology/amazon-union-staten-island.html).

Whitehead, Brian. 2019. "FAA Approves Eastgate Logistics Center Bound for San Bernardino Airport." *San Bernardino Sun*, December 30. Retrieved January 25, 2022 (https://www.sbsun.com/2019/12/30/faa-approves-eastgate -logistics-center-bound-for-san-bernardino-airport/).

Whitehead, Brian. 2020. "Critics Seek Court's Help to Stop Eastgate Project Bound for San Bernardino Airport." *San Bernardino Sun*, January 30. Retrieved January 25, 2022 (https://www.sbsun.com/2020/01/30/critics-seek -courts-help-to-stop-eastgate-project-bound-for-san-bernardino-airport/).

Whitehead, Brian. 2021a. "45-Day Warehouse Moratorium Fails by 1 Vote." *San Bernardino Sun*, June 3. Retrieved January 19, 2022 (https://www.sbsun

.com/2021/06/03/45-day-warehouse-moratorium-in-san-bernardino-fails-by
-1-vote/).

Whitehead, Brian. 2021b. "Amazon Hires 3700 Employees in Inland Empire."
San Bernardino Sun, April 7. Retrieved January 25, 2022 (https://www
.sbsun.com/2020/04/07/amazon-hires-3700-employees-in-inland-empire-to
-meet-coronavirus-demand-surge/).

Whitehead, Brian. 2022. "Fontana, State AG Settle Lawsuit over Warehouse
Project in Low-income Neighborhood." *Press Enterprise*, April 18. Retrieved
June 14 (https://www.pe.com/2022/04/18/fontana-state-ag-settle-lawsuit
-over-warehouse-project-in-low-income-neighborhood/).

Willsher, Kim. 2016. "Amazon Express Delivery Service Rattles Paris
Authorities." *The Guardian*, June 20. Retrieved July 30, 2022 (https://www
.theguardian.com/cities/2016/jun/20/amazon-prime-now-express-delivery
-service-france-paris).

Wilson, Leah and Loni Prinsloo. 2021. "Amazon's New Africa Site Draws Ire in
Indigenous People Protest." *Bloomberg News*, June 16. Retrieved January 21,
2022 (https://www.bloomberg.com/news/articles/2021-06-16/amazon-s-new
-africa-site-draws-ire-in-indigenous-people-protest).

Winther, Oscar O. 1953. "The Colony System of Southern California." *Agricultural History* 27(3):94–103.

WJZ-CBS Baltimore. 2018. "Two Killed at Amazon Facility Identified." November 2. Retrieved December 21, 2021 (https://baltimore.cbslocal.com/2018/11
/02/partial-building-collapse-at-baltimore-amazon-center/).

Woodcraft, Zoe. 2021. "Southern California Mega-Warehouse Will Heavily
Electrify Operations, Per Landmark Agreement Worth $47 Million."
Earthjustice, April 29. Retrieved December 4, 2022 (https://earthjustice.org
/news/press/2021/southern-california-mega-warehouse-will-heavily
-electrify-operations-per-landmark-agreement-worth-up-to-47).

Woodcraft, Zoe, Rachel Boyer, and Anthony Victoria. 2021. "Southern California's Air District Votes to Electrify and Clean Up Air Pollution from Mega-
Warehouses." Earthjustice, May 7. Retrieved December 4, 2022 (https://
earthjustice.org/news/press/2021/southern-californias-air-district-votes-to
-electrify-clean-up-air-pollution-from-mega-warehouses).

Woodhouse, Leighton. 2011. "The Destruction of the Inland Empire." *Huffington Post*, May 25. Retrieved December 17, 2021 (https://www.huffpost.com
/entry/the-destruction-of-the-in_b_374032).

Woodman, Spencer. 2015. "Exclusive: Amazon Makes Even Temporary Warehouse Workers Sign 18-month Non-competes." *The Verge*, March 26.
Retrieved December 21, 2021 (https://www.theverge.com/2015/3/26/8280309
/amazon-warehouse-jobs-exclusive-noncompete-contracts).

WSB-TV News Staff. 2022. "Metro Atlanta Amazon Workers Walk Out on
Prime Day to Protest for Better Pay, Security." July 14. Retrieved July 26,

2022 (https://www.wsbtv.com/news/local/dekalb-county/metro-atlanta
-amazon-workers-walk-out-prime-day-protest-better-pay-security
/5G7DBUUOBRGNLDGXJVAEDR6JPY/).

Wulfraat, Marc. 2021. "Amazon Global Supply Chain and Fulfillment Center
Network." Retrieved January 14, 2022 (https://www.mwpvl.com/html
/amazon_com.html).

Yuan, Quan. 2018a. "Environmental Justice in Warehousing Location: State of
the Art." *Journal of Planning Literature* 33(3):287–98.

Yuan, Quan. 2018b. "Location of Warehouses and Environmental Justice."
Journal of Planning Education and Research 33(3):287–98.

Yuan, Quan. 2019. "Planning Matters: Institutional Perspectives on Warehousing Development and Mitigating Its Negative Impacts." *Journal of the
American Planning Association* 85(4):525–43.

Zahn, Max and Sharif Paget. 2019. "'Colony of Hell': 911 Calls from inside
Amazon Warehouses." *Daily Beast*, March 11. Retrieved December 21, 2021
(https://www.thedailybeast.com/amazon-the-shocking-911-calls-from-inside
-its-warehouses).

ZipRecruiter. 2021. "Amazon Warehouse Salary in Riverside, CA." Retrieved
December 17, 2021 (https://www.ziprecruiter.com/Salaries/Amazon
-Warehouse-Salary-in-Riverside,CA).

Index

AB 701 (California, 2021, the Warehouse Worker Quotas law), 210, 212, 263n1

Adriana (interview participant), 85; on social isolation in the workplace, 168

ageism, 138–40

Aguierre, María del Rosario de, 31

Alejandra (interview participant), 81, 132–33; on the lack of safety in Amazon warehouses 162; sexual harassment of, 117–18; on supervisor bias toward attractive young women, 117; work career of, 115–17

Alta California colony, 31, 32

Alvarado, Joey, 75

Amazon: ageism at, 138–40; "Amazon capitalism," 6; and the "Amazon effect," 62; Amazon Europe, 245; Amazon facilities in Inland Southern California, 49–50*tab.*, 50–53; Climate Pledge of (2019), 60; diversity of Amazon's facilities in, 48–49; and the effects of Amazon's buildout, 62–63; electronic shopping platform of, 4; executive "S-team" of (including demographic breakdown of), 9–10; and the "flex up" or "flex down" policy of, 108; gender-inclusive bathroom policies at, 133; "high churn" employment of, 111–14, 275n19; impacts of the rapid growth of,

4–5, 6; increase in the stock prices of, 5; investments of in gasoline-diesel Sprinter Vans, 60; market percentage in the United States, 53; racism and xenophobia at, 133–38; second headquarters of (HQ$_2$), 16–17, 238

Amazon, community resistance to warehousing in Inland Southern California, 63, 183–88; involvement of labor activists in, 187–88, 200; long-standing public resistance to warehousing, 187; and mobilizing and uniting regional resistance to the warehouse industry, 219–21; mobilization of workers and improved labor practices, 200–203, 224–27; resisting Amazon and Moreno Valley's World Logistics Center, 197–98; in the United States, 230–40. *See also* Amazon, European and transnational resistance to; Amazon, opposition to warehousing due to environmental impacts; Targeting Amazon campaign

Amazon, electronic surveillance and rule by algorithm at, 98–109; and the electric monitoring of time off task (TOT), 104–7; and the importance of making rate, 100–101, 102–4, 108–9; and the stress of working under constant surveillance, 99

Amazon, European and transnational resistance to, 227–30; and the formation of European labor unions, 227; in France (the Yellow Vest Movement), 230; in Italy, 229; and the Make Amazon Pay coalition, 229–30; and the targeting of Amazon facilities on consumer holidays, 229; and the Transnational Social Strike, 229; and the work stoppage strike Germany, 227–28

Amazon, opposition to warehousing due to environmental impacts, 188–89; and Bloomington, California, 191–93; and Fontana, California, 193–97; and Mira Loma Village, 190–91

Amazon, resistance to outside of North America and Europe, 240–41; in India, 240; in South Africa, 240–41

Amazon, warehouse empire of, 39–41, 66–67, 208–9; and the rise of warehousing, 41–47

Amazon, warehousing issues of, 3, 8–9; concentration of in certain regions, 7; differences between the wealth of Bezos and Amazon warehouse employees, 5; employee turnover ("high churn") rates in, 111–14, 275n19; gender division of labor in warehouses, 122–25; warehouses primarily located in low-income neighborhoods of color, 13–14; workplace inequalities at Amazon and throughout the warehouse industry, 9–13

Amazon Employees for Climate Justice, 197, 237

Amazon fulfillment centers (FCs), ix, x, 14, 16, 40, 42fig., 47–48, 49tab., 51fig., 52, 63, 67, 76, 199, 245; in Bloomington, California, 193fig; in Beaumont, California, 251fig.; community resistance to development of, 238–39; discipline at, 97–98; in Eastvale, 61–62, 210fig.; JFK8 facility, 233, 234; LDJ₅ facility, 235; in March Air Reserve Base, 42fig., 43fig.; statistics concerning workplace injuries at, 156–58, 277n24; worker resistance at, 228–31

Amazonians United, 231–33; leadership of women of color within, 233

Amazon Labor Union (ALU [Staten Island]), 25, 218–19, 231, 234–36

Amazon managers, 10, 96, 121, 275n8; reliance of on lower-level supervisors, 99–100; and the Transportation Operations Management (TOM) team, 288n3

Amazon Prime, 43fig., 48, 50, 52, 213fig.

Amazon Prime Day, 64, 228, 229

Amazon's dominance of Inland Southern California's e-commerce companies: environmental and economic impacts of, 53–54; impacts of on the economy, 61–62; impacts on environmental and health disparities, 54–60

Amazon warehouse workers, 20, 23, 66, 246; Amazon's reliance on temporary agencies to minimize the cost of wages, 81–82, 245; common concerns among, 67–72, 69tab., 284n34; and the cultural influence of the "American Dream" on, 79; differences between temporary agency workers and those hired directly by Amazon, 81–82, 273n46; divisions between seasonal and permanent workers, 82–83; dramatic increase in the hiring of (2021), 74; exploitative employment practices of Amazon, 67; favoritism in the workplace, 120–21, 124, 144; friendly and helpful coworker relationships, 142–46; hazard pay for workers during the COVID-19 pandemic, 61, 73, 180; heterosexism and transphobia among, 131–33; high costs of health insurance offered to Amazon workers, 78; intergenerational divisions among workers, 139–40; interviewees' job assessments of working at Amazon, 71tab.; jobs lost by due to automation, 62; low wages of as a particularly problematic issue at Amazon, 77–78; motivations of, 96–97; "Pay to Quit" offers to, 87, 112; and peeing in bottles instead of using the bathroom due to work rate pressure, 105–7; "permanent" full-time workers, 74–75, 272n32; pregnancy-related and breastfeeding discrimination against women in the workplace, 129–31; and the requirement for employees to sign a "privacy notice," 287n114; resistance to Amazon policies by workers, 113; seasonal workers, 12–13, 80–83; temporary workers, 80–83; and unpaid personal time (UPT), 86, 87; wages and benefits of, 72–80; wages of compared to retail and food workers' compensation, 75, 272n24; workers' experiences and observations of workplace discrimination and iniquity, 118, 119tab.; workers' reliance on Medicaid and SNAP (Supplemental Nutrition Assistance Program), 78; workplace competition and disrespect among workers, 140–42; workplace socialization, 120, 140–42. *See also* Amazon warehouse workers, impacts on family life, education, and aspirations; Amazon warehouse workers, incentives of for harder work; Amazon warehouse workers, injuries and illnesses of

Amazon warehouse workers, impacts on family life, education, and aspirations, 83–84; and Amazon's tuition assistance program, 89–90; college education of workers, 87–88; education, training and future aspirations, 87–92; family life, 84–87; life after Amazon, 91–92; long-term career goals of workers and the cultural influence of the "American Dream" on, 79 of, 90–91; pregnancy discrimination at Amazon, 84, 129–31; sexism and sexual harassment faced by, 121–29, 238; and the strains of working overtime hours and the graveyard shift, 86–87. *See also* Amazon warehouse workers, incentives of for harder work

Amazon warehouse workers, incentives for harder work, 109–11; and the competition over "cherry picking," 109–10; food incentives, 110–11; free in-house training programs, 112–13; and the "Pay to Quit" program, 87, 112

Amazon warehouse workers, injuries and illnesses of, 147–50, 151*tab.*, 152, 180–82, 277n24; and the effect of noise pollution, 163–64; factors leading to the dangers of warehouse work, 160–61; and the gas leak incident, 164; and the lack of proper air conditioning leading to heat exhaustion, 155–56; mental stress and frustration, 165–67; and OSHA injury rate statistics and OSHA investigations, 157–60; pain and exhaustion, 152–56; pizza parties given by Amazon for "injury free" employees, 156–57; and poor response to workplace emergencies, 164; specific injuries and workplace hazards, 156–65; worker complaints concerning boredom, social isolation, and depression, 167–69. *See also* COVID-19 pandemic, fear and illness at Amazon during

Amazon Web Services (AWS), 128, 237–38

Amazon Workers International, 229

American Federation of Labor and Congress of Industrial Organizations (AFL-CIO), 202, 280n23, 282n84

American Lung Association, 214

Americans with Disabilities Act (ADA), 129, 131

Ana (interview participant): on the importance of meeting Amazon rate quotas, 102; inability of to balance work and college hours, 89; on the lack of safety in Amazon warehouses 163; on pain and exhaustion while working at Amazon, 152; on workplace socialization, 140–42

Andrea (interview participant), on the competition over "cherry picking," 110

Angel (interview participant), on workplace depression and boredom, 167–68

Angelo (interview participant), on broken safety rules at Amazon during the COVID-19 pandemic, 171–72

Anong (interview participant), 140

Asia, 33, 39

Asian Americans, 10, 22

Atchison, Topeka and Santa Fe Railroad, 27

Athena coalition, 208

"atmospheric sewers," 38

Atwood Center, 231–32

Baker, Dean, 73

Balderas, Angela, 3

Banning, California, 250–51

Banning Planning Commission, 250

Barrera, Yesenia, 1

Barstow, 32

Bear Flag Revolt, 31–32

Beaumont, California, 250, 251*fig.*

Bezos, Jeff, 5, 22, 66, 72–73, 147; business success of, 5–6; greed of, 79–80; net worth of (2020), 5, 264n12; wealth of, 5–6, 74, 79, 263n8

Bezos, Mackenzie, 5

Black Friday, 229, 230

Black Lives Matter (BLM) movement, 133, 225, 238

Blacks, 10, 22, 43, 250; Black warehouse workers, 28–29, 134–35; exclusion from US citizenship, 33; median income of (1975), 42

Blancas, Domingo, 205

Bloodworth, James, 105–6

Bloomington, California, 189, 250; challenges to the way of life in, 191–93

Bonta, Rob, 195, 196–97

Bracero program, 38, 62, 268n49

Brenda (interview participant), on boredom in the workplace, 167

Brianna (interview participant), 75, 87; on Amazon's safety rules for COVID-19, 177; on the lack of safety in Amazon

Brianna (interview participant) (*continued*)
    warehouses 163; on the retraction of
    Amazon's COVID-19 policies, 180; on sex-
    ual harassment in the workplace, 127–28;
    on pain and exhaustion while working at
    Amazon, 152
Bureau of Labor Statistics (BLS), 156, 254,
    275n19

California, 247; and the "California Dream" of
    home/farm ownership, 35–36; effect of
    World War II on, 37; sales tax collection
    in, 47–48
California, citrus industry in, 27–28, 31. *See
    also* "Orange Empire"
California Air Resources Board (CARB), 200
California Environmental Quality Act
    (CEQA), 190, 192, 194, 195, 196, 198, 239
California gold rush: extraordinary influx of
    immigrants because of, 32, 36; initial dis-
    covery of gold in the American River
    (1848), 32; population growth due to,
    31–33
California Labor Commission, 204
California Land Act (1852), 34, 267n31
California Silk Center Association, 26
California state constitution (1849), 33
California Trucking Association, 200
Californios, 27, 31, 32, 33, 34, 36
Camila (interview participant), 88, 100;
    exhaustion as a result of working at
    Amazon, 83–84; and the hassle she expe-
    rienced obtaining a COVID-19 leave of
    absence, 178; and her reprimand for too
    much TOT, 104; on pain and exhaustion
    while working at Amazon, 153; and
    peeing in bottles instead of using the
    bathroom due to work rate pressure, 107;
    on sexual harassment in the workplace,
    126; on workplace favoritism, 120
capitalism, 13; "Amazon capitalism," 6; free-
    market capitalism, 41; global capitalism,
    66; labor exploitation under capitalism,
    264n20; as the new slavery, 79; "one-
    click" capitalism, 249
Carousel Mall, 217
Carpenters Union Local 235, 282n79
Caryn (interview participant), on racial
    discrimination at Amazon, 137
Center for Biological Diversity, 194
Center for Community Action and Environ-
    mental Justice (CCAEJ), 17, 19, 21, 186–
    189, 208, 212–14, 216, 219–20, 267n12,

283n119 and n120; and Bloomington, Cal-
    ifornia, 191–93; and Fontana, California,
    194, 197; and Mira Loma Village, 190–91;
    and Indirect Sources, 199.
Centers for Disease Control and Prevention
    (CDC), 171
Central America, 45
Chaffey, George, 35
Change to Win's (CTWs) Warehouse Workers
    United (WWU), 202, 203, 204, 212,
    282n84
Chemical Control Corporation, 185, 279n10
Chinese Exclusion Act (1882), 36, 267n39
Citizens Clearinghouse for Hazardous Waste,
    185
citizenship: exclusion of Blacks from US
    citizenship, 33; Mexican, 34; US, 33
Clara (interview participant), 122, 139; on
    pain and exhaustion while working at
    Amazon, 153; and peeing in bottles
    instead of using the bathroom due to
    work rate pressure, 107; on the stress of
    being an Amazon supervisor, 167
climate justice movement, and climate
    strikes, 208, 230, 237; *See also* Amazon
    Employees for Climate Justice
coalitions, 4, 21, 25, 187, 193, 198, 280n23;
    coalition building, 6, 188; of labor unions,
    158. *See also* Athena coalition; Concerned
    Neighbors in Action (CNA); Concerned
    Neighbors of Bloomington; San Bernar-
    dino Airport Communities (SBAC)
Communication Workers of America (CWA),
    138–39
community activists, 239–40; female activists,
    185; labor activists, 187–88, 200. *See also*
    social justice activists
community benefits agreements (CBAs), 25,
    214–15, 216–17, 220
Comprehensive Environmental Response,
    Compensation, and Liability Act (1980),
    185
Compromise of 1850, 32, 267n24
Concerned Citizens of Bloomington, 250
Concerned Neighbors in Action (CNA), 184–
    85, 187
Concerned Neighbors of Bloomington,
    192–93
Confederation of All-India Traders, 240
Corina, Johnnie, 135–36, 146
Costco fulfillment center (FC) in Mira Loma,
    California, 45
Cothran, Phillip, 195

COVID-19 pandemic, 4, 5, 12, 19–21, 23–24, 52–53, 68, 134, 144–45, 157, 209–10, 223, 231; contested number of actual COVID-19 cases at Amazon, 175; and the "COVID bump," 60, 231; demand for home delivery during, 225; increasing resistance to Amazon during, 225–26, 233, 234; lack of transparency concerning positive COVID-19 cases at Amazon, 175–76; safety protocols at Amazon during, 142. *See also* COVID-19 pandemic, fear and illness at Amazon during

COVID-19 pandemic, fear and illness at Amazon during, 169–70; and Amazon's sanitation team, 170; and broken safety rules at Amazon, 171–73; COVID-19–related leaves and unfair terminations, 178–82; and fears of exposure to COVID-19 at Amazon 174–76; and the inefficiency of Amazon's safety measures during the pandemic, 170, 228, 248; and the role of "Safety Sabers" in, 169–70; stress and isolation concerning COVID-19 safety rules at Amazon, 176–77

Cox Communications and Media Group, 138–39

Craig, Brian, 183

Cunningham, Emily, 197

Cyber Monday, 4, 130, 160, 208, 216, 229

Daniel (interview participant): experience of as a picker and packer, 100; on the horrible working conditions at Amazon, 109; workplace discipline of, 101

Daniella (interview participant), 73–74; on racial discrimination at Amazon, 138

Davis, Alicia Boler, 133–34

De Lara, Juan, 44, 254

Delfanti, Alessandro, 243

Democrats, 16, 39, 40–41

Department of Housing and Urban Development, 281n39

Destiny (interview participant), 75; on the toll the graveyard shift exacts on her family life, 86–87; workplace injuries of, 147–50

Diana (interview participant): on the importance of meeting Amazon rate quotas, 103; on the lack of safety in Amazon warehouses 162; and peeing in bottles instead of using the bathroom due to work rate pressure, 106–7

Dinkins, Carol, 185

Disneyland, 45

distribution centers (DCs), 3–4, 13, 15, 45, 48, 49*tab*, 53, 58–62, 192, 194–95, 200, 205, 230, 233, 244, 263n5

Distribution Management Association (DMA), 44, 243

Doug (interview participant), on the importance of meeting Amazon rate quotas, 103

Duke Realty, 196

Dunaway, Wilma, 86

Earthjustice, 192, 198, 281n70,

Eastgate Air Cargo Logistics Center (San Bernardino International Airport), 212, 213–14, 213*fig.*, 238–39

Echeandía, José Maria de, 31

economic class, 9, 54

electric vehicles (EVs), 198

Eliva (interview participant), 85–86, 104; on broken safety rules at Amazon during the COVID-19 pandemic, 171; on the lack of safety in Amazon warehouses 163; on workplace discrimination, 137; on workplace favoritism, 120

Elizabeth (interview participant), on the competition over "cherry picking," 109–10

environmental justice (EJ), 3, 4, 24, 207, 215; activism in, 183, 187–88, 219, 226–27; female activists, 185; specific activist organizations involved in, 184–85, 191, 208, 214

Environmental Protection Agency (EPA), 184; Superfund National Priorities List of (1983), 185

Equal Employment Opportunity Commission (EEOC), 10, 129–30, 131, 134, 238; lawsuits filed by for employment discrimination against women, 128–29

Erica (interview participant), 99, 122; on broken safety rules at Amazon during the COVID-19 pandemic, 171; on coworker relationships, 143, 144; experience of as a sortation associate, 101

Estella (interview participant), 124

Esther (interview participant), 99; on pain and exhaustion while working at Amazon, 154

ethnicity, 7, 8–9, 33, 42, 53, 54, 55, 61, 66, 136, 140, 243

ethnographic community, case study of the methodology of, 18–21

Europe, 33

Facebook, 139; discrimination of against Blacks, Latinos, and Asian Americans at, 276n34

facility-based mobile source measures (FBMSM), 200

Federal Aviation Administration, 216

FedEx, 48, 194

Felipe (interview participant), 88; on high work rates at Amazon, 166; and peeing in bottles instead of using the bathroom due to work rate pressure, 107

Fernando (interview participant): on high work rates at Amazon, 166; on racial diversity at Amazon, 136, 137

Figueroa, José, 31

Fontana, California, 24, 39, 189; Planning Commission of, 194–95, 196–97; reinvention of, 193–97

Fontana City Council, 194, 195, 196

fulfillment centers (FCs), and spatial distribution of within Inland Southern California, 14; See also Amazon fulfillment centers (FCs); Costco fulfillment center (FC) in Mira Loma, California

FYC International, 128

Garcia, Peter, 195

General, Municipal, Boilermakers and Allied Trade Unions (GMBs), 228

General Data Protection Regulation (GDPR), 247, 248

Gibbs, Lois, 185

Glen Avon, 184, 186–87, 189

Gonzalez, Lorena, 210

Good Jobs First, 17, 238

Granillo, Paul, 52

Great Depression, 5

"great inflation" (1970s), 42–43, 268n68

Green Project, 280n37

Greves, James P., 26

Grossich, Gary, 192

Hannah (interview participant), on Amazon incentives for workers, 110

health concerns among interviewees (overall), 150–52, 151tab; See also Amazon warehouse workers, injuries and illnesses of,

heat exposure, and Amazon warehouse workers' experiences of dehydration and heat illnesses, 154–56, 205, 249; and demands among Inland Empire Amazon Workers United in San Bernardino, California, 218; and demands among

Amazonians United in Chicago, 233; and the development of indoor heat regulations in California, 155, 205, 220; Domingo Blancas and Cal/OSHA's ruling in favor of warehouse workers' legal complaint in Inland Southern California, 205; and increased risk of workplace accidents and heat illness, 155; and OSHA investigations of Amazon, in Breinigsville, Pennsylvania, 155–56

Herrera, Joel, 11

heterosexism, 131–33; 145

Hillwood Enterprises, 216

Hispanics, 36

Howard Industrial Partners, 193

Human Resources (HR), 81, 95, 102, 108, 112–13, 116, 126–28, 132, 137, 145, 178–79, 231, 255, 275n2, 288n3

Human Rights Campaign, 131

Humberto (interview participant), 80

Husing, John, 16

"hyper-exploitation," 9

IE Amazonians Unite, 209

immigrants, 11, 20, 31, 40, 114, 213, 235, 243; Chinese, 36; extraordinary influx of immigrants because of the California gold rush, 32; Latina/Latino, 122, 137; Mexican, 38; Somali Muslim, 231

Imperial County, California, 44

Industrial Workers of the World (IWW), 37

Inicjatywa Pracownicza (IP), 247–48

injury rates in the warehousing and transportation industry and specific warehouse occupations in the United States according to OSHA statistics, 156–57. See also Amazon warehouse workers, injuries and illnesses of

Inland Coalition for Immigrant Justice (ICIJ), 214

Inland Congregations United for Change (ICUC), 214, 217

Inland Empire Amazon Workers United, 218

Inland Empire Business Activity Index, 27–28

Inland Empire Central Labor Council, 214

Inland Empire Economic Partnership (IEEP), 16, 44, 243

Inland Southern California, 3, 6, 7, 8, 13–18; Amazon facilities in, 49–50tab., 49–50; Amazon facilities in "Metro" Inland Southern California, 51map.; "back lot" of, 54–55; coastal "mission zone" of, 30;

counties in, 14*map*; economic boom in, 41; effects of Amazon's expansion on, 222; effects of the Great Recession, 47; expansion of logistics and warehousing in, 14–15; growth of logistics expansion and population growth in, 46–47; logistics as its defining industry, 27–28; and the Santa Ana River overflow disaster, 3–35; unemployment in, 47; as a "warehouse empire," 15. *See also* Amazon, community resistance to warehousing in Inland Southern California; Inland Southern California, brief political and economic history of; Inland Southern California, social injustices and warehouse citing of Amazon in

Inland Southern California, brief political and economic history of, 29–30; of colonial Inland Southern California, 30–31; of early California statehood, 31–35; growth of warehouse workers in, 45–46; phenomenal growth of employment opportunities, in, 45

Isabella (interview participant): and the hassle she experienced obtaining a COVID-19 leave of absence, 178–79; on the isolating nature of Amazon's work environment, 168–69

IXDs, 48, 49–50*tab*, 52, 60, 193

Jacky (interview participant), 102
Jeffries, Kevin, 224
Jessica (interview participant), on the importance of meeting Amazon rate quotas, 102
Jesus (interview participant), 87
Jimmy (interview participant), 110; on the gender division of labor among warehouse workers, 122–23, 125; on the importance of meeting Amazon rate quotas, 100–101; on pain and exhaustion while working at Amazon, 152, 164–65
Jorge (interview participant), 124; on the importance of meeting Amazon rate quotas, 102–3; on the masculine work culture in Amazon warehouses, 125; on the pressure to have a low rate of errors, 103–4
Jose (interview participant), on broken safety rules at Amazon during the COVID-19 pandemic, 171
Josh (interview participant), 122, 136; on the pressure to have a low rate of errors, 103; on racial discrimination at Amazon, 137;

on sexual harassment in the workplace, 126–27
Juan (interview participant), 72; on the lack of safety in Amazon warehouses 163
Juanita (interview participant), on workplace favoritism, 120
Julio (interview participant), 64–66, 67; on the fears of exposure to COVID-19, 174; on the importance of meeting Amazon rate quotas, 102; on the lack of safety in Amazon warehouses 163; wages of, 77; on workplace favoritism, 120
Jurupa Valley, California, 184, 187, 190–91, 194; General Plans of, 190–91. *See also* Parents of Jurupa, Inc.

Kaiser Steel, 39–40; closure of, 41
Kelly (interview participant), on pain and exhaustion while working at Amazon, 153
Kirkby, Ruth, 184, 186

labor organizing/organizations, 3, 7, 19, 183, 188, 214, 226, 237, 250; and "union busting," 242. *See also individually listed specific labor organizations*
Laborers' International Union of North America (LiUNA), 195, 197, 216
Latin America, 39
Latinas, 140; exploitation of immigrant and native-born Latinas, 9, 122
Latinos, 43, 58, 63, 250; median income of (1975), 42–43
Latino warehouse workers, 22, 28–29; as outnumbering Blacks in Southern California, 11
Laura (interview participant), on the importance of meeting Amazon rate quotas, 102–3
LGBT or LGBTQ rights and Amazon's policies and practices, 131, 133, 240
LGBTQIA, 240, 286n76
Lichtenstein, Nelson, 249
"locally undesirable land uses" (LULUs), 59
logistics, 3, 53; and "green" warehousing, 189; logistic clusters in New Jersey, 11; logistics industry's growth, 28; median annual salary in the logistics industry, 60–61; third-party logistics ($_3$PL), 201–2; warehousing logistics, 207–8. *See also* logistics, critical issues concerning
logistics, critical issues concerning, 7–9; viewed of with critical theory and analysis, 8; workplace inequalities at Amazon

logistics, critical issues concerning (*continued*)
   and throughout the warehouse industry,
   9–13, 265n40
Long Beach harbor megaport, 15, 15*fig.*, 39,
   44, 45, 189, 243
Los Angeles City, 44
Los Angeles County, California, 44, 56
Los Angeles harbor megaport, 15, 39, 189,
   243; expansion of, 44–45
Love Canal, 185

MacGillis, Alec, 25, 55, 244
MacKenzie, Don, 250
Make Amazon Pay, 229–30, 241
Mao (interview participant), on impersonal
   relationships with supervisors and
   managers, 168
March Air Force Base, 41
March Air Reserve Base, 41–42, 42*fig.*, 43*fig.*
Maria (interview participant): appreciation
   for her Amazon job, 123; on the difficulty
   of balancing work and college, 89–90;
   on the Latina "clique" of older Latina
   workers, 140; on the stress of meeting
   productivity rates, 165
Martinez, Robert, 2–3
Mateo (interview participant): on the fears of
   exposure to COVID-19, 174–75; on sexual
   harassment in the workplace, 125–26
Matthew Gage Canal, 35
methodological appendix, 253–57, 258–61*tab.*
metropolitan planning organizations
   (MPOs), 199
Metropolitan Statistical Area (MSA), 55
Mexican Americans, 36, 38
Mexico, 33, 45; independence of from
   Spain, 31
Meza, Janet, 196–97
Michelle (interview participant), on work-
   place favoritism, 120
Miguel (interview participant): on discrimi-
   nation against Indian immigrants, 137; on
   racial diversity at Amazon, 136; on racist
   coworkers at Amazon, 138
minimum wage laws, 242
Mira Loma Village, 45, 189, 280n29; and the
   CCAEJ, 190–91; and WWU protests, 203,
   205
Mission Sobrante de San Jacinto, 31
Monterrey, 31–32
Moreno Valley, 24, 53–54; resistance to
   Amazon in, 197–98
Mormons, land acquisitions of, 35

Morris, Pat, 40
Musk, Elon, 79, 263n8

National Ambient Air Quality Standards
   (NAAQS), 55–56
National Association for the Advancement of
   Colored People (NAACP), 135
National Council of Occupational Safety and
   Health (National COSH), 157
National Environmental Protection Act
   (NEPA), 216
National Labor Relations Board (NLRB),
   233, 234
Native Americans, 10
Native Californians, 27, 30–31, 33, 267n25; as
   gente sin razon ("uncivilized people"), 30,
   33; and the harsh conditions of mission
   life, 30; and citrus industry, 36
nativity, 7, 9
natural disasters, 34–35
neoliberalism: neoliberal policies, 17, 224;
   reversing the neoliberal policy agenda,
   241–49
Newman, Penny, 59, 185, 186, 190, 279n13
Niekerk, David, 113
No Hate at Amazon, 237
non-compete agreements, 246–47
North, John W., 26, 35
Norton, Denard, 134–3
Norton Air Force Base, 41
Not In My Backyard (NIMBY), 54
No Way Gateway, 250
NO$_x$ (nitrogen oxides), 198

Occupational Safety and Health Adminis-
   tration (OSHA), 82, 156; Cal/OSHA,
   204–5, 209, 220; funding for, 248–49;
   statistics of concerning workplace
   injuries, 157–58
Oleander development project, 195–96
Olivia (interview participant), 71, 100, 104; on
   Amazon's safety rules for COVID-19, 177;
   on competition among workers, 141; on
   pain and exhaustion while working at
   Amazon, 154
Olmstead, Allan, 27
Ontario Mills, 45
Orange County, California, 43, 55
"Orange Empire," 35–39; agricultural shortages during, 38; and the building of irrigation ditches for water, 35–36; increasing
   reliance of on Mexican American workers,
   38; and the introduction of citrus crops in

California by Spanish missionaries, 35; peak of, 37; vast seasonal workforce of, 36

Orr, Jay, 52

paid time off (PTO), 65

Paola (interview participant), 81, 136; on coworker relationships, 144; on the difficulty of her Amazon warehouse job, 95–96, 97; long-term career goals of, 91; work history of, 93–95

Parents of Jurupa, Inc., 184, 187

particulates or particulate matter, 57; 59, 191, 250; and fine or PM$_{2.5}$, 46, 56, 189, 268n62

Partnership for Working Families, 199

patriarchy, 9

People's Collective for Environmental Justice (PC4EJ), 3, 4, 19, 55, 193, 197, 214, 217, 218, 220, 239

People's Council Tribunal, 1, 2fig., 3

Plascencia, Nannette, 219

Pleyers, Geoffrey, 226

political participation, racial and ethnic gaps in, 58

pollution: air pollution, 38–39, 45, 46; chemical pollutants, 183–84; pollution mitigation, 54; and regulation of warehouse facilities, 198–99

polychlorinated biphenyl (PCB), 183

Posey, Michelle, 130–31

Pride Month, 237

process associate or assistant (PA), 86, 99, 104, 107, 116–17, 121, 153, 167, 255, 288n3

Progressive International, 229

Promontory Point, 36

Proposition 13 (The People's Initiative to Limit Property Taxation), 43, 268–69n70

Quan Yuan, 13–14, 56

"race to the bottom," 286n100

racism, 9, 23, 118, 133–38, 145; environmental racism, 216

Rancho Jurupa, 35

Rancho San Bernardino, 35

Red Scare, the, 36–37

Republicans, 16, 39

Retail, Wholesale and Department Store Union (RWDSU), 232, 234

Reynoso, Ben, 217

Rhode, Paul, 27

Riverside Board of Supervisors, 58

Riverside County, California, 3, 10, 19, 26–27, 31, 35, 39, 41, 44, 46, 190; abundance of

low-wage work in, 45; demographic transition in, 40; home prices in (1984), 43; wages and salaries of blue-collar warehouse workers at Amazon, 11; warehouse-related facilities in, 28

Riverside-San Bernardino-Ontario Metropolitan Statistical Area (MSA), 55

Riverside Water Company, 35

Roberto (interview participant): on the greed of Jeff Bezos, 79–80; on workplace competition, 141; on workplace favoritism, 120

Roberts, John, 195

Robin (interview participant), on the lack of safety in Amazon warehouses 162–63

Rocha, Thomas, 192

Roman Catholic church, 34

Rosales, Beverly, 130

Sacramento, 36

Samantha (interview participant), 123

Samuel (interview participant): and peeing in bottles instead of using the bathroom due to work rate pressure, 107; on the stress of meeting productivity rates, 165–66; on workplace favoritism, 124

San Antonio Water Company, 35

San Bernardino Airport Communities (SBAC), 4, 21, 54, 214–15, 216–17, 218, 220

San Bernardino City Council, 217

San Bernardino County, California, 3, 10, 19, 31, 32, 39, 41, 44, 46; abundance of low-wage work in, 45; demographic transition in, 40; General Plan of, 217–18; home prices in (1984), 43; median household income in, 5; warehouse-related facilities in, 28

San Bernardino County Board of Supervisors, 192–93

Sanders, Bernie, 72

San Diego County, California, 43, 44, 55

San Gabriel Mountains, 36

San Joaquin Valley Air Pollution Control District's (APCD's) Indirect Source Review rule (Rule 9510), 200

Santa Ana Regional Water Quality Control Board (RWQCB), 183–84

Schawe-Lane, Allegra, 131

Schneider Logistics, 204–5

Sena, Elizabeth, 195

sexism, 23, 118, 121–29, 132, 139

Sierra Club, the, 21, 194, 196, 216; My Generation Campaign of, 199, 214

Simmons, Shaun, 131–32

slavery, 32; capitalism as the new slavery (the slave metaphor), 79, 272n42
Slover Distribution Center, 192, 196
Smalls, Christian (Chris), 79, 134, 219, 231, 233, 235
Smith, Noah, 54
Smith, Ronald, accidental death of in an Amazon facility, 82
SMX, 82
social justice activists, 226; view of Amazon's economic impact, 57–58, 59
Sofia (interview participant), 76–77
sortation, 48, 60, 67, 99, 101, 278n28
Soto, Brenda Huerta, 3
South America, 33
South Coast Air Basin, 198–99
South Coast Air Quality Management District (SCAQMD), 24, 59, 200, 220; Governing Board of, 199–200; Indirect Source Rule of (Rule 2305), 189, 198, 200; Proposed Rule 2301 (2009) of, 199; Warehouse Actions and Investments to Reduce Emissions (WAIRE) Program, 198–99
Southern California Association of Governments (SCAG), 44
Southern California Colony Association, 26, 35
Southern Pacific Railroad, 27
South Fontana Concerned Citizens Coalition, 195, 197
Spanish missionaries/missions, 36; introduction of citrus crops in California, 35
spatial inequalities, 13–18, 57tab.; feminist views of, 53–54
staffing services/agencies, 82, 245, 273n45
Stella (interview participant): on broken safety rules at Amazon during the COVID-19 pandemic, 172; on the constant surveillance at Amazon, 99
Strategic Organizing Center (SOC), 202, 277n26; statistics of concerning Amazon workplace injuries, 158–60
Stringfellow Acid Pits (SAP), 183–85 189; "ultramarathon" litigation over the SAP cleanup, 186
Struna, Jason, 11
Sustainable Communities & Climate Protection Act (SB 375, 2008), 199

Target, wages paid by compared to Amazon, 76
Targeting Amazon campaign, 207–10, 210fig., 211fig.; and building regional alliances for a sustainable economy, 212–19

Teamsters, 4, 203–4, 206–8, 210, 212–3, 218, 234, 236, 238–39
Teamsters Local 63, 2, 75, 201
Teamsters Local 1932, 21, 214, 216, 217
The Congress of Essential Workers (TCOEW), 233
Tibbets, Eliza, 35
time off task (TOT), 104–7, 141, 162, 173; bathroom breaks counted as TOT, 107–8; measurement of, 105
T-Mobile, 139
Torres, Ivette, 55
Toxics Coordinating Project, 187
Transnational Social Strike, 229
transphobia, 131–33
Treaty of Guadalupe Hidalgo, 33
Tyler (interview participant), 81

unfair labor practice (ULP), 205–6
UNI Global Union, 229
United Food and Commercial Workers Union (UFCW), 203–4, 206–7, 232
United 4 Change Coalition ONT8, 219
United Parcel Services (UPS), 48, 60
United States, 6, 33, 79, 241, 243; resistance to Amazon in, 230–40
University of California Riverside (UCR), 87–88, 273n60
University of Redlands, 55
unpaid personal time (UPT), 86, 87
US Immigration and Customs Enforcement (ICE), 208

Ventura County, California, 44
Ver.di, 228
Verizon, 128
Victoria, Anthony, 17, 197
Viviana (interview participant), 88–89; on broken safety rules at Amazon during the COVID-19 pandemic, 172; on the fears of exposure to COVID-19, 174; and the hassle she experienced obtaining a COVID-19 leave of absence, 179–80; on pain and exhaustion while working at Amazon, 152

Walmart Corporation, 60; and the Making Change at Walmart (MCAW) campaign, 203–7; wages paid by compared to Amazon, 76; and "Walmarch," 206
warehouse industry: disproportionate representation among Black and Latino warehouse workers in, 28–29; earnings in, 11;

gender division of labor in warehouses, 122–25; rise of connected to Amazon, 12, 15–16; wages in general compared to Amazon wages, 76; workplace inequalities at Amazon and throughout the warehouse industry, 9–13. *See also* distribution centers (DCs)

Warehouse Worker Quotas law (AB 701, California, 2021), 210, 212, 263n1

Warehouse Workers for Justice, 129

Warehouse Workers Protection Act (WWPA), 247

Warehouse Workers Resource Center (WWRC), 1, 4, 19, 21, 200, 203–10, 212–13, 214, 217, 218, 220, 220

Warehouse Workers Stand Up, 232

Warehouse Workers United (WWU), 21, 202–3

Warren, Acquanetta, 193–94, 195

Warren, Quinta, 57–58

"water spiders," 94, 116, 154, 162, 277n6

whites, median income of (1975), 42

women, 37, 139; and the California gold rush, 33–34; experiences at Amazon, 1–2; movement of from northern California to Los Angeles as the gold rush ended, 33. *See also* Amazon warehouse workers, sexism and sexual harassment faced by

Women's Land Army of America's "farmer-ettes," 36

World Logistics Center (WLC), 189, 197–98, 223

World War I (WWI), 37

World War II (WWII), 37–39

xenophobia, 133–38

Yellow Vest movement, 230

zoning laws, 58

Founded in 1893,
UNIVERSITY OF CALIFORNIA PRESS
publishes bold, progressive books and journals
on topics in the arts, humanities, social sciences,
and natural sciences—with a focus on social
justice issues—that inspire thought and action
among readers worldwide.

The UC PRESS FOUNDATION
raises funds to uphold the press's vital role
as an independent, nonprofit publisher, and
receives philanthropic support from a wide
range of individuals and institutions—and from
committed readers like you. To learn more, visit
ucpress.edu/supportus.